THE DIARY AND LETTERS OF MADAME D'ARBLAY [U+0080] VOLUME 2

THE DIARY AND LETTERS OF MADAME D'ARBLAY [U+0080] VOLUME 2

Fanny Burney

www.General-Books.net

Publication Data:

Title: The Diary and Letters of Madame D'arblay I Volume 2
Author: Burney, Fanny, 1752-1840
Reprinted: 2010, General Books, Memphis, Tennessee, USA
Subjects: Novelists, English – 19th century – Correspondence

THE DIARY AND LETTERS OF MADAME D'ARBLAY [U+0080] VOLUME 2

THE DIARY AND LETTERS OF MADAME D'ARBLAY (FRANCES BURNEY.)
WITH NOTES BY W. C. WARD, AND PREFACED BY LORD MACAULAY'S ESSAY.
IN THREE VOLUMES.
VOL. 2.
(1787-1792.)
WITH AN ENGRAVING OF GEORGE III., QUEEN CHARLOTTE, AND THEIR FAMILY.
LONDON: VIZETELLY CO., 16, HENRIETTA STREET,
COVENT GARDEN.
1891.
PRINTED BY J. S. VIRTUE COMPANY, LONDON, CITY ROAD.

10. (1787) COURT DUTIES AT ST. JAMES'S AND WINDSOR –9-48
The Queen's Birthday Drawing Room–A Serious Dilemma–Counsels of
a Court Official–Mr. Turbulent's Anxiety to Introduce Mr.
Wellbred–Colonel Wellbred is received at Tea–Eccentric Mr.

Bryant–Mr. Turbulent in a New Character–Bantering a Princess-
-Mr. Turbulent meets with a Rebuff–A Surprise at the Play–The
King's Birthday–The Equerries: Colonel Manners–The Duchess de
Polignac at Windsor–Colonel Manners' Musical Accomplishments-
-Mrs. Schwellenberg's "Lump of Leather"–Mrs. Schwellenberg's
Frogs–Mr. Turbulent's Antics.

**11 (1787-8) COURT DUTIES: SOME VARIATIONS IN THEIR ROUTINE–
49-85**
Meeting of the two Princes–Bunbury, the Caricaturist–Mrs.
Siddons proves disappointing on near acquaintance–Mr. Fairly's
Bereavement–Troublesome Mr. Turbulent–A Conceited Parson–Mr.
Turbulent becomes a Nuisance–Dr. Herschel and his Sister–Gay
and Entertaining Mr. Bunbury–The Prince of Wales at Windsor
again–False Rumours of Miss Burney's Resignation–Tyrannical
Mrs. Schwellenberg–Mrs. Schwellenberg's Capriciousness–New
Year's Day–Chatty Mr. Bryant again–Dr. Johnson's Letters to
Mrs. Thrale discussed–A Pair of Paragons–Mr. Turbulent's Self
Condemnation–Miss Burney among her Old Friends–Some Trivial
Court Incidents.

12 (1788) THE TRIAL OF WARREN HASTINGS–86-153
Westminster Hall at the opening of the Hastings Trial–Warren
Hastings appears at the Bar–The Lord Chancellor's Speech–The
Reading of the Charges commenced–An Old Acquaintance–William
Windham, Esq., M.P.–Windham inveighs against Warren Hastings-
-Miss Burney Battles for the Accused–A Wearied M.P.–Mr.
Crutchley reappears–Mr. Windham discusses the Impeachment-
-Windham affects to commiserate Hastings–Miss Burney is again
present at Hastings's Trial–Burke's Speech in support of the
Charges–Further Conversation with Mr. Windham–Miss Fuzilier
likely to become Mrs. Fairly–The Hastings Trial again: Mr. Fox
in a Rage–Mrs. Crewe, Mr. Burke and Mr. Windham–Miss Burney's
Unbiassed Sentiments–Burke and Sheridan meet with Cold
Receptions–At Windsor again–Death of Mrs. Delany–The
    page vi
    Hastings Trial and Mr. Windham again–"The Queen is so kind"–
Personal Resemblance between Windham and Hastings–Death of Young
Lady Mulgrave–Again at Windsor–Another Meeting with Mr.
Crutchley–Mr. Turbulent's troublesome Pleasantries–Colonel
Fairly and Second Attachments.

13. (1788) ROYAL VISIT TO CHELTENHAM–154–219
The Royal Party and their Suite–Loyalty not Damped by the Rain-
-Arrival at Fauconberg Hall–The Tea-Table Difficulty–A
t'ete-'a-t'ete wit" Colonel Fairly–The King's
Gentlemen and the Queen's Ladies–Royalty Crowded at Fauconberg
Hall–At the wells–Conversation and Flirtation with Colonel

Fairly–Miss Burney meets an old Friend–Colonel Fairly again–A
Visit to miss Palmer–"Original Love Letters"–The Founder of
Sunday Schools criticised–On the Walks–An Unexpected Visitor–
Courts and Court Life–The Vindictive Baretti–speculations upon
Colonel Fairly's Re-marrying–Colonel Fairly again presents
Himself–The Colonel and the "Original Love Letters"–The Gout
and the Love Letters again–A Dinner with Colonel Fairly and Miss
Planta–Royal Concern for the Colonel's Gout–young Republicans
Converted–The Princes' Animal Spirits–The Duke of York: Royal
Visit to the Theatre–An uncourtly visitor–Mr. Fairly reads
"Akenside" to Miss Burney–The Doctor's Embarrassment–From Grave
to Gay–A Visit to Worcester–The Queen and Mr. Fairly–Mr.
Fairly Moralizes–Major Price is tired of Retirement–The Return
to Windsor–At Windsor again: The Canon and Mrs. Schwellenberg–
Compliments from a famous Foreign Astronomer–The Prince eyes
miss Burney curiously–Colonel manners's Beating–mr. Fairly is
Discussed by his Brother Equerries–Baron Trenck: Mr. Turbulent's
Raillery–Amiable Mrs. Schwellenberg again–A Royal Joke–Colonel
Goldsworthy's Breach of Etiquette–Illness of Mrs. Schwellenberg-
-General Grenville's Regiment at Drill.

14. (1788-9) THE KING'S ILLNESS–220-299

Uncertain State of the King's Health–The King complains of Want of Sleep–Distress
of the Queen–First Outburst of the King's Delirium–An Anxious Night–The King's
Delirious Condition-The King refuses to see Dr. Warren–The Queen's anxiety to hear
Dr. Warren's opinion–The Queen removes to more distant Apartments–A Visit from
Mr. Fairly–The King's Night Watchers–A Change in Miss Burney's Duties–Mr. Fairly
Succeeds in Soothing the King–New Arrangements–The Princess Augusta's Birthday–
Strange Behaviour of the First Gentleman in Europe–Stringent New Regulations–Mrs.
Schwellenberg is back again–Public Prayers for the King decided upon–Sir Lucas
Pepys On the King's Condition- Further Changes at the Lodge–Mr. Fairly and the
Learned Ladies– Reports on the King's Condition–Mr. Fairly thinks the King
Page vii
needs Stricter Management–Mr. Fairly wants a Change–Removal of the King
to Kew determined upon–A Privy Council held–The Removal to Kew–A Mys-
terious Visitor–The King's Arrival–The Arrangements at Kew Palace–A Regency
hinted at–Mr. Fairly's Kind Offices–Mrs. Schwellenberg's Parlour–A new Physician Summoned–Mrs. Schwellenberg's Opinion of Mr. Fairly–The King's varying
Condition–Dr. Willis and his Son–Learning in Women–The Queen and Mr. Fairly's
Visits-A Melancholy Birthday–Mr. Fairly on Fans–Mr. Fairly continues his Visits: the Queen again Remarks upon them–The Search for Mr. Fairly–Miss Burney's
Alarm on being chased by the King–A Royal Salute and Royal Confidences– Cu-
riosity regarding Miss Burney's meeting with the King–The Regency Bill–Infinitely
Licentious!–Miss Burney is taxed with Visiting Gentlemen–Improvement in the King's
Health–Mr. Fairly and Mr. Windham–The King continues to improve–The King's
Health is completely Restored.

15. (1789) THE KING'S RECOVERY: ROYAL VISIT TO WEYMOUTH–300-333
The King's Reappearance–An Airing and its Consequences– Illuminations on the King's Recovery–Mr. Fairly on Miss Burney's Duties–A Visit from Miss Fuzilier–A Command from Her Majesty- -Colonel Manners mystifies Mrs. Schwellenberg–The Sailor Prince–Loyal Reception of the King in the New Forest–The Royal journey to Weymouth–Welcome to Weymouth–The Royal Plunge with Musical honours– "You must Kneel, Sir!"–Royal doings in and about Weymouth–A Patient Audience– A Fatiguing but Pleasant Day–Lulworth Castle–The Royal Party at the Assembly Rooms–A journey to Exeter and Saltram–May "One" come in?–An Excursion to Plymouth Dockyard–A Visit to a Seventy-four–A Day at Mount Edgecumbe–Mr. Fairly on a Court Life–A Brief Sojourn at Longleat–Tottenham Court: Return to Windsor.

16. (1789-90) MR. FAIRLY'S MARRIAGE: THE HASTINGS TRIAL–334-365
Rumours of Mr. Fairly's impending Marriage–A Royal Visit to the Theatre: jammed in the Crowd–In the Manager's Box–Mr. Fairly's Marriage imminent–Court Duties discussed–Mr. Fairly's Strange Wedding–Renewal of the Hastings Trial: A Political Impromptu–An Illbred Earl of Chesterfield–Miss Burney in a New Capacity–The long-forgotten Tragedy: Miss Burnei again as Reader–Colonel Manners in his Senatorial Capacity–A Conversation with Mr. Windham at the Hastings Trial–A Glimpse of Mrs. Piozzi–Captain Burney wants a Ship to go to Court–Captain Burney and Mr. Windham–Mr. Windham speaks on a Legal Point–An Emphatic Peroration-An Aptitude for Logic and for Greek–More Talk with Mr. Windham.

Page viii

17. (1790-1) MISS BURNEY RESIGNS HER PLACE AT COURT–366-409
A Melancholy Confession–Captain Burney's Laconic Letter and Interview–Burke's Speech on the French Revolution–An Awkward Meeting–A New Visit from Mrs. Fairly–One Tragedy Finished and Another Commenced–Miss Burney's Resignation Memorial–Mr. Windham Intervenes–An Amusing Interview with Mr. Boswell–Ill, Unsettled, and Unhappy–A Medical Opinion on Miss Burney's Condition–Miss Burney breaks the Matter to the Queen–The Memorial and Explanatory Note–The Keeper of the Robes' Consternation–Leave of Absence is Suggested–A Royal Gift to the Master of the Horse–Conferences with the Queen–Miss Burney determines on Seclusion–The Hastings Trial Resumed: The Accused makes his Defence–Mr. Windham is Congratulated on his Silence– Miss Burney makes her Report–Prince William insists on the King's Health being Drunk–The Queen's Health–The Procession to the Ball-room: Absence of the Princes–Boswell's Life of johnson–The Close of Miss Burney's Court Duties–Miss Burney's

Successor: A Pension from the Queen–Leavetakings–Farewell to
Kew–The Final Parting.

18. (1791-2) REGAINED LIBERTY–410-468

Released from Duty–A Western journey: Farnham Castle–A Party of
French Fugitives–Winchester Cathedral–Stonehenge, Wilton, and
Milton Abbey–Lyme and Sidmouth–Sidmouth Loyalty–Powderham
Castle and Collumpton Church–Glastonbury Abbey–Wells
Cathedral–Bath Revisited–A Visit from Lady Spencer–Bath Sunday
Schools–Georgiana, Duchess of Devonshire–Bishop Percy–The
Duchess of Devonshire again–Dr. Burney's Conversation with Mr.
Burke: Remarks by Miss Burney–Literary Recreation–Sir Joshua
Reynoldsls Blindness–Among Old Friends–A Summons from the
Queen–Mr. Hastings's Defence–Diverse Views–Mr. Law's Speech
Discussed–Mr. Windham on the French National Assembly–"A
Barbarous Business!"–Death of Sir Joshua Reynolds–Mr. Windham
twitted on his Lack of Compassion–A Point of Ceremonial–Mrs.
Schwellenberg and Mlle. Jacobi–A Long Talk with the King and
Queen–Madame de Genlis: a Woeful Change–The Weeping Beauty
Again–Madame de la Fite and Mrs. Hastings–The Impetuous Orator-
-Mimicry of Dr. Johnson–The King's Birthday–Mr. Hastings's
Speech–A Well-preserved Beauty–The Burkes–Burke's
Conversational Powers–A Wild Irish Girl–Erskine's Egotism–
Caen-wood—An Adventure with Mrs. Crewe–An Invitation from
Arthur Young.

SECTION 10. (1787)
COURT DUTIES AT ST. JAMES'S AND WINDSOR.
THE QUEEN'S BIRTHDAY DRAWING ROOM.

January. Go back to the 16th, when I went to town, accompanied only by Mr. de Luc.
I saw my dear father the next morning, who gave me a poem on the queen's birthday, to
present. It was very pretty; but I felt very awkward in offering it to her, as it was from
so near a relation, and without any particular reason or motive. Mr. Smelt came and
stayed with me almost all the morning, and soothed and solaced me by his charming
converse. The rest of the day was devoted to milliners, mantua-makers, and such
artificers, and you may easily conjecture how great must be my fatigue. Nevertheless,
when, in the midst of these wasteful toils, the Princess Augusta entered my room, and
asked me, from the queen, if I should wish to see the ball the next day, I preferred
running the risk of that new fatigue, to declining an honour so offered: especially as
the Princess Augusta was herself to open the ball.

A chance question this night from the queen, whom I now again attended as usual,
fortunately relieved me from my embarrassment about the poem. She inquired of me if
my father was still writing? "A little," I answered, and the next morning, Thursday, the
18th, when the birth-day was kept, I found her all sweetness and serenity; mumbled out
my own little compliment, which she received as graciously as if she had understood
and heard it; and then,

when she was dressed, I followed her through the great rooms, to get rid of the wardrobe woman, and there taking the poem from my pocket, I said "I told your majesty that my father had written a little!–and here–the little is!"

She took it from me with a smile and a curtsey, and I ran off. She never has named it since; but she has spoken of my father with much sweetness and complacency. The modest dignity of the queen, upon all subjects of panegyric, is truly royal and noble.

I had now, a second time, the ceremony of being entirely new dressed. I then went to St. James's, where the queen gave a very gracious approbation of my gewgaws, and called upon the king to bestow the same; which his constant goodhumour makes a matter of great ease to him.

The queen's dress, being for her own birthday, was extremely simple, the style of dress considered. The king was quite superb, and the Princesses Augusta and Elizabeth were ornamented with much brilliancy.

Not only the princess royal was missed at this exhibition, but also the Prince of Wales. He wrote, however, his congratulations to the queen, though the coldness then subsisting between him and his majesty occasioned his absence from Court. I fear it was severely felt by his royal mother, though she appeared composed and content.

The two princesses spoke very kind words, also, about my frippery on this festival; and Princess Augusta laid her positive commands upon me that I should change my gown before I went to the lord chamberlain's box, where only my head could be seen. The counsel proved as useful as the consideration was amiable.

When the queen was attired, the Duchess of Ancaster was admitted to the dressing room, where she stayed, in conversation with their majesties and the princesses, till it was time to summon the bed-chamber women. During this, I had the office of holding the queen's train. I knew, for me, it was a great honour, yet it made me feel, once more, so like a mute upon the stage, that I could scarce believe myself only performing my own real character.

Mrs. Stainforth and I had some time to stand upon the stairs before the opening of the doors. We joined Mrs. Fielding and her daughters, and all entered together, but the crowd parted us - they all ran on, and got in as they could, and I Page 11 remained alone by the door. They soon found me out, and made signs to me, which I saw not, and then they sent me messages that they had kept room for me just by them. I had received orders from the queen to go out at the end of the second country dance ; I thought, therefore, that as I now was seated by the door, I had better be content, and stay where I could make my exit in a moment, and without trouble or disturbance. A queer-looking old lady sat next me, and I spoke to her now and then, by way of seeming to belong to somebody. She did not appear to know whether it were advisable for her to answer me or not, seeing me alone, and with high head ornaments; but as I had no plan but to save appearances to the surrounders, I was perfectly satisfied that my very concise propositions should meet with yet more laconic replies.

Before we parted, however, finding me quiet and inoffensive, she became voluntarily sociable, and I felt so much at home, by being still in a part of the palace, that I needed nothing further than just so much notice as not to seem an object to be avoided.

The sight which called me to that spot perfectly answered all my expectations: the air, manner, and countenance of the queen, as she goes round the circle, are truly graceful and engaging: I thought I could understand, by the motion of her lips, and the expression of her face, even at the height and distance of the chamberlain's box, the gracious and pleasant speeches she made to all whom she approached. With my glass, you know, I can see just as other people see with the naked eye.

The princesses looked extremely lovely, and the whole Court was in the utmost splendour.

A SERIOUS DILEMMA.

At the appointed moment I slipped through the door, leaving my old lady utterly astonished at my sudden departure, and I passed, alone and quietly, to Mr. Rhamus's apartment, which was appropriated for the company to wait in. Here I desired a servant I met with to call my man: he was not to be found. I went down the stairs, and made them call him aloud, by my name; all to no purpose. Then the chairmen were called, but called also in vain!

What to do I knew not ; though I was still in a part of the
Page 12
palace, it was separated by many courts, avenues, passages, and alleys, from the queen's or my own apartments- and though I had so lately passed them, I could not remember the way, nor at that late hour could I have walked, dressed as I then was, and the ground wet with recent rain, even if I had had a servant: I had therefore ordered the chair allotted me for these days; but chair and chairmen and footmen were alike out of the way.

My fright lest the queen should wait for me was very serious. I believe there are state apartments through which she passes, and therefore I had no chance to know when she retired from the ball-room. Yet could I not stir, and was forced to return to the room whence I came, in order to wait for John, that I might be out of the way of the cold winds which infested the hall.

I now found a young clergyman, standing by the fire. I suppose my anxiety was visible, for he instantly inquired if he could assist me. I declined his offer, but walked up and down, making frequent questions about my chair and John.

He then very civilly said, "You seem distressed, ma'am; would you permit me the honour to see for your chair, or, if it is not come, as you seem hurried, would you trust me to see you home?"

I thanked him, but could not accept his services. He was sorry, he said, that I refused him, but could not wonder, as he was a stranger. I made some apologising answer, and remained in that unpleasant situation till, at length, a hackneychair was procured me. My new acquaintance would take no denial to handing me to the chair. When I got in, I told the men to carry me to the palace.

"We are there now!" cried they; "what part of the palace?"

I was now in a distress the most extraordinary : I really knew not my own direction! I had always gone to my apartment in a chair, and had been carried by chairmen officially appointed; and, except that it was in St. James's palace, I knew nothing of my own situation.

"Near the park," I told them, and saw my new esquire look utterly amazed at me.

"Ma'am," said he, " half the palace is in the park."

"I don't know how to direct," cried I, in the greatest
embarrassment, "but it is somewhere between Pall Mall and the
park."
Page 13
"I know where the lady lives well enough," cried one of the chairmen, "'tis in St.
James's street."

"No, no," cried I, "'tis in St. James's palace."

"Up with the chair!" cried the other man, "I know best—'tis in
South Audley-street; I know the lady well enough."

Think what a situation at the moment! I found they had both been drinking the
queen's health till they knew not what they said and could with difficulty stand. Yet
they lifted me up, and though I called in the most terrible fright to be let out, they
carried me down the steps.

I now actually screamed for help, believing they would carry me off to South
Audley-street; and now my good genius, who had waited patiently in the crowd,
forcibly stopped the chairmen, who abused him violently, and opened the door himself,
and I ran back to the hall.

You may imagine how earnestly I returned my thanks for this most seasonable
assistance, without which I should almost have died with terror, for where they might
have taken or dropped me, or how or where left me, who could say?

He begged me to go again upstairs, but my apprehension about the queen prevented
me. I knew she was to have nobody but me, and that her jewels, though few, were to
be intrusted back to the queen's house to no other hands. I must, I said, go, be it in
what manner it might. All I could devise was to summon Mr. Rhamus, the page. I
had never seen him, but my attendance upon the queen would be an apology for the
application, and I determined to put myself under his immediate protection.

Mr. Rhamus was nowhere to be found ; he was already supposed to be gone to the
queen's house, to wait the arrival of his majesty. This news redoubled my fear; and
now my new acquaintance desired me to employ him in making inquiries for me as to
the direction I wanted.

It was almost ridiculous, in the midst of my distress, to be thus at a loss for an address
to myself! I felt averse to speaking my name amongst so many listeners, and only
told him he would much oblige me by finding out a direction to Mrs. Haggerdorn's
rooms. He went upstairs ; and returning, said he could now direct the chairmen, if I
did not fear trusting them.

I did fear—I even shook with fear; yet my horror of disappointing the queen upon
such a night prevailed over all my reluctance, and I ventured once more into the
chair, thanking this excellent Samaritan, and begging him to give the direction very
particularly.

Imagine, however, my gratitude and my relief, when, instead of hearing the direction, I heard only these words, " Follow me." And then did this truly benevolent young
man himself play the footman, in walking by the side of the chair till we came to an
alley, when he bid them turn; but they answered him with an oath, and ran on with
me, till the poles ran against a wall, for they had entered a passage in which there was
no outlet! I would fain have got out, but they would not hear me; they would only pull

the chair back, and go on another way. But my guardian angel told them to follow him, or not, at their peril ; and then walked before the chair.

We next came to a court where we were stopped by the sentinels. They said they had orders not to admit any hackney chairs. The chairmen vowed they would make way; I called out aloud to be set down; the sentinels said they would run their bayonets through the first man that attempted to dispute their orders. I then screamed out again to be set down, and my new and good friend peremptorily forced them to stop, and opening the door with violence, offered me his arm, saying, "You had better trust yourself with me, ma'am!"

Most thankfully I now accepted what so fruitlessly I had declined, and I held by his arm, and we walked on together, but neither of us knew whither, nor the right way from the wrong 1 It was really a terrible situation.

The chairmen followed us, clamorous for money, and full of abuse. They demanded half a crown - my companion refused to listen to such an imposition : my shaking hand could find no purse, and I begged him to pay them what they asked, that they might leave us. He did ; and when they were gone, I shook less, and was able to pay that one part of the debt I was now contracting.

We wandered about, heaven knows where, in a way the most alarming and horrible to myself imaginable: for I never knew where I was.–It was midnight. I concluded the queen waiting for me.–It was wet. My head was full dressed. I was under the care of a total stranger; and I knew not which side to take, wherever we came. Inquiries were vain. The sentinels alone were in sight, and they are so continually changed that they knew no more of Mrs. Haggerdorn than if she had never resided here.

At length I spied a door open, and I begged to enter it at a venture, for information. Fortunately a person stood in the passage who instantly spoke to me by my name; I never

heard that sound with more glee: to me he was a stranger, but I suppose he had seen me in some of the apartments. I begged him to direct me straight to the queen's rooms: he did ; and I then took leave of my most humane new friend, with a thousand acknowledgments for his benevolence and services.

Was it not a strange business ? I can never say what an agony Of fright it cost me at the time, nor ever be sufficiently grateful for the kind assistance, so providentially afforded me.'

COUNSELS OF A COURT OFFICIAL.

The general directions and counsel of Mr. Smelt, which I have scrupulously observed ever since, were, in abridgment, these:-

That I should see nobody at all but by appointment. This, as he well said, would obviate, not only numerous personal inconveniences to myself, but prevent alike surprises from those I had no leave to admit, and repetitions of visits from others who might inadvertently come too often. He advised me to tell this to my father, and beg it might be spread, as a settled part of my situation, among all who inquired for me.

That I should see no fresh person whatsoever without an immediate permission from the queen, nor any party, even amongst those already authorised, without apprising her of such a plan.

That I should never go out without an immediate application to her, so that no possible inquiry for me might occasion surprise or disappointment.

These, and other similar ties, perhaps, had my spirits been better, I might less readily have acceded to : as it was, I would have bound myself to as many more.

At length, however, even then, I was startled when Mr. Smelt, with some earnestness, said, "And, with respect to your parties, such as you may occasionally have here, you have but one rule for keeping all things smooth, and all partisans unoffended, at a distance–which is, to have no men–none!

I stared a little, and made no answer.

"Yes," cried he, "Mr. Locke may be admitted; but him only. Your father, you know, is of course."

Still I was silent: after a pause of some length, he plumply Yet with an evidently affected unmeaningness, said, "Mr. Cambridge– as to Mr. Cambridge–"

I stopped him short at once; I dared not trust to what

might follow, and eagerly called Out, "Mr. Cambridge, Sir, I cannot exclude! So much friendship and kindness I owe, and have long owed him, that he would go about howling at my ingratitude, could I seem so suddenly to forget it!"

My impetuosity in uttering this surprised, but silenced him; he said not a word more, nor did I.

MR. TURBULENT's ANXIETY TO INTRODUCE MR. WELLBRED. Windsor, Sunday, Jan. 28.-I was too ill to go to church. I was now, indeed, rarely well enough for anything but absolute and unavoidable duties ; and those were still painfully and forcibly performed.

I had only Miss Planta for my guest, and when she went to the princesses I retired for a quiet and solitary evening to my own room. But here, while reading, I was interrupted by a tat-tat at my door. I opened it and saw Mr. Turbulent. . . . He came forward, and began a gay and animated conversation, with a flow of spirits and good humour which I had never observed in him before.

His darling colonel(230) was the subject that he still harped upon; but it was only with a civil and amusing raillery, not, as before, with an overpowering vehemence to conquer. Probably, however, the change in myself might be as observable as in him,– since I now ceased to look upon him with that distance and coldness which hitherto he had uniformly found in me.

I must give you a little specimen of him in this new dress.

After some general talk,

"When, ma'am," he said, "am I to have the honour of introducing Colonel Wellbred to you?"

"Indeed, I have not settled that entirely!"

"Reflect a little, then, ma'am, and tell me. I only wish to know when."

"Indeed to tell you that is somewhat more than I am able to do; I must find it out myself, first."

" Well, ma'am, make the inquiry as speedily as possible, I beg. What say you to now? shall I call him up?

"No, no,–pray let him alone."

"But will you not, at least, tell me your reasons for this conduct?"

"Why, frankly, then, if you will hear them and be quiet, I will confess them."

I then told him, that I had so little time to myself, that to gain even a single evening was to gain a treasure; and that I had no chance but this. "Not," said I, "that I wish to avoid him, but to break the custom of constantly meeting with the equerries."

"But it is impossible to break the custom, ma'am; it has been so always: the tea-table has been the time of uniting the company, ever since the king came to Windsor."

" Well, but everything now is upon a new construction. I am not positively bound to do everything Mrs. Haggerdorn did, and his having drank tea with her will not make him conclude he must also drink tea with me."

No, no, that is true, I allow. Nothing that belonged to her can bring conclusions round to you. But still, why begin with Colonel Wellbred? You did not treat Colonel Goldsworthy so?"

"I had not the power of beginning with him. I did what I could,
I assure you."

"Major Price, ma'am?–I never heard you avoided him."

"No; but I knew him before I came, and he knew much of my family, and indeed I am truly sorry that I shall now see no more of him. But Colonel Wellbred and I are mutually strangers."

"All people are so at first, every acquaintance must have a beginning."

"But this, if you are quiet, we are most willing should have none."

"Not he, ma'am–he is not so willing; he wishes to come. He asked me, to-day, if I had spoke about it."

I disclaimed believing this; but he persisted in asserting it, adding "For he said if I had spoke he would come."

"He is very condescending," cried I, "but I am satisfied he would not think of it at all, if you did not put it in his head."

"Upon my honour, You are mistaken; we talk just as much of it down there as up here."

"you would much oblige me if you would not talk of it,- neither there nor here."

"Let me end it, then, by bringing him at once!"

"No, no, leave us both alone: he has his resources and his engagements as much as I have; we both are best as we now are."

"But what can he say, ma'am? Consider his confusion and disgrace! It is well known, in the world, the private life that the royal family live at Windsor, and who are the attendants that belong to them; and when Colonel Wellbred quits his waiting–three months' waiting and is asked how he likes Miss Burney, he must answer he has never seen her! And what, ma'am, has Colonel Wellbred done to merit such a mortification?"

It was impossible not to laugh at such a statement of the case; and again he requested to bring him directly. "One quarter of an hour will content me ; I only wish to introduce him–for the sake of his credit in the world; and when once you have met, you need meet no more; no consequences whatever need be drawn to the detriment of your solitude."

I begged him to desist, and let us both rest.

"But have you, yourself, ma'am, no curiosity—no desire to see Colonel Wellbred?"

"None in the world."

"If, then, hereafter you admit any other equerry—"

"No, no, I intend to carry the new construction throughout."

"Or if you suffer anyone else to bring you Colonel Wellbred."

"Depend upon it I have no such intention."

"But if any other more eloquent man prevails—"

" Be assured there is no danger."

"Will you, at least, promise I shall be present at the meet—?"

" There will be no meeting."

"You are certainly, then, afraid of him?"

I denied this, and, hearing the king's supper called, he took his leave ; though not before I very seriously told him that, however amusing all this might be as pure badinage, I Should be very earnestly vexed if he took any steps in the matter without my consent.

COLONEL WELLBRED IS RECEIVED AT TEA.

Feb. 2.-MISS Planta came to tea, and we went together to the eating-parlour, which we found quite empty. Mr. Turbulent's studious table was all deserted, and his books laid waste; but in a very few minutes he entered again, with his arms spread wide, his face all glee, and his voice all triumph, calling out,

"Mr. Smelt and Colonel Wellbred desire leave to wait upon miss Burney to tea!"

A little provoked at this determined victory over my will and my wish, I remained silent,- but Miss Planta broke forth into open upbraidings:

"Upon my word, Mr. Turbulent, this is really abominable it is all your own doing— and if I was Miss Burney I would not bear it!" and much more, till he fairly gave her to understand she had nothing to do with the matter.

Then, turning to me, "What am I to say, ma'am? am I to tell Colonel Wellbred you hesitate?" He protested he came upon the embassy fairly employed.

"Not fairly, I am sure, Mr. Turbulent The whole is a device and contrivance of your own! Colonel Wellbred would have been as quiet as myself, had you left him alone."

"Don't throw it all upon me, ma'am; 'tis Mr. Smelt. But what are they to think of this delay? are they to suppose it requires deliberation whether or not you can admit a gentleman to your tea-table?"

I begged him to tell me, at least, how it had passed, and in what manner he had brought his scheme about. But he would give me no satisfaction; he only said "You refuse to receive him, ma'am?– shall I go and tell him you refuse to receive him?"

"O No,

This was enough -. he waited no fuller consent, but ran off. Miss Planta began a good-natured repining for me. I determined to fetch some work before they arrived; and in coming for it to my own room, I saw Mr. Turbulent, not yet gone downstairs. I really believe, by the strong marks of laughter on his countenance, that he had stopped to compose himself before he could venture to appear in the equerryroom!

I looked at him reproachfully, and passed on; he shook his head at me in return, and hied downstairs. I had but just time to rejoin Miss Planta when he led the way to the two Other gentlemen: entering first, with the most earnest curiosity, to watch the scene. Mr. Smelt followed, introducing the colonel.

I could almost have laughed, so ridiculous had the behaviour of Mr. Turbulent, joined to his presence and watchfulness, rendered this meeting; and I saw in Colonel Wellbred the most evident marks of similar sensations: for he coloured

violently on his entrance, and seemed in an embarrassment that, to any one who knew not the previous tricks of Mr. Turbulent, must have appeared really distressing. And, in truth, Mr. Smelt himself, little imagining what had preceded the interview, was so much struck with his manner and looks, that he conceived him to be afraid of poor little me, and observed, afterwards, with what "blushing diffidence" he had begun the acquaintance!

I, who saw the true cause through the effect, felt more provoked than ever with Mr. Turbulent, since I was now quite satisfied he had been as busy with the colonel about me, as with me about the colonel.

He is tall, his figure is very elegant, and his face very handsome: he is sensible, well-bred, modest, and intelligent. I had always been told he was very amiable and accomplished, and the whole of his appearance confirmed the report.

The discourse was almost all Mr. Smelt's, the colonel was silent and reserved, and Mr. Turbulent had resolved to be a mere watchman. The king entered early and stayed late, and took away with him, on retiring, all the gentlemen.

Feb. 3.-As the tea hour approached, to-day, Mr. Turbulent grew very restless. I saw what was passing in his mind, and therefore forbore ordering tea; but presently, and suddenly, as if from some instant impulse, he gravely came up to me, and said

"Shall I go and call the colonel, ma'am?"

"No, sir!" was my johnsonian reply.

"What, ma'am!–won't you give him a little tea?"

"No, no, no!–I beg you will be at rest!"

He shrugged his shoulders, and walked away; and Mr. Smelt, smiling, said, "Will you give us any?"

"O yes, surely cried I, and was going away to ring for the man.

I believe I have already mentioned that I had no bell at all, except in my bedroom, and that only for my maid, whom I was obliged to summon first, like Smart's monkey–

"Here, Betty!–Nan!–

Go, call the maid, to call the man!"

For Mrs. Haggerdorn had done without, twenty-six years, by always keeping her servant in waiting at the door. I could never endure inflicting such a hardship, and therefore had always to run to my bedroom, and wait the progress of the maid's arrival, and then of her search of the man, ere ever

I could give him an order. A mighty tiresome and inconvenient ceremony. Mr Turbulent insisted upon saving me this trouble, and went 'out himself to speak to John. But you will believe me a little amazed, when, in a very few minutes, he returned again, accompanied by his colonel! My surprise brought the colour both into my own cheeks and those of my guests. Mr. Smelt looked pleased; and Mr. Turbulent, though I saw he was half afraid of what he was doing, could by no means restrain a most exulting smile, which was constantly in play during the whole evening.

Mr. Smelt instantly opened a conversation, with an ease and good breeding which drew every one into sharing it. The colonel was far less reserved and silent, and I found him very pleasing, very unassuming, extremely attentive, and sensible and obliging. The moment, however, that we mutually joined in the discourse, Mr. Turbulent came to my side, and seating himself there, whispered that he begged my pardon for the step he had taken. I made him no answer, but talked on with the colonel and Mr. Smelt. He. then whispered me again, "I am now certain of your forgiveness, since I see your approbation!" And when still I said nothing, he interrupted every speech to the colonel with another little whisper, saying that his end was obtained, and he was now quite happy, since he saw he had obliged me!

At length he proceeded so far, with so positive a determination to be answered, that he absolutely compelled me to say I forgave him, lest he should go on till the colonel heard him.

ECCENTRIC MR. BRYANT.

Feb. 9-This morning, soon after my breakfast, the princess royal came to fetch me to the queen. She talked of Mrs. Delany all the way, and in terms of affection that can never fail to raise her in the minds of all who hear her. The queen was alone; and told me she had been so much struck with the Duke of Suffolk's letter to his son, in the Paston collection,(231)

Page 22

that she wished to hear my opinion of it. She then condescended to read it to me. It is indeed both instructive and interesting. She was so gracious, when she dismissed me, as to lend me the book, desiring me to have it sent back to her apartment when I went to dinner.

I had invited Mr. Bryant to dinner. He came an hour before, and I could not read "Paston," but rejoiced the more in his living intelligence. We talked upon the "Jew's Letters," which he had lent me. Have I mentioned them? They are a mighty well written defence of the Mosaic law and mission, and as orthodox for Christians as for Jews, with regard to their main tenor, which is to refute the infidel doctrine of Voltaire up to the time of our Saviour.

Before our dinner we were joined by 'Mr. Smelt ; and the conversation was then very good. The same subject was continued, except where it was interrupted by Mr. Bryant's speaking of his own works, which was very frequently, and with a droll sort of simplicity that had a mixture of nature and of humour extremely amusing. He told us, very frankly his manner of writing; he confessed that what he first committed to paper seldom could be printed without variation or correction, even to a single line: he copied everything over, he said, himself, and three transcribings were the fewest he could ever make do; but, generally, nothing went from him to the press under seven.

Mr. Turbulent and Miss Planta came to dinner, and it was very cheerful. Ere it was over John told me somebody wanted me. I desired they might be shewn to my room till the things were removed; but, as these were some time taking away, I called John to let me know who it was. "The princess royal, ma'am," was his answer, with perfect ease.

Up I started, ashamed and eager, and flew to her royal highness instantly : and I found her calmly and quietly waiting, shut up in my room, without any candles, and almost wholly in the dark, except from the light of the fire! I made all possible apologies, and doubled and trebled them upon her Smilingly saying "I would not let them tell you who it was, nor hurry you, for I know 'tis so disagreeable to be called Page 23

away in the middle of dinner." And then, to reconcile me to the little accident, she took hold of both my hands.

She came to me from the queen, about the "Paston Letters," which John had not carried to the right page.

Very soon after came the king, who entered into a gay disquisition with Mr. Bryant upon his school achievements to which he answered with a readiness and simplicity highly entertaining.

"You are an Etonian, Mr. Bryant," said the king, "but pray, for what were you most famous at school?"

We all expected, from the celebrity of his scholarship, to hear him answer his Latin Exercises but no such thing.

"Cudgelling, Sir. I was most famous for that."

While a general laugh followed this speech, he very gravely proceeded to particularize his feats though unless you could see the diminutive figure, the weak, thin, feeble, little frame, whence issued the proclamation of his prowess, you can but very Inadequately judge the comic effect of his big talk.

"Your majesty, sir, knows General Conway? I broke his head for him, sir."

The shout which ensued did not at all interfere with the steadiness of his further detail.

"And there's another man, Sir, a great stout fellow, Sir, as ever you saw–Dr. Gibbon, of the Temple: I broke his head too, sir.–I don't know if he remembers it."

The king, afterwards, inquired after his present family, meaning his dogs, which he is famed for breeding and preserving.

"Why, sir," he answered, "I have now only twelve. Once, I recollect, when your majesty was so gracious as to ask me about them, I happened to have twenty-two; and so I told you, sir. Upon my word, Sir, it made me very uneasy afterwards when I came to reflect upon it: I was afraid your majesty might think I presumed to joke!"

The king then asked him for some account of the Marlborough family, with which he is very particularly connected and desired to know which among the young Lady Spencers was his favourite.

"Upon my word, sir, I like them all! Lady Elizabeth is a charming young lady–I believe, Sir, I am most in her favour; I don't know why, Sir. But I happened to write a letter to the duke, sir, that she took a fancy to; I don't know the reason, sir, but she begged it. I don't know what was in the letter, sir-I could never find out; but she took a prodigious fancy to it, sir."

The king laughed heartily, and supposed there might be some compliments to herself in it.

"Upon my word' sir," cried he, "I am afraid your majesty will think I was in love with her! but indeed, sir, I don't know what was in the letter."

The converse went on in the same style, and the king was so much entertained by Mr. Bryant, that he stayed almost the whole evening,

MR TURBULENT IN A NEW CHARACTER.

Friday, Feb. 16.-The instant I was left alone with Mr. Turbulent he demanded to know my "project for his happiness;" and he made his claim in a tone so determined, that I saw it would be fruitless to attempt evasion or delay.

"Your captivity, then, sir," cried I-"for such I must call your regarding your attendance to be indispensable is at an end: the equerry-coach is now wholly in your power. I have spoken myself upon the subject to the queen, as you bid–at least, braved me to do; and I have now her consent to discharging you from all necessity of travelling in our coach."(232)

He looked extremely provoked, and asked if I really meant to inform him I did not choose his company? I laughed the question off, and used a world of civil argument to persuade him I had only done him a good office: but I was fain to make the whole debate as sportive as possible, as I saw him disposed to be seriously affronted.

A long debate ensued. I had been, he protested, excessively ill-natured to him. "What an impression," cried he, "must this make upon the queen! After travelling, with apparent content, six years With that oyster Mrs. Haggerdorn–now–now that travelling is become really agreeable–in that coach –I am to be turned out of it! How must it disgrace me in her opinion!"

She was too partial, I said, to "that oyster," to look upon the matter in such a degrading light nor would she think of it

at all, but as an accidental matter. I then added, that the reason that he had hitherto been destined to the female coach was, that Mrs. Schwellenberg and Mrs. Haggerdorn were always afraid of travelling by themselves; but that as I had more courage, there was no need of such slavery.

"Slavery!"–repeated he, with an emphasis that almost startled me,–"Slavery is pleasure–is happiness–when directed by our wishes!"

And then, with a sudden motion that made me quite jump, he cast himself at my feet, on both his knees–

"Your slave," he cried, "I am content to be! your slave I am ready to live and die!"

I begged him to rise, and be a little less rhapsodic. "I have emancipated you," I cried; "do not, therefore, throw away the freedom you have been six years sighing to obtain. You are now your own agent–a volunteer–"

"If I am," cried he, impetuously, "I dedicate myself to you!–A volunteer, ma'am, remember that! I dedicate myself to you, therefore, of my own accord, for every journey! You shall not get rid of me these twenty years."

I tried to get myself away-but he would not let me move and he began, with still increasing violence of manner, a most fervent protestation that he would not be set aside, and that he devoted himself to me entirely. And, to say the simple truth, ridiculous as all this was, I really began to grow a little frightened by his vehemence and his posture - till, at last, in the midst of an almost furious vow, in which he dedicated himself to me for ever, he relieved me, by suddenly calling upon Jupiter, Juno, Mars, and Hercules, and every god, and every goddess, to witness his oath. And then, content with his sublimity, he arose.

Was it not a curious scene? and have I not a curious fellow traveller for my little journeys? Monday, Feb. 19.-This morning I Proposed to my fellow travellers that we should begin our journey on foot. The wonderment with which they heard a proposal so new was diverting : but they all agreed to it; and though they declared that my predecessor, Mrs. Haggerdorn, would have thought the person fit for Bedlam who should have suggested such plan, no one could find any real objection, and off we set, ordering the coach to proceed slowly after us.

The weather was delightful, and the enterprise served to shorten and enliven the expedition, and pleased them all, Page 26

Mr. Turbulent began, almost immediately, an attack about his colonel : upon quite a new ground, yet as restless and earnest as upon the old one. He now reproached my attention to him, protesting I talked to him continually, and spun out into an hour's discourse what might have been said in three minutes.

"And was it my spinning?" I could not forbear saying.

"Yes, ma'am: for you might have dropped it."

"How?–by not answering when spoken to?"

"by not talking to him, ma'am, more than to any one else."

"And pray, Mr. Turbulent, solve me, then, this difficulty; what choice has a poor female with whom she may converse? Must she not, in company as in dancing, take up with those Who choose to take up with her?"

He was staggered by this question, and while he wavered how to answer it, I pursued my little advantage–

"No man, Mr. Turbulent, has any cause to be flattered that a woman talks with him, while it is only in reply; for though he may come, go, address or neglect, and do as he will,– she, let her think and wish what she may, must only follow as he leads."

He protested, with great warmth, he never heard any thing so proudly said in Ins life. But I would not retract.

"And now, ma'am," he continued, "how wondrous intimate you are grown! After such averseness to a meeting–such struggles to avoid him; what am I to think of the sincerity of that pretended reluctance?"

"You must think the truth," said I, "that it was not the colonel, but the equerry, I wished to avoid; that it was not the individual, but the official necessity of receiving company, that I wished to escape."

BANTERING A PRINCESS.

March 1.- With all the various humours in which I had already seen Mr. Turbulent, he gave me this evening a surprise, by his behaviour to one of the princesses, nearly the same that I had experienced from him myself. The Princess Augusta came, during coffee, for a knotting shuttle of the queen's. While she was speaking to me, he stood behind and exclaimed, 'a demi voix, as if to himself, "Comme elle est jolie ce soir, son Altesse Royale!" And then, seeing her blush extremely, he clasped his hands, in high pretended confusion,

and hiding his head, called Out, "Que ferai-je? The princess has heard me!"

"Pray, Mr. Turbulent," cried she, hastily, "what play are you to read to-night?"

"You shall choose, ma'am; either 'La Coquette corrigée,' or–" [he named another I have forgotten.]

"O no!" cried she, "that last is shocking! don't let me hear that!"

"I understand you, ma'am. You fix, then, upon 'La Coquette?' 'La Coquette' is your royal highness's taste?"

"No, indeed, I am sure I did not say that."

"Yes, ma'am, by implication. And certainly, therefore, I will read it, to please your royal highness!"

"No, pray don't; for I like none of them."

"None of them, ma'am?"

"No, none;–no French plays at all!" And away she was running, with a droll air, that acknowledged she had said something to provoke him.

"This is a declaration, ma'am, I must beg you to explain!" cried he, gliding adroitly between the princess and the door, and shutting it With his back.

"No, no, I can't explain it;–so pray, Mr. Turbulent, do open the door."

"Not for the world, ma'am, with such a stain uncleared upon your royal highness's taste and feeling!"

She told him she positively could not stay, and begged him to let her pass instantly. But he would hear her no more than he has heard me, protesting he was too much shocked for her, to suffer her to depart without clearing her own credit!

He conquered at last, and thus forced to speak, she turned round to us and said, "Well–if I must, then–I will appeal to these ladies, who understand such things far better than I do, and ask them if it is not true about these French plays, that they are all so like to one another, that to hear them in this manner every night is enough to tire one?"

"Pray, then, madam," cried he, "if French plays have the misfortune to displease you, what national plays have the honour Of your preference?"

I saw he meant something that she understood better than me, for she blushed again, and called out "Pray open the door at once! I can stay no longer; do let me go, Mr. Turbulent!" Page 28

"Not till you have answered that question, ma'am' what country has plays to your royal highness's taste?"

"Miss Burney," cried she impatiently, yet laughing, "pray do you take him away!–Pull him!"

He bowed to me very invitingly for the office but I frankly answered her, "Indeed, ma'am, I dare not undertake him! I cannot manage him at all."

"The country! the country! Princess Augusta! name the happy country!" was all she could gain.

"Order him away, Miss Burney," cried she. "It is your room: order him away from the door."

"Name it, ma'am, name it!" exclaimed he; "name but the chosen nation!"

And then, fixing her with the most provoking eyes, "Est-ce la Danemarc?" he cried.

She coloured violently, and quite angry with him, called out, "Mr. Turbulent, how can you be such a fool!" And now I found . . . the prince royal of Denmark was in his meaning, and in her understanding!

He bowed to the ground, in gratitude for the term "fool," but added with pretended Submission to her will, "Very well, ma'am, s'il ne faut lire que les comédies Danoises."

" Do let me go!" cried she, seriously; and then he made way, with a profound bow as she passed, saying, "Very well, ma'am, 'La Coquette,' then? your royal highness chooses 'La Coquette corrigée?'"

"Corrigée? That never was done!" cried she, with all her sweet good-humour, the moment she got out - and off she ran, like lightning, to the queen's apartments.

What say you to Mr. Turbulent now?

For my part, I was greatly surprised. I had not imagined any man, but the king or Prince of Wales, had ever ventured at a badinage of this sort with any of the princesses; nor do I suppose any other man ever did. Mr. Turbulent is so great a favourite with all the royal family that he safely ventures upon whatever he pleases, and doubtless they find, in his courage and his rhodomontading, a novelty extremely amusing to them.

MR. TURBULENT MEETS WITH A REBUFF.

March–I must now, rather reluctantly I own, come to recite a quarrel, a very serious quarrel, in which I have been involved with my most extraordinary fellow-traveller. One evening at Windsor Miss Planta left the room, while I was winding some silk. I was content to stay and finish the skein, though my remaining companion was in a humour too flighty to induce me to continue with him a moment longer. Indeed I had avoided pretty successfully all tête-à-têetes with him since the time when his eccentric genius led to such eccentric conduct in our long conference in the last month.

This time, however, when I had done my work, he protested I should stay and chat with him. I pleaded business–letters– hurry–all in vain: he would listen to nothing, and when I tried to move was so tumultuous in his opposition, that I was obliged to re-seat myself to appease him.

A flow of compliments followed, every one of which I liked less and less; but his spirits seemed uncontrollable, and, I suppose, ran away with all that ought to check them. I laughed and rallied as long as I possibly could, and tried to keep him in order, by not seeming to suppose he wanted aid for that purpose: yet still, every time I tried to rise, he stopped me, and uttered at last Such expressions of homage–so like what Shakspeare says of the school-boy, who makes "a sonnet on his mistress' eyebrow," which is always his favourite theme–that I told him his real compliment was all to my temper, in imagining it could brook such mockery.

This brought him once more on his knees, with such a volley of asseverations of his sincerity, uttered with such fervour and eloquence, that I really felt uneasy, and used every possible means to get away from him, rallying him however all the time, and disguising the consciousness I felt of my inability to quit him. More and more vehement, however, he grew, till I could be no longer passive, but forcibly rising, protested I would not stay another minute. But you may easily imagine my astonishment and provocation, when, hastily rising himself, he violently seized hold of me, and compelled me to return to my chair, with a force and a freedom that gave me as much surprise as offence.

All now became serious. Raillery, good-humour, and even pretended ease and unconcern, were at an end. The positive displeasure I felt I made positively known;

and the voice manner, and looks with which I insisted upon an immediate' release were so changed from what he had ever heard or observed in me before, that I saw him quite thunderstruck with the alteration; and all his own violence subsiding, he begged my pardon with the mildest humility.

He had made me too angry to grant it, and I only desired

him to let me instantly go to my room. He ceased all personal opposition, but going to the door, planted himself before it, and said, "Not in wrath! I cannot let you go away in wrath!"

"You must, sir," cried I, "for I am in wrath!" He began a thousand apologies, and as many promises of the most submissive behaviour in future; but I stopped them all, with a peremptory declaration that every minute he detained me made me but the more seriously angry. His vehemence now was all changed into strong alarm, and he opened the door, profoundly bowing, but not speaking, as I passed him.

I am sure I need not dwell upon the uncomfortable sensations I felt, in a check so rude and violent to the gaiety and entertainment of an acquaintance which had promised me my best amusement during our winter campaigns. I was now to begin upon quite a new system, and instead of encouraging, as hitherto I had done, everything that could lead to vivacity and spirit, I was fain to determine upon the most distant and even forbidding demeanour with the only life of our parties, that he might not again forget himself.

This disagreeable conduct I put into immediate practice. I stayed in my own room till I heard every one assembled in the next : I was then obliged to prepare for joining them, but before I opened the door a gentle rap at it made me call out "Who's there?" and Mr. Turbulent looked in.

I hastily said I was coming instantly, but he advanced softly into the room, entreating forgiveness at every step. I made no other answer than desiring he would go, and saying I should follow. He went back to the door, and, dropping on one knee, said, "Miss Burney! surely you cannot be seriously angry?-'tis so impossible you should think I meant to offend you!"

I said nothing, and did not look near him, but opened the door, from which he retreated to make way for me, rising a little mortified, and exclaiming, "Can you then have such real ill-nature? How little I suspected it in you!"

"'Tis you," cried I, as I passed on, "that are ill-natured!"

I meant for forcing me into anger; but I left him to make the meaning out, and walked into the next room. He did not immediately follow, and he then appeared so much disconcerted that I saw Miss Planta incessantly eyeing him, to find out what was the matter. I assumed an unconcern I did not Page 31

feel for I was really both provoked and sorry, foreseeing what a breach this folly must make in the comfort of my Windsor expeditions,

He sat down a little aloof, and entered into no conversation all the evening; but just as tea was over, the hunt of the next being mentioned he suddenly, asked Miss Planta to request leave for him of the queen to ride out with the party.

"I shall not see the queen," cried she; "you had much better ask Miss Burney."

This was very awkward. I was in no humour to act for him at this time, nor could he muster courage to desire it; but upon Miss Planta's looking at each of us with some surprise, and repeating her amendment to his proposal, he faintly said, "Would Miss Burney be so good as to take that trouble?"

An opportunity offering favourably, I spoke at night to the queen, and she gave leave for his attending the chase. I intended to send this permission to Miss Planta, but I had scarce returned to my own room from her majesty, before a rap at my door was followed by his appearance. He stood quite aloof, looking grave and contrite. I Immediately called out "I have spoken, sir, to the queen, and you have her leave to go." He bowed very profoundly, and thanked me, and was retreating, but came back again, and advancing, assumed an air of less humility, and exclaimed, "Allons donc, Mademoiselle, j'espère que vous n'êtes plus si méchante qu'hier au soir!"

I said nothing; he came nearer, and, bowing upon his own hand, held it out for mine, with a look of most respectful Supplication. I had no intention of cutting the matter so short, yet from shame to sustain resentment, I was compelled to hold out a finger: he took it with a look of great gratitude, and very reverently touching the tip of my glove with his lip, instantly let it go, and very solemnly said, "Soyez sûr que je n'ai jamais eu la moindre idée de vous offenser." and then he thanked me again for his licence, and went his way.

A SURPRISE AT THE PLAY.

I had the pleasure of two or three visits from Mr. Bryant, whose loyal regard for the king and queen makes him eagerly accept every invitation, from the hope of seeing them in my room; and one of the days they both came in to speak to him, and were accompanied by the two eldest princesses, who stood

chatting with me by the door the whole time, and saying comical things upon royal personages in tragedies, particularly Princess Augusta, who has a great deal of sport in her disposition. She very gravely asserted she thought some of those princes on the stage looked really quite as well as some she knew off it.

Once about this time I went to a play myself, which surely I may live long enough and never forget. It was "Seduction," a very clever piece, but containing a dreadful picture of vice and dissipation in high life, written by Mr. Miles Andrews, with an epilogue–O, such an epilogue! I was listening to it with uncommon attention, from a compliment paid in it to Mrs. Montagu, among other female writers; but imagine what became of my attention when I suddenly was struck with these lines, or something like them:–

Let sweet Cecilia gain your just applause, Whose every passion yields to Reason's laws."

To hear, wholly unprepared and unsuspicious, such lines in a theatre–seated in a royal box–and with the whole royal family and their suite immediately opposite me–was it not a singular circumstance? To describe my embarrassment would be impossible. My whole head was leaning forward, with my opera glass in my hand, examining Miss Farren, who spoke the epilogue. Instantly I shrank back, so astonished and so ashamed of my public situation, that I was almost ready to take to my heels and run, for it seemed as if I were there purposely in that conspicuous place–

"To list attentive to my own applause."

The king immediately raised his opera-glass to look at me, laughing heartily–the queen's presently took the same direction–all the princesses looked up, and all the attendants, and all the maids of honour!

I protest I was never more at a loss what to do with myself: nobody was in the front row with me but Miss Goldsworthy, who instantly seeing how I was disconcerted, prudently and good-naturedly forbore taking any notice of me. I sat as far back as I could, and kept my fan against the exposed profile for the rest of the night, never once leaning forward, nor using my glass.

None of the royal family spoke to me on this matter till a few days after; but I heard from Mrs. Delany they had all declared

themselves sorry for the confusion it had caused me. And some time after the queen could not forbear saying, "I hope, Miss Burney, YOU minded the epilogue the other night?"

And the king, very comically, said, "I took a peep at you!–I could not help that. I wanted to see how you looked when your father first discovered your writing–and now I think I know!"

THE KING's BIRTHDAY.

St. James's Palace, June 4-Take a little of the humours of this day, with respect to myself, as they have arisen. I quitted my downy pillow at half-past six o'clock, for bad habits in sickness have lost me half an hour of every morning; and then, according to an etiquette I discovered but on Friday night, I was quite new dressed: for I find that, on the king's birthday, and on the queen's, both real and nominal, two new attires, one half, the other full dressed, are expected from all attendants that come into the royal presence.

This first labour was happily achieved in such good time, that I was just seated to my breakfast–a delicate bit of roll half-eaten, and a promising dish of tea well stirred–when I received my summons to attend the queen.

She was only with her wardrobe-woman, and accepted most graciously a little murmuring congratulation upon the- day, which I ventured to whisper while she looked another way. Fortunately for me, she is always quick in conceiving what is meant, and never wastes time in demanding what is said. She told me she had bespoke Miss Planta to attend at the grand toilette at St. James's, as she saw my strength still diminished by my late illness. Indeed it still is, though in all other respects I am perfectly well.

The queen wore a very beautiful dress, of a new manufacture, of worked muslin, thin, fine, and clear, as the chambery gauze. I attended her from the blue closet, in which she dresses, through the rooms that lead to the breakfast apartment. In One of these while she stopped for her hair-dresser to finish her head-dress, the king joined her. She spoke to him in German, and he kissed her hand.

The three elder princesses came in soon after: they all went up, with congratulatory smiles and curtsies, to their royal father, who kissed them very affectionately; they then, as usual every Morning, kissed the queen's hand. The door was thrown open Page 34

to the breakfast-room, which is a noble apartment, fitted up with some of Vandyke's best works; and the instant the king, who led the way, entered, I was surprised by a sudden sound of music, and found that a band of musicians were stationed there to welcome him. The princesses followed, but Princess Elizabeth turned round to me to say she could hardly bear the sound: it was the first morning of her coming down to breakfast for many months, as she had had that repast in her own room ever since her dangerous illness. It overcame her, she said, more than the dressing, more than the early rising, more than the whole of the hurry and fatigue of all the rest of a public birthday. She loves the king most tenderly; and there is a something in receiving any person who is loved, by sudden music, that I can easily conceive to be very trying to the nerves.

Princess Augusta came back to cheer and counsel her; she begged her to look out at the window, to divert her thoughts, and said she would place her where the sound might be less affecting to her.

A lively "How d'ye do, Miss Burney? I hope you are quite well now?" from the sweet Princess Mary, who was entering the ante-room, made me turn from her two charming sisters; she passed on to the breakfast, soon followed by Princess Sophia, and then a train of their governesses, Miss Goldsworthy, Mademoiselle Montmoulin, and Miss Gomme, all in full dress, with fans. We reciprocated little civilities, and I had then the pleasure to see little Princess Amelia, with Mrs. Cheveley, who brought up the rear. Never, in tale or fable, were there six sister princesses more lovely.

As I had been extremely distressed upon the queen's birthday, in January, where to go or how to act, and could obtain no information from my coadjutrix, I now resolved to ask for directions from the queen herself; and she readily gave them, in a manner to make this day far more comfortable to me than the last. She bade me dress as fast as I could, and go to St. James', by eleven o'clock; but first come into the room to her. Then followed my grand toilette. The hair-dresser was waiting for me, and he went to work first, and I second, with all our might and main. When my adorning tasks were accomplished, I went to the blue closet. No one was there, I then hesitated whether to go back or seek the queen. I have a dislike insuperable to entering a royal presence, except by an

immediate Summons: however, the directions I had had prevailed, and I- went into the adjoining apartment. There stood Madame de la Fite! she was talking in a low voice with M. de Luc. They told me the queen was in the next room, and on I went.

She was seated at a glass, and the hair-dresser was putting on her jewels, while a clergyman in his canonicals was standing near and talking to her. I imagined him some bishop unknown to me, and stopped; the queen looked round, and called out "it's Miss Burney!–come in, Miss Burney." in I came, curtseying respectfully to a bow from the canonicals, but I found not out till he answered something said by the queen, that it was no other than Mr. Turbulent.

Madame de la Fite then presented herself at the door (which was open for air) of the ante-room. The queen bowed to her, and said she would see her presently: she retired, and her majesty, in a significant low voice, said to me, "Do go to her, and keep her there a little!" I obeyed, and being now in no fright nor hurry, entered into conversation with her sociably and comfortably.

I then went to St. James's. The queen was most brilliant in attire; and when she was arrayed, Mr. West(233) was allowed to enter the dressing-room, in order to give his opinion of the disposition -of her jewels, which indeed were arranged with great taste and effect.

The three princesses, Princess Royal, Augusta, and Elizabeth, were all very splendidly decorated, and looked beautiful. They are indeed uncommonly handsome, each in their different Way-the princess royal for figure, the Princess Augusta for countenance, and the Princess Elizabeth for face.

THE EQUERRIES: COLONEL MANNERS.

Friday, June 8-This day we came to Windsor for the Summer, during which we only go to town for a Drawing-room once a fortnight, and to Kew in the way. Mrs. Schwellenberg remained in town, not well enough to move.

The house now was quite full, the king having ordered a party to it for the Whitsun holidays. This party was Colonel

Manners, the equerry in waiting; Colonel Ramsden, a good-humoured and well-bred old officer of the king's household; Colonels Wellbred and Goldsworthy, and General Budé.

Colonel Ramsden is gentle and pleasing, but very silent; General Budé is always cheerful, but rises not above a second; Colonel Hotham has a shyness that looks haughty, and therefore distances; Colonel Goldsworthy reserves his sport and humour for particular days and particular favourites; and Colonel Wellbred draws back into himself unless the conversation promises either instruction or quiet pleasure; nor would any one of these, during the whole time, speak at all, but to a next neighbour, nor even then, except when that neighbour suited his fancy.

You must not, however, imagine we had no public speakers; M. del Campo harangued aloud to whoever was willing to listen, and Colonel Manners did the same, without even waiting for that proviso. Colonel Manners, however, I must introduce to you by a few specimens: he is so often, in common with all the equerries, to appear on the scene, that I wish you to make a particular acquaintance with him.

One evening, when we were all, as usual, assembled, he began a discourse upon the conclusion of his waiting, which finishes with the end of June:–"Now I don't think," cried he, "that it's well managed: here we're all in waiting for three months at a time, and then for nine months there's nothing!"

"Cry your mercy!" cried Colonel Goldsworthy, "if three months- -three whole months–are not enough for you, pray take a few more from mine to make up your market!"

"No, no, I don't mean that;–but why can't we have our waitings month by month?– would not that be better?"

"I think not!–we should then have no time unbroken."

"Well, but would not that be better than what it is now? Why, we're here so long, that when one goes away nobody knows one!– one has quite to make a new acquaintance! Why, when I first come out of waiting, I never know where to find anybody!"

The Ascot races were held at this time; the royal family were to be at them one or two of the days. Colonel Manners earnestly pressed Miss Port to be there. Colonel Goldsworthy said it was quite immaterial to him who was there, for when he was attending royalty he never presumed to think of any private comfort.

"Well, I don't see that!" cried Colonel Manners,–"for if
I was you, and not in my turn for waiting, I should go about just as I liked;–but
now, as for me, as it happens to be my own turn, Why I think it right to be civil to the
king."

We all looked round;–but Colonel Goldsworthy broke forth aloud– "Civil, quotha?"
cried he; "Ha! ha! civil, forsooth!–You're mighty condescending!–the first equerry
I ever heard talk of his civility to the king!–'Duty,' and 'respect,' and 'humble
reverence,'–those are words we are used to,–but here come you with Your civility!—
-Commend me to such affability!"

you see he is not spared; but Colonel Goldsworthy is the wag professed of their
community, and privileged to say what he pleases. The other, with the most perfect
good-humour, accepted the joke, without dreaming of taking offence at the sarcasm.

Another evening the king sent for Colonel Ramsden to play at backgammon.

"Happy, happy man!" exclaimed Colonel Goldsworthy, exultingly; but scarce had
he uttered the words ere he was summoned to follow himself. "What! already!" cried
he,–"without even my tea! Why this is worse and worse!–no peace in Israel!–only
one half hour allowed for comfort, and now that's swallowed! Well, I must go;–make
my complaints aside, and my bows and smiles in full face!"

Off he went, but presently, in a great rage, came back, and, while he drank a hot
dish of tea which I instantly presented him, kept railing at his stars for ever bringing
him under a royal roof. "If it had not been for a puppy," cried he, "I had never got
off even to scald my throat in this manner But they've just got a dear little new ugly
dog: so one puppy gave Way to t'other, and I just left them to kiss and hug it, while I
stole off to drink this tea! But this is too much!—no peace for a moment!– no peace
in Israel!"

When this was passed, Colonel Wellbred renewed some of the conversation of the
preceding day with me; and, just as he named Dr. Herschel Colonel Manners broke
forth with his dissenting opinions. "I don't give up to Dr. Herschel at all," cried he;
"he is all system; and so they are all: and if they can but make out their systems, they
don't care a pin for anything else. As to Herschel, I liked him well enough till he came
to his volcanoes in the moon, and then I gave him up, I saw he was just like the rest.
How should he know anything Of the matter? There's no such thing as pretending to
measure, at such a distance as that?"

Colonel Wellbred, to whom I looked for an answer, instead of making any, waited
in quiet silence till he had exhausted all he had to say upon the subject, and then,
turning to me, made some inquiry about the Terrace, and went on to other general
matters. But, some time after, when all were engaged, and this topic seemed quite
passed, he calmly began, in general terms, to lament that the wisest and best of people
were always so little honoured or understood in their own time, and added that he had
no doubt but Sir Isaac Newton had been as much scoffed and laughed at formerly as
Herschel was now; but concluded, in return, Herschel, hereafter, would be as highly
reverenced as Sir Isaac was at present. . . .

We had then some discourse upon dress and fashions. Virtuosos being next named,
Colonel Manners inveighed against them quite violently, protesting they all wanted
common honour and honesty; and to complete the happy subject, he instanced, in

particular, Sir William Hamilton, who, he declared, had absolutely robbed both the king and state of Naples!

After this, somebody related that, upon the heat in the air being mentioned to Dr. Heberden, he had answered that he supposed it proceeded from the last eruption in the volcano in the moon: "Ay," cried Colonel Manners, "I suppose he knows as much of the matter as the rest of them: if you put a candle at the end of a telescope, and let him look at it, he'll say, what an eruption there is in the moon! I mean if Dr, Herschel would do it to him; I don't say he would think so from such a person as me."

"But Mr. Bryant himself has seen this volcano from the telescope."

"Why, I don't mind Mr. Bryant any more than Dr. Heberden: he's just as credulous as t'other."

I wanted to ask by what criterion he settled these points in so superior a manner:–but I thought it best to imitate the silence of Colonel Wellbred, who constantly called a new subject, upon every pause, to avoid all argument and discussion while the good-humoured Colonel Manners was just as ready to start forward in the new subject, as he had been in that which had been set aside.

One other evening I invited Madame de la Fite: but it did not prove the same thing; they have all a really most undue dislike of her, and shirk her conversation and fly to one another, to discourse on hunting and horses.

THE DUCHESS DE POLIGNAC AT WINDSOR.

The following Sunday, June 17, I was tempted to go on the Terrace, in order to se the celebrated Madame de Polignac,(234) and her daughter, Madame de Guiche. They were to be presented, with the Duke de Polignac, to their majesties, upon the Terrace. Their rank entitled them to this distinction; and the Duchess of Ancaster, to whom they had been extremely courteous abroad, came to Windsor to introduce them. They were accompanied to the Terrace by Mrs. Harcourt and the general 'with whom they were also well acquainted.

They went to the place of rendezvous at six o'clock; the royal party followed about seven, and was very brilliant upon the occasion. The king and queen led the way, and the Prince of Wales, who came purposely to honour the interview, appeared at it also, in the king's Windsor uniform. Lady Weymouth was in waiting upon the queen. The Duchess of Ancaster, Lady Charlotte Bertie, and Lady Elizabeth Waldegrave, with some other ladies, I think, attended: but the two eldest princesses, to the very great detriment of the scenery, were ill, and remained at home. Princess Elizabeth and Mary were alone in the queen's suite.

I went with Miss Port and Mrs. and Miss Heberden. The crowd was so great, it was difficult to move. Their majesties and their train occupied a large space, and their attendants

had no easy task in keeping them from being incommoded by the pressing of the people. They stopped to converse with these noble travellers for more than an hour. Madame la Duchesse de Polignac is a very well-looking woman, and Madame de Guiche is very pretty. There were other ladies and gentlemen in their party. But I was much amused by their dress, which they meant should be entirely 'a l'Angloise–for which purpose they had put on plain undress gowns, with close ordinary black silk bonnets! I am sure they must have been quite confused when they saw the queen and princesses, with their ladies, who were all dressed with uncommon care, and very splendidly.

But I was glad, at least, they should all witness, and report, the reconciliation of the king and the Prince of Wales, who frequently spoke together, and were both in good spirits.

COLONEL MANNERS' MUSICAL ACCOMPLISHMENTS.

Miss Port and myself had, afterwards, an extremely risible evening with Colonels Goldsworthy, Wellbred, and Manners the rest were summoned away to the king, or retired to their own apartments. Colonel Wellbred began the sport, undesignedly, by telling me something new relative to Dr. Herschel's volcanoes. This was enough for Colonel Manners, who declared aloud his utter contempt for such pretended discoveries. He was deaf to all that could be said in answer, and protested he wondered how any man of common sense could ever listen to such a pack of stuff.

Mr. de Luc's opinion upon the subject being then mentioned–he exclaimed, very disdainfully, "O, as to Mr. de Luc, he's another man for a system himself, and I'd no more trust him than anybody: if you was only to make a little bonfire, and put it upon a hill a little way off, you might make him take it for a volcano directly!–And Herschel's not a bit better. Those sort of philosophers are the easiest taken in in the world." Our next topic was still more ludicrous. Colonel Manners asked me if I had not heard something, very harmonious at church in the morning? I answered I was too far off, if he meant from himself.

"Yes," said he; "I was singing with Colonel Wellbred; and he said he was my second.–How did I do that song?"

"Song?–Mercy!" exclaimed Colonel Goldsworthy, "a song at church!–why it was the 104th Psalm!"

"But how did I do it, Wellbred; for I never tried at it before?"

"why–pretty well," answered Colonel Wellbred, very composedly; "Only now and then you run me a little into 'God save the king.'"

This dryness discomposed every muscle but of Colonel Manners, who replied, with great simplicity, "Why, that's because that's the tune I know best!"

"At least," cried I, "'twas a happy mistake to make so near their majesties."

"But: pray, now, Colonel Wellbred, tell me sincerely)–could you really make out what I was singing?"

"O yes," answered Colonel Wellbred; "with the words."

"Well, but pray, now, what do you call my voice?"

"Why–a–a–a counter-tenor."

"Well, and is that a good voice?"

There was no resisting,-even the quiet Colonel Wellbred could not resist laughing out here. But Colonel Manners, quite at his ease, continued his self-discussion.

"I do think, now, if I was to have a person to play over a thing to me again and again, and then let me sing it, and stop me every time I was wrong, I do think I should be able to sing 'God save the king' as well as some ladies do, that have always people to show them."

"You have a good chance then here," cried I, "of singing some pieces of Handel, for I am sure you hear them again and again!"

"Yes, but that is not the thing for though I hear them do it' so often over, they don't stop for me to sing it after them, and then to set me right. Now I'll try if you'll know what this is."

He then began humming aloud, "My soul praise," etc., so very horribly, that I really found all decorum at an end, and laughed, with Miss Port, 'a qui mieux mieux. Too much engaged to mind this, he very innocently, when he had done, applied to us all round for our opinions.

Miss Port begged him to sing another, and asked for that he had spouted the other day, "Care, thou bane of love and joy."

He instantly complied; and went on, in such shocking, discordant and unmeaning sounds, that nothing in a farce could be more risible: in defiance however of all interruptions, he Continued till he had finished one stanza; when Colonel Goldsworthy loudly called out,–"There,–there's enough!–have mercy!"

"Well, then, now I'll try something else."

"O, no!" cried Colonel Goldsworthy, hastily, "thank you, thank you for this,-but I won't trouble you for more–I'll not bear another word."

Colonel Wellbred then, with an affected seriousness, begged to know, since he took to singing, what he should do for a shake, which was absolutely indispensable.

"A shake?" he repeated, "what do you mean?"

"Why–a shake with the voice, such as singers make."

"Why, how must I do it?"

"O, really, I cannot tell you."

"Why, then, I'll try myself–is it so?"

And he began such a harsh hoarse noise, that Colonel Goldsworthy exclaimed, between every other sound,–"No, no,–no more!" While Colonel Wellbred professed teaching him, and gave such ridiculous lessons and directions,-now to stop short, now to swell,-now to sink the voice, etc., etc., that, between the master and the scholar, we were almost demolished.

MRS. SCHWELLENBERG'S "LUMP OF LEATHER."

Tuesday, June 19.-We were scarcely all arranged at tea when Colonel Manners eagerly said, "Pray, Mrs. Schwellenberg, have you lost anything?"

"Me?–no, not I

"No?–what, nothing?"

"Not I!"

"Well, then, that's very odd! for I found something that had your name writ upon it."

"My name? and where did you find that?"

"Why–it was something I found in my bed."

"In your bed?–O, very well! that is reelly comeecal?"

"And pray what was it?" cried Miss Port.

"Why–a great large, clumsy lump of leather."

"Of leadder, sir?–of leadder? What was that for me?"

"Why, ma'am, it was so big and so heavy, it was as much as I could do to lift it!"

"Well, that was nothing from me! when it was so heavy, you might let it alone!"

"But, ma'am, Colonel Wellbred said it was somewhat of yours."

"Of mine?–O, ver well! Colonel Wellbred might not say such thing! I know nothing, Sir, from your leadder, nor from your bed, sir,–not I!"

"Well, ma'am, then your maid does. Colonel Wellbred says he supposes it was she."

"Upon my vord! Colonel Wellbred might not say such things from my maid! I won't not have it so!"

"O yes, ma'am; Colonel Wellbred says she often does SO. He says she's a very gay lady."

She was quite too much amazed to speak: one of her maids, Mrs. Arline, is a poor humble thing, that would not venture to jest, I believe, with the kitchen maid, and the other has never before been at Windsor.

"But what was it?" cried Miss Port.

"Why, I tell you–a great, large lump of leather, with 'Madame Schwellenberg' wrote upon it. However, I've ordered it to be sold."

"To be sold? How will you have it sold, Sir? You might tell me that, when you please."

"Why, by auction, ma'am."

"By auction, Sir? What, when it had my name upon it? Upon my vord!–how come you to do dat, sir? Will you tell me, once?"

"Why, I did it for the benefit of my man, ma'am, that he might have the money."

"But for what is your man to have it, when it is mine?"

"Because, ma'am, it frightened him so."

"O, ver well! Do you rob, sir? Do you take what is not your own, but others', sir, because your man is frightened?"

"O yes, ma'am! We military men take all we can get!"

"What! in the king's house, Sir!"

"Why then, ma'am, what business had it in my bed? My room's my castle: nobody has a right there. My bed must be my treasury; and here they put me a thing into it big enough to be a bed itself."——

"O! vell! (much alarmed) it might be my bed-case, then!" (Whenever Mrs. Schwellenberg travels, she carries her bed in a large black leather case, behind her servants' carriage.)

" Very likely, ma'am."

"Then, sir," very angrily, "how Come you by it?"

"Why, I'll tell you, ma'am. I was just going to bed; so MY servant took one candle, and I had the other. I had just had my hair done, and my curls were just rolled up, and he

was going away; but I turned about, by accident, and I saw a great lump in my bed; so I thought it was my clothes. 'What do you put them there for?' says I. 'Sir,' says he, 'it looks as if there was a drunken man in the bed.' 'A drunken man?' says I; 'Take the poker, then, and knock him on the head!'"

"Knock him on the head?" interrupted Mrs. Schwellenberg, "What! when it might be some innocent person? Fie! Colonel Manners. I thought you had been too good-natured for such thing–to poker the people in the king's house!"

"Then what business have they to get into my bed, ma'am? So then my man looked nearer, and he said, 'Sir, why, here's your night-cap and here's the pillow!–and here's a great, large lump of leather!' 'Shovel it all out!' says I. 'Sir,' says he, 'It's Madame Schwellenberg's! here's her name on it.' 'Well, then,' says I, 'sell it, to-morrow, to the saddler.'"

"What! when you knew it was mine, sir? Upon my vord, you been ver good!" (bowing very low).

"Well, ma'am, it's all Colonel Wellbred, I dare say; so, suppose you and I were to take the law of him?"

"Not I, sir!" (Scornfully).

"Well, but let's write him a letter, then, and frighten him: let's tell him it's sold, and he must make it good. You and I'll do it together."

"No, sir; you might do it yourself. I am not so familiar to write to gentlemens."

"Why then, you shall only sign it, and I'll frank it."

Here the entrance of some new person stopped the discussion.

Happy in his success, he began, the next day, a new device: he made an attack in politics, and said, he did not doubt but Mr. Hastings would come to be hanged; though, he assured us, afterwards, he was firmly his friend, and believed no such thing.(236)

Even with this not satisfied, he next told her that he had just heard Mr. Burke was in Windsor. Mr. Burke is the name in the world most obnoxious, both for his Reform bill,(237) which deeply affected all the household, and for his prosecution of Mr. Hastings; she therefore declaimed against him very warmly.

"Should you like to know him, ma'am?" cried he.

"Me?–No; not I."

"Because, I dare say, ma'am, I have interest enough with him to procure you his acquaintance. Shall I bring him to the Lodge to see you?"

"When you please, sir, you might keep him to yourself!"

"Well, then, he shall come and dine with me,'and after it drink tea with you."

"No, no, not I! You might have him all to yourself."

"but if he comes, you must make his tea."

"There is no such 'must,' sir! I do it for my pleasure–only when I please, sir!"

At night, when we were separating, he whispered Miss Port that he had something else in store for the next meeting, when he intended to introduce magnetising.

MRS. SCHWELLENBERG's FROGS.

July 2.-What a stare was drawn from our new equerry(238) by Major Price's gravely asking Mrs. Schwellenberg, after the health of her frogs? She answered they were very well, and the major said, " You must know, Colonel Gwynn, Mrs. Schwellenberg keeps a pair of frogs,"

"Of frogs?–pray what do they feed upon?"

"Flies, sir," she answered.

"And pray, ma'am, what food have they in winter?"

"Nothing other."

The stare was now still wider.

"But I can make them croak when I will," she added, "when I only go so to my snuff-box, knock, knock, knock, they croak all what I please."

"Very pretty, indeed!" exclaimed Colonel Goldsworthy.

"I thought to have some spawn," she continued; "but then Maria Carlton, what you call Lady Doncaster, came and frightened them; I was never so angry!"

"I am sorry for that," cried the major, very seriously, "for else I should have begged a pair."

"So you meant, ma'am, to have had a breed of them," cried Colonel Goldsworthy; "a breed of young frogs? Vastly clever, indeed!;

Then followed a formal enumeration of their virtues and endearing little qualities, which made all laugh except the new equerry, who sat in perfect amaze.

Then, suddenly, she stopped short, and called out, "There! now I have told you all this, you might tell something to me. I have talked enoff; now you might amuse me."

July 19.-In the afternoon, while I was working in Mrs. Schwellenberg's room, Mr. Turbulent entered, to summon Miss Planta to the princesses; and, in the little while of executing that simple commission, he made such use of his very ungovernable and extraordinary eyes, that the moment he was gone, Mrs. Schwellenberg demanded "for what he looked so at me?"

I desired to know what she meant.

"Why, like when he was so cordial with you? Been you acquainted?"

"O, yes!" cried I, "I spent three hours twice a-week upon the road with him and Miss Planta, all the winter; and three or four dinners and afternoons besides."

"O that's nothing! that's no acquaintance at all. I have had people to me, to travel and to dine, fourteen and fifteen years, and yet they been never so cordial!"

This was too unanswerable for reply; but it determined me to try at some decided measure for restraining or changing looks and behaviour that excited such comments. And I thought my safest way would be fairly and frankly to tell him this very inquiry. It might put him upon his guard from such foolishness, without any more serious effort.

July 20.-This evening Mrs. Schwellenberg was not well, and sent to desire I would receive the gentlemen to tea, and make her apologies. I immediately summoned my lively, and lovely young companion, Miss Port, who hastens at every call with good-humoured delight.

We had really a pleasant evening, though simply from the absence of spleen and jealousy, which seemed to renew and invigorate the spirits of all present: namely, General Budé, Signor del Campo, and Colonel Gwynn. They all stayed very late but when they made their exit, I dismissed my gay assistant and thought it incumbent on me to show myself upstairs; a reception was awaiting me!-so grim! But, what O heaven! how depressing, how cruel, to be fastened thus on an associate so exigeante, so tyrannical, and so ill-disposed!

I feared to blame the equerries for having detained me, as they were already so much out of favour. I only, therefore, mentioned M. del Campo, who, as a foreign minister, might be allowed so much civility as not to be left to himself: for I was openly reproached- that I had not quitted them to hasten to her! Nothing, however, availed; and after vainly trying to appease her, I was obliged to go to my own room, to be in attendance for my royal summons.

July 21.-I resolved to be very meek and patient, as I do, now and then, when I am good, and to bear this hard trial of causeless offence without resentment; and, therefore, I went this afternoon as soon as I had dined, and sat and worked, and forced conversation, and did my best, but with very indifferent success; when, most perversely, who should be again announced -but Mr. Turbulent. As I believe the visit was not, just after those "cordial" looks, supposed to be solely for the lady of the apartment, his reception was no better than mine had been the preceding days! He did not, however, regard it, but began a talk, in which he made it his business to involve me, by perpetual reference to my opinion. This did not much conciliate matters; and his rebuffs, from time to time, were so little ceremonious, that nothing but the most confirmed contempt could have kept off an angry resentment. I could sometimes scarcely help laughing at his utterly careless returns to an imperious haughtiness, vainly meant to abash and distance him. I took the earliest moment in my power to quit the room and the reproach with which he looked at my exit, for leaving him to such a tête-à-tête, was quite risible. He knew he could not, in decency, run away immediately, to and he seemed ready to commit some desperate act for having drawn himself into such a difficulty. I am always rejoiced when his flights and follies bring their own punishment.

MR. TURBULENT'S ANTICS.

July 25-Mr. Turbulent amused himself this morning with giving me yet another panic. He was ordered to attend the queen during her hair-dressing, as was Mr. de Luc. I remained in the room the queen conversed with us all three, as occasions arose, with the utmost complacency; but this person, instead of fixing there his sole attention, contrived, by standing behind her chair, and facing me, to address a language of signs to me the whole time, casting up his eyes, clasping],is hands, and placing himself in various fine attitudes, and all with a humour so burlesque, that it was impossible to take it either ill or seriously. Indeed, when I am on the very point of the most alarmed displeasure with him, he always falls upon some such ridiculous devices of affected homage, that I grow ashamed of my anger, and hurry it over, lest he should perceive it, and attribute it to a misunderstanding he might think ridiculous in his turn.

How much should I have been discountenanced had her majesty turned about and perceived him!

(230) Colonel Greville, called in the "Diary" "Colonel Wellbred," one of the king's equerries, whom M. de Guiffardiere ("Mr. Turbulent") was particularly anxious to introduce to Miss Burney.-ED.

(231) I "The Paston Letters" were first published, from the original manuscripts, in 1787. They were chiefly written by or to members of the Paston family in Norfolk during the reigns of Henry VI., Edward IV., Richard III., and Henry VII. The letter above alluded to is No. 91 in the collection. It is a letter of good Counsel to his young son, written in a very tender and religious strain, by the Duke of Suffolk, on the 30th of April, 1450, the day on which he quitted England to undergo his five years' banishment. The duke had been impeached of high treason, and condemned to this term of banishment, through the king's interposition, to save him from a worse fate.

But his fate was not to be eluded. He set sail on the 30th of April, was taken on the sea by his enemies, and beheaded on the 2nd of May following.-ED.

(232) Miss Burney had obtained the tacit consent of the queen that M. de Guiffardiere should travel occasionally with the equerries, instead of taking his usual place in the coach assigned to the keepers of the robes. Her real motive in making the application had been a desire to see less of this boisterous gentleman, but she had put it upon his attachment to Colonel Greville-ED.

(233) Benjamin -west, R.A., who succeeded Reynolds as President of the Royal Academy, on the death of the latter in 1792. This mediocre painter was a prodigious favourite with George III., for whom many of his works were executed.-ED.

(234) The Duchess Jules de Polignac, the celebrated favourite of Marie Antoinette. She and her husband, who had been raised by the queen from a condition of positive poverty, were hated in France, both as Court favourites, and on account of the wealth which, it was believed, they had taken advantage of their position to amass. "Mille 6cus," cried Mirabeau, "A la famille d'Assas pour avoir sauv6 l'etat; un million a la famille Polignac pour l'avoir perdu!"

The ostensible object of the duches,'s visit to England was to drink the Bath Waters, but there are good grounds for believing that her real purpose was to make an arrangement with M. de la Motte for the suppression of some scurrilous Memoirs which it was rumoured his wife had written, and in which, among other things, Marie Antoinette was accused of being the principal culprit in the notorious Diamond Necldace fraud. M. de la Motte states in his autobiography that he met the Duchess Jules and her Sister-in-law, the Countess Diane, at the Duchess of Devonshire's (the beautiful Georgiana), at the request of the latter, when certain overtures were made to him, and trustworthy authorities assert that a large sum of money was afterwards paid to the De la Mottes, to suppress the Memoirs which were however eventually published. When the French Revolution broke out the Polignacs were among the first to emigrate. The duchess died at Vienna in December, 1793, a few months after Marie Antoinette had perished on the scaffold.-ED.

(235) Mrs. Schwellenberg had returned to Windsor the day before.-ED.

(236) The storm had been gathering round Hastings ever since his return to England in June, 1785, within a week of which Burke had given notice in the House of Commons of a motion affecting the conduct of the late Governor-General in India. His impeachment was voted in May, 1787, and preparations for his trial were now going actively forward. We shall find hereafter, in the Diary, some sketches, from Fanny's point of view, of scenes in this famous trial, which commenced in February, 1788.-ED.

(237) This was an old grievance. In 1780 Burke had introduced a hill "for the better regulation of his majesty's civil establishments, and of certain public offices; for the limitation of pensions, and the suppression of sundry useless, expensive and inconvenient places; and for applying the monies saved thereby to the public service." The bill was defeated at the time, but was re-introduced with certain alterations, and finally passed both houses by a large majority in 1782.-ED.

(238) Colonel Gwynn who had just arrived at Windsor to succeed
Colonel Manners in the office of equerry in waiting to the King.

Colonel Gwynn was the husband of Mary Horneck, Goldsmith's "Jessamy Bride."-ED.

SECTION 11. (1787-8.)
COURT DUTIES: SOME VARIATIONS IN THEIR ROUTINE.
MEETING OF THE TWO PRINCES.

To-day, after a seven years' absence, arrived the Duke of York. I saw him alight from his carriage, with an eagerness, a vivacity, that assured me of the affectionate joy with which he returned to his country and family. But the joy of his excellent father!-O, that there is no describing It was the glee of the first youth–nay, of ai ardent and innocent infancy,–so pure it seemed, so warm, so open, so unmixed! Softer joy was the queen's–mild, equal, and touching while all the princesses were in one universal rapture.

To have the pleasure of seeing the royal family in this happy assemblage, I accompanied Miss Port on the Terrace. It was indeed an affecting sight to view the general content; but that of the king went to my very heart, so delighted he looked-so proud Of his son–so benevolently pleased that every one should witness his satisfaction. The Terrace was very full; all Windsor and its neighbourhood poured in upon it, to see the prince whose whole demeanour seemed promising to merit his flattering reception–gay yet grateful–modest, yet unembarrassed

Early the next morning arrived the Prince of Wales, who had travelled all night from Brighthelmstone. The day was a day Of complete happiness to the whole of the royal family; the king was in one transport of delight, unceasing, invariable;

and though the newly-arrived duke was its source and Support the kindness of his heart extended and expanded to his eldest' born, whom he seemed ready again to take to his paternal breast; indeed, the whole world seemed endeared to him by the happiness he now felt in it.

Sunday, Aug. 5.-General Grenville brought in the duke this evening to the tea-room. I was very much pleased with his behaviour, which was modest, dignified, and easy. Might he but escape the contagion of surrounding examples, he seems promising of all his fond father expects and merits. . . .

Kew, Aug. 7-The next day the now happy family had the delight of again seeing the two princes in its circle. They dined here; and the Princess Augusta, who came to Mrs. Schwellenberg's room in the evening, on a message, said, "There never had been so happy a dinner since the world was created," The king, In the evening, again drove out the queen and princesses. The Prince of Wales, seeing Mr. Smelt in our room (which, at Kew, is in the front of the house, as well as at Windsor), said he would come in and ask him how he did. Accordingly, in he came, and talked to Mr. Smelt for about a quarter of an hour; his subjects almost wholly his horses and his rides. He gave some account of his expedition to town to meet his brother. He was just preparing, at Brighton, to give a supper entertainment to Madame La Princesse de Lamballe,–when he perceived his courier. "I dare say," he cried, "my brother's come!" set off instantly to excuse himself to the princess, and arrived at Windsor by the time of early prayers, at eight o'clock the next morning.

"To-day, again," he said, "I resolved to be in town to meet my brother; we determined to dine somewhere together, but had not settled where; so hither we came.

When I went last to Brighton, I rode one hundred and thirty miles, and then danced at the ball,. I am going back directly; but I shall ride to Windsor again for the birthday, and shall stay there till my brother's, and then back on Friday. We are going now over the way: my brother wants to see the old mansion."

The Prince of Wales's house is exactly opposite to the Lodge

The duke then came in, and bowed to every one present, very attentively; and presently after, they went over the way, arm in arm; and thence returned to town.

I had a long and painful discourse afterwards with Mr. Smelt, deeply interested in these young princes , upon the many dangers awaiting the newly-arrived, who seemed alike

unfitted and unsuspicious for encountering them. Mr. Smelt's heart ached as if he had been their parent, and the regard springing from his early and long care of them seemed all revived in his hopes and fears of what might ensue from this reunion.

I rejoiced at the public reconciliation with the Prince of Wales, which had taken place during my illness, and which gave the greater reason for hope that there might not now be a division!

BUNBURY, THE CARICATURIST.

Windsor, Aug. 14.-General Budé came in, with two strangers, whom he introduced to us by the names of Bunbury and Crawfurd. I was very curious to know if this was the Bunbury;(239) and I conjectured it could be no other. When Colonel Gwynn joined us, he proposed anew the introduction; but nothing passed to ascertain my surmise. The conversation was general And good-humoured, but without anything striking, or bespeaking character or genius. Almost the whole consisted of inquiries what to do, whither to go, and how to proceed; which, though natural and sensible for a new man, were undistinguished by any humour, or keenness of expression or manner.

Mr. Crawfurd spoke not a word. He is a very handsome young man, just appointed equerry to the Duke of York.

I whispered my inquiry to Colonel Gwynn as soon as I found an opportunity, and heard, "Yes,–'tis Harry Bunbury, sure enough!"

So now we may all be caricatured at his leisure! He is made another of the equerries to the Duke. A man with such a turn, and with talents so inimitable in displaying it, was rather a dangerous character to be brought within a Court!

Aug. 15.-My sole conversation this evening was with Mr. Bunbury, who drew a chair next mine, and chatted incessantly, with great good humour, and an avidity to discuss the subjects he started, which were all concerning plays and Players.

Presently the voice of the Duke of York was heard, calling aloud for Colonel Goldsworthy. Off he ran. Mr. Bunbury laughed, but declared he would not take the hint: "What," cried he, "if I lose the beginning?(240)–I think I know it pretty well by heart'-'Why did I marry' '"–And then he began to spout, and act, and rattle away, with all his might,-till the same voice called out "Bunbury !–you'll be too late!"–And off he flew, leaving his tea untasted–so eager had he been in discourse.

MRS. SIDDONS PROVES DISAPPOINTING ON NEAR ACQUAINTANCE.

Wednesday, Aug. 15.-Mrs. Schwellenberg's illness occasioned my attending the queen alone; and when my official business was ended, she graciously detained me, to read to me a new paper called "Olla Podrida," which is now Publishing periodically. Nothing very bright–nothing very deficient.

In the afternoon, while I was drinking coffee with Mrs. Schwellenberg,–or, rather, looking at it, since I rarely, swallow any,–her majesty came Into the room, and soon after a little German discourse with Mrs. Schwellenberg told me Mrs. Siddons had been ordered to the Lodge, to read a play, and desired I would receive her in my room

I felt a little queer in the office ; I had only seen her twice or thrice, in large assemblies, at Miss Monckton's, and at Sir Joshua Reynolds's, and never had been introduced to her, nor spoken with her. However, in this dead and tame life I now lead, such an interview was by no means undesirable.

I had just got to the bottom of the stairs, when she entered the passage gallery. I took her into the tea-room, and endeavoured to make amends for former distance and taciturnity, by an open and cheerful reception. I had heard from sundry people (in old days) that she wished to make the acquaintance; but I thought it then one of too conspicuous a sort for the quietness I had so much difficulty to preserve in my ever increasing connections. Here all was changed; I received her by the queen's commands, and was perfectly well inclined to reap some pleasure from the meeting.

But, now that we came so near, I was much disappointed in my expectations. I know not if my dear Fredy has met with her in private, but I fancy approximation is not highly in her favour. I found her the heroine of a tragedy,–sublime, elevated, and solemn. In face and person truly noble and commanding; in manners quiet and stiff; in voice deep and dragging; and in conversation, formal, sententious, calm, and

dry. I expected her to have been all that is interesting; the delicacy and sweetness with which she seizes every opportunity to strike and to captivate upon the stage had persuaded me that her mind was formed with that peculiar susceptibility which, in different modes, must give equal powers to attract and to delight in common life. But I was very much mistaken. As a stranger I must have admired her noble appearance and beautiful countenance, and have regretted that nothing in her conversation kept pace with their promise and, as a celebrated actress I had still only to do the same.

Whether fame and success have spoiled her, or whether she only possesses the skill of representing and embellishing materials with which she is furnished by others, I know not but still I remain disappointed.

She was scarcely seated, and a little general discourse begun, before she told me–at once–that "There was no part she had ever so much wished to act as that of Cecilia."

I made some little acknowledgment, and hurried to ask when she had seen Sir Joshua Reynolds, Miss Palmer, and others with whom I knew her acquainted.

The play she was to read was "The Provoked Husband." She appeared neither alarmed nor elated by her summons, but calmly to look upon it as a thing of course, from her celebrity.

I should very much have liked to have heard her read the play, but my dearest Mrs. Delany spent the whole evening with me, and I could therefore take no measures for finding out a convenient adjoining room. Mrs. Schwellenberg, I heard afterwards, was so accommodated, though not well enough for the tea-table.

MR. FAIRLY'S BEREAVEMENT.

Aug. 23.-At St. James's I read in the newspapers a paragraph that touched me much for the very amiable Mr. Fairly: it was the death of his wife, which happened on the Duke of York's birth-day, the 16th.(242) Mr. Fairly has devoted his whole time, strength, thoughts, and cares solely to nursing and attending her during a long and most painful illness which she sustained. They speak of her here as being amiable, but so

cold and reserved, that she was little known, and by no means in equal favour with her husband, who stands, upon the whole the highest in general esteem and regard of any individual of the household. I find every mouth open to praise and pity, love and honour him.

TROUBLESOME MR. TURBULENT.

Upon returning to Kew, I had a scene for which I was little enough, indeed, prepared, though willing, and indeed, earnest to satisfy Mr. Turbulent, I wished him to make an alteration of behaviour. After hastily changing my dress, I went, as usual, to the parlour, to be ready for dinner; but found there no Mrs. Schwellenberg; she was again unwell; Miss Planta was not ready, and Mr. Turbulent was reading by himself.

Away he flung his book in a moment, and hastening to shut the door lest I should retreat, he rather charged than desired me to explain my late "chilling demeanour."

Almost startled by his apparent entire ignorance of deserving it, I found an awkwardness I had not foreseen in making myself understood. I wished him rather to feel than be told the improprieties I meant to obviate - and I did what was possible by half evasive, half expressive answers, to call back his own recollection and consciousness. In vain, however, was the attempt; he protested himself wholly innocent, and that he would rather make an end of his existence than give me offence.

He saw not these very protestations were again doing it, and he grew so vehement in his defence, and so reproachful in his accusation of unjust usage, that I was soon totally in a perplexity how to extricate myself from a difficulty I had regarded simply as his own. The moment he saw I grew embarrassed, he redoubled his challenges to know the cause of my "ill-treatment." I assured him, then, I could never reckon silence ill-treatment.

"Yes," he cried, "yes, from you it is ill-treatment, and it has given me the most serious uneasiness." "I am sorry," I said, "for that, and did not mean it."

"Not mean it?" cried be. "Could you imagine I should miss your conversation, your ease, your pleasantness, your gaiety, and take no notice of the loss?"

Then followed a most violent flow of compliments, ending with a fresh demand for an explanation, made with an energy

that, to own the truth, once more quite frightened me. I endeavoured to appease him, by general promises of becoming more voluble - and I quite languished to say to him the truth at once; that his sport, his spirit, and his society would all be acceptable to me, would he but divest them of that redundance of -gallantry which rendered them offensive : but I could only think how to say this—I could not bring it out.

This promised volubility, though it softened him, he seemed to receive as a sort of acknowledgment that I owed him some reparation for the disturbance I had caused him. I stared enough at such an interpretation, which I could by no means allow; but no sooner did I disclaim it than all his violence was resumed, and he urged me to give in my charge against him with an impetuosity that almost made me tremble.

I made as little answer as possible, finding everything I said seemed but the more to inflame his violent spirit; but his emotion was such, and the cause so inadequate, and my uncertainty so unpleasant what to think of him altogether, that I was seized with sensations so nervous, I Could almost have cried. In the full torrent of his offended justification against my displeasure towards him, he perceived my increasing distress how to proceed, and, suddenly stopping, exclaimed in quite another tone, "Now, then, ma'am, I see your justice returning; you feel that you have used me very ill!"

To my great relief entered Miss Planta. He contrived to say, "Remember, you promise to explain all this."

I made him no sort of answer, and though he frequently, in the course of the evening, repeated, "I depend upon your promise! I build upon a conference," I sent his dependence and his building to Coventry, by not seeming to hear him.

I determined, however, to avoid all tête-à-têtes with him whatsoever, as much as was in my power. How very few people are fit for them, nobody living in trios and quartettos can imagine!

A CONCEITED PARSON.

Windsor.-Who should find me out now but Dr. Shepherd.(243) He is here as canon, and was in residence. He told me he had long wished to come, but had never been able to find the

way of entrance before. He made me an immense length of visit, and related to me all the exploits of his life,-so far as they were prosperous. In no farce did a man ever more floridly open upon his own perfections. He assured me I should be delighted to know the whole of his life; it was equal to anything; and everything he had was got by his own address and ingenuity.

"I could tell the king," cried he, "more than all the chapter. I want to talk to him, but he always gets out of my way; he does not know me; he takes me for a mere common person, like the rest of the canons here, and thinks of me no more than if I were only fit for the cassock;–a mere Scotch priest! Bless 'em!–they know nothing about me. You have no conception what things I have done! And I want to tell 'em all this;–It's fitter for them to hear than what comes to their ears. What I want is for somebody to tell them what I am."

They know it already, thought I.

Then, when he had exhausted this general panegyric, he descended to some few particulars; especially dilating upon his preaching, and applying to me for attesting its excellence.

"I shall make one sermon every year, precisely for you!" he cried; "I think I know what will please you. That on the creation last Sunday was just to your taste. You shall have such another next residence. I think I preach in the right tone–not too slow, like that poor wretch Grape, nor too fast like Davis and the rest of 'em; but yet fast enough never to tire them. That's just my idea of good preaching."

Then he told me what excellent apartments he had here and how much he should like my opinion in fitting them up.

MR. TURBULENT BECOMES A NUISANCE.

Aug.30.-Mrs. Schwellenberg invited Mr. Turbulent to dinner, for she said he had a large correspondence, and might amuse her. He came early; and finding nobody in the eating-parlour, begged to wait in mine till Mrs. Schwellenberg came downstairs. This was the last thing I wished; but he required no answer, and instantly resumed the Kew discussion, entreating me to tell him what he had done. I desired him to desist–in vain, he affirmed I had promised him an explanation, and he had therefore a right to it.

"You fully mistook me, then," cried I, "for I meant no

Page 57

such thing then; I mean no such thing now; and I never shall mean any such thing in future. Is this explicit? I think it best to tell you so at once, that you may expect nothing more, but give over the subject, and talk of something else. What is the news?"

"I'll talk of nothing else!–it distracts me;–pray No, no, tell Me!–I call upon your good-nature!"

"I have none–about this! "

"Upon your goodness of heart!"

"'Tis all hardness here!"

"I will cast myself at your feet,–I will kneel to you!" And he was preparing his immense person for prostration, when Goter(244) opened the door. Such an interruption to his heroics made me laugh heartily; nor could he help joining himself; though the moment she was gone he renewed his importunity with unabated earnestness.

"I remember," he cried, "it was upon the Terrace you first shewed me this disdain; and there, too, you have shown it me repeatedly since, with public superciliousness. . . . You well know you have treated me ill,–you know and have acknowledged it!"

"And when?" cried I, amazed and provoked; "when did I do what could never be done?"

"At Kew, ma'am, you were full of concern–full of remorse for the treatment you had given me!–and you owned it!"

"Good heaven, Mr. Turbulent, what can induce you to say this?"

"Is it not true?"

"Not a word of it! You know it is not!"

"Indeed," cried he, "I really and truly thought so–hoped so;–I believed you looked as if you felt your own ill-usage,- and it gave to me a delight inexpressible!"

This was almost enough to bring back the very same supercilious Distance of which he complained; but, in dread of fresh explanations, I forbore to notice this flight, and only told him he might be perfectly satisfied, since I no longer Persevered in the taciturnity to which he objected.

"But how," cried he, "do you give up, without deigning to assign one reason for It"?

"The greater the compliment!" cried I, laughing; "I give up to your request."

"Yes, ma'am, upon my speaking,-but why did you keep Me so long in that painful suspense?"

"Nay," cried I, "could I well be quicker? Till you spoke could I know if you heeded it?"

"Ah, ma'am–is there no language but of words? Do you pretend to think there is no other?'–Must I teach it you,,–teach it to Miss Burney who speaks, who understands it so well?–who is never silent, and never can b silent?"

And then came his heroic old homage to the poor eyebrows vehemently finishing with, "Do you, can you affect to know no language but speech?"

" Not," cried I, coolly, " without the trouble of more investigation than I had taken here."

He called this "contempt," and, exceedingly irritated, de sired me, once more, to explain, from beginning to end, how he had ever offended me.

"Mr. Turbulent," cried I, "will you be satisfied if I tell you it shall all blow over?"

"Make me a vow, then, you will never more, never while you live, resume that proud taciturnity."

"No, no,–certainly not; I never make vows; it is a rule with me to avoid them."

"Give me, then, your promise,–your solemn promise,–at least I may claim that?"

"I have the same peculiarity about promises; I never make them."

He was again beginning to storm, but again I assured him I would let the acquaintance take its old course, if he would but be appeased, and say no more; and, after difficulties innumerable, he at length gave up the point: but to this he was hastened, if not driven, by a summons to dinner.

DR. HERSCHEL AND HIS SISTER.

Sept.-Dr. Herschel is a delightful man; so unassuming with his great knowledge, so willing to dispense it to the ignorant, and so cheerful and easy in his general manners, that were he no genius it would be impossible not to remark him as a pleasing and sensible man. I was equally pleased with his sister, whom I had wished to see very much, for her great celebrity in her brother's science. She is very little, very gentle, very modest, and very ingenious; and her manners are those of a person unhackneyed and unawed by the world, yet desirous to meet

and to return its smiles. I love not the philosophy that braves it. This brother and sister seem gratified with its favour, at the same time that their own pursuit is all-sufficient to them without it.

I inquired of Miss Herschel if she was still comet-hunting, or content now with the moon? The brother answered that he had the charge of the moon, but he left to his sister to sweep the heavens for comets.

Their manner of working together is most ingenious and curious. While he makes his observations without-doors, he has a method of communicating them to his sister so immediately, that she can instantly commit them to paper, with the precise moment in which they are made. By this means he loses not a minute, when there is anything particularly worth observing, by writing it down, but can still proceed, yet still have his accounts and calculations exact. The methods he has contrived to facilitate this commerce I have not the terms to explain, though his simple manner of showing them made me, fully, at the time, comprehend them.

The night, unfortunately, was dark, and I could not see the moon with the famous new telescope. I mean not the great telescope through which I had taken a walk, for that is still incomplete, but another of uncommon powers. I saw Saturn, however, and his satellites, very distinctly, and their appearance was very beautiful.

GAY AND ENTERTAINING MR. BUNBURY.

Sept.-I saw a great deal of Mr. Bunbury in the course of this month, as he was in waiting upon the Duke of York, who spent great part of it at Windsor, to the inexpressible delight of his almost idolising father. Mr. Bunbury did not open upon me with that mildness and urbanity that might lead me to forget the strokes of his pencil, and power of his caricature: he early avowed a general disposition to laugh at, censure, or despise all around him. He began talking of everybody and everything about us, with the decisive freedom of a confirmed old intimacy.

"I am in disgrace here, already!" he cried almost exultingly.

"In disgrace?" I repeated.

"Yes,–for not riding out this morning!–I was asked–what Could I have better to do?–Ha! ha!"

The next time that I saw him after your departure from Windsor,(245) he talked a great deal of painting and painters, and then said, "The draftsman of whom I think the most highly of any in the world was in this room the other day, and I did not know it, and was not introduced to him!"

I immediately assured him I never held the honours of the room when its right mistress was in it, but that I would certainly have named them to each other had I known he desired it. "O, yes,"' cried he, "of all things I wished to know him. He draws like the old masters. I have seen fragments in the style of many of the very best and first productions of the greatest artists of former times. He could deceive the most critical judge. I wish greatly for a sight of his works, and for the possession of one of them, to add to my collection, as I have something from almost everybody else and a small sketch of his I should esteem a greater curiosity than all the rest put together."(246)

Moved by the justness of' this praise, I fetched him the sweet little cadeaux so lately left me by Mr. William's kindness. He was very much pleased, and perhaps thought I might bestow them. O, no–not one stroke of that pencil could I relinquish!

Another evening he gave us the history, of his way of life at Brighthelmstone. He spoke highly of the duke, but with much satire of all else, and that incautiously, and evidently with an innate defiance of consequences, from a consciousness of secret powers to overawe their hurting him.

Notwithstanding the general reverence I pay to extraordinary talents, which lead me to think it even a species of impertinence to dwell upon small failings in their rare possessors, Mr. Bunbury did not gain my good-will. His serious manner is supercilious and haughty, and his easy conversation wants rectitude in its principles. For the rest, he is entertaining and gay, full of talk, sociable, willing to enjoy what is going forward, and ready to speak his opinion with perfect unreserve.

Plays and players seem his darling theme; he can rave about them from morning to night, and yet be ready to rave again when morning returns, He acts as he talks, spouts as he recollects, and seems to give his whole soul to dramatic feeling and expression. This is not, however, his only subject Love and romance are equally clear to his discourse, though they cannot be introduced with equal frequency. Upon these topics he loses himself wholly–he runs into rhapsodies that discredit him at once as a father, a husband, and a moral man. He asserts that love Is the first principle of life, and should take place of every other; holds all bonds and obligations as nugatory that would claim a preference; and advances such doctrines of exalted sensations in the tender passion as made me tremble while I heard them.

He adores Werter, and would scarce believe I had not read it- -still less that I had begun It and left it off, from distaste at its evident tendency. I saw myself sink instantly in his estimation, though till this little avowal I had appeared to Stand in it very honourably.

THE PRINCE OF WALES AT WINDSOR AGAIN.

One evening, while I was sitting with Mrs. Delany, and her fair niece, when tea was over, and the gentlemen all withdrawn, the door was Opened, and a star entered, that I perceived presently to be the Prince of Wales. He was here to hunt with his royal father and brother. With great politeness he made me his first bow, and then advancing to Mrs. Delany, insisted, very considerately, on her sitting still, though he stood himself for half an hour–all the time he stayed. He entered into discourse very good-humouredly, and with much vivacity; described to her his villa at Brighthelmstone, told several anecdotes of adventures there, and seemed desirous to entertain both her and myself . . . . .

NOV. 8.-At near one o'clock in the morning, while the wardrobe woman was pinning up the queen's hair, there was a sudden rap-tap at the dressing-room door. Extremely surprised, I looked at the queen, to see what should be done; she did not speak. I had never heard such a sound before, for at the royal doors there Is always a peculiar kind of scratch used, instead of tapping. I heard it, however, again,–and the queen called out, "What is that?" I Was really startled, not conceiving who could take so strange a liberty as to come to the queen's apartment without the announcing of a page - and no page, I was very sure, would make such a noise. Page 62

Again the sound was repeated, and more smartly. I grew quite alarmed, imagining some serious evil at hand–either regarding the king or some of the princesses. The queen, however, bid me open the door. I did–but what was MY surprise to see there a large man, in an immense wrapping great coat, buttoned up round his chin, so that he was almost hid between cape and hat!

I stood quite motionless for a moment–but he, as if also surprised, drew back; I felt quite sick with sudden terror–I really thought some ruffian had broke into the house, or a madman.

"Who is it?" cried the queen.

"I do not know, ma'am," I answered.

"Who is it?" she called aloud; and then, taking off his hat, entered the Prince of Wales!

The queen laughed very much, so did I too, happy in this unexpected explanation.

He told her, eagerly, he merely came to inform her there were the most beautiful northern lights to be seen that could possibly be imagined, and begged her to come to the gallery windows.

FALSE RUMOURS OF Miss BURNEY'S RESIGNATION. Wednesday, Sept. 14–
We went to town for the drawing-room, and I caught a most severe cold, by being oblige to have the glass down on my side, to suit Mrs. Schwellenberg, though the sharpest wind blew in that ever attacked a poor phiz. However, these are the sort

of desagremens I can always best bear; and for the rest, I have now pretty constant civility.

My dear father drank tea with me - but told me of a paragraph in "The World," that gave me some uneasiness; to this effect:–"We hear that Miss Burney has resigned her place about the queen, and is now promoted to attend the princesses, an office far more suited to her character and abilities, which will now be called forth as they merit."–Or to that purpose. As "The World" is not taken in here, I flattered myself it would not be known; for I knew how little pleasure such a paragraph would give, and was very sorry for it.

The next day, at St. James's, Miss Planta desired to speak to me, before the queen arrived. She acquainted me Of the same "news," and said, "Everybody spoke of it;" and the queen might receive twenty letters of recommend, to

my place before night. Still I could only be sorry. Another paragraph had now appeared, she told me, contradicting the first, and saying, "The resignation of Miss Burney is premature; it only arose from an idea of the service the education of the princesses might reap from her virtues and accomplishments."

I was really concerned - conscious how little gratified my royal mistress would be by the whole :-and, presently, Miss Planta came to me again, and told me that the princesses had mentioned it! They never read any newspapers; but they had heard of it from the Duke of York. I observed the queen was most particularly gracious with me, softer, gentler, more complacent than ever; and, while dressing, she dismissed her wardrobe-woman, and, looking at me very steadfastly, said, "Miss Burney, do you ever read newspapers?"

"Sometimes," I answered, "but not often: however. I believe I know what your majesty means!"

I could say no less; I was so sure of her meaning.

"Do you?" she cried.

"Yes, ma'am, and I have been very much hurt by it: that is, if your majesty means anything relative to myself?"

"I do!" she answered, still looking at me with earnestness. "My father, ma'am," cried I, "told me of it last night, with a good deal of indignation."

"I," cried she, "did not see it myself: you know how little I read the newspapers."

"Indeed," cried I, "as it was in a paper not taken in here, I hoped it would quite have escaped your majesty."

".So it did: I only heard of it."

I looked a little curious, and she kindly explained herself.

"When the Duke of York came yesterday to dinner, he said almost immediately, 'Pray, ma'am, what has Miss Burney left You for?' 'Left me?' 'Yes, they say she's gone; pray what's the reason?' 'Gone?' 'Yes, it's at full length in all the newspapers: is not she gone?' 'Not that I know of.'"

"All the newspapers" was undoubtedly a little flourish of the duke; but we jointly censured and lamented the unbridled liberty of the press, in thus inventing, contradicting, and bringing on and putting off, whatever they pleased.

I saw, however, she had really been staggered: she concluded, I fancy, that the paragraph arose from some latent Muse, which might end in matter of fact; for she talked to me of Mrs. Dickenson, and of all that related to her retreat, and

dwelt upon the subject with a sort of solicitude that seemed apprehensive–if I may here use such a word-of a similar action. It appeared to me that she rather expected some further assurance on my part that no such view or intention had given rise to this pretended report; and therefore, when I had again the honour of her conversation alone, I renewed the subject, and mentioned that my father had had some thoughts of contradicting the paragraph himself.

"And has he done it ? " cried she quite eagerly.

"No, ma'am; for, upon further consideration, he feared it might only excite fresh paragraphs, and that the whole would sooner die, if neglected."

"So," said she, "I have been told; for, some years ago, there was a paragraph in the papers I wanted myself to have had contradicted, but they acquainted me it was best to be patient, and it would be forgot the sooner."

"This, however, ma'am, has been contradicted this morning."

"By your father?" cried she, again speaking eagerly.

"No, ma'am; I know not by whom."

She then asked how it was done. This was very distressing but I was forced to repeat It as well as I could, reddening enough, though omitting, you may believe, the worst.

just then there happened an interruption; which was vexatious, as it prevented a concluding speech, disclaiming all thoughts of resignation, which I saw was really now become necessary for the queen's satisfaction; and since it was true–why not say it? And, accordingly, the next day, when she was most excessively kind to me, I seized an opportunity, by attending her through the apartments to the breakfast-room, to beg, permission to speak to her. It was smilingly granted me.

"I have now, ma'am, read both the paragraphs."

"Well?" with a look of much curiosity.

"And indeed I thought them both very impertinent. They say that the idea arose from a notion of my being promoted to a place about the princesses!"

"I have not seen either of the paragraphs," she answered, "but the Prince of Wales told me of the second yesterday."

"They little know me, ma'am," I cried, "who think I should regard any other place as a promotion that removed me from your majesty."

Page 65

"I did not take it ill, I assure you," cried she, gently.

"Indeed, ma'am, I am far from having a wish for any such promotion–far from it! your majesty does not bestow a smile upon me that does not secure and confirm my attachment."

one of her best smiles followed this, with a very condescending little bow, and the words, "You are very good," uttered in a most gentle Voice; and she went on to her breakfast.

I am most glad this complete explanation passed. Indeed it is most true I would not willingly quit a place about the queen for any place; and I was glad to mark that her smiles were to me the whole estimate of its value.

This little matter has proved, in the end, very gratifying to me for it has made clear beyond all doubt her desire of retaining me, and a considerably increased degree of attention and complacency have most flatteringly shown a wish I should be retained by attachment.

TYRANNICAL MRS. SCHWELLENBERG.

Nov. 27-I had a terrible journey indeed to town, Mrs. Schwellenberg finding it expedient to have the glass down on my side, whence there blew in a sharp wind, which so painfully attacked my eyes that they were inflamed even before we -arrived in town.

Mr. de Luc and Miss Planta both looked uneasy, but no one durst speak; and for me, it was among the evils that I can always best bear yet before the evening I grew so ill that I could not propose going to Chelsea, lest I should be utterly unfitted for Thursday's drawing-room.

The next day, however, I received a consolation that has been some ease to my mind ever since. My dear father spent the evening with me, and was so incensed at the state of my eyes, which were now as piteous to behold as to feel, and at the relation of their usage, that he charged me, another time, to draw up my 'glass in defiance of all opposition, and to abide by all consequences, since my place was wholly immaterial when put in competition with my health.

I was truly glad of this permission to rebel, and it has given Me an internal hardiness in all similar assaults, that has at least relieved my mind from the terror of giving mortal offence where most I owe implicit obedience, should provocation overpower my capacity of forbearance.

When we assembled to return to Windsor, Mr. de Luc was

in real consternation at sight of my eyes; and I saw an indignant glance at my coadjutrix, that could scarce content itself without being understood. Miss Planta ventured not at such a glance, but a whisper broke out, as we were descending the stairs, expressive of horror against the same poor person–poor person indeed–to exercise a power productive only of abhorrence, to those who view as well as to those who feel it!

Some business of Mrs. Schwellenberg's occasioned a delay of the journey, and we all retreated back; and when I returned to my room, Miller, the old head housemaid, came to me, with a little neat tin saucepan in her hand, saying, "Pray, ma'am, use this for your eyes; 'tis milk and butter, much as I used to make for Madame Haggerdorn when she travelled in the winter with Mrs. Schwellenberg."

Good heaven! I really shuddered when she added, that all that poor woman's misfortunes with her eyes, which, from inflammation after inflammation, grew nearly blind, were attributed by herself to these journeys, in which she was forced to have the glass down at her side in all weathers, and frequently the glasses behind her also! Upo n my word this account of my predecessor was the least exhilarating intelligence I could receive! Goter told me, afterwards, that all the servants in the house had remarked I was going just the same way!

Miss Planta presently ran into my room, to say she had hopes we should travel without this amiable being; and she had left me but a moment when Mrs. Stainforth succeeded her, exclaiming, "O, for heaven's sake, don't leave her behind; for heaven's sake, Miss Burney, take her with you!"

'Twas impossible not to laugh at these opposite' interests, both, from agony of fear, breaking through all restraint. Soon after, however, we all assembled again, and got into the coach. Mr.' de Luc, who was my vis-'a-vis, instantly pulled up the glass.

"Put down that glass!" was the immediate order.

He affected not to hear her, and began conversing. She enraged quite tremendously, calling aloud to be obeyed without delay. He looked compassionately at me, and shrugged his shoulders, and said, "But, ma'am-"

"Do it, Mr. de Luc, when I tell you! I will have it! When you been too cold, you might bear it!"

""It is not for me, ma'am, but poor Miss Burney."

"O, poor Miss Burney might bear it the same! put it down, Mr. de
Luc! without, I will get out! put it down, when I tell

you! It is my coach! I will have it selfs! I might go alone in it, or with one, or with what you call nobody, when I please!"

Frightened for good Mr. de Luc, and the more for being much obliged to him, I now interfered, and begged him to let down the glass. Very reluctantly he complied, and I leant back in the coach, and held up my muff to my eyes. What a journey ensued! To see that face when lighted up with fury is a sight for horror! I was glad to exclude it by my muff.

Miss Planta alone attempted to speak. I did not think it incumbent on me to "make the agreeable," thus used; I was therefore wholly dumb : for not a word, not an apology, not one expression of being sorry for what I suffered, was uttered. The most horrible ill-humour, violence, and rudeness, were all that were shown. Mr. de Luc was too much provoked to take his usual method of passing all off by constant talk and as I had never seen him venture to appear provoked before, I felt a great obligation to his kindness. When we were about half way, we stopped to water the horses. He then again pulled up the glass, as if from absence. A voice of fury exclaimed, "Let it down! without I won't go!"

"I am sure," cried he, "all Mrs. de Luc's plants will be killed by this frost For the frost was very severe indeed.

Then he proposed my changing places with Miss Planta, who sat opposite Mrs. Schwellenberg, and consequently on the sheltered side. "Yes!" cried Mrs. Schwellenberg, "MISS Burney might sit there, and so she ought!"

I told her, briefly, I was always sick in riding backwards.

"O, ver well! when you don't like it, don't do it. You might bear it when you like it? what did the poor Haggerdorn bear it! when the blood was all running down from her eyes!"

This was too much! "I must take, then," I cried, "the more warning!" After that I spoke not a word. I ruminated all the rest of the way upon my dear father's recent charge and permission. I was upon the point continually of availing myself of both, but alas! I felt the deep disappointment I should give him, and I felt the most cruel repugnance to owe a resignation to a quarrel.

These reflections powerfully forbade the rebellion to which this unequalled arrogance and cruelty excited me; and after revolving them again and again, I—-accepted a bit of cake which she suddenly offered me as we reached Windsor, and

determined, since I submitted to my monastic destiny from motives my serious thoughts deemed right, I would not be prompted to oppose it from mere feelings of resentment to one who, strictly, merited only contempt. . . .

I gulped as well as I could at dinner; but all civil fits are again over. Not a word was said to me: yet I was really very ill all the afternoon; the cold had seized my elbows, from holding them up so long, and I was stiff and chilled all over.

In the evening, however, came my soothing Mrs. Delany. Sweet soul ! she folded me in her arms, and wept over my shoulder! Too angry to stand upon ceremony she told Mrs. Schwellenberg, after our public tea, she must retire to my room, that she might speak with me alone. This was highly resented, and I was threatened, afterwards, that she would come to tea no more, and we might talk our secrets always.

Mr. de Luc called upon me next morning, and openly avowed his indignation, protesting it was an oppression he could not bear to see used, and reproving me for checking him when he would have run all risks. I thanked him most cordially; but assured him the worst of all inflammations to me was that of a quarrel, and I entreated him, therefore, not to interfere. But we have been cordial friends from that time forward.

Miss Planta also called, kindly bringing me some eye-water, and telling me she had "Never so longed to beat anybody in her life; and yet, I assure you," she added, "everybody remarks that she behaves, altogether, better to you than to any body!"

O heavens!

MRS. SCHWELLENBERG'S CAPRICIOUSNESS.

Saturday, Dec. 1.-'Tis strange that two feelings so very opposite as love and resentment should have nearly equal power in inspiring courage for or against the object that excites them yet so it is. In former times I have often, on various occasions, felt it raised to anything possible, by affection, and now I have found it mount to the boldest height, by disdain For, be it known, such gross and harsh usage I experienced at the end of last month, since the inflammation of the eyes which I bore much more composedly than sundry personal indignities that followed, that I resolved upon a new mode of

conduct–namely, to go out every evening, in Order to show that I by no means considered myself as bound to stay at home after dinner, if treated very ill; and this most courageous plan I flattered myself must needs either procure me a liberty of absence, always so much wished, or occasion a change of behaviour to more decency and endurability. I had received for to-day an invitation to meet Lady Bute and Lady Louisa Stuart at my dearest Mrs. Delany's, and I should have wished it at all times, so much I like them both. I had no opportunity to speak first to my royal mistress, but I went to her at noon, rather more dressed than usual, and when I saw her look a little surprised, I explained my reason. She seemed very well satisfied with it, but my coadjutrix appeared in an astonishment unequalled, and at dinner, when we necessarily met again, new testimonies of conduct quite without example were exhibited: for when Mrs. Thackeray and Miss Planta were helped, she helped herself, and appeared publicly to send me to Coventry–though the sole provocation was intending to forego her society this evening!

I sat quiet and unhelped a few minutes, considering what to do: for so little was my appetite, I was almost tempted to go without dinner entirely. However, upon further reflection, I concluded it would but harden her heart still more to have this fresh affront so borne, and so related, as it must have been, through Windsor, and therefore I calmly begged some greens from Miss Planta.

The weakness of my eyes, which still would not bear the light, prevented me from tasting animal food all this time.

A little ashamed, she then anticipated Miss Planta's assistance, by offering me some French beans. To curb my own displeasure, I obliged myself to accept them. Unfortunately, however, this little softening was presently worn out, by some speeches which it encouraged from Mrs. Thackeray, who seemed to seize the moment of permission to acknowledge that I was in the room, by telling me she had lately met some of my friends in town, among whom Mrs. Chapone and the Burrows family had charged her with a thousand regrets for My Seclusion from their society, and as many kind compliments and good wishes.

This again sent me to Coventry for the rest of the dinner. When it was over, and we were all going upstairs to coffee, I spoke to Columb,(247) in passing, to have a chair for me at seven o'clock.

"For what, then," cried a stern voice behind me, "for What go you upstairs at all, when you don't drink coffee?

Did she imagine I should answer "For your society, ma'am"? No–I turned back quick as lightning, and only saying, "Very well, ma'am," moved towards my own room.

Again a little ashamed of herself, she added, rather more civilly, "For what should you have that trouble?"

I simply repeated my "Very well, ma'am," in a voice of, I believe, rather pique than calm acquiescence, and entered my own apartment, unable to enjoy this little release, however speedy to obtain it, from the various, the grievous emotions of my mind, that this was the person, use me how she might, with whom I must chiefly pass my time!

So unpleasant were the sensations that filled me, that I could recover no gaiety, even at the house of my beloved friend, though received there by her dear self, her beautiful niece, and Lady Bute and Lady Louisa, in the most flattering manner. . . .

The behaviour of my coadjutrix continued in the same strain– -really shocking to endure. I always began, at our first meeting, some little small speech, and constantly received so harsh a rebuff at the second word, that I then regularly seated myself by a table, at work, and remained wholly silent the rest of the day. I tried the experiment of making my escape; but I was fairly conquered from pursuing it. The constant black reception depressed me out of powers to exert for flight; and therefore I relinquished this plan, and only got off, as I could, to my own room, or remained dumb in hers.

To detail the circumstances of the tyranny and the grossieret'e I experienced at this time would be afflicting to my beloved friends, and oppressive to myself, I am fain, however, to confess they vanquished me. I found the restoration of some degree of decency quite necessary to my quiet, since such open and horrible ill-will from one daily in my sight even affrighted me: it pursued me in shocking visions even when I avoided her presence; and therefore I was content to put upon myself the great and cruel force of seeking to conciliate a person who had no complaint against me, but that she had given me an inflammation of the eyes, which had been witnessed and resented by her favourite Mr. de Luc. I rather believe that latter circumstance was what incensed her so inveterately.

The next extraordinary step she took was one that promised me amends for all: she told me that there was no occasion we should continue together after coffee, unless by her invitation. I eagerly exclaimed that this seemed a most feasible way of producing some variety in our intercourse, and that I would adopt it most readily. She wanted instantly to call back her words : she had expected I should be alarmed, and solicit her leave to be buried -with her every evening! When she saw me so eager in acceptance, she looked mortified and disappointed ; but I would not suffer her to retract, and I began, at once, to retire to my room the moment coffee was over.

This flight of the sublime, which, being her own, she could not resent, brought all round: for as she saw me every evening prepare to depart with the coffee, she constantly began, at that period, some civil discourse to detain me. I always suffered it to succeed, while civil, and when there was a failure, or a pause, I retired.

By this means I recovered such portion of quiet as is compatible with a situation like mine: for she soon returned entirely to such behaviour as preceded the offence of my eyes; and I obtained a little leisure at which she could not repine, as a caprice of her own bestowed it. . . .

To finish, however, with respect to the présidente, I must now acquaint you that, as my eyes entirely grew -well, her incivility entirely wore off, and I became a far greater favourite than I had ever presumed to think myself till that time! I was obliged to give up my short-lived privilege of retirement, and live on as before, making only my two precious little visits to my beloved comforter and supporter, and to devote the rest of my wearisome time to her presence–better satisfied, however, since I now saw that open war made me wretched, even When a victor, beyond what any subjection could do that had peace for its terms.

This was not an unuseful discovery, for it has abated all propensity to experiment in shaking off a yoke which, however hard to bear, is so annexed to my place, that I must take one with the other, and endure them as I can.

My favour, now, was beyond the favour of all others; I was "good Miss Berner," at every other word, and no one else was listened to if I would speak, and no one else was Accepted for a partner if I would play! I found no cause to Which I could attribute this change. I believe the whole mere Matter of caprice.

New YEAR's DAY.

Queen's Lodge, Windsor, Tuesday, Jan. 1, 1788-I began the new year, as I ended the old one, by seizing the first moment it presented to my own disposal, for flying to Mrs. Delany, and begging her annual benediction. She bestowed it with the sweetest affection, and I spent, as usual all the time with her I had to spare. . . .

In the evening, by long appointment, I was to receive Mr. Fisher and his bride.(248) Mrs. Schwellenberg, of her own accord desired me to have them in my room, and said she would herself make tea for the equerries in the eating-parlour. Mrs. Delany and Miss Port came to meet them. Mrs. Fisher seems good-natured, cheerful, and obliging, neither well nor ill in appearance, and, I fancy, not strongly marked in any way. But she adores Mr. Fisher, and has brought him a large fortune.

The Princess Amelia was brought by Mrs. Cheveley, to fetch Mrs. Delany to the queen. Mrs. Fisher was much delighted in seeing her royal highness, who, when in a grave humour, does 'the honours of her rank with a seriousness extremely entertaining. She commands the company to sit down, holds out her little fat hand to be kissed, and makes a distant courtesy, with an air of complacency and encouragement that might suit any princess of five times her age.

I had much discourse, while the rest were engaged, with Mr. Fisher, about my ever-valued, ever-regretted Mrs. Thrale. Can I call her by another name, loving that name so long, so well, for her and her sake? He gave me concern by information that she is now publishing, not only the "Letters " of Dr. Johnson, but her own. How strange!

Jan. 4.-In the morning, Mrs. Schwellenberg presented me, from the queen, with a new year's gift. It is plate, and very elegant. The queen, I find, makes presents to her whole household every year: more or less, according to some standard of their claims which she sets up, very properly, in her own mind.

CHATTY MR. BRYANT AGAIN.

Jan. 8.-I met Mr. Bryant, who came, by appointment to give me that pleasure. He was in very high spirits, full Of anecdote and amusement. He has as much good-humoured chit-chat and entertaining gossiping as if he had given no time to the classics and his studies, instead of having nearly devoted his life to them. One or two of his little anecdotes I will try to recollect.

in the year thirty-three of this century, and in his own memory, there was a cause brought before a judge, between two highwaymen, who had quarrelled about the division of their booty; and these men had the effrontery to bring their dispute to trial. "In the petition of the plaintiff," said Mr. Bryant, "he asserted that he had been extremely ill-used by the defendant: that they had carried on a very advantageous trade together, upon Black-heath, Hounslow-heath, Bagshot-heath, and other places; that their business chiefly consisted in watches, wearing apparel, and trinkets of all sorts, as well as large concerns between them in cash; that they had agreed to an equitable partition of all profits, and that this agreement had been violated. So impudent a thing, the judge said, was never before brought out in a court, and so he refused to pass sentence in favour of either of them, and dismissed them from the court."

Then he told us a great number of comic slip-slops, of the first Lord Baltimore, who made a constant misuse of one word for another: for instance, "I have been," says he, "upon a little excoriation to see a ship lanced; and there is not a finer going vessel upon the face of God's earth: you've no idiom how well it sailed."

Having given us this elegant specimen of the language of one lord, he proceeded to give us one equally forcible of the understanding of another. The late Lord Plymouth, meeting in a country town with a puppet-show, was induced to see it; and, from the high entertainment he received through Punch, he determined to buy him, and accordingly asked his price, and paid it, and carried the puppet to his country-house, that he might be diverted with him at any odd hour. Mr. Bryant protests he met the same troop Just as the purchase had been made, and went himself to the puppet-show, which was exhibited senza punch!

Next he spoke upon the Mysteries, or origin of our theatrical entertainments, and repeated the plan and conduct Of several Of these strange compositions, in particular one he remembered which was called "Noah's Ark," and in which that patriarch and his sons, just previous to the Deluge, made it all their delight to speed themselves into the ark without Mrs. Noah, Page 74

whom they wished to escape; but she surprised them just as they had embarked, and made so prodigious a racket against the door that, after a long and violent contention, she forced them to open it, and gained admission, having first content, them by being kept out till she was thoroughly wet to the skin. These most eccentric and unaccountable dramas filled up the chief of our conversation.

DR. JOHNSON's LETTERS To MRS. THRALE DISCUSSED. Wednesday, Jan. 9.-To-day Mrs. Schwellenberg did me a real favour, and with real good nature; for she sent me the "Letters" of my poor lost friends, Dr. Johnson and Mrs. Thrale,(249) which she knew me to be almost pining to procure. The book belongs to the Bishop of Carlisle, who lent it to Mr. Turbulent, from whom it was again lent to the queen, and so passed on to Mrs. Schwellenberg. It is still unpublished.(249)

With what a sadness have I been reading!–what scenes in it revived!–what regrets renewed! These letters have not been more improperly published in the whole, than they are injudiciously displayed in their several parts. She has all–every word–and thinks that, perhaps, a justice to Dr. Johnson, which, in fact, is the greatest injury to his memory. The few she has selected of her own do her, indeed, much credit; she has discarded all that were trivial and merely local, and given only such as contain something instructive, amusing, or ingenious.

About four of the letters, however, of my ever-revered Dr. Johnson are truly worthy his exalted powers: one is upon death, in considering its approach as we are surrounded, or not by mourners; another, upon the sudden and premature loss of poor Mrs. Thrale's darling and only son.(250)

Our name once occurs: how I started at its sight It is to mention the party that planned the first visit to our house: Miss Owen, Mr. Seward, Mrs. and Miss Thrale, and Dr. Johnson. How well shall we ever, my Susan, remember that morning!

I have had so many attacks upon her subject, that at last I fairly begged quarter,–and frankly owned to Mrs. Schwellenberg that I could not endure to speak any more upon the matter, endeavouring, at the same time, to explain to her my

long and intimate connection with the family. Yet nothing I could say put a stop to "How can you defend her in this?–how can you justify her in that?"" etc. Alas! that I cannot defend her is precisely the reason I can so ill bear to speak of her. How differently and how sweetly has the queen conducted herself -upon this occasion! Eager to see the "Letters," she began reading them with the utmost avidity : a natural curiosity arose to be informed of several names and several particulars, which she knew I could satisfy; yet, when she perceived how tender a string she touched, she soon suppressed her inquiries, or only made them with so much gentleness towards the parties mentioned, that I could not be distressed in my answers; and even In a short time I found her questions made so favourable a disposition, that I began secretly to rejoice in them, as the means by which I reaped opportunity of clearing several points that had been darkened by calumny, and of softening others that had been viewed wholly through false lights.

Jan. 10.-When we were summoned to the tea-room I met Miss de Luc coming out. I asked if she did not stay tea? "O How can I," cried she, in a voice of distress, "when already, as there is company here without me, Mrs. Schwellenberg has asked me what I came for?" I was quite shocked for her, and could only shrug in dismay and let her pass. When there is no one else she is courted to stay!

Mr. and Mrs. Fisher came soon after; and the Princesses Augusta and Amelia fetched away Mrs. Delany.

Soon after Colonel Wellbred came, ushering in Mr. Fairly and his young son, who is at Eton school. I had seen Mr. F. but once since his great and heavy loss, though now near half a year had elapsed. So great a personal alteration in a few months I have seldom seen: thin, haggard, worn with care, grief, and watching– his hair turned grey–white, rather, and some of his front teeth vanished. He seemed to have suffered, through his feelings, the depredations suffered by Others through age and time. His demeanour, upon this trying occasion, filled me with as much admiration as his countenance did with compassion : calm, composed, and gentle, he seemed bent on appearing not only resigned, but cheerful. I might even have supposed him verging on being happy, had not the havoc of grief on his face, and the tone of deep melancholy in his voice, assured me his Solitude was all sacred to his sorrows.

Mr. Fisher was very sad himself, grieving at the death of Dr. Harley, Dean of Windsor and Bishop of Hereford. He began, however, talking to me of these "Letters," and, with him, I could speak of them, and of their publisher, without reserve: but the moment they were named Mrs. Schwellenberg uttered such hard and harsh things, that I could not keep my seat and the less, because, knowing my strong friendship there in former days, I was sure it was meant I should be hurt, I attempted not to speak, well aware all defence is irritation, where an attack is made from ill-nature, not justice.

The gentle Mr. Fisher, sorry for the cause and the effect of this assault, tried vainly to turn it aside: what began with censure soon proceeded to invective; and at last, being really sick from crowding recollections of past scenes, where the person now thus vilified had been dear and precious to my very heart, I was forced, abruptly, to walk out of the room.

It was indifferent to me whether or not my retreat was noticed. I have never sought to disguise the warm friendship that once subsisted between Mrs. Thrale and myself, for I always hoped that, where it was known, reproach might be spared to a name I can never hear without a secret pang, even when simply mentioned. Oh, then, how severe a one is added, when its sound is accompanied by the hardest aspersions!

I returned when I could, and the subject was over.
When all were gone Mrs. Schwellenberg said, "I have told it Mr.
Fisher that he drove you out from the room, and he says he won't
not do it no more."

She told me next—that in the second volume I also was mentioned. Where she may have heard this I cannot gather, but it has given me a sickness at heart inexpressible. It is not that I expect severity: for at the time of that correspondence—at all times, indeed, previous to the marriage with Piozzi, if Mrs. Thrale loved not F. B., where shall we find faith in words, or give credit to actions? But her present resentment, however unjustly incurred, of my constant disapprobation of her conduct, may prompt some note, or other mark, to point out her change of sentiments—but let me try to avoid such painful expectations; at least, not to dwell upon them.

O, little does she know how tenderly at this moment I could run again into her arms, so often opened to receive me with a cordiality I believed inalienable. And it was sincere then, I am satisfied: pride, resentment of disapprobation, and consciousness of unjustifiable proceedings — these have now

changed her: but if we met, and she saw and believed my faithful regard, how would she again feel all her own return!

Well, what a dream am I making!

Jan. 11.-Upon this ever-interesting subject, I had to-day a very sweet scene with the queen. While Mrs. Schwellenberg and myself were both in our usual attendance at noon, her majesty inquired of Mrs. Schwellenberg if she had yet read any of the "Letters"?

"No," she answered, "I have them not to read."

I then said she had been so obliging as to lend them to me, to whom they were undoubtedly of far greater personal value.

"That is true," said the queen; "for I think there is but little in them that can be of much consequence or value to the public at large."

"Your majesty, you will hurt Miss Burney if you speak about that; poor Miss Burney will be quite hurt by that."

The queen looked much surprised, and I hastily exclaimed, "O, no!—not with the gentleness her majesty names it."

Mrs. Schwellenberg then spoke in German; and, I fancy, by the names she mentioned, recounted how Mr. Turbulent and Mr. Fisher had "driven me out of the room."

The queen seemed extremely astonished, and I was truly vexed at this total misunderstanding; and that the goodness she has exerted upon this occasion should seem so little to have succeeded. But I could not explain, lest it should seem to reproach what was meant as kindness in Mrs. Schwellenberg, who had not yet discovered that it was not the subject, but her own manner of treating it, that was so painful to me.

However, the instant Mrs. Schwellenberg left the room, and we remained alone, the queen, approaching me in the softest manner, and looking earnestly in my face, said, "You could not be offended, surely, at what I said."

"O no, ma'am," cried I, deeply indeed penetrated by such unexpected condescension. "I have been longing to make a speech to your majesty upon this matter; and it was but yesterday that I entreated Mrs. Delany to make it for me, and to express to your majesty the very deep sense I feel of the lenity with which this Subject has been treated in my hearing."

"Indeed," cried she, with eyes strongly expressive of the complacency with which she heard me, "I have always spoke as little as possible upon this affair. I remember but twice that I have named it: once I said to the Bishop of Carlisle,

that I thought most of these letters had better have been spared the printing; and once to Mr. Langton, at the Drawing-room, I said, 'Your friend Dr. Johnson, sir, has had many friends busy to publish his books, and his memoirs, and his meditations, and his thoughts; but I think he wanted one friend more.' 'What for? ma'am,' cried he; 'A friend to suppress them,' I answered. And, indeed, this is all I ever said about the business."

A PAIR OF PARAGONS.

..I was amply recompensed in spending an evening the most to my natural taste of any I have spent officially under the royal roof. How high Colonel Wellbred stands with me you know; Mr. Fairly., with equal gentleness, good breeding, and delicacy, adds a far more general turn for conversation, and seemed not only ready, but pleased, to open upon subjects of such serious import as were suited to his state of mind, and could not but be edifying, from a man of such high moral character, to all who heard him.

Life and death were the deep themes to which he .led; and the little space between them, and the little value of that space were the subject of his comments. The unhappiness of man at least after the ardour of his first youth, and the near worthlessness of the world, seemed so deeply impressed on his mind, that no reflection appeared to be consolatory to it, save the necessary shortness of our mortal career. . . .

"Indeed," said he, "there is no time—I know of none—in which life is well worth having. The prospect before us is never such as to make it worth preserving, except from religious motives."

I felt shocked and sorry. Has he never tasted happiness, who so deeply drinks of sorrow? He surprised me, and filled me, indeed, with equal wonder and pity. At a loss how to make an answer sufficiently general, I made none at all, but referred to Colonel Wellbred: perhaps he felt the same difficulty, for he said nothing; and Mr. Fairly then gathered an answer for himself, by saying, "Yes, it may, indeed, be attainable in the only actual as well as only right way to seek it,—that of doing good!"

"If," cried Colonel Wellbred, afterwards, "I lived always in London, I should be as tired of life as you are: I always sicken of it there, if detained beyond a certain time."

They then joined in a general censure of dissipated life, and a general distaste of dissipated characters, which seemed, however, to comprise almost all their acquaintance; and this presently occasioned Mr. Fairly to say,

"It is, however, but fair for you and me to own, Wellbred, that if people in general ,'are bad, we live chiefly amongst those who are the worst."

Whether he meant any particular set to which they belong, or whether his reflection went against people in high life, such 'as constitute their own relations and connexions in general, I cannot say, as he did not explain himself.

Mr. Fairly, besides the attention due to him from all, in consideration of his late loss, merited from me peculiar deference, in return for a mark I received of his disposition to think favourably of me from our first acquaintance: for not more was I surprised than pleased at his opening frankly upon the character of my coadjutrix, and telling me at once, that when first he saw me here, just before the Oxford expedition, he had sincerely felt for and pitied me. . . .

Sunday, Jan. 13.-There is something in Colonel Wellbred so elegant, so equal, and so pleasing, it is impossible not to see him with approbation, and to speak of him with praise. But I found in Mr. Fairly a much greater depth of understanding, and all his sentiments seem formed upon the most perfect basis of religious morality.

During the evening, in talking over plays and players, we all three united warmly in panegyric of Mrs. Siddons; but when Mrs. Jordan was named, Mr. Fairly and myself were left to make the best of her. Observing the silence of Colonel Wellbred, we called upon him to explain it.

"I have seen her," he answered, quietly, "but in one part."

"Whatever it was," cried Mr. Fairly, "it must have been well done."

"Yes," answered the colonel, "and so well that it seemed to be her real character: and I disliked her for that very reason, for it was a character that, off the stage or on, is equally distasteful to me–a hoyden."

I had had a little of this feeling myself when I saw her in "The Romp,"(251) where she gave me, in the early part, a real disgust; but afterwards she displayed such uncommon humour that it brought me to pardon her assumed vulgarity, in favour of a representation of nature, which, In its particular class, seemed to me quite perfect.

MR. TURBULENT'S SELF CONDEMNATION.

At the usual tea-time I sent Columb, to see if anybody had come upstairs. He brought me word the eating-parlour was empty. I determined to go thither at once, with my work, that there might be no pretence to fetch me when the party assembled; but upon opening the door I saw Mr. Turbulent there, and alone!

I entered with readiness into discourse with him, and showed a disposition to placid good-will, for with so irritable a spirit resentment has much less chance to do good than an appearance of not supposing it deserved. Our conversation was in the utmost gravity. He told me he was not happy, though owned he had everything to make him so; but he was firmly persuaded that happiness in this world was a real stranger. I combated this misanthropy in general terms; but he assured me that such was his unconquerable opinion of human life.

How differently did I feel when I heard an almost similar sentiment from Mr. Fairly! In him I imputed it to unhappiness of circumstances, and was filled with compassion for his fate: in this person I impute it to something blameable within, and I tried by all the arguments I could devise to give him better notions. For him, however, I soon felt pity, though not of the same composition : for he frankly said he was good enough to be happy-that he thought human frailty incompatible with happiness, and happiness with human frailty, and that he had no wish so strong as to turn monk!

I asked him if he thought a life of uselessness and of goodness the same thing?

"I need not be useless," he said; "I might assist by my counsels. I might be good in a monastery–in the world I cannot! I am not master of my feelings: I am run away by passions too potent for control!"

This was a most unwelcome species of confidence, but I affected to treat it as mere talk, and answered it only slightly, telling him he spoke from the gloom of the moment.

"No," he answered, "I have tried in vain to conquer them. I have made vows–resolutions–all in vain! I cannot keep them!"

"Is not weakness," cried I, "sometimes fancied, merely to save the pain and trouble of exerting fortitude."

"No, it is with me inevitable. I am not formed for success in self-conquest. I resolve–I repent–but I fall! I blame–reproach–I even hate myself–I do everything, in short, yet cannot save myself! Yet do not," he continued, seeing me shrink, "think worse of me than I deserve: nothing of injustice, of ill-nature, of malignancy–I have nothing of these to reproach myself with."

"I believe you," I cried, "and surely, therefore, a general circumspection, an immediate watchfulness—"

"No, no, no–'twould be all to no purpose."

"'Tis that hopelessness which is most your enemy. If you would but exert your better reason–"

"No, madam, no!–'tis a fruitless struggle. I know myself too well–I can do nothing so right as to retire–to turn monk– hermit."

"I have no respect," cried I, "for these selfish seclusions. I can never suppose we were created in the midst of society, in order to run away to a useless solitude. I have not a doubt but you may do well, if you will do well."

Some time after he suddenly exclaimed, "Have you–tell me–have you, ma'am, never done what you repent?"

O "yes!–at times."

"You have?" he cried, eagerly.

"O yes, alas!–yet not, I think, very often–for it is not very often I have done anything!"

"And what is it has saved you?"

I really did not know well what to answer him; I could say nothing that would not sound like parade, or implied superiority. I suppose he was afraid himself of the latter ; for, finding me silent, he was pleased to answer for me.

"Prejudice, education, accident!–those have saved you."

"Perhaps so," cried I. "And one thing more, I acknowledge myself obliged to, on various occasions–fear. I run no risks that I see–I run–but it is always away from all danger that I perceive."

"You do not, however, call that virtue, ma'am–you do not call that the rule of right?"

"No–I dare not–I must be content that it is certainly not the rule of wrong."

He began then an harangue upon the universality of depravity and frailty that I heard with much displeasure; for, it seems to me, those most encourage such general ideas of general worthlessness who most wish to found upon them partial excuses for their own.

MISS BURNEY AMONG HER OLD FRIENDS.

Jan. 31.–And now I must finish my account of this month by my own assembly at my dear Mrs. Ord's.

I passed through the friendly hands of Miss Ord to the most cordial ones of Mrs. Garrick,(252) who frankly embraced me, saying, "Do I see you, once more, before I die, my tear little spark? for your father is my flame, all my life, and you are a little spark of that flame!"

She added how much she had wished to visit me at the queen's house, when she found I no longer came about the world; but that she was too discreet, and I did not dare say "Do come!" unauthorized.

Then came Mr. Pepys, and he spoke to me instantly, of the 'Streatham Letters.' He is in agony as to his own fate, but said there could be no doubt of my faring well. Not, I assured him, to my own content, if named at all.

We were interrupted by Sir Joshua Reynolds. I was quite glad to see him; and we began chatting with all our old spirit, and he quite raved against my present life of confinement, an the invisibility it had occasioned, etc., etc.

The approach of Mrs. Porteus stopped this. She is always most obliging and courteous, and she came to inquire whether now she saw I really was not wholly immured, there was any chance of a more intimate cultivation of an acquaintance long begun, but stopped in its first progress. I could only make a general answer of acknowledgment to her kindness. Her bishop, whom I had not seen since his preferment from Chester to London, joined us, and most good-naturedly entered into discourse upon my health.

I was next called to Mrs. Montagu, who was behind with no one in kind speeches, and who insisted upon making me a visit at the queen's house, and would take no denial to my fixing my own time, whenever I was at leisure, and sending her word; and she promised to put off any and every engagement for that Purpose. I could make no other return to such

civility, but to desire to postpone it till my dear Mr. and Mrs. Locke came to town, and could meet her.

Mrs. Boscawen(253) was my next little t'ete-'a-t'ete, but I had only begun it when Mr. Cambridge came to my side.

"I can't get a word!" cried he, with a most forlorn look, "and yet I came on purpose!" I thanked him, and felt such a real pleasure in his sight, from old and never-varying regard, that I began to listen to him with my usual satisfaction. He related to me a long history of Lavant, where the new-married Mrs. Charles Cambridge is now very unwell: and then he told me many good things of his dear and deserving daughter; and I showed him her muff, which she had worked for me, in embroidery, and we were proceeding a little in the old way, when I saw Mrs. Pepys leaning forward to hear us; and then Lady Rothes, who also seemed all attention to Mr. Cambridge and his conversation.

The sweet Lady Mulgrave came for only a few words, not to take me, she said, from older claimants; the good and wise Mrs. Carter(254) expressed herself with equal kindness and goodness on our once more meeting; Miss Port, looking beautiful as a little angel, only once advanced to shake hands, and say, "I can see you another time, so I won't be unreasonable now."

Mr. Smelt, who came from Kew for this party, made me the same speech, and no more, and I had time for nothing beyond a "how do do " with Mr. Langton, his Lady

Rothes,(255) Mr. Batt, Mr. Cholmondoley, Lord Mulgrave, Sir Lucas Pepys, and Lady Herries.

Then up came Mrs. Chapone, and, after most cordially shaking hands with me, "But I hope," she cried, "you are not always to appear only as a comet, to be stared at, and then vanish? If you are, let me beg at least to be brushed by your tail, and not hear you have disappeared before my telescope is ready for looking at you!" When at last I was able to sit down, after a short conference with every one, it was next to Mr. Walpole,(256) who had secured

me a place by his side ; and with him was my longest conversation, for he was in high spirits, polite, ingenious, entertaining, quaint, and original.

But all was so short!–so short!–I was forced to return home so soon! 'Twas, however, a very great regale to me, and the sight of so much kindness, preserved so entire after so long an absence, warmed my whole heart with pleasure and satisfaction. My dearest father brought me home.

SOME TRIVIAL COURT INCIDENTS.

Friday, Feb. 1.-To-day I had a summons in the morning to Mrs. Schwellenberg, who was very ill; so ill as to fill me with compassion. She was extremely low-spirited, and spoke to me with quite unwonted kindness of manner, and desired me to accept a sedan-chair, which had been Mrs. Haggerdorn's, and now devolved to her, saying, I might as well have it while she lived as when she was dead, which would soon happen.

I thanked her, and wished her, I am sure very sincerely, better. Nor do I doubt her again recovering, as I have frequently seen her much worse. True, she must die at last, but who must not?

Feb. 2.-The king always makes himself much diversion with Colonel Goldsworthy, whose dryness of humour and pretended servility of submission, extremely entertain him. He now attacked him upon the enormous height of his collar, which through some mistake of his tailor, exceeded even the extremity of fashion. And while the king, who was examining and pulling it about, had his back to us, Colonel Wellbred had the malice to whisper me, "Miss Burney, I do assure you it is nothing to what it was; he has had two inches cut off since morning!

Fortunately, as Colonel Wellbred stood next me, this was not heard for the king would not easily have forgotten. He soon after went away, but gave no summons to his gentlemen.

And now Colonel Wellbred gave me another proof of his extraordinary powers of seeing. You now know, my dear friends, that in the king's presence everybody retreats back, as far as they can go, to leave him the room to himself. In all this, through the disposition of the chairs, I was placed so much behind Colonel Wellbred as to conclude myself out of his sight; but the moment the king retired, he said, as

we all dropped on our seats, "Everybody is tired–Miss Burney the most–for she has stood the stillest. Miss Planta has leant on her chair, Colonel Goldsworthy against the wall, myself occasionally on the screen, but Miss Burney has stood perfectly still–I perceived that without looking."

'Tis, indeed, to us standers, an amazing addition to fatigue to keep still.

We returned to town next day. In the morning I had had a very disagreeable, though merely foolish, embarrassment. Detained, by the calling in of a poor woman about a

THE DIARY AND LETTERS OF MADAME D'ARBLAY | VOLUME 2 **59**

subscription, from dressing myself, I was forced to run to the queen, at her summons, without any cap. She smiled, but said nothing. Indeed, she is all indulgence in those points of externals, which rather augments than diminishes my desire of showing apparent as well as my feeling of internal respect but just as I had assisted her with her peignoir, Lady Effingham was admitted, and the moment she sat down, and the hair-dresser began his office, a page announced the Duke of York, who instantly followed his name.

I would have given the world to have run away, but the common door of entrance and exit was locked, unfortunately, on account of the coldness of the day; and there was none to pass, but that by which his royal highness entered, and was standing. I was forced. therefore, to remain, and wait for dismission.

Yet I was pleased, too, by the sight of his affectionate manner to his royal mother. He flew to take and kiss her hand, but she gave him her cheek; and then he began a conversation with her, so open and so gay, that he seemed talking to the most intimate associate.

His subject was Lady Augusta Campbell's elopement from. the masquerade. The Duchess of Ancaster had received masks at her house on Monday, and sent tickets to all the queen's household. I, amongst the rest, had one; but it was impossible I could be spared at such an hour, though the queen told me that she had thought of my going, but could not manage it, as Mrs. Schwellenberg was so ill. Miss Planta went, and I had the entire equipment of her. I started the Project of dressing her at Mrs. Delany's, in all the most antique and old-fashioned things we could borrow; and this was Put very happily in execution, for she was, I have heard, one of the best and most grotesque figures in the room.

(239) Henry William Bunbury, the well-known caricaturist. He was connected by marriage with Colonel Gwynn, having married, in 1771, Catherine, the "Little Comedy," sister of the "Jessamy Bride."-ED.

(240) i.e., of the Play which was to be read by Mrs. Siddons. See P- 55.-ED.

(241) This excellent comedy was completed by Colley Cibber, from an unfinished play of Sir John Vanbrugh's.-ED.

(242) See note 210, ante, vol. 1, P. 370.-ED.

(243) Mr. Anthony Shepherd, Plumian Professor of Astronomy at Cambridge. We meet with him occasionally in the "Early Diary:" "dullness itself" Fanny once calls him (in 1774).-ED.

(244) Fanny's maid.-ED.

(245) Susan Phillips and the Lockes had stayed at Windsor from the 10th to the 17th of September.-ED.

(246) This magnificent panegyric relates to a young amateur, William Locke, the son of Fanny's friends, Mr. and Mrs. Locke. But there was more than a little of the amateur about Mr. Bunbury himself. His works bear no comparison with those of the great masters of caricatured Rowlandson and Gulray.-ED.

(247) Fanny's man-servant, a Swiss.-ED.

(248) Mr. Fisher was a canon at Windsor, and an amateur landscape-painter. He had recently married.-ED.

(249) "Letters to and from Dr. Johnson," published by Mrs. Piozzi in 1788.-ED.

(250) Thrale's only son died, a child, in March, 1776.–ED.

(251) A farce, adapted from Bickerstaff's opera, "Love in the City."-ED.

(252) Eva Maria Feigel, a Viennese dancer, whom Garrick married in 1749. Fanny writes of her in 1771: "Mrs. Garrick is the most attentively polite and perfectly well-bred woman in the world; her speech is all softness; her manners all elegance; her smiles all sweetness. There is something so peculiarly graceful in her motion, and pleasing in her address, that the most trifling words have weight and power, when spoken by her, to oblige and even delight." ("Early Diary," vol. i. p. 111.) She died in 1822; her husband in 1779.-ED.

(253) The Hon. Mrs. Boscawen, widow of Admiral Boscawen.-ED.

(254) Elizabeth Carter, the celebrated translator of Epictetus. She was now in her seventieth year, and had been for many years an esteemed friend of Dr. Johnson. She died in 1806.-ED. , '

(255) Mr. Langton's wife was the Countess dowager of Rothes, widow of the eighth earl. Lady Jane Leslie, who married Sir Lucas Pepys, the physician, also enjoyed, in her own right, the title of Countess of Rothes.-ED.

(256) Horace Walpole. -E D.

SECTION 12. (1788.)

THE TRIAL OF WARREN HASTINGS.

Warren Hastings was a lad of seventeen when, in 1750, he was first sent out to India as a writer in the East India Company's service. His abilities attracted the notice of Clive, and, after the downfall of the Nawab Suraj-u-Dowlah, Hastings was chosen to represent the Company at the Court of Mir Jafir, the new Nawab of Bengal. In 1761 he was appointed Member of Council at Calcutta, and he returned to England in 1765, unknown as yet to fame, but with an excellent reputation both for efficiency and integrity. He left Bengal in a state of anarchy. The actual power was in the possession of a trading company, whose objects were at once to fill their coffers, and to avoid unnecessary political complications. The show of authority was invested in a Nawab who was a mere puppet in the hands of the English company. Disorder was rampant throughout the provinces, and the unhappy Hindoos, unprotected by their native princes, were left a helpless prey to the rapacity of their foreign tyrants.

At a time when to enrich himself with the plunder of the natives was the aim of every servant of the East India Company, it is much to the honour of Hastings that he returned home a comparatively poor man. In England he indulged his taste for literary society, busied himself with a scheme for introducing at

Page 87 oxford the study of the Persian language and literature, and made the acquaintance of Dr. Johnson. But generosity and imprudence together soon reduced his small means. He applied to the Directors of the Company for employment, was appointed to a seat on the Council at Madras, and made his second voyage to India in 1769. Among his fellow-passengers on board the "Duke of Grafton" was Madame Imhoff, whom he afterwards married.

At Madras Hastings managed the export business of the Company with conspicuous success, and so completely to the satisfaction of the Directors, that, two years later, he was promoted to the governorship of Bengal, and sent to exercise his administrative ability and genius for reform -%N here they were then 'greatly needed-at Calcutta.

With this appointment his historic career may be said to commence. He found himself at the outset in a situation of extreme difficulty. He was required to establish something-resembling a stable government in place of the prevailing anarchy, and, above all things, with disordered finances, to satisfy the expectations of his' employers by constant remittances of money. Both these tasks he accomplished, but the difficulties in the way of the latter led him to the commission of those acts for which he was afterwards denounced by his enemies as a monster of injustice and barbarity. Hastings's conduct with respect to the Great Mogul has been sketched by Macaulay in words which imply a reprehension in reality undeserved. Little remained at this time of the magnificent empire of Aurungzebe beyond a title and a palace at Delhi. In 1765 Lord Clive had ceded to the titular master of the Mogul empire the districts of Corah and Allahabad, lying to the south of Oude, and westwards of Benares. The cession had been made in pursuance of the same policy which Hastings afterwards followed; that, namely, of sheltering the British possessions behind a barrier of friendly states, which should be sufficiently strong to withstand the incursions of their hostile neighbours, and particularly of the Mahrattas, the most warlike and dreaded of the native powers. But Clive's purpose had been completely frustrated; for the Mogul, far from shielding the English, had not been able to hold his own against the Mahrattas, to whom he had actually ceded the very territories made over to him by the Company. Under these circumstances the English authorities can hardly be blamed for causing their troops to re-occupy the districts in question, nor can it fairly be imputed as a crime to Hastings that in September, 1773, he concluded with the Vizier of Oude the treaty of Benares, by which he sold Allahabad and Corah to that friendly potentate for about half a million sterling.

But the next act of foreign policy on the part of the Governor of Bengal—his share in the subjugation of the Rohillas—does not admit of so favourable an interpretation. The Rohillas occupied territory lying under the southern slopes of the Himalayas, to the north-west of Oude. The dominant race in Rohilcund was of

Afghan origin, although the majority of the population was Hindoo. Of the rulers of Rohilcund Hastings himself wrote, in terms which we may accept as accurate, "They are a tribe of Afghans or Pathans, freebooters who conquered the country about sixty years ago, and have ever since lived upon the fruits of it, without contributing either to its cultivation or manufactures, or even mixing with the native inhabitants."(257)

In 1772, the Rohillas, hard pressed by their foes, the Mahrattas, sought the assistance of the Vizier of Oude, Shuja-u-Dowlah, to whom they agreed to pay, in return for his aid, a large sum of money. This agreement was signed in the presence of an English general, and an English brigade accompanied the vizier's army, which co-operated with the Rohilla forces, and obliged the Mahrattas to withdraw. But when Shula-u-Dowlah demanded his promised hire, he received from the Rohillas plenty of excuses but no money. Hereupon he resolved to annex Rohilcund to his own dominions, and, to ensure success, he concerted measures with Hastings, who, willing at once to strengthen a friendly power and to put money into his own exchequer, placed an English brigade at the vizier's disposal for a consideration Of 400,000 pounds. In the spring of 1774 the invasion took place. The desperate bravery of the Rohillas was of no avail against English discipline, and the country was so reduced to submission. Macaulay's stirring account of the barbarities practised by the invaders has been proved to be greatly exaggerated. Disorders, however, there were: the people were plundered, and some of the villages were burnt by the vizier's troops. Many of the Rohilla families were exiled, but the Hindoo inhabitants of Rohilcund were left to till their fields as before, and were probably not greatly affected by their change of master.

Hastings's conduct in this affair is, from the most favourable point of view, rather to be excused than applauded. It may have been politic under the circumstances, but it was hardly in accordance with a high standard of morality to let out on hire an English force for the subjugation of a people who, whatever grounds of complaint the Vizier of Oude might have had against them, had certainly given no provocation whatsoever to the English Government. As to the plea which has been put forward in his favour, that the Rohillas were merely the conquerors, and not the original owners of Rohilcund, it is sufficiently answered, by Macaulay's query, "What were the English themselves?"

In 1773 Lord North's "Regulating Act" introduced considerable changes in the constitution of the Indian government, and marked the first step in the direction of a transfer of the control over Indian affairs from the Company to the Crown. By this act "the governorship of Bengal, Bahar, and Orissa was vested in the Governor-General, with four Councillors, having authority over

Madras and Bombay ; and all correspondence relating to civil government or military affairs was to be laid by the Directors of the Company in London before his -Majesty's Ministers, who Could disapprove or cancel any rules or orders. A Supreme Court of judicature, appointed by the Crown, was established in Calcutta."(258) The Governor-General was appointed for a term of five years, and the first Governor-General was Hastings. Of the four councillors with whom he was associated, three were sent out from England to take their places at the board, and landed at Calcutta, together with the judges of the Supreme Court, in October, 1771. Indisputably the ablest, and, as it proved, historically the most noteworthy of these three, was Philip Francis, the supposed author of "Junius's Letters."

Even before the council commenced its duties dissensions arose. The newcomers, Francis, Clavering, and Monson, were in constant opposition to the Governor-General. Indeed, the hostility between Hastings and Francis rose by degrees to such a height that, some years later, they met in a duel, in which Francis was severely wounded. For the present, however, the opponents of Hastings formed a majority on the council, and his authority was in eclipse. His ill-wishers in the country began to bestir themselves, and a scandalous and, there is no doubt, utterly untrue charge of accepting bribes was brought against him by an old enemy, the Maharajah Nuncomar. Hastings replied by prosecuting Nuncomar and his allies for conspiracy. The accused were admitted to bail, but a little later Nuncomar was arrested on a charge of having forged a bond some years previously, tried before an English jury, condemned to death, and hanged, August 5, 1775, his application for leave to appeal having been rejected by the Chief justice, Sir Elijah Impey. Hastings solemnly declared his innocence of any share in this transaction, nor is there any evidence directly implicating him. On the other hand, it must he remembered that Nuncomar had preferred a most serious charge against Hastings; that the majority on the council were only too ready to listen to any charge, well or ill founded, against the Governor-General; and that Nuncomar's triumph would, in all probability, have meant Hastings's ruin. Even Mr. Forrest admits that "it is extremely probable, as Francis stated, that if Nuncomar had never stood forth in politics, his other offences would not have hurt him."(259) Macaulay comments upon the scandal of this stringent enforcement Of the English law against forgery under circumstances so peculiar, and in a country where the English law was totally unknown.(260) That Nuncomar was fairly tried and convicted

in the ordinary course of law is now beyond doubt, but we still hold that it was Impey's clear duty to respite his prisoner. That he did not do so is a fact which, beyond all others, gave colour to the assertion of Hastings's enemies, that the execution of Nuncomar was the result of a secret understanding between the Governor-General of Bengal and the Chief justice of the Supreme Court. But, however brought about, the death of Nuncomar was to the opponents of Hastings a blow from which they never recovered. The death of Monson, in September, 1776, and that of Clavering, a year later, placed him in a majority on the council ; his authority was more undisputed than ever ; and at the expiration of his term he was re-appointed Governor-General.

During the years 1780 and 1781 British rule in India passed through the most dangerous crisis that had befallen it since the days of Clive. A formidable confederacy had been formed between the Nizam, the Mahrattas, and the famous Hyder Ali, Sultan of Mysore, with the object of crushing their common enemy, the English. The hostility of these powerful states had been provoked by the blundering and bad faith of the governments of Bombay and Madras, which had made, and broken, treaties with each of them in turn. "As to the Mahrattas," to quote the words of Burke, "they had so many cross treaties with the states general of that nation, and with each of the chiefs, that it was notorious that no one of these agreements could be kept without grossly violating the rest."(261) The war in which the Bombay Government had engaged with the Mahrattas had been as unsuccessful in its prosecution as it was impolitic in its commencement, until, early in 1780, a force under General Goddard was dispatched from Bengal to co-operate with the Bombay troops. Goddard's arrival turned the tide of events. The province of Gujerat was reduced, the Mahratta chiefs, Sindia and Holkar, were defeated, and everything portended a favourable termination of the war, when the whole face of affairs was changed by news from the south.

Hyder Ali, the most able and warlike of the native princes, swept down upon the Carnatic in July, 1780, at the head of a disciplined army of nearly 100,000 men. He was now an old man, but age had not broken his vigour. He rapidly overran the country; an English force, under Colonel Baillie, which opposed him, was cut to pieces, and Madras itself was threatened. The prompt measures adopted by Hastings on this occasion saved the colony. Reinforcements were hurried to Madras; the veteran, Sir Eyre Coote, was entrusted with the command of the army; and the triumphant

career of Hyder Ali was checked by the victory of Porto Novo, July 1st, 1781. The end of the war, however, was yet far off. Peace was concluded with the Mahrattas, on terms honourable to them, in 1782, but in the south the struggle was still maintained by Hyder Ali and his French allies, and after Hyder Ali's death, in December of that year, by his son Tippoo; nor was it brought to a termination until after the general peace Of 1783.

To support the financial strain of these wars Hastings had recourse to measures which, with the colouring given to them by his enemies, gave subsequent rise to two of the heaviest charges brought forward by the managers of his impeachment. His first victim was Cheyt Sing, the Rajah of Benares, a tributary of the English Government. Cheyt Sing had been formerly a vassal of the Vizier of Oude, and when, in 1775, the vizier transferred his sovereign rights over Benares to the English, the Bengal Government confirmed the possession of the city and its dependencies to Cheyt Sing and his heirs for ever, stipulating only for the payment of an annual tribute, and undertaking that the regular payment of this tribute should acquit the Rajah of further obligations. It was afterwards contended on behalf of Hastings that this undertaking did not annul the right of the superior power to call upon its vassal for extraordinary aid on extraordinary occasions, and this view was upheld by Pitt.

Hastings began operations in 1778 by demanding of the Rajah, in addition to his settled tribute, a large contribution towards the war expenses. The sum was paid, but similar requisitions in the following years were met with procrastination or evasion, and a demand that the Rajah should furnish a contingent of cavalry was not complied with. This conduct on the part of Cheyt Sing appeared to the Governor-General and his Council "to require early punishment, and, as his wealth was great and the Company's exigencies pressing," in 1781 a fine of fifty lakhs, of rupees (500,000 pounds) was laid upon the unlucky Rajah; Hastings himself proceeding to Benares, with a small escort, to enforce payment. Cheyt Sing received his unwelcome visitor with due respect, but with ambiguous answers, and Hastings, most imprudently, gave the order for the Rajah's arrest. The Rajah submitted, but his troops and the population of Benares rose to the rescue : a portion of Hastings's little force was massacred, the Rajah regained his liberty, and the Governor-General found safety only in flight. The insurrection rapidly spread to the country around, and assumed dangerous proportions, but the promptitude and vigour of-Hastings soon restored order. Cheyt Sing was deposed, compelled to flee his country, his estates were confiscated, and a new Rajah of Benares was appointed in his stead.

The charge subsequently preferred against Hastings in connection with this affair turned upon the question whether Cheyt Sing Was, as the prosecutors affirmed, a sovereign prince who owed no duty to the Bengal government beyond the payment (which he
had regularly performed) of a fixed annual tribute; or as Hastings contended, a mere feudal vassal, bound to furnish aid when called upon by his over-lord. Pitt, as we have said, took the latter view, yet he gave his support to the charge on the ground that the fine imposed upon the Rajah of Benares was excessive., Upon the whole, it would appear that Hastings was acting within his rights in demanding an extraordinary subsidy from the Rajah but the enormous amount of the fine, and the harshness and in' dignity with which Cheyt Sing was treated, point to a determination on the part of the Governor-General to ruin a subject prince, with whom, moreover, it was known he had personal grounds of pique.

The deposition of Cheyt Sing was followed by an act on which was afterwards founded the most sensational of all the charges brought against Warren Hastings. Shuja-u-Dowlah, the Nawab Vizier of Oude, to whom Hastings had sold the Rohillas, died in 1775, and was succeeded by his son Asaph-u-Dowlah. At the time of his death Shuja-u-Dowlah was deeply in debt, both to his own army and to the Bengal Government. The treasure which he left was estimated at two millions sterling, but this vast sum of money and certain rich estates were appropriated by his mother and widow, the begums, or princesses, of Oude, under the pretence of a will which may possibly have existed, but was certainly never Produced. With this wealth at their disposal the begums enjoyed a practical independence of the new vizier, who was no match in energy and resolution for his mother and grandmother. A small portion, however, of the money was paid over to the vizier, on the understanding, guaranteed by the Bengal Government, that the begums should be left in undisturbed enjoyment of the remainder of their possessions. Hastings believed, and, it would seem, on good grounds, that the younger begum had busied herself actively in fomenting the insurrection which broke out upon the arrest of Cheyt Sing at Benares. He conceived a plan by which he might at once punish the rebellious princesses, and secure for the exchequer at Calcutta the arrears of debt due from the Government of Oude. He withdrew the guarantee, and urged the Vizier to seize upon the estates possessed by the begums. Asaph-u-Dowlah came willingly into the arrangement, but, when it became necessary to act, his heart failed him. Hastings, however, was not to be trifled with. English troops were employed: the begums were closely confined in their palace at Fyzabad; and, to the lasting disgrace of Hastings, their personal attendants were starved and even tortured, until they consented to surrender their money and estates. Hastings's conduct in withdrawing the guarantee was not without justification ; the means which he suffered to be employed in carrying out his purpose, and for the employment of which he must be held primarily responsible, were utterly indefensible.

Page 93 Long before his return to England, the Governor-General's proceedings had engaged no little share of public attention in this country. In Parliament the attack was led by Burke and Fox;

Hastings's chief defender was one Major Scott, an Indian officer whom he had sent over to England as his agent in 1780, and who maintained his patron's cause by voice and pen, in Parliament and in the press, with far more energy than discretion. In 1784 Mrs. Hastings arrived in England, bringing home with her, says Wraxall, "about 40,000 pounds, acquired without her husband's privity or approval;" and a year later her husband followed her, having resigned his Governor-Generalship. The fortune which he now possessed was moderate, his opportunities considered, and had been honourably acquired; for his motives had never been mercenary, and the money which he had wrung from Indian princes had invariably been applied to the service of the Company or the necessities of his administration. He was received with honour by the Directors and with favour by the Court. There was talk of a peerage for him, and he believed himself not only beyond danger, but in the direct road to reward and distinction. But all this was the calm which preceded the storm. The enemies of Hastings were active and bitterly in earnest, and they were receiving invaluable assistance from his old opponent in council, Francis, who had returned to England in 1781. In April, 1786, the charges, drawn up by Burke, were laid on the table of the House of Commons. The first charge, respecting the Rohilla war, was thrown out by the House, ministers siding with the accused. But on the second charge, relating to the

Rajah of Benares, the Prime Minister, Pitt, declared against Hastings on the ground that, although the Governor-General had the right to impose a fine upon his vassal, the amount of the fine was excessive, and the motion was affirmed by a majority of forty votes. Early the next session, in February, 1787, Sheridan moved the third charge, touching the begums of Oude, in a speech which was pronounced the most brilliant ever delivered in the House of Commons. The majority against Hastings was on this occasion increased to one hundred and seven, Pitt, as before, supporting the motion. Other charges of oppression and corruption were then gone into and affirmed, and in May, by order of the House, Burke formally impeached Warren Hastings of high crimes and misdemeanours at the bar of the House of Lords. The accused was admitted to bail, himself in 20,000 pounds, and two sureties in 10,000 pounds each. The Committee of Management, elected by the Commons to conduct the impeachment, included Burke and Fox, Sheridan and Windham, and the trial was opened before the Lords, in Westminster Hall, on the 13th of February, 1788.

After two days occupied in reading the charges and the defendant's replies, Burke arose and opened the case for the prosecution in a speech full of eloquent exaggeration and honourable

zeal in the cause of an oppressed people. He spoke during days, after which the Benares charge was brought forward by Fox and Grey (afterwards Earl Grey), the youngest of the managers, and that relating to the Begums by Adam and Sheridan. The court then adjourned to the next session. But it is unnecessary here to follow the details of this famous trial which "dragged its slow length along" for seven years. In the spring of 1795 Hastings was acquitted, by a large majority, on all counts; and, although his conduct had, in some particulars, been far from faultless, and the sincerity of his principal accusers was beyond question, his acquittal must be owned as just as it was honourable, especially when we remember that his action had been entirely uninfluenced by considerations of private advantage, that he had endured for so many anxious years the burden of an impeachment, that he was ruined in fortune by the expenses of the trial, and that his great services to his country had been left wholly without reward.

His poverty, however, was relieved by the Directors of the East India Company, who bestowed upon him a pension of 4,000 a year, and he passed the remainder of his long life in honourable retirement. He died in 1818, his wife, to whom he was always devotedly attached, surviving him by a few Years.

The following section contains little besides the account of Fanny's visits to Westminster Hall during the early days of the trial. One other event, however, it relates, of sorrowful significance to the diarist. By the death of Mrs. Delany, on the 11th of April, 17; she lost at once a dear and venerated friend, and her only occasional refuge from the odious tyranny of Court routine.-ED.]

WESTMINSTER HALL AT THE OPENING OF THE HASTINGS TRIAL. February 13th. O what an interesting transaction does this day open! a day, indeed, of strong emotion to me, though all upon matters foreign to any immediate concern of my own— if anything may be called foreign that deeply interests us, merely because it is not personal.

The trial, so long impending, of Mr. Hastings, opened to-day.

The queen yesterday asked me if I wished to be present at the beginning, or had rather take another day. I was greatly obliged by her condescension, and preferred the opening. I thought it would give me a general view of the court, and the manner of proceeding, and that I might read hereafter the speeches and evidence. She then told me she had six tickets from Sir Peter Burrell, the grand chamberlain, for every day; that three were for his box, and three for his gallery. She asked me who I would go with, and promised me a box-ticket not only for myself, but my companion. Nor was this consideration all she showed me for she added, that as I might naturally wish for my father, she would have me send him my other ticket.

I thanked her very gratefully, and after dinner went to St. Martin's-street; but all there was embarrassing: my father could not go; he was averse to be present at the trial, and he was a little lame from a fall. In the end I sent an express to Hammersmith, to desire Charles(262) to come to me the next morning by eight o'clock. I was very sorry not to have my father, as he had been named by the queen; but I was glad to have Charles.

I told her majesty at night the step I had ventured to take, and she was perfectly content with it. "But I must trouble you," she said, "with Miss Gomme, who has no other way to go."

This morning the queen dispensed with all attendance from me after her first dressing, that I might haste away. Mrs. Schwellenberg was fortunately well enough to take the whole duty, and the sweet queen not only hurried me off, but sent me some cakes from her own breakfast-table, that I might

carry them, in my pocket, lest I should have no time for eating before I went.

Charles was not in time, but we all did well in the end We got to Westminster Hall between nine and ten O'clock; and, as I know my dear Susan, like my-self, was never at a trial, I will give some account of the place and arrangements'; and whether the description be new to her or old, my partial Fredy will not blame it.

The grand chamberlain's box Is in the centre of the upper end of the Hall: there we sat, Miss Gomme and myself, immediately behind the chair placed for Sir Peter Burrell. To the left, on the same level, were the green benches for the House of Commons, which occupied a third of the upper end of the Hall, and the whole of the left side: to the right of us, on the same level, was the grand chamberlain's gallery.

The right side of the Hall, opposite to the green benches for the commons, was appropriated to the peeresses and peers' daughters. The bottom of the Hall contained the royal family's box and the lord high steward's, above which was a large gallery appointed for receiving company with peers' tickets.

A gallery also was run along the left side of the Hall, above the green benches, which is called the Duke of Newcastle's box, the centre of which was railed off into a separate apartment for the reception of the queen and four eldest princesses, who were then incog., not choosing to appear in state, and in their own box.

Along the right side of the Hall ran another gallery, over the seats of the peeresses, and this was divided into boxes for various people—the lord chamberlain, (not the great chamberlain,) the surveyor, architect, etc.

So much for all the raised buildings ; now for the disposition of the Hall itself, or ground. In the middle was placed a large table, and at the head of it the seat for the chancellor, and round it seats for the judges, the masters in chancery, the clerks, and all who belonged to the law; the upper end, and the right side of the room, was allotted to the peers in their robes; the left side to the bishops and archbishops.

Immediately below the great chamberlain's box was the place allotted for the prisoner. On his right side was a box for his own counsel, on his left the box for the managers, or committee, for the prosecution; and these three most important of all the divisions in the Hall were all directly adjoining to where I was seated.

Almost the moment I entered I was spoken to by a lady I Page 97 did not recollect, but found afterwards to be Lady Claremont and this proved very agreeable, for she took Sir Peter's place: and said she would occupy it till he claimed it; and then, when just before me, she named to me all the order of the buildings, and all the company, pointing out every distinguished person, and most obligingly desiring me to ask her any questions I wanted to have solved, as she knew, she said, "all those creatures that filled the green benches, looking so little like gentlemen, and so much like hair-dressers," These were the Commons. In truth, she did the honours of the Hall to me with as much good nature and good breeding as if I had been a foreigner of distinction, to whom she had dedicated her time and attention. My acquaintance with her had been made formerly at Mrs. Vesey's.

The business did not begin till near twelve o'clock. The opening to the whole then took place, by the entrance of the managers of the prosecution; all the company were already long in their boxes or galleries. I shuddered, and drew Involuntarily back, when, as the doors were flung open, I saw Mr. Burke, as head of the committee, make his solemn entry. He held a scroll in his hand, and walked alone, his brow knit with corroding care and deep labouring thought,—a brow how different to that which had proved so alluring to my warmest admiration when first I met him! so highly as he had been my favourite, so captivating as I had found his manners; and conversation in our first acquaintance, and so much as I had owed to his zeal and kindness to me and my affairs in its progress! How did I grieve to behold him now the cruel prosecutor (such to me he appeared) of an injured and innocent man!

Mr. Fox followed next, Mr. Sheridan, Mr. Windham, Messrs. Anstruther, Grey, Adam, Michael Angelo Taylor, Pelham, Colonel North, Mr. Frederick Montagu, Sir Gilbert Elliot, General Burgoyne, Dudley Long, etc. They were all named over to me by Lady Claremont, or I should not have recollected even those of my acquaintance, from the shortness of my sight,

When the committee box was filled the House of Commons at large took their seats on their green benches, which stretched, as I have said, along the whole left side of the Hall, and, taking in a third of the upper end, joined to the great Chamberlain's box, from which nothing separated them but a Partition of about two feet in height.

Then began the procession, the clerks entering first, then the lawyers according to their rank, and the peers, bishops, and officers, all in their coronation robes; concluding with the princes of the blood,–Prince William, son to the Duke of Gloucester, coming first, then the Dukes of Cumberland, Gloucester, and York, then the Prince of Wales; and the whole ending by the chancellor, with his train borne. They then all took their seats.

WARREN HASTINGS APPEARS AT THE BAR.

A sergeant-at- arms arose, and commanded silence in court, on pain of imprisonment. Then some other officer, in a loud voice, called out, as well as I can recollect, words to this purpose:– "Warren Hastings, esquire, come forth! Answer to the charges brought against you; save your bail, or forfeit your recognizance."

Indeed I trembled at these words, and hardly Could keep my place when I found Mr. Hastings was being brought to the bar. He came forth from some place immediately under the great chamberlain's box, and was preceded by Sir Francis Molyneux, gentleman-usher of the black rod; and at each side of him walked his bail, Messrs. Sulivan and Sumner.

The moment he came in sight, which was not for full ten minutes after his awful summons, he made a low bow to the chancellor and court facing him. I saw not his face, as he was directly under me. He moved on slowly, and, I think, supported between his two bails, to the opening of his own box; there, lower still, he bowed again; and then, advancing to the bar, he leant his hands upon it, and dropped on his knees; but a voice in the same minute proclaiming he had leave to rise, he stood up almost instantaneously, and a third time, profoundly bowed to the court.

What an awful moment this for such a man!–a man fallen from such height of power to a situation so humiliating–from the almost unlimited command of so large a part of the eastern World to be cast at the feet of his enemies, of the great tribunal of his country, and of the nation at large, assembled thus in a body to try and to judge him! Could even his prosecutors at that moment look on–and not shudder at least, if they did not blush?

The crier, I think it was, made, in a loud and hollow voice, a public proclamation, "That Warren Hastings, esquire, late governor-general of Bengal, was now on his trial for high

Page 99 crimes and misdemeanours, with which he was charged by the commons of Great Britain; and that all persons whatsoever who had aught to allege against him were now to stand forth."

A general silence followed, and the chancellor, Lord Thurlow, now made his speech. I will give it you to the best of my power from memory; the newspapers have printed it far less accurately than I have retained it, though I am by no means exact or secure.

THE LORD CHANCELLOR'S SPEECH.

Warren Hastings, you are now brought into this court to answer to the charge, brought against you by the knights, esquires, burgesses, and commons of Great Britain–charges now standing only as allegations, by them to be legally proved, or by you to be disproved. Bring forth your answer and defence, with that seriousness, respect, and truth, due to accusers so respectable. Time has been allowed you for preparation, proportioned to the intricacies in which the transactions are involved, and to the remote distances whence your documents may have been searched and required. You will be allowed bail, for the better forwarding your defence, and-whatever you can require will still be yours, of time, witnesses, and all things else you may hold necessary. This is not granted you as any indulgence: it is entirely your due: it is the privilege which every British subject has a right to claim, and which is due to every one who is brought before this high tribunal."

This speech, uttered in a calm, equal, solemn manner, and in a voice mellow and penetrating, with eyes keen and black, yet softened into some degree of tenderness while fastened full upon the prisoner–this speech, its occasion, its portent, and its object, had an effect upon every hearer of producing the most respectful attention, and, out of the committee box at least, the strongest emotions in the cause of Mr. Hastings. Again Mr. Hastings made the lowest reverence to the court, and, leaning over the bar answered, with much agitation, through evident efforts to suppress it, "My lords –Impressed–deeply impressed– I come before your lordships, equally confident in my own integrity, and in the justice of the court before which I am to clear it."

"Impressed" and "deeply impressed," too, was my mind, by this short yet comprehensive speech, and all my best wishes

for his clearance and redress rose warmer than ever in my heart.

THE READING OF THE CHARGES COMMENCED.

A general silence again ensued, and then one of the lawyers opened the cause. He began by reading from an immense roll of parchment the general charges against Mr. Hastings, but he read in so monotonous a chant that nothing more could I hear or understand than now and then the name of Warren Hastings.

During this reading, to which I vainly lent all my attention, Mr. Hastings, finding it, I presume, equally impossible to hear a word, began to cast his eyes around the house, and having taken a survey of all in front and at the sides, he turned about and looked up; pale looked his face–pale, ill, and altered. I was much affected by the sight of that dreadful harass which was written on his countenance. Had I looked at him without restraint, it could not have been without tears. I felt shocked, too, shocked and ashamed, to be seen by him in that place. I had wished to be present from an earnest interest in the business, joined to a firm confidence in his powers of defence; but his eyes were not those I wished to meet in Westminster Hall. I called upon Miss Gomme and Charles to assist me in looking another way, and in conversing with me as I turned aside, and I kept as much aloof as possible till he had taken his survey, and placed himself again in front.

From this time, however, he frequently looked round, and I was soon without a doubt that he must see me. . . . In a few minutes more, while this reading was still continued, I perceived Sir Joshua Reynolds in the midst of the committee. He, at the same moment, saw me also, and not only bowed, but smiled and nodded with his usual good-humour and intimacy, making at the same time a sign to his ear, by which I understood he had no trumpet; whether he had forgotten or lost it I know not.

I would rather have answered all this dumb show anywhere else, as my last ambition was that of being noticed from such a box. I again entreated aid in turning away; but Miss Gomme, who is a friend of Sir Gilbert Elliot, one of the managers and an ill-wisher, for his sake, to the opposite cause, would only laugh, and ask why I should not be owned by them.

I did not, however, like it, but had no choice from my near

situation; and in a few seconds I had again a bow, and a profound one, and again very ridiculously I was obliged to inquire of Lady Claremont who my own acquaintance might be. Mr. Richard Burke, senior, she answered. He is a brother of the great–great in defiance of all drawbacks–Edmund Burke.

Another lawyer now arose, and read so exactly in the same manner, that it was utterly impossible to discover even whether it was a charge or an answer. Such reading as this, you may well suppose, set every body pretty much at their ease and but for the interest I took in looking from time to time at Mr. Hastings, and watching his countenance, I might as well have been away. He seemed composed after the first half-hour, and calm; but he looked with a species of indignant contempt towards his accusers, that could not, I think, have been worn had his defence been doubtful. Many there are who fear for him; for me, I own myself wholly confident in his acquittal.

AN OLD ACQUAINTANCE.

Soon after, a voice just by my side, from the green benches, said, "Will Miss Burney allow me to renew my acquaintance with her?" I turned about and saw Mr. Crutchley.

All Streatham rose to my mind at sight of him. I have never beheld him since the Streatham society was abolished. We entered instantly upon the subject of that family, a Subject ever to me the most Interesting. He also had never seen poor Mrs. Thrale since her return to England; but he joined with me very earnestly in agreeing that, since so unhappy a step was now past recall, it became the duty, however painful a one, of the daughters, to support, not cast off and contemn, one who was now as much their mother as when she still bore their own name.

"But how," cried he, "do you stand the fiery trial of this Streatham book that is coming upon us?"

I acknowledged myself very uneasy about it, and he assured me all who had ever been at Streatham were in fright and consternation. We talked all these matters over more at length, till I was called away by an "How d'ye do, Miss Burney?" from the committee box! And then I saw young Mr. Burke, who had jumped up on the nearest form to speak to me.

Pleasant enough! I checked my vexation as well as I was able, since the least shyness on my part to those with whom formerly I had been social must instantly have been attributed to Court influence; and therefore, since I could not avoid the notice, I did what I could to talk with him as heretofore. He is besides so amiable a young man that I could not be sorry to see him again, though I regretted it should be Just In that place, and at this time.

While we talked together, Mr. Crutchley went back to his more distant seat, and the moment I was able to withdraw from young Mr. Burke, Charles, who sat behind me, leant down and told me a gentleman had just desired to be presented to me.

"Who?" quoth I.

" Mr. Windham," he answered.

I really thought he was laughing, and answered accordingly, but he assured me he was in earnest, and that Mr. Windham had begged him to make the proposition. What could I do? There was no refusing; yet a planned meeting with another of the committee, and one deep in the prosecution, and from whom one of the hardest charges has come(263)—could anything be less pleasant as I was then situated? The great chamberlain's box is the only part of the Hall that has any communication with either the committee box or the House of Commons, and it is also the very nearest to the prisoner.

WILLIAM WINDHAM) ESQ., M.P.

Mr. Windham I had seen twice before-both times at Miss Monckton's; and anywhere else I should have been much gratified by his desire of a third meeting, as he is one of the most agreeable, spirited, well-bred, and brilliant conversers I have ever spoken with. He is a neighbour, too, now, of

Charlotte's. He is member for Norwich, and a man of family and fortune, with a very pleasing though not handsome face, a very elegant figure, and an air of fashion and vivacity.

The conversations I had had with him at Miss Monckton's had been, wholly- by his own means, extremely spirited and entertaining. I was sorry to see him make one of a set that appeared so inveterate against a man I believe so injuriously treated; and my concern was founded upon the good thoughts I had conceived of him, not merely from his social talents, which are yet very uncommon, but from a reason clearer to my remembrance. He loved Dr. Johnson,-and Dr. Johnson returned his affection. Their political principles and connexions were opposite, but Mr. Windham respected his venerable friend too highly to discuss any points that could offend him ; and showed for him so true a regard, that, during all his late illnesses, for the latter part of his life, his carriage and himself were alike at his service, to air, visit, or go out, whenever he was disposed to accept them.

Nor was this all; one tender proof he gave of warm and generous regard, that I can never forget, and that rose instantly to my mind when I heard his name, and gave him a welcome in my eyes when they met his face : it is this: Dr. Johnson, in his last visit to Lichfield, was taken ill, and waited to recover strength for travelling back to town in his usual vehicle, a stage-coach– as soon as this reached the ears of Mr. Windham, he set off for Lichfield in his own carriage, to offer to bring hint back to town in it, and at his own time.

For a young man of fashion, such a trait towards an old, however dignified philosopher, must surely be a mark indisputable of an elevated mind and character; and still the more strongly it marked a noble way of thinking, as it was done in favour of a person in open opposition to his own party, and declared prejudices.

Charles soon told me he was it my elbow. He had taken the place Mr. Crutchley had just left. The abord was, oil my , part, very awkward, from the distress I felt lest Mr. Hastings should look up, and from a conviction that I must not name Page 104

that gentleman, of whom alone I could then think, to a person in a committee against him.

He, however, was easy, having no embarrassing thoughts, since the conference was of his own seeking. 'Twas so long since I had seen him, that I almost wonder he remembered me. After the first compliments he looked around him, and exclaimed "What an assembly is this! How striking a spectacle! I had not seen half its splendour down there. You have it here to great advantage; you lose some of the lords, but you gain all the ladies. You have a very good place here,"

"Yes and I may safely say I make a very impartial use of it for since here I have sat, I have never discovered to which side I have been listening!"

He laughed, but told me they were then running through the charges.

"And is it essential," cried I, "that they should so run them through that nobody can understand them? Is that a form of law?"

He agreed to the absurdity - and then, looking still at the spectacle, which indeed is the most splendid I ever saw, arrested his eyes upon the chancellor.

"He looks very well from hence," cried he; "and how well he acquits himself on these solemn occasions! With what dignity, what loftiness, what high propriety, he comports himself!"

This praise to the chancellor, who is a known friend to Mr. Hastings, though I believe he would be the last to favour him unjustly now he is on trial, was a pleasant sound to my ear, and confirmed my original idea of the liberal disposition of my new associate. i joined heartily in the commendation, and warmly praised his speech.

"Even a degree of pompousness," cried I, "in such a court as this, seems a propriety."

"Yes," said he "but his speech had one word that might as well have been let alone: 'mere allegations' he called the charges; the word 'mere,' at least, might have been spared, especially as it is already strongly suspected on which side he leans!"

I protested, and with truth, I had not heard the word in his speech; but he still affirmed it.

"Surely," I said, "he was as fair and impartial as possible: he called the accusers 'so respectable!'"

"Yes, but 'mere–mere' was no word for this occasion and it could not be unguarded, for he would never come to

Page 105 speak in such a court as this, without some little thinking beforehand. However, he is a fine fellow,–a very fine fellow! and though, in his private life, guilty of so many inaccuracies, in his public capacity I really hold him to be unexceptionable."

This fairness, from an oppositionist professed, brought me at once to easy terms with him. I begged him to inform me for what reason, at the end of the chancellor's speech, there had been a cry of "Hear! hear! hear him!" which had led me to expect another speech, when I found no other seemed intended. He laughed very much, and confessed that, as a parliament man, he was so used to that absurdity, that he had ceased to regard it; for that it was merely a mark of approbation to a speech already spoken; "And, in fact, they only," cried he, "say 'Hear!' when there is nothing more to be heard!" Then, still looking at the scene before him, he suddenly laughed, and said, "I must not, to Miss Burney, make this remark, but-it is observable that in the king's box sit the Hawkesbury family, while, next to the Speaker, who is here as a sort of representative of the king, sits Major Scott!"

I knew his inference, of Court influence in favour of Mr. Hastings, but I thought it best to let it pass quietly. I knew, else, I should only be supposed under the same influence myself. Looking still on, he next noticed the two archbishops. "And see," cried he, "the Archbishop of York, Markham,–see how he affects to read the articles of impeachment, as if he was still open to either side! My good lord archbishop! your grace might, with perfect safety, spare your eyes, for your mind has been made up upon this subject before ever it was investigated. He holds Hastings to be the greatest man in the world–for Hastings promoted the interest of his son in the East Indies!"

WINDHAM INVEIGHS AGAINST WARREN HASTINGS. Somewhat sarcastic, this - but I had as little time as power for answering, since now, and suddenly, his eye dropped down upon poor Mr. Hastings; the expression of his face instantly lost the gaiety and ease with which it had addressed me; he stopped short in his remarks; he fixed his eyes steadfastly on this new, and but too interesting object, and after viewing him

106

some time in a sort of earnest silence, he suddenly exclaimed as if speaking to himself, and from an impulse irresistible "What a sight is that! to see that man, that small portion of human clay, that poor feeble machine of earth, enclosed now in that little space, brought to that bar, a prisoner in a spot six foot square–and to reflect on his late power! Nations at his command! Princes prostrate at his feet!–What a change! how Must he feel it!–"

He stopped, and I said not a word. I was glad to see him thus impressed; I hoped it might soften his enmity. I found, by his manner, that he had never, from the committee box, looked at him. He broke forth again, after a pause of Some length,–"Wonderful indeed! almost past credibility, is such a reverse! He that, so lately, had the Eastern world nearly at his beck; he, under whose tyrant power princes and potentates sunk and trembled; he, whose authority was without the reach of responsibility!–"

Again he stopped, seeming struck, almost beyond the power of speech, with meditative commiseration ; but then, suddenly rousing himself, as if recollecting his "almost blunted purpose," he passionately exclaimed, "Oh could those–the thousands, the millions, who have groaned and languished under the iron rod of his oppressions--could they but–whatever region they inhabit– be permitted one dawn of light to look into this Hall, and see him there! There–where he now stands–It might prove, perhaps, some recompense for their sufferings!"

I can hardly tell you, my dearest Susan, how shocked I felt at these words! words so hard, and following sensations so much more pitying and philosophic! I cannot believe Mr. Hastings guilty; I feel in myself a strong internal evidence of his innocence, drawn from all I have seen of him; I can only regard the prosecution as a party affair; but yet, since his adversaries now openly stake their names, fame, and character against him, I did not think it decent to intrude such an opinion. I could only be sorry, and silent.

Still he looked at him, earnest in rumination, and as if unable to turn away his eyes; and presently he again exclaimed, "How wonderful an instance of the instability of mortal power is presented]In that object! From possessions so extensive, from a despotism so uncontrolled. to see him, now there, in that small circumference! In the history Of human nature how memorable will be the records of this day!

a day that brings to the great tribunal of the nation a man whose power, so short a time since, was of equal magnitude with his crimes!"

Good heaven! thought I, and do you really believe all this? Can Mr. Hastings appear to you such a monster? and are you not merely swayed by party? I could not hear him without shuddering, nor see him thus in earnest without alarm. I thought myself no longer bound to silence, since I saw, by the continuance as well as by the freedom of his exclamations, he conceived me of the same sentiments with himself; and therefore I hardily resolved to make known to him that mistake, which, indeed, was a liberty that seemed no longer impertinent, but a mere act of justice and honesty.

His very expressive pause, his eyes still steadfastly fixed on Mr. Hastings, gave me ample opportunity for speaking - though I had some little difficulty how to get out what I wished to say. However, in the midst of his reverie, I broke forth, but not without great hesitation, and, very humbly, I said, "Could you pardon me, Mr. Windham, If I should forget, for a moment, that you are a committee man, and speak to you frankly?"

He looked surprised, but laughed at the question, and very eagerly called out "Oh yes, yes, pray speak out, I beg it!"

"Well, then, may I venture to say to you that I believe it utterly impossible for any one, not particularly engaged on the contrary side, ever to enter a court of justice, and not instantly, and involuntarily, wish well to the prisoner!"

His surprise subsided by this general speech, which I had not courage to put in a more pointed way, and he very readily answered, "'Tis natural, certainly, and what must almost unavoidably be the first impulse; yet, where justice—"

I stopped him; I saw I was not comprehended, and thought else he might say something to stop me.

"May I," I said, " go yet a little farther ?

"Yes," cried he, with a very civil smile, "and I feel an assent beforehand."

" Supposing then, that even you, if that may be supposed, could be divested of all knowledge of the particulars of this affair, and in the same state of general Ignorance that I confess myself to be, and could then, like me, have seen Mr. Hastings make his entrance into this court, and looked at him when he was brought to that bar; not even you, Mr. Windham, could then have reflected on such a vicissitude for him, on all he has

left and all he has lost, and not have given him, like me, all your best wishes the moment you beheld him."

The promised assent came not, though he was too civil to contradict me ; but still I saw he Understood me only in a general sense. I feared going farther : a weak advocate is apt to be a mischievous one and, as I knew nothing, it was not to a professed enemy I could talk of what I only believed. Recovering, now, from the strong emotion with which the sight of Mr. Hastings had filled him, he looked again around the court, and pointed out several of the principal characters present, with arch and striking remarks upon each of them, all uttered with high spirit, but none with ill-nature.

("Pitt," cried he, "is not here!–a noble stroke that for the annals of his administration! A trial is brought on by the whole House of Commons In a body, and he is absent at the very opening! However," added he, with a very meaning laugh, "I'm glad of it, for 'tis to his eternal disgrace!"

Mercy! thought I, what a friend to kindness Is party!

"Do you see Scott?" cried he.

"No, I never saw him; pray show him to me,"

"There he is, in green; just now by the Speaker, now moved by the committee; in two minutes more he will be somewhere else, skipping backwards and forwards; what a grasshopper it is!"

"I cannot look at him," cried I, "without recollecting a very extraordinary letter from him, that I read last summer in the newspaper, where he answers some attack that he says has been made upon him, because the term is used of 'a very insignificant fellow,' and he printed two or three letters in 'The Public Advertiser,' in following days, to prove, with great care and pains, that he knew it was all meant as an abuse of himself, from those words!"

"And what," cried he, laughing, "do you say to that notion now you see him?"

"That no one," cried I, examining him with my glass, "can possibly dispute his claim!"

What pity that Mr. Hastings should have trusted his cause to so frivolous an agent! I believe, and indeed it is the general belief, both of foes and friends, that to his officious and injudicious zeal the present prosecution is wholly owing.

Next, Mr. Windham pointed out Mr. Francis to me. 'TIS a singular circumstance, that the friend who most loves and the enemy Who most hates Mr. Hastings should bear the same

name!(264) Mr. Windham, with all the bias of party, gave me then the highest character of this Mr. Francis, whom he called one of the most ill-used of men. Want of documents how to answer forced me to be silent, oppositely as I thought. But it was a very unpleasant situation to me, as I saw that Mr. Windham still conceived me to have no other interest than a common, and probably to his mind, a weak compassion for the prisoner–that prisoner who, frequently looking around, saw me, I am certain, and saw with whom I was engaged.

The subject of Mr. Francis again drew him back to Mr. Hastings, but with more severity of mind. "A prouder heart," cried he, "an ambition more profound, were never, I suppose, lodged in any mortal mould than in that man! With what a port he entered! did you observe him? his air! I saw not his face, but his air his port!"

"Surely there," cried I, "he could not be to blame! He comes upon his defence; ought he to look as if he gave himself up?"

"Why no; 'tis true he must look what vindication to himself he can; we must not blame him there."

Encouraged by this little concession, I resolved to venture farther, and once more said "May I again, Mr. Windham, forget that you are a committee-man, and say something not fit for a committee man to hear?"

"O yes!" cried he, laughing very much, and looking extremely curious.

"I must fairly, then, own myself utterly ignorant upon this subject, and–and–may I go on?"

"I beg you will!"

"Well, then,–and originally prepossessed in favour of the object!"

He quite started, and with a look of surprise from which all pleasure was separated, exclaimed–"Indeed!"

"Yes!" cried I, "'tis really true, and really out, now!"

"For Mr. Hastings, prepossessed!" he repeated, in a tone that seemed to say–do you not mean Mr. Burke?

"Yes," I said, "for Mr. Hastings! But I should not have presumed to own it just at this time,–so little as I am able to do honour to my prepossession by any materials to defend it,–but that you have given me courage, by appearing so free from all malignity in the business. Tis, therefore, Your own fault!"

"But can you speak seriously," cried he, " "when You say you know nothing of this business?"

"Very seriously: I never entered into it at all; it was always too intricate to tempt me."

"But, surely you must have read the charges?"

"No; they are so long, I had never the courage to begin."

The conscious look with which he heard this, brought–all too late–to my remembrance, that one of them was drawn up, and delivered in the House, by himself! I was really very sorry to have been so unfortunate; but I had no way to call back the words, so was quiet, perforce.

"Come then," cried he, emphatically, "to hear Burke! come and listen to him, and you will be mistress of the whole. Hear Burke, and read the charges of the Begums, and then you will form your judgment without difficulty."

I would rather (thought I) hear him upon any other subject: but I made no answer; I only said, "Certainly, I can gain nothing by what is going forward to-day. I meant to come to the opening now, but it seems rather like the shutting up!"

He was not to be put off. "You will come, however, to hear Burke? To hear truth, reason, justice, eloquence! You will then see, in other colours, 'That man!' There is more cruelty, more oppression, more tyranny, in that little machine, with an arrogance, a self-confidence, unexampled, unheard of!"

MISS BURNEY BATTLES FOR THE ACCUSED.

"Indeed, sir!" cried I; "that does not appear, to those who know him and–I–know him a little."

"Do you?" cried he earnestly; "personally, do you know him?"

"Yes; and from that knowledge arose this prepossession I have confessed."

"Indeed, what you have seen of him have you then so much approved?"

"Yes, very much! I must own the truth!"

"But you have not seen much of him?"

"No, not lately. My first knowledge of him was almost immediately upon his coming from India; I had heard nothing of all these accusations; I had never been in the way of hearing them, and knew not even that there were any to be heard. I saw him, therefore, quite without prejudice, for or against him ; and indeed, I must own, he soon gave me a strong interest in his favour."

The surprise with which he heard me must have silenced me on the subject, had it not been accompanied with an attention so earnest as to encourage me still to proceed. It is evident to me that this committee live so much shut Lip with one another, that they conclude all the world of the same opinions with themselves, and universally imagine that the tyrant they think themselves pursuing is a monster in every part of his life, and held in contempt and abhorrence by all mankind. Could I then be sorry, seeing this, to contribute my small mite towards clearing, at least, so very wide a mistake? On the contrary, when I saw he listened, I was most eager to give him all I could to hear,

"I found him," I continued, "so mild, so gentle, so extremely pleasing in his manners–"

"Gentle!" cried he, with quickness.

"Yes, Indeed; gentle even to humility–"

"Humility? Mr. Hastings and humility!"

"Indeed it is true; he is perfectly diffident in the whole of his manner, when engaged in conversation; and so much struck was I, at that very time, by seeing him so simple, so unassuming, when just returned from a government that had accustomed him to a power superior to our monarchs here, that it produced an effect upon my mind in his favour which nothing can erase!"

"Yes, Yes!" cried he, with great energy, "you will give it up! you must lose it, must give it up! it will be plucked away, rooted wholly out of your mind ."

"Indeed, sir," cried I, steadily, "I believe not!"

"You believe not?" repeated he, with added animation; "then there will be the more glory in making you a convert!"

If "conversion" is the word, thought I, I would rather make than be made.

"But –Mr. Windham," cried I, "all my amazement now is at your condescension in speaking to me upon this business at all, when I have confessed to you my total ignorance of the subject, and my original prepossession in favour of the object. Why do you not ask me when I was at the play ? and how I liked the last opera?"

He laughed; and we talked on a little while in that strain, till again, suddenly fixing his eyes on poor Mr. Hastings, his gaiety once more vanished, and he gravely and severely examined his countenance. "'Tis surely," cried he, "an unpleasant one. He does not know, I suppose, 'tis reckoned like his own!"

"How should he," cried I, "look otherwise than unpleasant here?"

"True," cried he; "yet still, I think, his features, his look, his whole expression, unfavourable to him. I never saw him but once before; that was at the bar of the House of Commons and there, as Burke admirably said, he looked, when first he glanced an eye against him, like a hungry tiger, ready to howl for his prey!"

"Well," cried I, "I am sure he does not look fierce now!
Contemptuous, a little, I think he does look!"

I was sorry I used this word; yet its truth forced it to escape me. He did not like it; he repeated it; he could not but be sure the contempt could only be levelled at his prosecutors. I feared discussion, and flew off as fast as I could, to softer ground. "It was not," cried I, "with that countenance he gave me my prepossession! Very differently, indeed, he looked then!"

"And can he ever look pleasant? can that face ever obtain an expression that is pleasing?"

"Yes, indeed and in truth, very pleasant! It was in the country I first saw him, and without any restraint on his part; I saw him, therefore, perfectly natural and easy. And no one, let me say, could so have seen him without being pleased with him–his quietness and serenity, joined to his intelligence and information–"

"His information?–in what way?"

"In such a way as suited his hearer: not upon committee business–of all that I knew nothing. The only conversation in which I could mix was upon India, considered simply as, a country in which he had travelled; and his communications upon the people, the customs, habits, cities, and whatever I could name, were so instructive as well as entertaining, that I think I never recollect gaining more intelligence, or more pleasantly conveyed, from any conversation in which I ever have been engaged."

To this he listened with an attention that, but for the secret zeal which warmed me must have silenced and shamed me. I am satisfied this committee have concluded Mr. Hastings a mere man of blood, with slaughter and avarice for his sole ideas! The surprise with which he heard this just testimony to his social abilities was only silent from good-breeding, but his eyes expressed what his tongue withheld; something that satisfied me he concluded

I had undesignedly been duped by him. I answered this silence by saying "There was no object for hypocrisy, for it was quite in retirement I met with him : it was not lately ; it is near two years since I have seen him; he had therefore no point to gain with me, nor was there any public character, nor any person whatever, that Could induce him to act a part; yet was he all I have said-informing, Communicative, instructive, and at the same time, gentle and highly pleasing."

"Well," said he, very civilly, "I begin the less to wonder, now, that You have adhered to his side; but–"

"To see him, then," cried I, stopping his 'but,'–"to see him brought to that bar! and kneeling at it!–indeed, Mr. Windham, I must own to you, I could hardly keep my seat–hardly forbear rising and running out of the Hall."

"Why, there," cried he, "I agree with you! 'Tis certainly a humiliation not to be wished or defended: it is, indeed, a mere ceremony, a mere formality; but it is a mortifying one, and so obsolete, so unlike the practices of the times, so repugnant from a gentleman to a gentleman, that I myself looked another way: it hurt me, and I wished it dispensed with."

"O, Mr. Windham," cried I, surprised and pleased, "and can you be so liberal?"

"Yes," cried he, laughing, "but 'tis only to take you in!"

Afterwards he asked what his coat was, whether blue Or purple; and said, "is it not customary for a prisoner to come black?"

"Whether or not," quoth I, "I am heartily glad he has not done it; why should he seem so dismal, so shut out from hope?"

"Why, I believe he is in the right. I think he has judged that not ill."

"O, don't be so candid," cried I, "I beg you not."

"Yes, yes, I must; and you know the reason," cried he, gaily; but presently exclaimed, "one unpleasant thing belong-

ing to being a manager is that I must now go and show myself in the committee." And then he very civilly bowed, and went down to his box, leaving me much persuaded that I had never yet been engaged in a conversation so curious, from its circumstances, in my life. The warm well-wisher myself of the prisoner, though formerly the warmest admirer of his accuser, engaged, even at his trial and in his presence, in so open a discussion with one of his principal prosecutors; and the queen herself in full view, unavoidably beholding me in close and eager conference with an avowed member of the opposition!

These circumstances made me at first enter into discourse with Mr. Windham with the utmost reluctance ; but though I wished to shun him, I could not, when once attacked, decline to converse with him. It would but injure the cause of Mr. Hastings to seem to fear hearing the voice of his accusers; and it could but be attributed to undue court-influence had I avoided any intercourse with an acquaintance so long ago established as a member of the opposition.

A WEARIED M.P.-MR. CRUTCHLEY REAPPEARS.

In the midst of the opening of a trial such as this, so important to the country as well as to the individual who is tried, what will you say to a man–a member of the House of Commons who kept exclaiming almost perpetually, just at my side, "What a bore!- -when will it be over?–Must one come any more?–I had a great mind not to have come at all.–Who's that?–Lady Hawkesbury and the Copes?–Yes.–A pretty girl, Kitty.–Well, when will they have done?–I wish they'd call the question–I should vote it a bore at once!

just such exclamations as these were repeated, without intermission, till the gentleman departed: and who should it be that spoke with so much legislative wisdom but Mr. W—!

In about two or three hours–this reading still lasting–Mr. Crutchley came to me again. He, too, was so wearied, that he was departing; but he stayed some time to talk over our constant topic–my poor Mrs. Thrale. How little does he suspect the interest I unceasingly take in her–the avidity with which I seize every opportunity to gather the smallest intelligence concerning her!

One little trait of Mr. Crutchley, so characteristic of that queerness which distinguishes him, I must mention. He said

he questioned whether he should comme any more: I told him I had imagined the attendance of every member to be indispensable. "No," cried he, "ten to one if another day they are able to make a house!"

"The Lords, however, I suppose, must come?"

"Not unless they like it."

" But I hear if they do not attend they have no tickets."

"Why, then, Miss Primrose and Miss Cowslip must stay away too!"

I had the pleasure to find him entirely for Mr. Hastings, and to hear he had constantly voted on his side through every stage of the business. He is a very independent man, and a man of real good character, and, with all his oddity, of real understanding. We compared notes very amicably upon this subject, and both agreed that those who looked for every flaw in the conduct of a man in so high and hazardous a station, ought first to have weighed his merits and his difficulties.

MR. WINDHAM DISCUSSES THE IMPEACHMENT.

A far more interesting conference, however, was now awaiting me. Towards the close of the day Mr. Windham very unexpectedly came again from the committee-box, and seated himself by my side. I was glad to see by this second visit that my frankness had not offended him. He began, too, in so open and social a manner, that I was satisfied he forgave it.

"I have been," cried he, "very busy since I left you.–writing– reading–making documents."

I saw he was much agitated ; the gaiety which seems natural to him was flown, and had left in its place the most evident and unquiet emotion. I looked a little surprised, and rallying himself, in a few moments he inquired if I wished for any refreshment, and proposed fetching me some. But, well as I liked him for a conspirator, I could not break bread with him!

I thought now all was over of communication between us, but I was mistaken. He spoke for a minute or two upon the crowd–early hour of coming–hasty breakfasting and such general nothings; and then, as if involuntarily, he returned to the sole subject on his mind.

"Our plan," cried he, "is all changing: we have all been busy–we are coming into a new method. I have been making preparations–I did not intend speaking for a considerable time–not till after the circuit, but now, I may be called upon, I know not how soon."

Then he stopped–ruminating–and I let him ruminate without interruption for some minutes, when he broke forth with these reflections: "How strange, how infatuated a frailty has man with respect to the future! Be our views, our designs, our anticipations what they may, we are never prepared for it!–It always takes us by surprise–always comes before we look for it!"

He stopped; but I waited his explanation without speaking, and, after pausing thoughtfully for some time, he went on:

"This day–for which we have all been waiting so anxiously, so earnestly–the day for which we have fought, for which we have struggled–a day, indeed, of national glory, in bringing to this great tribunal a delinquent from so high an office–this day, so much wished, has seemed to me, to the last moment, so distant, that now–now that it Is actually arrived, it takes me as if I had never thought of it before–it comes upon me all unexpected, and finds me unready!"

Still I said nothing, for I did not fully comprehend him, till he added, "I will not be so affected as to say to you that I have made no preparation–that I have not thought a little upon what I have to do; yet now that the moment is actually come–"

Again he broke off. but a generous sentiment was, bursting from him, and would not be withheld.

"It has brought me," he resumed, "a feeling of which I am not yet quite the master! What I have said hitherto, when I have spoken in the house, has been urged and stimulated by the idea of pleading for the injured and the absent, and that gave me spirit. Nor do I tell you (with a half-conscious smile) that the ardour of the prosecution went for nothing–a prosecution in favour of oppressed millions! But now,. when I am to speak here, the thought of that man, close to my side–culprit as he is–that man on whom all the odium is to fall–gives me, I own, a sensation that almost disqualifies me beforehand!" . . .

"That this day was ever brought about," continued he, "must ever remain a noble memorial of courage and perseverance in the Commons. Every possible obstacle has been thrown in our way– every art of government has been at work to impede us–nothing has been left untried to obstruct us–every check and clog of power and influence."

"Not by him," cried I, looking at poor Mr. Hastings; "he has raised no impediments–he has been wholly careless."

"Come," cried he, with energy, "come and hear Burke!–Come but and hear him!–'tis an eloquence irresistible!–a torrent that sweeps all before it with the force of a whirlwind! It will Cure You, indeed, of your prepossession, but it will give you truth and right in its place. What discoveries has he not made!—what gulfs has he not dived into! Come and hear him, and your conflict will end!" I could hardly stand this, and, to turn it off', asked him if Mr. Hastings was to make his own defence?

"No," he answered, "he will only speak by counsel. But do not regret that, for his own sake, as he is not used to public speaking, and has some impediment in his speech besides. He writes wonderfully—there he shines—and with a facility quite astonishing. Have you ever happened to see any of his writings?"

"No: only one short account, which he calls 'Memoirs relative to some India transactions,' and that struck me to be extremely unequal—in some places strong and finely expressed, In others obscure and scarce intelligible."

"That is just the case—that ambiguity runs through him in everything. Burke has found an admirable word for it in the Persian tongue, for which we have no translation, but it means an intricacy involved so deep as to be nearly unfathomable—an artificial entanglement."

I inquired how it was all to end—whether this reading was to continue incessantly, or any speaking was to follow it?

"I have not inquired how that is," he answered, "but I believe you will now soon be released."

"And will the chancellor speak to adjourn?"

"I cannot tell what the form may be, or how we are to be dissolved. I think myself there is nothing more difficult than how to tell people they may go about their business. I remember, when I was in the militia, it was just what I thought the most awkward, when I had done with my men. Use gives one the habit; and I found, afterwards, there was a regular mode for it: but, at first, I found it very embarrassing how to get rid of them."

Nothing excites frankness like frankness ; and I answered him in return with a case of my own. "When first I came to my present residence I was perpetually," I said, "upon the point of making a blunder with the queen; for when, after she had honoured me with any conversation, she used to say 'Now I won't keep you—now I will detain you no longer,' .

Page 118 I was always ready to answer, 'Ma'am, I am in no haste,- ma'am, I don't wish to go!' for I was not, at first, aware that it was only her mode of dismissing people from her presence."

WINDHAM AFFECTS TO COMMISERATE HASTINGS.

Again he was going: but glancing his eyes once more down upon Mr. Hastings, he almost sighed—he fetched, at least, a deep breath, while he exclaimed with strong emotion, "What a place for a man to stand in to hear what he has to hear!—'tis almost too much!"

It would not be easy to tell you how touching at such a time was the smallest concession from an avowed opponent, and I could not help exclaiming again, "O, Mr. Windham, you must not be so liberal!"

"O!" cried he, smiling, and recovering himself, "'tis all the deeper malice, only to draw you in!"

Still, however, he did not go : he kept gazing upon Mr. Hastings till he seemed almost fascinated to the spot; and presently after, growing more and more open in his discourse, he began to talk to me of Sir Elijah Impey. I presume my dearest friends, little as they hear of politics and state business, must yet know that the House of Commons is threatening Sir Elijah with an impeachment, to succeed that of Mr. Hastings, and all upon East India transactions of the same date.(265)

When he had given me his sentiments upon this subject, which I had heard with that sort of quietness that results from total ignorance of the matter, joined to total ignorance of the person concerned, he drew a short comparison, which, nearly, from him, and at such a moment, drew the tears from my eyes—nearly do I say?—Indeed more than that!

"Sir Elijah," cried he, "knows how to go to work, and by getting the lawyers to side with him professionally, has set

about his defence in the most artful manner. He is not only wicked, but a very pitiful fellow. Let him but escape fine or imprisonment, and he will pocket all indignity, and hold himself happy in getting off: but Hastings (again looking steadfastly at him)— Hastings has feeling—'tis a proud feeling, an ambitious feeling—but feeling he has! Hastings—come to him what may— fine, imprisonment, whatsoever is inflicted—all will be nothing. The moment of his punishment—I think it, upon my honour!—was the moment that brought him to that bar!"

When he said "I think it, upon my honour," he laid his hand on his breast, as if he implied, "I acquit him henceforward."

Poor Mr. Hastings! One generous enemy he has at least, who pursues him with public hate, but without personal malignity! yet sure I feel he can deserve neither!

I did not spare to express my sense of this liberality from a foe; for, indeed, the situation I was in, and the sight of Mr. Hastings, made it very affecting to me. He was affected too, himself; but presently, rising, he said with great quickness, "I must shake all. this off; I must have done with it—dismiss it— forget that he is there."

"O, no," cried I, earnestly, "do not forget it!"

"Yes, yes; I must."

" No, remember it rather," cried I; "I could almost (putting up my hands as if praying) do thus and then, like poor Mr. Hastings just now to the house, drop down on my knees to you, to call out 'Remember it.'"

"Yes, Yes," cried he, precipitately, "how else shall I go on? I must forget that he is there, and that you are here." And then he hurried down to his committee.

Was it not a most singular scene ?

I had afterwards to relate great part of this to the queen herself. She saw me engaged in such close discourse, and with such apparent interest on both sides, with Mr. Windham, that I knew she must else form conjectures innumerable. So candid, so liberal is the mind of the queen, that she not only heard me with the most favourable attention towards Mr. Windham, but was herself touched even to tears by the relation.

We stayed but a short time after this last conference ; for nothing more was attempted than reading on the charges and answers, in the same useless manner,

MISS BURNEY IS AGAIN PRESENT AT HASTINGS'S TRIAL... The interest of this trial was so much upon my mind, that I have not kept even a memorandum of what passed from the 13th of February to the day when I went again to Westminster Hall; nor, except renewing the Friday Oratorios with Mrs. Ord, do I recollect one circumstance.

The second time that the queen, who saw my wishes, indulged me with one of her tickets, and a permission of absence for the trial, was to hear Mr. Burke, for whom my curiosity and my interest stood the highest. One ticket, however, would not do; I could not go alone, and the queen had bestowed all her other' tickets before she discovered that this was a day in my particular wishes. She entered into my perplexity with a sweetness the most gracious, and when I knew not how to obviate it, commanded me to write to the Duchess of Ancaster, and beg permission to be put under the wing of her grace, or any of her friends that were going to the Hall.

The duchess, unluckily, did not go, from indisposition, nor any of her family; but she sent me a very obliging letter, and another ticket from Sir Peter Burrell, to use for a companion.

I fixed upon James, who, I knew, wished to hear Mr. Burke for once, and we went together very comfortably. When the managers, who, as before, made the first procession, by entering their box below us, were all arranged, one from among them, whom I knew not, came up into the seats of the House of Commons by our side, and said, "Captain Burney, I am very glad to see you."

"How do you do, sir ?" answered James; "here I am, come to see the fine show."

Upon this the attacker turned short upon his heel, and abruptly walked away, descending into the box, which he did not quit any more. I inquired who he was; General Burgoyne, James told me. "A manager!" cried I, "and one of the chargers! and you treat the business of the Hall with such contempt to his face!"

James laughed heartily at his own uncourtly address, but I would not repent, though he acknowledged he saw the offence his slight and slighting speech had given.

Fearful lest he should proceed in the same style with my friend Mr. Windham, I kept as aloof as possible, to avoid his notice, entreating James at the same time to have the complaisance to be silent upon this subject, should he discover me and approach. My own sentiments were as opposite to those of the managers as his, and I had not scrupled to avow honestly my dissent; but I well knew Mr. Windham might bear, and even respect, from a female, the same openness of opposition that might be highly offensive to him from a man. But I could obtain no positive promise; he would only compromise with my request, and agree not to speak unless applied to first. This, however, contented me, as Mr. Windham was too far embarked in his undertaking to solicit any opinion upon it from accidentally meeting any common acquaintance.

From young Burke and his uncle Richard I had bows from the committee box. Mr. Windham either saw me not, or was too much engaged in business to ascend.

BURKE'.S SPEECH IN SUPPORT OF THE CHARGES. At length the peers' procession closed, the prisoner was brought in, and Mr. Burke began his speech. It was the second day of his harangue;(266) the first I had not been able to attend.

All I had heard of his eloquence, and all I had conceived of his great abilities, was more than answered by his performance. Nervous, clear, and striking was almost all that he uttered: the main business, indeed, of his coming forth was frequently neglected, and not seldom wholly lost , but his excursions were so fanciful, so entertaining, and so ingenious, that no miscellaneous hearer, like myself, could blame them. It is true he was unequal, but his inequality produced an effect which, in so long a speech, was perhaps preferable to greater consistency since, though it lost attention in its falling off, it recovered it with additional energy by some ascent unexpected and wonderful. When he narrated, he was easy, flowing, and natural; when he declaimed, energetic, warm, and brilliant. The sentiments he interspersed were as nobly conceived as they were highly coloured; his satire had a poignancy of wit that made it as entertaining as it was penetrating; his allusions and quotations, as far as they were English and within my reach, were apt and ingenious - and the wild and sudden flights of his fancy, bursting forth from his creative imagination in language fluent, forcible, and varied, had a charm for my ear and my attention wholly new and perfectly irresistible.

Were talents such as these exercised in the service of truth,

unbiased by party and prejudice, how could we sufficiently applaud their exalted possessor? But though frequently he made me tremble by his strong and horrible representations, his own violence recovered me, by stigmatizing his assertions with personal ill-will and designing illiberality. Yet, at times I confess, with all that I felt, wished, and thought concerning Mr. Hastings, the whirlwind of his eloquence nearly drew me into its vortex. I give no particulars of the speech, because they will all be printed.

The observations and whispers of our keen as well as honest James, during the whole, were highly characteristic and entertaining.

"When will he come to the point?"-"These are mere words!"–"This is all sheer detraction!"–"All this is nothing to the purpose!" etc., etc.

"Well, ma'am, what say you to all this? how have you been entertained?" cried a voice at my side; and I saw Mr. Crutchley, who came round to speak to me.

"Entertained?" cried I, "indeed, not at all, it is quite too serious and too horrible for entertainment: you ask after my amusement as if I were at an opera or a comedy."

"A comedy?" repeated he, contemptuously, "no, a farce! It is not high enough for a comedy. To hear a man rant such stuff. But you should have been here the first day he spoke; this is milk and honey to that. He said then, ' His heart was as black–as– black!' and called him the captain-general of iniquity."

"Hush! hush!" cried I, for he spoke very loud; "that young man you see down there, who is looking up, is his son."

"I know it," cried he, "and what do I care?"

How I knew Mr. Crutchley again, by his ready talent of defiance,

and disposition to contempt ! I was called aside from him by

James.

Mr. Crutchley retired, and Mr. Windham quitted his den, and approached me, with a smile of good-humour and satisfaction that made me instantly exclaim, "No exultation, Mr. Windham, no questions; don't ask me what I think of the speech; I can bear no triumph just now."

"No, indeed," cried he, very civilly, "I will not, I promise you, and you may depend upon me."

He then spoke to James, regretting with much politeness that he had seen so little of him when he was his neighbour in Norfolk, and attributing it to the load of India business he had carried into the country to study. I believe I have mentioned

that Felbrig, Mr. Windham's seat, is within a few miles of my brother-in-law, Mr. Francis's house at Aylsham.

After this, however, ere we knew where we were, we began commenting upon the speech. It was impossible to refuse applause to its able delivery and skilful eloquence; I, too, who so long had been amongst the warmest personal admirers of Mr. Burke, could least of all withhold from him the mite of common justice. In talking over the speech, therefore, while I kept clear of its purpose, I gave to its execution the amplest praise; and I secretly grieved that I held back more blame than I had commendation to bestow.

He had the good breeding to accept it just as I offered it, without claiming more, or endeavouring to entangle me in my approbation. He even checked himself, voluntarily, when he was asking me some question of my conversion, by stopping short, and saying, "But, no, it is not fair to press you; I must not do that."

"You cannot," cried I, "press me too much, with respect to my admiration of the ability of the speaker; I never more wished to have written short-hand. I must content myself, however, that I have at least a long memory."

He regretted very much that I had missed the first opening of the speech, and gave me some account of it, adding, I might judge what I had lost then by what I had heard now.

I frankly confessed that the two stories which Mr. Burke had narrated had nearly overpowered me; they were pictures of cruelty so terrible.

"But General Caillot," cried he, smiling, "the hero of one of them, you would be tempted to like: he is as mild, as meek, as gentle in his manners–"

I saw he was going to say "As your Mr. Hastings;" but I interrupted him hastily, calling out, "Hush! hush! Mr. Windham; would you wish me in future to take to nothing but lions?

FURTHER CONVERSATION WITH MR. WINDHAM.

We then went into various other particulars of the speech, till Mr. Windham observed that Mr. Hastings was looking up, and, after examining him some time, said he did not like his countenance. I could have told him that he is generally reckoned extremely like himself but after such an observation I would not venture, and only said, "Indeed, he is cruelly altered: it

was not so he looked when I conceived for him that prepossession I have owned to you."

"Altered, is he?" cried he, biting his lips and looking somewhat shocked.

"Yes, and who can wonder? Indeed, it is quite affecting to see him sit there to hear such things."

"I did not see him," cried he, eagerly "I did not think it right to look at him during the speech, nor from the committeebox; and, therefore, I constantly kept my eyes another way."

I -had a great inclination to beg he would recommend a little of the same decency to some of his colleagues, among whom are three or four that even stand on the benches to examine him, during the severest strictures, with opera-glasses. Looking at him again now, myself, I could not see his pale face and haggard eye without fresh concern, nor forbear to exclaim, "Indeed, Mr. Windham, this is a dreadful business!" He seemed a little struck with this exclamation; and, lest it should offend him, I hastened to add, in apology, "You look so little like a bloody-minded prosecutor, that I forget I ought not to say these things to you."

"Oh!" cried he, laughing, "we are only prosecutors there–(pointing to the committee-box), we are at play up here." . . .

I wished much to know when he was himself to speak, and made sundry inquiries relative to the progress of the several harangues, but all without being comprehended, till at length I cried, "In short, Mr. Windham, I want to know when everybody speaks."

He started, and cried with precipitancy, "Do you mean me?"

"Yes."

"No, I hope not; I hope you have no wants about my miserable speaking?"

I Only laughed, and we talked for some time of other things; and then, suddenly, he burst forth with, "But you have really made me a little uneasy by what you dropped just now."

"And what was that?"

"Something like an intention of hearing me."

"Oh, if that depended wholly on myself, I should certainly do it."

"No, I hope not! I would not have you here on any account. If you have formed any expectations, it will give me great concern."

"Pray don't be uneasy about that; for whatever expectations I may have formed, I had much rather have them disappointed."

" Ho! ho!–you come, then," cried he, pointedly, "to hear me, by way of soft ground to rest upon, after the hard course you will have been run with these higher-spirited speakers?" . . . He desired me not to fail to come and hear Fox. My chances, I told him, were very uncertain, and Friday was the earliest of them. "He speaks on Thursday," cried he, "and indeed you should hear him."

"Thursday is my worst chance of all," I answered, "for it is the Court-day."

"And is there no dispensation ? " cried he ; and then, recollecting himself, and looking very archly at Mr. Fox, who was just below us, he added, "No,–true–not for him!"

"Not for any body!" cried I; "on a Court-day my attendance is as necessary, and I am dressed out as fine, and almost as stiff, as those heralds are here." I then told him what were my Windsor days, and begged he would not seize one of them to speak himself.

"By no means," cried he, quite seriously, "would I have you here!–stay away, and only let me hope for your good wishes."

" I shall be quite sincere," cried I, laughing, "and own to you that stay away I shall not, if I can possibly come; but as to my good wishes, I have not, in this case, one to give you!"

He heard this with a start that was almost a jump. "What!" he exclaimed, "would you lay me under your judgment without your mercy?–Why this is heavier than any penal statute."

He spoke this with an energy that made Mr. Fox look up, to see to whom he addressed his speech: but before I could answer it, poor James, tired of keeping his promised circumspection, advanced his head to join the conversation; and so much was I alarmed lest he should burst forth into some unguarded expression of his vehement hatred to the cause, which could not but have irritated its prosecutors, that the moment I perceived his motion and intention, I abruptly took my leave of Mr. Windham, and surprised poor James into a necessity of following me.

Indeed I was now most eager to depart, from a circumstance that made me feel infinitely awkward. Mr. Burke himself was just come forward, to speak to a lady a little below me; Mr. Windham had instantly turned towards me, with a look of congratulation that seemed rejoicing for me, that the orator

of the day, and of the cause, was approaching,; but I retreated involuntarily back, and shirked meeting his eyes. He perceived in an instant the mistake he was making, and went on with his discourse as if Mr. Burke was out of the Hall. In a minute, however, Mr. Burke himself saw me, and he bowed with the most marked civility of manner; my courtesy was the most ungrateful, distant, and cold ; I could not do otherwise ; so hurt I felt to see him the head of such a cause, so impossible I found it to titter one word of admiration for a performance whose nobleness was so disgraced by its tenour, and so conscious was I the whole time that at such a moment to say nothing must seem almost an affront, that I hardly knew which way to look, or what to do with myself.(267) ' In coming downstairs I met Lord Walsingham and Sir Lucas Pepys. "Well, Miss Burney," cried the first, "what say you to a governor-general of India now?"

"Only this," cried I, "that I do not dwell much upon any question till I have heard its answer!"

Sir Lucas then attacked me too. All the world against poor Mr. Hastings, though without yet knowing what his materials may be for clearing away these aspersions!

Miss FUZILIER LIKELY TO PECONIE MRS, FAIRLY, February.-Her majesty at this time was a little indisposed, and we missed going to Windsor for a fortnight, during which I received visits of inquiry from divers of her ladies–Mrs. Brudenell, bed-chamber woman; Miss Brudenell, her daughter, and a maid of honour elect, would but one of that class please to marry or die; Miss Tryon and Miss Beauclerk, maids of honour, neither of them in a firm way to oblige Miss Brudenell, being nothing approaching to death, though far advanced from marriage; and various others.

Miss Brudenell's only present hope is said to be in Miss Fuzilier,(268) who is reported, with what foundation I know not,

to be likely to become Mrs. Fairly. She is pretty, learned, and accomplished ; yet, from the very little I have seen of her, I should not think she had heart enough to satisfy Mr. Fairly, in whose character the leading trait is the most acute sensibility,

However, I have heard he has disclaimed all such intention, with high indignation at the report, as equally injurious to the delicacy both of Miss Fuzilier and himself, so recently after his loss.

THE HASTINGS TRIAL AGAIN: MR. FOX IN A RAGE. And now for my third Westminster Hall, which, by the queen's own indulgent order, was with dear Charlott and Sarah. It was also to hear Mr. Fox, and I was very glad to let Mr. Windham see a "dispensation" was attainable, though the cause was accidental, since the queen's cold prevented the Drawing-room.(269)

We went early, yet did not get very good places. The managers at this time were all in great wrath at a decision made the night before by the Lords, upon a dispute between them and the counsel for Mr. Hastings, which turned entirely in favour of the latter.(270) When they entered their committee-box, led on as usual by Mr. Burke, they all appeared in the extremest and most angry emotion.

When they had caballed together some time, Mr. Windham came up among the Commons, to bow to some ladies of his acquaintance, and then to speak to me ; but he was so agitated and so disconcerted, he could name nothing but their recent provocation from the Lords. He seemed quite enraged, and broke forth with a vehemence I should not much have liked to have excited. They had experienced, he said, in the late decision, the Most injurious treatment that could be offered them: the Lords had resolved upon saving Mr. Hastings, and the chancellor had taken him under the grossest protection.

"In short," said he, "the whole business is taken out of our hands, and they have all determined to save him."

"Have they indeed?" cried I, with Involuntary eagerness.

"Yes," answered he, perceiving how little I was shocked for him, "it is now all going your way."

I could not pretend to be sorry, and only inquired if Mr. Fox was to speak.

"I know not," cried he, hastily, "what is to be done, who will speak, or what will be resolved. Fox is in a rage! Oh, a rage!"

"But yet I hope he will speak. I have never heard him."

"No? not the other day?"

"No; I was then at Windsor."

"Oh yes, I remember you told me you were going. You have lost every thing by it! To-day will be nothing, he is all rage! On Tuesday he was great indeed. You should have heard him then. And Burke, You should have heard the conclusion of Burke's speech; 'twas the noblest ever uttered by man!"

"So I have been told."

"To-day you will hear nothing–know nothing,–there will be no opportunity,- Fox is all fury."

I told him he almost frightened me; for he spoke in a tremor himself that was really unpleasant.

"Oh!" cried he, looking at me half reproachfully, half goodhumouredly, "Fox's fury is with the Lords–not there!" pointing to Mr. Hastings.

I saw by this he entered into my feelings in the midst of his irritability, and that gave me courage to cry out, "I am glad of that at least!:

Mr. Fox spoke five hours, and with a violence that did not make me forget what I had heard of his being in such a fury but I shall never give any account of these speeches, as they will all be printed. I shall only say a word of the speakers as far as relates to my own feelings about them, and that briefly will be to say that I adhere to Mr. Burke, whose oratorical powers appear to me far more gentleman-like, scholar-like, and fraught with true genius than those of Mr. Fox. it may be I am prejudiced by old kindnesses of Mr. Burke, and it may be that the countenance of Mr. Fox may have turned me against him, for it struck me to have a boldness in it quite hard and callous. However, it is little matter how much my judgment in this point may err. With you, my dear friends, I have Page 129

nothing further to do than simply to give it ; and even should it be wrong, it will not very essentially injure you in your politics.

MRS. CREWE, MR. BURKE, AND MR. WINDHAM.

Again, on the fourth time of my attendance at Westminster Hall, honest James was my esquire.

We were so late from divers accidents that we did not enter till the same moment with the prisoner. In descending the steps I heard my name exclaimed with surprise, and looking before me, I saw myself recognised by Mrs. Crewe. "Miss Burney," she cried, "who could have thought of seeing you here!"

Very obligingly she made me join her immediately, which, as I was with no lady, was a very desirable circumstance; and though her political principles are well known, and, of course, lead her to side with the enemies of Mr. Hastings, she had the good sense to conclude me on the other side, and the delicacy never once to distress me by any discussion of the prosecution.

I was much disappointed to find nothing intended for this day's trial but hearing evidence; no speaker was preparing; all the attention was devoted to the witnesses.

Mr. Adam, Mr. Dudley Long, and others that I know not, Came from the committee to chat with Mrs. Crewe; but soon after one came not so unknown to me–Mr. Burke; and Mrs. Crewe, seeing him ascend, named him to me, but was herself a little surprised to see it was his purpose to name himself, for he immediately made up to me, and with an air of such frank kindness that, could I have forgot his errand in that Hall, would have made me receive him as formerly, when I was almost fascinated with him. But far other were my sensations. I trembled as he approached me, with conscious change of sentiments, and with a dread of his pressing from me a disapprobation he might resent, but which I knew not how to disguise.

"Near-sighted as I am," cried he, "I knew you immediately. I knew you from our box the moment I looked up; yet how long it is, except for an instant here, since I have seen you!"

"Yes," I hesitatingly answered, "I live in a monastery now."

He said nothing to this. He felt, perhaps, it was meant to express my inaccessibility.

I inquired after Mrs. Burke. He recounted to me the particulars of his sudden seizure when he spoke last, from the cramp in his stomach, owing to a draught of cold water which he drank in the midst of the heat of his oration.

I could not even wear a semblance of being sorry for him on this occasion; and my cold answers made him soon bend down to speak with Mrs. Crewe.

I was seated in the next row to her, just above.

Mr. Windham was now talking with her. My whole curiosity and desire being to hear him, which had induced me to make a point of coming this time, I was eager to know if my chance was wholly gone. "You are aware," I cried, when he spoke to me, "what brings me here this morning

No;" he protested he knew not.

Mrs. Crewe, again a little surprised, I believe, at this second opposition acquaintance, began questioning how often I had attended this trial.

Mr. Windham, with much warmth of regret, told her very seldom, and that I had lost Mr. Burke on his best day.

I then turned to speak to Mr. Burke, that I might not seem listening, for they interspersed various civilities upon my peculiar right to have heard all the great speeches, but Mr. Burke was in so profound a reverie he did not hear me.

I wished Mr. Windham had not either, for he called upon him aloud, "Mr. Burke, Miss Burney speaks to you!"

He gave me his immediate attention with an air so full of respect that it quite shamed me.

"Indeed," I cried, " I had never meant to speak to Mr. Burke again after hearing him in Westminster Hall. I had meant to keep at least that " geographical timidity."

I alluded to an expression in his great speech of "geographical morality" which had struck me very much.

He laughed heartily, instantly comprehending me, and assured me it was an idea that had occurred to him on the moment he had uttered it, wholly without study.

A little general talk followed; and then, one of the lords rising to question some of the evidence, he said he must return to his committee and business,-very flatteringly saying, in quitting his post, "This is the first time I have played truant from the manager's box."

However I might be obliged to him, which sincerely I felt, I was yet glad to have him go. My total ill will to all he was about made his conversation merely a pain to me.

I did not feel the same With regard to Mr. Windham. He is not the prosecutor, and seems endowed with so much liberality and candour that it not Only encourages me to speak to him what I think, but leads me to believe he will one day or other reflect upon joining a party so violent as a stain to the independence of his character.

Almost instantly he came forward, to the place Mr. Burke had vacated.

"Are you approaching," I cried, "to hear my upbraidings?"

"Why–I don't know," cried he, looking half alarmed.

"Oh! I give you warning, if you come you must expect them; so my invitation is almost as pleasant as the man's in 'Measure for Measure,' who calls to Master Barnardine, 'Won't you come down to be hanged?'"

"But how," cried he, "have I incurred your upbraidings?"
"
By bringing me here," I answered, "only to disappoint me."

"Did I bring you here?"

"Yes, by telling me you were to speak to-day."

He protested he could never have made such an assertion. I explained myself, reminding him he had told me he was certainly to speak before the recess; and that, therefore, when I was informed this was to be the last day of trial till after the recess, I concluded I should be right, but found myself so utterly wrong as to hear nothing but such evidence as I Could not even understand, because it was so uninteresting I could not even listen to it.

"How strangely," he exclaimed, "are we all moulded, that nothing ever in this mortal life, however pleasant in itself, and however desirable from its circumstances, can come to us without alloy– not even flattery; for here, at this moment, all the high gratification I should feel, and I am well disposed to feel it thoroughly in supposing you could think it worth your while to come hither in order to hear me, is kept down and subdued by the consciousness how much I must disappoint you."

"Not at all," cried I; "the worse you speak, the better for my side of the question."

He laughed, but confessed the agitation of his spirits was so great in the thought of that speech, whenever he was to make it, that it haunted him in fiery dreams in his sleep.

"Sleep!" cried I; "do you ever sleep?"

He stared a little, but I added with pretended dryness, "Do any of you that live down there in that prosecutor's den ever sleep in your beds? I should have imagined that, had you

even attempted it, the anticipating ghost of Mr. Hastings would have appeared to you in the dead of the night, and have drawn your curtains, and glared ghastly in your eyes. I do heartily wish Mr. Tickell would send You that 'Anticipation' at once!"

This idea furnished us with sundry images, till, looking down upon Mr. Hastings, with an air a little moved, he said, "I am afraid the most insulting thing we do by him is coming up hither to show ourselves so easy and disengaged, and to enter into conversation with the ladies."

"But I hope," cried I, alarmed, "he does not see that."

"Why your caps," cried he, "are much in your favour for concealment; they are excellent screens to all but the first row!"

I saw him, however, again look at the poor, and, I sincerely believe, much-injured prisoner, and as I saw also he still bore With my open opposition, I could not but again seize a favourable moment for being more serious With him.

"Ah, Mr. Windham," I cried, "I have not forgot what dropped from you on the first day of this trial."

He looked a little surprised. "You," I continued, "probably have no remembrance of it, for you have been living ever since down there; but I was more touched with what you said then, than with all I have since heard from all the others, and probably than with all I shall hear even from you again when you mount the rostrum."

"You conclude," cried he, looking very sharp, "I shall then be better steeled against that fatal candour?"

"In fact," cried I, "Mr. Windham, I do really believe your steeling to he factitious; notwithstanding you took pains to assure me your candour was but the deeper malice; and yet I will own, when once I have heard your speech, I have little expectation of ever having the honour of conversing with you again."

"And why?" cried- he, starting back "what am I to say that you denounce such a forfeit beforehand?"

I could not explain; I left him to imagine; for, should he prove as violent and as personal as the rest, I had no objection to his previously understanding I could have no future pleasure in discoursing with him.

"I think, however," I continued, with a laugh, "that since I have settled this future taciturnity, I have a fair right in the meanwhile to say whatever comes uppermost."

He agreed to this with great approvance.

"Molière, you know, in order to obtain a natural opinion of his plays, applied to an old woman: you upon the same principle, to obtain a natural opinion of political matters, should apply to an ignorant one–for you will never, I am sure, gain it down there."

He smiled, whether he would or not, but protested this was the severest stricture upon his committee that had ever yet been uttered.

MISS BURNEY'S UNBIASED SENTIMENTS.

I told him as it was the last time he was likely to hear unbiased sentiments upon this subject, it was right they should be spoken very intelligibly. " And permit me," I said, " to begin with what strikes me the most. Were Mr. Hastings really the culprit he is represented, he would never stand there."

"Certainly," cried he, with a candour he could not suppress, "there seems something favourable in that; it has a Pod look; but assure yourself he never expected to see this day."

"But would he, if guilty, have waited its chance? Was not all the world before him? Could he not have chosen any other place of residence ?"

"Yes–but the shame, the disgrace of a flight?"

"What is it all to the shame and disgrace of convicted guilt?"

He made no answer.

"And now," I continued, "shall I tell you, just in the same simple style, how I have been struck with the speakers and speeches I have yet heard?" He eagerly begged me to go on.

"The whole of this public speaking is quite new to me. I was never in the House of Commons. It is all a new creation to me."

"And what a creation it is he exclaimed. "how noble, how elevating! and what an inhabitant for it!"

I received his compliment with great courtesy, as an encouragement. for me to proceed. I then began upon Mr. Burke; but I must give you a very brief summary of my speech, as it could only be intelligible at full length from your having heard his. I told him that his opening had struck me with the highest admiration of his powers, from the eloquence, the imagination, the fire, the diversity of expression, and the ready flow of language, with which he seemed gifted, in a most superior manner, for any and every purpose to which rhetoric

could lead. "And when he came to his two narratives," I continued, "whence he related the particulars of those dreadful murders, he interested, he engaged, he at last overpowered me; I felt my cause lost. I Could hardly keep on my seat. My eyes dreaded a single glance towards a man so accused as Mr. Hastings; I wanted to sink on the floor, that they might be saved so painful a sight. I had no hope he could clear himself; not another wish in his favour remained. But When from this narration Mr. Burke proceeded to his own comments and declamation–when the charges of rapacity, cruelty, tyranny were general, and made with all the violence of personal detestation, and continued and aggravated without any further fact or illustration; then there appeared more of study than of truth, more of invective than of justice; and, in short, so little of proof to so much of passion, that in a very short time I began to lift up my head, my seat was no longer uneasy, my eyes were indifferent which way they looked, or what object caught them; and before I was myself aware of the declension of Mr. Burke's powers over my feelings, I found myself a mere spectator in a public place, and looking all around it, with my opera-glass in my hand."

His eyes sought the ground on hearing this, and with no other comment than a rather uncomfortable shrug of the shoulders, he expressively and concisely said–"I comprehend you perfectly!"

This was a hearing too favourable to stop me; and Mr. Hastings constantly before me was an animation to my spirits which nothing less could have given me, to a manager of such a committee.

I next, therefore, began upon Mr. Fox; and I ran through the general matter of his speech, with such observations as had occurred to me in hearing it. "His violence," I said, "had that sort of monotony that seemed to result from its being factitious, and I felt less pardon for that than for any extravagance in Mr. Burke, whose excesses seemed at least to be unaffected, and, if they spoke against his judgment, spared his probity. Mr. Fox appeared to have no such excuse; he looked all good humour and negligent ease the instant before he began a speech of uninterrupted passion and vehemence, and he wore the same careless and disengaged air the very instant he had finished. A display of talents in which the inward man took so little share could have no powers of persuasion to those who saw them in that light and therefore.

however their brilliancy might be admired, they were useless to their cause, for they left the mind of the hearer in the same state that they found it."

After a short vindication of his friends, he said, "You have never heard Pitt? You would like him beyond any other competitor."

And then he made his panegyric in very strong terms, allowing him to be equal, ready, splendid, wonderful!–he was in constant astonishment himself at his powers and success;–his youth and inexperience never seemed against him: though he mounted to his present height after and in opposition to such a vortex of splendid abilities, yet, alone and unsupported, he coped with them all! And then, with conscious generosity, he finished a most noble éloge with these words: "Take–you may take–the testimony of an enemy–a very confirmed enemy of Mr. Pitt's!"

Not very confirmed, I hope! A man so liberal can harbour no enmity of that dreadful malignancy that sets mitigation at defiance for ever.

He then asked me if I had heard Mr. Grey?

" No," I answered ; " I can come but seldom, and therefore I reserved myself for to-day."

"You really fill me with compunction," he cried. "But if, indeed, I have drawn you into so cruel a waste of your time, the only compensation I can make you will be carefully to keep from you the day when I shall really speak."

"No," I answered, "I must hear you; for that is all I now wait for to make up my final opinion."

"And does it all rest with me?–'Dreadful responsibility'–as Mr. Hastings powerfully enough expresses himself in his narrative."

"And can you allow an expression of Mr. Hastings's to be powerful?–That is not like Mr. Fox, who, in acknowledging some one small thing to be right, in his speech, checked himself for the acknowledgment by hastily saying 'Though I am no great admirer of the genius and abilities of the gentleman at the bar;'–as if he had pronounced a sentence in a parenthesis, between hooks,–so rapidly he flew off to what he could positively censure."

" And hooks they were indeed he cried.

"Do not inform against me," I continued, "and I will give you a little more of Molière's old woman."

He gave me his parole, and looked very curious,

"Well then,–amongst the things most striking to an unbiased spectator was that action of the orator that led him to look full at the prisoner upon every hard part of the charge. There was no courage in it, since the accused is so situated he must make no answer; and, not being courage, to Molière's old woman it could only seem cruelty!"

He quite gave up this point without a defence, except telling me it was from the habit of the House of Commons, as Fox, who chiefly had done this, was a most good-humoured man, and by nothing but habit would have been betrayed into such an error.

"And another thing," I cried, "which strikes those ignorant of senatorial licence, is this,–that those perpetual repetitions, from all the speakers, of inveighing against the power, the rapacity, the tyranny, the despotism of the gentleman at the bar, being uttered now, when we see him without any power, without even liberty-con fined to that spot, and the only person in this large assembly who may not leave it when he will–when we see such a contrast to all we hear we think the simplest relation would be sufficient for all purposes of justice, as all that goes beyond plain narrative, instead of sharpening indignation, only calls to mind the greatness of the fall, and raises involuntary commiseration!"

"And you wish," he cried, "to hear me? How you add to my difficulties!–for now, instead of thinking of Lords, Commons, bishops, and judges before me, and of the delinquent and his counsel at my side, I shall have every thought and faculty swallowed up in thinking of who is behind me!"

This civil speech put an end to Molière's old woman and her comments; and not to have him wonder at her unnecessarily, I said, "Now, then, Mr. Windham, shall I tell you fairly what it is that induced me to say all this to you?–Dr. Johnson!–what I have heard from him of Mr. Windham has been the cause of all this hazardous openness."

"'Twas a noble cause," cried he, well pleased, "and noble has been its effect! I loved him, indeed, sincerely. He has left a chasm in my heart-a chasm in the world

! There was in him what I never saw before, what I never shall find again! I lament every moment as lost, that I might have spent in his society, and yet gave to any other."

How it delighted me to hear this just praise, thus warmly uttered!–I could speak from this moment upon no other subject. I told him how much it gratified me; and we agreed

in comparing notes upon the very few opportunities his real remaining friends could now meet with of a similar indulgence, since so little was his intrinsic worth understood, while so deeply all his foibles had been felt, that in general it was merely a matter of pain to hear him even named.

How did we then emulate each other in calling to mind all his excellences!

"His abilities," cried Mr. Windham, "were gigantic, and always at hand no matter for the subject, he had information ready for everything. He was fertile,–he was universal."

My praise of him was of a still more solid kind,–his principles, his piety, his kind heart under all its rough coating: but I need not repeat what I said,–my dear friends know every word.

I reminded him of the airings, in which he gave his time with his carriage for the benefit of Dr. Johnson's health. "What an advantage!" he cried, "was all that to myself! I had not merely an admiration, but a tenderness for him,–the more I knew him, the stronger it became. We never disagreed ; even in politics, I found it rather words than things in which we differed."

"And if you could so love him," cried I, "knowing him only in a general way, what would you have felt for him had you known him at Streatham?"

I then gave him a little history of his manners and way of life, there,–his good humour, his sport, his kindness, his sociability, and all the many excellent qualities that, in the world at large, were by so many means obscured.

He was extremely interested in all I told him, and regrettingly said he had only known him in his worst days, when his health was upon its decline, and infirmities were crowding- fast upon him.

"Had he lived longer," he cried, "I am satisfied I should have taken to him almost wholly. I should have taken him to my heart! have looked up to him, applied to him, advised with him in all the most essential occurrences of my life! I am sure, too,– though it is a proud assertion,–he would have liked me, also, better, had we mingled more. I felt a mixed fondness and reverence growing so strong upon me, that I am satisfied the closest union would have followed his longer life."

I then mentioned how kindly he had taken his visit to him at Lichfield during a severe illness, "And he left you," I said, "a book ? "

"Yes," he answered, "and he gave me one, also, just before he died. 'You will look into this Sometimes,' he said, 'and not refuse to remember whence you had it.' "(271)

And then he added he had heard him speak of me,–and with so much kindness, that I was forced not to press a recapitulation: yet now I wish I had heard it.

just before we broke up, "There Is nothing," he cried, with energy, "for which I look back upon myself with severer discipline than the time I have thrown away in other pursuits, that might else have been devoted to that wonderful man!" He then said he must be gone,–he was one in a committee of the House, and could keep away no longer.

BURKE AND SHERIDAN MEET WITH COLD RECEPTIONS. I then again joined in with Mrs. Crewe, who, meantime, had had managers without end to converse with her. But, very soon after, Mr. Burke mounted to the House of Commons(272) again, and took the place left by Mr. Windham. I inquired very much after Mrs. Burke, and we talked of the spectacle, and its fine effect; and I ventured to mention, allusively, some of the digressive parts of the great speech in which I had heard him: but I saw him anxious for speaking more to the point, and as I could not talk to him–the leading prosecutor–with that frankness of opposing sentiments which I used to Mr. Windham, I was anxious only to avoid talking at all; and so brief was my speech, and so long my silences, that, of course, he was soon wearied into a retreat. Had he not acted such a part, with what pleasure should I have exerted myself to lengthen his stay!

Yet he went not in wrath: for, before the close, he came yet a third time, to say "I do not pity you for having to sit there so long, for, with you, sitting can now be no punishment."

"No," cried I, "I may take rest for a twelvemonth back." His son also came to speak to me; but, not long after,

Mrs. Crewe called upon me to say, "Miss Burney, Mr. Sheridan begs me to introduce him to you, for he thinks you have forgot him."

I did not feel very comfortable in this; the part he acts would take from me all desire for his notice, even were his talents as singular as they are celebrated. Cold, therefore, was my reception of his salutations, though as civil as I could make it. He talked a little over our former meeting at Mrs. Cholmondeley's, and he reminded me of what he had there urged and persuaded with all his might, namely, that I would write a comedy; and he now reproached me for my total disregard of his counsel and opinion.

I made little or no answer, for I am always put out by such sort of discourse, especially when entered upon with such abruptness. Recollecting, then, that "Cecilia" had been published since that time, he began a very florid flourish, saying he was in my debt greatly, not only for reproaches about what I had neglected, but for fine speeches about what I had performed. I hastily interrupted him with a fair retort, exclaiming,–"O if fine speeches may now be made, I ought to begin first—but know not where I should end!" I then asked after Mrs. Sheridan, and he soon after left me.

Mrs. Crewe was very obligingly solicitous our renewed acquaintance should not drop here; she asked me to name any day for dining with her, or to send to her at any time when I could arrange a visit: but I was obliged to decline it, on the general score of wanting time.

In the conclusion of the day's business there was much speaking, and I heard Mr. Fox, Mr. Burke, and several others; but the whole turned extremely in favour of the gentleman at the bar, to the great consternation of the accusers, whose own witnesses gave testimony, most unexpectedly, on the side of Mr. Hastings.

We came away very late; my dear James quite delighted with this happy catastrophe.

AT WINDSOR AGAIN.

March.-In our first journey to Windsor this month Mrs. Schwellenberg was still unable to go, and the party was Miss Planta, Colonel Wellbred, Mr. Fairly, Sir Joseph Banks, and Mr. Turbulent.

Sir Joseph was so exceedingly shy that we made no sort of acquaintance. If instead of going round the world he had only fallen from the moon, he could not appear less versed in the usual modes of a tea-drinking party. But what, you will say, has a tea-drinking party to do with a botanist, a man of science, a president of the Royal Society?

I left him , however, to the charge of Mr. Turbulent, the two colonels becoming, as usual, my joint supporters. And Mr. Turbulent, in revenge, ceased not one moment to watch Colonel Wellbred, nor permitted him to say a word, or to hear an answer, without some most provoking grimace. Fortunately, upon this subject he cannot confuse me; I have not a sentiment about Colonel Wellbred, for or against, that shrinks from examination.

To-night, however, my conversation was almost wholly with him. I would not talk with Mr. Turbulent; I could not talk with Sir Joseph Banks - and Mr. Fairly did not talk with me : he had his little son with him; he was grave and thoughtful, and seemed awake to no other pleasure than discoursing with that sweet boy.

I believe I have forgotten to mention that Mrs. Gwynn had called upon me one morning, in London, and left me a remarkably fine impression of Mr. Bunbury's "Propagation of a Lie," which I had mentioned when she was at Windsor, with regret at having never seen it. This I had produced here a month ago, to show to our tea-party, and just as it was in the hands of Colonel Wellbred, his majesty entered the room; and, after looking at it a little while, with much entertainment, he took it away to show it to the queen and princesses. I thought it lost; for Colonel Wellbred said he concluded it would be thrown amidst the general hoard of curiosities, which, when once seen, are commonly ever after forgotten, yet which no one has courage to name and to claim.

This evening, however, the colonel was successful, and recovered me my print. It is so extremely humorous that I was very glad to receive it, and in return I fetched my last sketches, which Mr. William Locke had most kindly done for me when here last autumn, and indulged Colonel Wellbred with looking at them, charging him at the same time to guard them from a similar accident. I meant to show them myself to my royal mistress, who is all care, caution, and delicacy, to restore to the right owner whatever she receives with a perfect knowledge who the right owner is,

Page 141

The second volume of the "Letters" of my reverenced Dr. Johnson was now lent me by her majesty; I found in them very frequent mention of our name, but nothing to alarm in the reading it.

DEATH OF MRS. DELANY.

April.-I have scarce a memorandum of this fatal month, in which I was bereft of the most revered of friends, and, perhaps, the most perfect of women.(273) I am yet scarce able to settle whether to glide silently and resignedly—as far as I can—past all this melancholy deprivation, or whether to go back once more to the ever-remembered, ever-sacred scene that closed the earthly pilgrimage of my venerable, my sainted friend.

I believe I heard the last words she uttered : I cannot learn that she spoke after my reluctant departure. She finished with that cheerful resignation, that lively hope, which always broke forth when this last–awful–but, to her, most happy change seemed approaching.

Poor Miss Port and myself were kneeling by her bedside. She had just given me her soft hand; without power to see either of us, she felt and knew us. O, never can I cease to cherish the remembrance of the sweet, benign, holy voice with which she pronounced a blessing upon us both! We kissed her–and, with a smile all beaming–I thought it so–of heaven, she seemed then to have taken leave of all earthly solicitudes. Yet then, even then, short as was her time on earth, the same soft human sensibility filled her for poor human objects. She would not bid us farewell–would not tell us she should speak with us no more– she only said, as she turned gently away from us, "And now–I'll go to sleep!"–But, O, in what a voice she said it! I felt what the sleep would be; so did poor Miss Port.

Poor, sweet, unfortunate girl! what deluges of tears did she shed over me! I promised her in that solemn moment my eternal regard, and she accepted this, my first protestation of any kind made to her, as some solace to her sufferings. Sacred shall I hold it!–sacred to my last hour. I believe, indeed, that angelic being had no other wish equally fervent.

How full of days and full of honours was her exit! I should blush at the affliction of my heart in losing her, could I ever

believe excellence was given us here to love and to revere, yet gladly to relinquish. No, I cannot think it: the deprivation may be a chastisement, but not a joy. We may submit to it with patience; but we cannot have felt it with warmth where we lose it without pain, Outrageously to murmur, or sullenly to refuse consolation–there, indeed, we are rebels against the dispensations of providence–and rebels yet more weak than wicked; for what and whom is it we resist? what and who are we for such resistance ?

She bid me–how often did she bid me not grieve to lose her! Yet she said, in my absence, she knew I must, and sweetly regretted how much I must miss her. I teach myself to think of her felicity; and I never dwell upon that without faithfully feeling I would not desire her return. But, in every other channel in which my thoughts and feelings turn, I miss her with so sad a void! She was all that I dearly loved that remained within my reach; she was become the bosom repository of all the livelong day's transactions, reflections, feelings, and wishes. Her own exalted mind was all expanded when we met. I do not think she concealed from me the most secret thought of her heart; and while every word that fell from her spoke wisdom, piety, and instruction, her manner had an endearment, her spirits a native gaiety, and her smile, to those she loved, a tenderness so animated.

Blessed spirit! sweet, fair, and beneficent on earth!–O, gently mayest thou now be at rest in that last home to which fearfully I look forward, yet not hopeless; never that–and sometimes with fullest, fairest, sublimest expectations! If to her it be given to plead for those she left, I shall not be forgotten in her prayer. Rest to her sweet soul! rest and everlasting peace to her gentle spirit!

I saw my poor lovely Miss Port twice in every day, when in town, till after the last holy rites had been performed. I had no peace away from her; I thought myself fulfilling a wish of that sweet departed saint, in consigning all the time I had at my own disposal to solacing and advising with her beloved niece, who received this little offering with a sweetness that once again twined her round my heart. . . .

Poor Mrs. Astley, the worthy humble friend, rather than servant, of the most excellent departed, was the person whom, next to the niece, I most pitied. She was every way to be lamented: unfit for any other service, but unprovided for in this, by the utter and most regretted inability of her much

attached mistress, who frequently told me that leaving poor Astley unsettled hung heavy on her mind.

My dearest friends know, the success I had in venturing to represent her worth and situation to my royal mistress. In the moment when she came to my room to announce his majesty's gracious intention to pension Mrs. Astley here as housekeeper to the same house, I really could scarce withhold myself from falling prostrate at her feet : I never felt such a burst of gratitude but where I had no ceremonials to repress it. Joseph, too, the faithful footman, I was most anxious to secure in some good service– and I related my wishes for him to General Cary, who procured for him a place with his daughter, Lady Amherst.

I forget if I have ever read you the sweet words that accompanied to me the kind legacies left me by my honoured friend. I believe not. They were ordered to be sent me with the portrait of Sacharissa, and two medallions of their majesties: they were originally written to accompany the legacy to the Bishop of Worcester, Dr. Hurd, as you may perceive by the style, but it was desired they might also be copied:–

"I take this liberty, that my much esteemed and respected friend may sometimes recollect a person who was so sensible of the honour of her friendship and who delighted so much in her conversation and works."

Need I–O, I am sure I need not say with what tender, grateful, sorrowing joy I received these sweet pledges of her invaluable regard!

To these, by another codicil, was added the choice of one of her mosaic flowers. And verbally, on the night but one before she died, she desired I might have her fine quarto edition of Shakespeare, sweetly saying she had never received so much pleasure from him in any other way as through my reading.

THE HASTINGS TRIAL AND MR. WINDHAM AGAIN. The part of this month in which my Susanna was in town I kept no journal at all. And I have now nothing to add but to copy those memorandums I made of the trial on the day I went to Westminster Hall with my two friends,(274) previously to

the deep calamity on which I have dwelt. They told me they could not hear what Mr. Windham said; and there is a spirit in his discourse more worth their hearing than any other thing I have now to write.

You may remember his coming straight from the managers, in their first procession to their box, and beginning at once a most animated attack–scarcely waiting first to say "How do!"–before he exclaimed "I have a great quarrel with you–I am come now purposely to quarrel with you–you have done me mischief irreparable–you have ruined me!"

"Have I?"

"Yes: and not only with what passed here, even setting that aside, though there was mischief enough here; but you have quite undone me since!"

I begged him to let me understand how.

"I will," he cried. "When the trial broke up for the recess I went into the country, purposing to give my whole time to study and business; but, most unfortunately, I had just sent for a new set of 'Evelina;' and intending only to look at it, I was so cruelly caught that I could not let it out of my hands, and have been living with nothing but the Branghtons ever since."

I could not but laugh, though on this subject 'tis always awkwardly.

"There was no parting with it," he continued. "I could not shake it off from me a moment!–see, then, every way, what mischief you have done me!"

He ran on to this purpose much longer, with great rapidity, and then, suddenly, stopping, again said, "But I have yet another quarrel with you, and one you must answer. How comes it that the moment you have attached us to the hero and the heroine–the instant you have made us cling to them so that there is no getting disengaged–twined, twisted, twirled them round our very heart-strings–how is it that then you make them undergo such persecutions? There is really no enduring their distresses, their Suspenses, their perplexities. Why are you so cruel to all around–to them and their readers?"

I longed to say–Do you object to a persecution?–but I know he spells it prosecution.

I could make no answer: I never can. Talking over one's own writings seems to me always ludicrous, because it cannot be impartially, either by author or commentator; one feeling,

the other fearing, too much for strict truth and unaffected candour.

When we found the subject quite hopeless as to discussion, he changed it, and said "I have lately seen some friends of yours, and I assure you I gave you an excellent character to them: I told them you were firm, fixed, and impenetrable to all conviction."

An excellent character, indeed! He meant to Mr. Francis and Charlotte.

Then he talked a little of the business of the day and he told me that Mr. Anstruther was to speak.

"I was sure of it," I cried,, "by his manner when he entered the managers' box. I shall know when you are to speak, Mr. Windham, before I hear you.,"

He shrugged his shoulders a little uncomfortably. I asked him to name to me the various managers. He did ; adding, "Do you not like to sit here, where you can look down upon the several combatants before the battle?"

When he named Mr. Michael Angelo Taylor, I particularly desired he might be pointed out to me, telling him I had long wished to see him, from the companion given to him in one of the "Probationary Odes," where they have coupled him with my dear father, most impertinently and unwarrantably.

"That, indeed," he cried, "is a licentiousness in the press quite intolerable–to attack and involve private characters in their public lampoons! To Dr. Burney they could have no right; but Mr. Michael Angelo Taylor is fair game enough, and likes that or any other way whatever of obtaining notice. You know what Johnson said to Boswell of preserving fame?"

"No."

"There were but two ways," he told him, "of preserving; one was by sugar, the other by salt. 'Now,' says he, 'as the sweet way, Bozzy, you are but little likely to attain, I would have you plunge into vinegar, and get fairly pickled at once.' And such has been the plan of Mr. Michael Angelo Taylor. With the sweet he had, indeed, little chance, so he soused into the other, head over ears."

We then united forces in repeating passages from various of the "Probationary Odes," and talking over various of the managers, till Mr. Anstruther was preparing to speak, and Mr. Windham went to his cell.

I am sure you will remember that Mr. Burke came also,

and the panic with which I saw him, doubled by my fear lest he should see that panic.

When the speech was over, and evidence was filling up the day's business, Mr. Windham returned. Some time after, but I have forgotten how, we were agreeing in thinking suspense, and all obscurity, in expectation or in opinion, almost the thing's most trying to bear in this mortal life, especially where they lead to some evil construction.

"But then," cried he, "on the other hand, there is nothing so pleasant as clearing away a disagreeable prejudice; nothing SO exhilarating as the dispersion of a black mist, and seeing all that had been black and gloomy turn out bright and fair."

"That, Sir," cried I, "is precisely what I expect from thence," pointing to the prisoner.

What a look he gave me, yet he laughed irresistibly.

"However," I continued, "I have been putting my expectations from your speech to a kind of test."

"And how, for heaven's sake?"

"Why, I have been reading–running over, rather–a set of speeches, in which almost the whole House made a part, upon the India bill ; and in looking over those I saw not one that had not in it something positively and pointedly personal, except Mr. Windham's."

"O, that was a mere accident."

"But it was just the accident I expected from Mr. Windham. I do not mean that there was invective in all the others, for in some there was panegyric–plenty! but that panegyric was always so directed as to convey more of severe censure to one party than of real praise to the other. Yours was all to the business, and hence I infer you will deal just so by Mr. Hastings."

"I believe," cried he, looking at me very sharp, "you only want to praise me down. You know what it is to skate a man down?"

"No, indeed."

"Why, to skate a man down is a very favourite diversion among a certain race Of wags. It is only to praise, and extol, and stimulate him to double and treble exertion and effort, till, in order to show his desert of such panegyric, the poor dupe makes so many turnings and windings, and describes circle after circle with such hazardous dexterity, that, at last, down he drops in the midst of his flourishes, to his own eternal disgrace, and their entire content."

I gave myself no vindication from this charge but a laugh; and we returned to discuss speeches and speakers, and I expressed again my extreme repugnance against all personality in these public harangues, except in simply stating facts. " What say you, then," cried he, " to Pitt?" He then repeated a warm and animated praise of his powers and his eloquence, but finished with this censure: "He takes not," cried he, "the grand path suited to his post as prime minister, for he is personal beyond all men ; pointed, sarcastic, cutting ; and it is in him peculiarly unbecoming. The minister should be always conciliating; the attack, the probe, the invective, belong to the assailant." Then he instanced Lord North, and said much more on these political matters and maxims than I can possibly write, or could at the time do more than hear; for, as I told him, I not only am no politician, but have no ambition to become one, thinking it by no means a female business.

"THE QUEEN IS so KIND."

When he went to the managers' box, Mr. Burke again took his place, but he held it a very short time, though he was in high good humour and civility. The involuntary coldness that results from internal disapprobation must, I am sure, have been seen, so thoroughly was it felt. I can only talk on this matter with Mr. Windham, who, knowing my opposite principles, expects to hear them, and gives them the fairest play by his good humour, candour, and politeness. But there is not one other manager with whom I could venture such openness.

That Mr. Windham takes it all in good part is certainly amongst the things he makes plainest, for again, after Mr. Burke's return to the den, he came back.

"I am happy," cried I, "to find you have not betrayed me."

"Oh, no; I would not for the world."

"I am quite satisfied you have kept my counsel; for Mr. Burke has been with me twice, and speaking with a good humour I could not else have expected from him. He comes to tell me that he never pities me for sitting here, whatever is going forward, as the sitting must be rest; and, indeed, it seems as if my coming hither was as much to rest my frame as to exercise my mind."

"That's a very good idea, but I do not like to realize it ; I do not like to think of you and fatigue together. Is it so? Do you really want rest?"

"O, no."

"O, I am well aware yours is not a mind to turn complainer but yet I fear, and not for your rest only, but your time. How is that; have you it, as you Ought, at your own disposal?"

"Why not quite," cried I, laughing. Good heaven! what a question, in a situation like mine!

"Well, that is a thing I cannot bear to think of—that you should want time."

"But the queen," cried I, is so kind."

"That may be," interrupted he, "and I am very glad of it but still, time—and to you!"

"Yet, after all, in the whole, I have a good deal, though always Uncertain. for, if sometimes I have not two minutes when I expect two hours, at other times I have two hours where I expected only two minutes."

"All that is nothing, if you have them not with certainty. Two hours are of no more value than two minutes, if you have them not at undoubted command."

Again I answered, "The queen is so kind;" determined to sound that sentence well and audibly into republican ears.

"Well, well," cried he, "that may be some compensation to you, but to us, to all others, what compensation is there for depriving you of time?"

"Mrs. Locke, here," cried I, "always wishes time could be bought, because there are so many who have more than they know what to do with, that those who have less might be supplied very reasonably."

"'Tis an exceeding good idea," cried he, "and I am sure, if it could be purchased, it ought to be given to YOU by act of parliament, as a public donation and tribute." There was a fine flourish!

PERSONAL RESEMBLANCE BETWEEN WINDHAM AND HASTINGS. A little after, while we were observing Mr. Hastings, Mr. Windham exclaimed, "He's looking up; I believe he is looking for you."

I turned hastily away, fairly saying, "I hope not."

"Yes, he is; he seems as if he wanted to bow to you." I shrank back. "No, he looks off; he thinks you in too bad company!" "Ah, Mr. Windham," cried I, "you should not be so hardhearted towards him, whoever else may; and I could tell you, and I will tell you if you please, a very forcible reason." He assented. "You must know, then, that people there are in this world who scruple not to assert that there is a very strong personal resemblance between Mr. Windham and Mr. Hastings; nay, in the profile, I see it myself at this moment and therefore ought not you to be a little softer than the rest, if merely in sympathy?"

He laughed very heartily; and owned he had heard of the resemblance before.

"I could take him extremely well," I cried, "for your uncle."

"No, no; if he looks like my elder brother, I aspire at no more."

"No, no; he is more like your uncle; he has just that air; he seems just of that time of life. Can You then be so unnatural as to prosecute him with this eagerness?"

And then, once again, I ventured to give him a little touch of Molière's old woman, lest he should forget that good and honest dame; and I told him there was one thing she particularly objected to in all the speeches that had yet been made, and hoped his speech would be exempt from.

He inquired what that was.

"Why, she says she does not like to hear every orator compliment another; every fresh speaker say, he leaves to the superior ability of his successor the prosecution of the business." "O, no," cried he, very readily, "I detest all that sort of adulation. I hold it in the utmost contempt."

"And, indeed, it will be time to avoid it when your turn comes, for I have heard it in no less than four speeches already." And then he offered his assistance about servants and carriages, and we all came away, our different routes; but my Fredy and Susan must remember my meeting with Mr. Hastings in coming out, and his calling after me, and saying, with a very comic sort of politeness, "I must come here to have the pleasure of seeing Miss Burney, for I see her nowhere else."

What a strange incident would have been formed had this rencontre happened thus if I had accepted Mr. Windham's offered services ! I am most glad I had not ; I should have felt myself a conspirator, to have been so met by Mr. Hastings.

DEATH OF YOUNG LADY MULGRAVE.

May.-On the 17th of this month Miss Port bade her sad reluctant adieu to London. I gave what time I could command from Miss Port's departure to my excellent and maternal Mrs. Ord, who supported herself with unabating fortitude and resignation. But a new calamity affected her much, and affected me greatly also, though neither she nor I were more than distant spectators in comparison with the nearer mourners; the amiable and lovely Lady Mulgrave gave a child to her lord, and died, in the first dawn of youthful beauty and sweetness, exactly a year after she became his wife. 'Twas, indeed, a tremendous blow. It was all our wonder that Lord Mulgrave kept his senses, as he had not been famed for patience or piety; but I believe he was benignly inspired with both, from his deep admiration of their excellence in his lovely wife.

AGAIN AT WINDSOR.

I must mention a laughable enough circumstance. Her majesty inquired of me if I had ever met with- Lady Hawke? "Oh yes," I cried, "and Lady Say and Sele too." " She has just desired permission to send me a novel of her own Writing," answered her majesty.

"I hope," cried I, "'tis not the 'Mausoleum of Julia!'"

But yes, it proved no less ! and this she has now published and sends about. You must remember Lady Say and Sele's quotation from it.(275) Her majesty was so gracious as to lend it me, for I had some curiosity to read it. It is all of a piece: all love, love, love, unmixed and unadulterated with any more worldly materials.

I read also the second volume of the "Paston Letters," and found their character the same as in the first, and therefore read them with curiosity and entertainment.

The greater part of the month was spent, alas! at Windsor, with what a dreary vacuity of heart and of pleasure I need not say. The only period of it in which my spirits could be commanded to revive was during two of the excursions in which Mr. Fairly was of the party; and the sight of him, calm, mild, nay cheerful, under such superior sorrows– –struck me with that sort of edifying admiration that led me, perforce, to the best

exertion in my power for the conquest of my deep depression. If I did this from conscience in private, from a sense of obligation to him in public I reiterated my efforts, as I received from him all the condoling softness and attention he could possibly have bestowed upon me had my affliction been equal or even greater than his own.

ANOTHER MEETING WITH MR. CRUTCHLEY.

On one of the Egham race days the queen sent Miss Planta and me on the course, in one of the royal coaches, with Lord Templeton and Mr. Charles Fairly,(276) for our beaux. Lady Templeton was then at the Lodge, and I had the honour of two or three conferences with er during her stay. On the course, we were espied by Mr. Crutchley, who instantly devoted himself to my service for the morning–taking care of our places, naming jockeys, horses, bets, plates, etc., and talking between times of Streatham and all the Streathamites. We were both, I believe, very glad of this discourse. He pointed out to me where his house stood, in a fine park, within sight of the race-ground, and proposed introducing me to his sister, who was his housekeeper, and asking me if, through her invitation, I would come to Sunning Hill park. I assured him I lived so completely in a monastery that I could make no new acquaintance. He then said he expected soon Susan and Sophy Thrale on a visit to his sister, and he presumed I would not refuse coming to see them. I truly answered I should rejoice to do it if in my power, but that most probably I must content myself with meeting them on the Terrace. He promised to bring them there with his sister, though he had given up that walk these five years.

It will give me indeed great pleasure to see them again.

MR. TURBULENT'S TROUBLESOME PLEASANTRIES. My two young beaux Stayed dinner with us, and I afterwards strolled upon the lawn with them till tea-time. I could not go on the Terrace, nor persuade them to go on by themselves. We backed as the royal party returned home; and when they had all entered the house, Colonel Wellbred, who had stood aloof, quitted the train to join our little society. "Miss

Burney," he cried, "I think I know which horse you betted upon!
Cordelia!"

"For the name's sake you think it," I cried; and he began some questions and comments upon the races, when suddenly the window of the tea-room opened, and the voice of Mr. Turbulent, with a most sarcastic tone, called out, "I hope Miss Burney and Colonel Wellbred are well!"

We could neither Of us keep a profound gravity, though really he deserved it from us both. I turned from the Colonel, and said I was coming directly to the tea-room.

Colonel Wellbred would have detained me to finish Our race discourse, for he had shut the window when he had made his speech, but I said it was time to go in.

"Oh no," cried he, laughing a little, "Mr. Turbulent only wants his own tea, and he does not deserve it for this!"

In, however, I went, and Colonel Manners took the famous chair the instant I was seated. We all began race talk, but Mr. Turbulent, approaching very significantly, said, "Do you want a chair On the other side, ma'am? Shall I tell the colonel-to bring one?"

"No, indeed cried I, half seriously, lest he should do it. . . .

Colonel Wellbred, not knowing what had passed, came to that same other side, and renewed his conversation. In the midst of all this Mr. Turbulent hastily advanced with a chair, saying, "Colonel Wellbred, I cannot bear to see you standing so long."

I found it impossible not to laugh under My hat, though I really wished to bid him stand in a corner for a naughty boy. The colonel, I suppose, laughed too, whether he would or not, for I heard no answer. However, he took the chair, and finding me wholly unembarrassed by this polissonnerie, though not wholly unprovoked by it, he renewed his discourse, and kept his seat till the party, very late, broke up; but Colonel Manners, who knew not what to make of all this, exclaimed, "Why, ma'am, you cannot keep Mr. Turbulent in much order."

June.-Mrs. Schwellenberg came to Windsor with us after the birthday, for the rest of the summer.

Mr. Turbulent took a formal leave of me at the same time, as his wife now came to settle at Windsor, and he ceased to belong to our party. He only comes to the princesses at stated hours, and then returns to his own home. He gave me many serious thanks for the time passed with me, spoke in flourishing

terms of its contrast to former times, and vowed no compensation could ever be made him for the hours he had thrown away by compulsion on "The Oyster."(277) His behaviour altogether was very well–here and there a little eccentric, but, in the main, merely good-humoured and high-spirited.

COLONEL FAIRLY AND SECOND ATTACHMENTS.

I am persuaded there is no manner of truth in the report relative to Mr. Fairly and Miss Fuzilier, for he led me into a long conversation with him one evening when the party was large, and all were otherwise engaged, upon subjects of this nature, in the course of which he asked me if I thought any second attachment could either be as strong or as happy as a first.

I was extremely surprised by the question, and quite unprepared how to answer it, as I knew not with what feelings or intentions I might war by any unwary opinions. I did little, therefore, but evade and listen, though he kept up the discourse in a very animated manner, till the party all broke up.

Had I spoken without any consideration but what was general and genuine, I should have told him that my idea was simply this, that where a first blessing was withdrawn by providence, not lost by misconduct, it seemed to me most consonant to reason, nature, and mortal life, to accept what could come second, in this as in all other deprivations. Is it not a species of submission to the divine will to make ourselves as happy as we can in what is left us to obtain, where bereft of what we had sought? My own conflict for content in a life totally adverse to my own inclinations, is all built on this principle, and when it succeeds, to this owes its success.

I presumed not, however, to talk in this way to Mr. Fairly, for I am wholly ignorant in what manner or to what degree his first attachment may have rivetted his affections; but by the whole of what passed it seemed to me very evident that he was not merely entirely without any engagement, but entirely at this time without any plan or scheme of forming any; and probably he never may.

(257) "Selections from the State Papers preserved in the Foreign Department of the Government of India, 1772-1785," Edited by G. W. Forrest, VOL i. P, 178.

(258) "Warren Hastings," by Sir Alfred Lyall, p. 54.

(259) Selections from State Papers," vol. i. p. xlviii.

(260) In his defence at the bar of the House of Commons, (Feb. 4th, 1788) Sir Elijah Impey attempted to justify his conduct by precedent, but the single precedent on which he relied does not prove much in his favour. A Hindoo, named Radachund Metre, was condemned to death for forgery in 1765, but was pardoned on this very ground, that capital punishment for such a crime was unheard of in India.

(261) Speech on Mr. Fox's East India Bill, Dec. 1st, 1783,

(262) Fanny's brother, the scholar. He was, at this time, master of a school at Hammersmith-ED.

(263) Windham had introduced and carried through the House of Commons the charge respecting Fyzoolla Khan, the Nawab of Rampore; but this charge, with many others of the original articles of impeachment, was not proceeded upon at the trial. Fyzoolla Khan was one of the Rohilla chiefs, who, more fortunate than the rest, had

been permitted by treaty, after the conquest of Rohilcund in 17 74, to retain possession of Rampore as a vassal of the Vizier of Oude. By this treaty the Nawab of Rampore was empowered to maintain an army of 5,000 horse and foot in all and in return he bound himself to place from 2,000 to 3,000 troops at the disposal of the Vizier whenever that assistance might be required. In November, 1780, the Vizier, or rather, Hastings, speaking by the mouth of the Vizier, called upon Fyzoolla Khan to furnish forthwith a contingent of 5,000 horse. The unhappy Nawab offered all the assistance in his power, but not only Was the demand unwarranted by the terms of the treaty, but the number of horse required was far greater than he had the means to furnish. Thereupon Mr. Hastings gave permission to the Vizier to dispossess his vassal of his dominions. This iniquitous scheme, however, was never carried out, and in 1782, Fyzoolla Khan made his peace with the Governor-General, and procured his own future exemption from military service, by payment of a large sum of money.-ED.

(264) Mr. Hastings's enemy was Mr. afterwards Sir Philip Francis, by some people supposed to have been the author of "Junius's Letters." The best friend of Mr. Hastings here alluded to was Clement Francis, Esq. of Aylsham, in Norfolk, who married Charlotte, fourth daughter of Dr. Burney. [Francis, though an active supporter of the impeachment, was not one of the "managers." He had been nominated to the committee by Burke, but rejected by the House, on the ground of his well-known animosity to Hastings.-ED.)

(265) After all, Impey escaped impeachment. In December, 1787, Sir Gilbert Elliot, one of the managers of Hastings' impeachment, brought before the House of Commons six charges against Impey, of which the first, and most serious, related to the death of Nuncomar. The charges were referred to a committee, before which Impey made his defence, February 4, 1788. On May 9, a division was taken on the first charge, and showed a majority of eighteen in favour of Impey. The subject was resumed, May 27, and finally disposed of by the rejection of sir Gilbert Elliot's motion without a division-ED.

(266) Saturday, February 16, 1788.-ED.

(267) Macaulay attributes perhaps too exclusively to Court influence Fanny's pre-possession in favour of Hastings. It should be remembered that her family and many of her friends were, equally with herself, partisans of Hastings, to whom, moreover, she had been first introduced by a much valued friend, Mr. Cambridge (see ante, vol. i., P. 326).-ED.

(268) "Miss Fuzilier" is the name given in the "Diary" to Miss Charlotte Margaret Gunning, daughter of Sir Robert Gunning. She married Colonel Digby ("Mr. Fairly") in 1790.-ED.

(269) This would seem to fix the date as Thursday, February 21, Thursday being mentioned by Fanny as the Court-day (see ante, p. 125). According, however, to Debrett's "History of the Trial," Fox spoke on the charge relating to Cheyt Sing on Friday, February 22, the first day of the Court's sitting since the preceding Tuesday.-ED. '

(270) The managers had desired that each charge should be taken separately, and replied to, before proceeding to the next. Hastings's counsel, on the other hand,

demanded that all the charges should be presented before the defence was opened. The Lords, by a large majority, decided against the managers.-ED.

(271) Windham relates that when he called upon Dr. Johnson, six days before his death, Johnson put into his hands a copy of the New Testament, saying "Extremum hoc mumus morientis habeto." See the extracts from Windham's journal in Croker's "Boswell," v., 326. In a codicil to Johnson's will, dated Dec. 9, 1784, we find, among other bequests of books, "to Mr. Windham, Poete Greci Henrici per Henriculum Stephanum."-ED.

(272) i.e. to the benches assigned to the Commons in Westminster Hall. These immediately adjoined the chamberlain's box in which Miss Burney was seated.-ED.

(273) Mrs. Delany died on the 15th of April, 1788.-ED.

(274) Her sister Susan and Mrs. Locke. The day referred to must have been Friday, April 11th, on which day Mr. Anstruther spoke on the charge relating to Cheyt Sing.-ED. (275) See ante, vol. 1, p. 220.-ED.

(276) The young son of Colonel Digby.-ED.

(277) Mrs. Haggerdorn, Fanny's predecessor in office. See ante, p. 26.-ED.

SECTION 13

(1788.)

ROYAL VISIT TO CHELTENHAM.

(Since her establishment at Court we have not yet found Fanny so content with her surroundings as she shows herself in the following section of the " Diary." The comparative quiet of country life at Cheltenham was far more to her taste than the tiresome splendours of Windsor and St. James's. She had still, it is true, her official duties to perform : it was Court life still, but Court life en déshabille. But her time was otherwise more at her own disposal, and, above all things, the absence of "Cerbera," as she nicknamed the amiable Mrs. Schwellenberg and the presence of Colonel Digby, contributed to restore to her harassed mind that tranquillity which is so pleasantly apparent in the following pages.

In the frequent society of Colonel Digby Fanny seems to have found an enjoyment peculiarly adapted to her reserved and sensitive disposition. The colonel was almost equally retiring and sensitive with herself, and his natural seriousness was deepened by sorrow for the recent loss of his wife. A similarity of tastes, as well as (in some respects) of disposition, drew him continually to Fanny's tea-table, and the gentleness of his manners, the refined and intellectual character of his conversation, so unlike the Court gossip to which she was usually condemned to remain a patient listener, caused her more and more to welcome his visits and to regret his departure. "How unexpected an indulgence," she writes, "a luxury, I may say, to me, are these evenings now becoming!" The colonel reads to her- -poetry, love-letters, even sermons, and while she listens to such reading, and such a reader, her work goes on with an alacrity that renders it all pleasure. The friendship which grew up between them was evidently, at least on the part of Fanny, of a more than ordinarily tender description. Whether, had circumstances permitted, it might have ripened into a feeling yet more tender, must remain a matter of speculation. Circumstances did not permit, and in after years both married elsewhere.-ED.] Page 155

THE ROYAL PARTY AND THEIR SUITE.

July.-Early in this month the king's indisposition occasioned the plan of his going to Cheltenham, to try the effect of the waters drank upon the spot. It was settled that the party should be the smallest that was possible, as his majesty was to inhabit the house of Lord Fauconberg, vacated for that purpose, which was very small. He resolved upon only taking his equerry in waiting and pages, etc. Lord Courtown, his treasurer of the household, was already at Cheltenham, and therefore at hand to attend. The queen agreed to carry her lady of the bedchamber in waiting, with Miss Planta and F. B., and none others but wardrobe-women for herself and the princesses.

Mr. Fairly was here almost all the month previously to our departure. At first it was concluded he and Colonel Gwynn, the equerry in waiting, were to belong wholly to the same table with Miss Planta and me, and Mr. Fairly threatened repeatedly how well we should all know one another, and how well he would study and know us all au fond.

But before we set out the plan was all changed, for the king determined to throw aside all state, and make the two gentlemen dine at his own table. "We shall have, therefore," said Mr. Fairly, with a very civil regret, "no tea-meetings at Cheltenham."

This, however, was an opening- to me of time and leisure such as I had never yet enjoyed.

Now, my dearest friends, I open an account which promises at least all the charms of novelty, and which, if it fulfils its promise, will make this month rather an episode than a continuation of my prosaic performance. So now for yesterday, Saturday, July 12.

We were all up at five o'clock; and the noise and confusion reigning through the house, and resounding all around it, from the quantities of people stirring, boxes nailing, horses neighing, and dogs barking, was tremendous.

I must now tell you the party:–Their majesties; the princesses Royal, Augusta, and Elizabeth; Lady Weymouth, Mr. Fairly, Colonel Gwynn, Miss Planta, and a person you have sometimes met; pages for king, queen, and princesses, ward- robe-women for ditto, and footmen for all. A smaller party for a royal excursion cannot well be imagined. How we shall all manage heaven knows. Miss Planta and myself are allowed no maid; the house would not hold one.

The royal party set off first, to stop and breakfast at Lord Harcourt's at Nuneham. You will easily believe Miss Planta and myself were not much discomfited in having orders to proceed straight forward. You know we have been at Nuneham!

Mrs. Sandys, the queen's wardrobe-woman, and Miss Macentomb, the princesses', accompanied us. At Henley-on-Thames, at an inn beautifully situated, we stopped to breakfast, and at Oxford to take a sort of half dinner.

LOYALTY NOT DAMPED BY THE RAIN.

The crowd gathered together upon the road, waiting for the king and queen to pass, was immense, and almost unbroken from Oxford to Cheltenham. Every town and village within twenty miles seemed to have been deserted, to supply all the pathways with groups of anxious spectators. Yet, though so numerus, so quiet were they, and so new to the practices of a hackneyed mob, that their curiosity never induced them to venture within some yards of the royal carriage, and their satisfaction never broke forth into tumult and acclamation.

In truth, I believe they never were aware of the moment in which their eagerness met its gratification. Their majesties travelled wholly without guards or state; and I am convinced, from the time we advanced beyond Oxford, they were taken only for their own attendants.

All the towns through which we passed were filled with people, as closely fastened one to another as they appear in the pit of the playhouse. Every town seemed all face; and all the way upon the road we rarely proceeded five miles without encountering a band of most horrid fiddlers, scraping "God save the king" with all their might, out of tune, out of time, and all in the rain; for, most unfortunately, there were continual showers falling all the day. This was really a subject for serious regret, such numbers of men, women, and children being severely sufferers; yet standing it all through with such patient loyalty, that I am persuaded not even a hail or thunder storm would have dispersed them.

The country, for the most part, that we traversed, was ex-

tremely pretty; and, as we advanced nearer to our place Of destination, it became quite beautiful.

ARRIVAL AT FAUCONBERG HALL.

When we arrived at Cheltenham, which is almost all one street, extremely long, clean and well paved, we had to turn out of the public way about a quarter of a mile, to proceed to Fauconberg Hall, which my Lord Fauconberg has lent for the king's use during his stay at this place.

it is, indeed, situated on a most sweet spot, surrounded with lofty hills beautifully variegated, and bounded, for the principal object, with the hills of Malvern, Which, here barren, and there cultivated, here all chalk, and there all verdure, reminded me of How hill, and gave Me an immediate sensation of reflected as well as of visual pleasure, from giving to my new habitation some resemblance of NorbUry park.

When we had mounted the gradual ascent on which the house stands, the crowd all around it was as one head! We stopped within twenty yards of the door, uncertain how to proceed. All the royals were at the windows; and to pass this multitude–to wade through it, rather,–was a most disagreeable operation. However, we had no choice: we therefore got out, and, leaving the wardrobe-women to find the way to the back-door, Miss Planta and I glided on to the front one, where we saw the two gentlemen and where, as soon as we got up the steps, we encountered the king. He inquired most graciously concerning our journey; and Lady Weymouth came down-stairs to summon me to the queen, who was in excellent spirits, and said she would show me her room.

"This, ma'am!" cried I, as I entered it–"is this little room for your majesty?"

"O stay," cried she, laughing, "till you see your own before you call it 'little'."

Soon after, she sent me upstairs for that purpose ; and then, to be sure, I began to think less diminutively of that I had just quitted.

Mine, with one window, has just space to crowd in a bed, a chest of drawers, and three small chairs. The prospect from the window, is extremely pretty, and all IS new and clean. So I doubt not being very comfortable, as I am senza Cerbera,(278)–though having no maid is a real evil to one so little her own mistress as myself. I little wanted the fagging of my own clothes and dressing, to add to my daily fatigues.

I began a little unpacking and was called to dinner. Columb, happily, is allowed me, and he will be very useful, I am sure. Miss alone dined with me, and we are to be companions constant at all meals, and t'ete-'a-t'ete, during this sejour. She is friendly and well disposed, and I am perfectly content; and the more, as I know she will not take up my leisure Unnecessarily, for she finds sauntering in the open air very serviceable to her health, and she has determined to make that her chief occupation. Here, therefore, whenever I am not in attendance, or at meals, I expect the singular comfort of having my time wholly unmolested, and at my own disposal.

THE TEA-TABLE DIFFICULTY.

A little parlour, which formerly had belonged to Lord Fauconberg's housekeeper, is now called mine, and here Miss Planta and myself are to breakfast and dine. But for tea we formed a new plan: as Mr. Fairly had himself told me he understood there would be no tea-table at Cheltenham, I determined to stand upon no ceremony with Colonel Gwynn, but fairly and at once take and appropriate my afternoons to my own inclinations. To prevent, therefore, any surprise or alteration, we settled to have our tea upstairs.

But then a difficulty arose as to where ? We had each equally small bed-rooms, and no dressing-room; but, at length, we fixed on the passage, near a window looking over Malvern hills and much beautiful country.

This being arranged, we went mutually on with our unpackings, till we were both too thirsty to work longer. Having no maid to send, and no bell to ring for my man, I then made out my way downstairs, to give Columb directions for our teaequipage.

After two or three mistakes, of peering into royal rooms, I at length got safe to my little parlour, but still was at a loss where to find Columb; and while parading in and out, in hopes of meeting with some assistant, I heard my name inquired for from the front door. I looked out, and saw Mrs. Tracy, senior bedchamber-woman to the queen. She is at Cheltenham for her health, and came to pay her duty in inquiries, and so forth.

I conducted her to my little store-room, for such it looks, from its cupboards and short checked window curtains; and we chatted upon the place and the expedition, till Columb came to tell me that Mr. Fairly desired to speak with me. I waited upon him immediately, in the passage leading to the kitchen stairs, for that was my salle d'audience.

He was with Lord Courtown; they apologised for disturbing me, but Mr. Fairly said he came to solicit leave that they might join my tea-table for this night only, as they would give orders to be supplied in their own apartments the next day, and not intrude upon me any more, nor break into my time and retirement.

This is literally the first instance I have met, for now two whole years, of being understood as to my own retiring inclinations; and it is singular I should first meet with it from the only person who makes them waver.

I begged them to come in, and ordered tea. They are well acquainted with Mrs. Tracy, and I was very glad she happened to stay.

Poor Miss Planta, meanwhile, I was forced to leave in the lurch; for I could not propose the bed-room passage to my present company, and she was undressed and unpacking.

Very soon the king, searching for his gentlemen, found out my room, and entered. He admired It prodigiously, and inquired concerning all our accommodations. He then gave Mr. Fairly a commission to answer an address, or petition, or some such thing to the master of the ceremonies, and, after half an hour's chat, retired.

Colonel Gwynn found us out also, but was eager to find out more company, and soon left us to go and look over the books at the rooms, for the list of the company here.

A TETE-A-TETE WITH COLONEL FAIRLY.

After tea Mrs. Tracy went, and the king sent for Lord Courtown. Mr. Fairly was going too, and I was preparing to return upstairs to my toils; but he presently changed his design, and asked leave to stay a little longer, if I was at leisure. At leisure I certainly was not but I was most content to work double tides for the pleasure of his company, especially where given thus voluntarily, and not accepted officially.

What creatures are we all for liberty and freedom! Rebels
partout!
"Soon as the life-blood warms the heart,
The love of liberty awakes!"

Ah, my dear friends! I wrote that with a sigh that might have pierced through royal walls!

From this circumstance we entered into discourse with no little spirit. I felt flattered, and he knew he had given me de quoi: so we were both in mighty good humour. Our sociability, however, had very soon an interruption. The king re-entered ; he started back at sight of our diminished party, and exclaimed, with a sort of arch surprise, "What! only You two?"

Mr. Fairly laughed a little, and Ismiled ditto! But I had rather his majesty had made such a comment on any other of his establishment, if make it he must; since I am sure Mr. Fairly's aversion to that species of raillery is equal to my Own.

The king gave some fresh orders about the letter, and instantly went away. As soon as he was gone, Mr. Fairly,–perhaps to show himself superior to that little sally,–asked me whether he might write his letter in my room?

"O yes," cried I, with all the alacrity of the same superiority.

He then went in search of a page, for pen and ink, and told me, on returning, that the king had just given orders for writing implements for himself and Colonel Gwynn to be placed in the dining-parlour, of which they were, henceforth, to have the use as soon as the dinner-party had separated; and after to-night, therefore, he should intrude himself upon me no more. I had half a mind to say I was very sorry for it! I assure you I felt so.

He pretended to require my assistance in his letter, and consulted and read over all that he writ. So I gave my opinion as he went on, though I think it really possible he might have done without me!

Away then he went with it, to dispatch it by a royal footman; and I thought him gone, and was again going myself, when he returned,–surprising me not a little by saying. as he held the door in his hand, "Will there be any–impropriety–in my staying here a little logger?" I must have said no, if I had thought yes; but it would not have been so plump and ready a no! and I should not, with

quite so courteous a grace, have added that his stay could do me nothing but honour.

On, therefore, we sat, discoursing on various subjects, till the twilight made him rise to take leave. He was in much better spirits than I have yet seen him, and I know not when I have spent an hour more socially to my taste. Highly cultivated by books, and uncommonly fertile in stores of internal resource, he left me nothing to wish, for the time I spent with him, but that "the Fates, the Sisters Three, and suchlike branches of learning," would interfere against the mode of future separation planned for the remainder of our expedition. Need I more strongly than this mark the very rare pleasure I received from his conversation?

Not a little did poor Miss Planta marvel what had become of me; and scarce less was her marvel when she had heard my adventures. She had told me how gladly the gentlemen would seize the opportunity of a new situation, to disengage themselves from the joint tea-table, and we had mutually agreed to use all means possible for seconding this partition; but I had been too well satisfied this night, to make any further efforts about the matter, and I therefore inwardly resolved to let the future take care of itself–certain it could not be inimical to me, since either it must give me Mr. Fairly in a party, or time for my own disposal in solitude.

This pleasant beginning has given a spirit to all my expectations and my fatigues in this place; and though it cost me near two hours from my downy pillow to recover lost time, I stole them without repining, and arose–dead asleep–this morning, without a murmur.

THE KING's GENTLEMEN AND THE QUEEN's LADIES. Sunday, July 13–I was obliged to rise before six o'clock, that I might play the part of dresser to myself, before I played it to the queen; so that did not much recruit the fatigues of yesterday's rising and journey! Not a little was I surprised to be told, this morning, by her majesty, that the gentlemen were to breakfast with Miss Planta and me, every morning, by the king's orders.

When I left the queen, I found them already in my little parlour. Mr. Fairly came to the door to meet me, and hand me into the room, telling me of the new arrangement of the king, with an air of very civil satisfaction. Colonel Gwynn

appeared precisely as I believe he felt,-perfectly indifferent to the matter. Miss Planta joined us, and Columb was hurried to get ready, lest the king should summon his esquires before they had broken their fast. Mr. Fairly undertook to settle our seats, and all the etiquette of the tea-table; and I was very well content, for when he had placed me where he conceived I should be most commodiously situated, he fixed upon the place next me for himself, and desired we might all keep to our posts. It was next agreed, that whoever came first to the room should order and make the tea; for I must often be detained by my waiting, and the king is so rapid in his meals, that whoever attends him must be rapid also, or follow fasting. Mr. Fairly said he should already have hastened Columb, had he not apprehended it might be too great a liberty ; for they had waited near half an hour, and expected a call every half minute. I set him perfectly at his ease upon this subject, assuring him I should be very little at mine if he had ever the same scruple again. He had been in waiting, he said, himself, ever since a quarter after five o'clock in the morning, at which time he showed himself under the king's window, and walked before the house till six! I was beginning to express my compassion for this harass, but he interrupted me with shrewdly saying, "

"O, this will save future fatigue, for it will establish me such a character for early rising and punctuality, that I may now do as I will: 'tis amazing what privileges a man obtains for taking liberties, when once his character is established for taking none."

Neither Miss Planta nor myself could attempt going to church, we had both so much actual business to do for ourselves, in unpacking, and fitting up our rooms, etc. The rest of the day was all fasting, till the evening, and then–who should enter my little parlour, after all the speechifying Of only one night," made yesterday, but Mr. Fairly, Colonel Gwynn, and Lord Courtown! Whether this, again, is by the king's command, or in consequence of the morning arrangement, I know not: but not a word more has dropped of "no evening tea-table;" so, whether we are to unite, or to separate, in future, I know not, and, which is far more extraordinary, I care not! Nobody but you could imagine what a compliment that is, from me! I had made Miss Planta promise, in case such a thing should happen, to come down; and she was very ready, and

we had a very cheerful evening. Great difficulties, however, arose about our tea-equipage, So few things are brought, or at least are yet arrived, that Columb is forced to be summoned every other moment, and I have no bell, and dare not, for this short time, beg for one, as my man herds with the King's men; besides, I have no disposition to make a fuss here, where every body takes up with every thing that they get.

In lamenting, however, the incessant trouble I was obliged to give the gentlemen, of running after Columb, I told Mr. Fairly my obligation, at Windsor, to Colonel Wellbred, for my bell there.

"O yes," cried he, laughing, "I am not surprised; Colonel Wellbred is quite the man for a 'belle!'"

"Yes," cried I, "that he is indeed, and for a 'beau' too."

"O ho! you think him so, do you?" quoth he: to which my prompt assent followed.

ROYALTY CROWDED AT FAUCONBERG HALL.

The royal family had all been upon the walks. I have agreed with myself not to go thither till they have gone through the news- mongers' drawing up of them and their troop. I had rather avoid all mention and after a few days, I may walk there as if not belonging to them, as I am not of place or rank to follow in their train.

But let me give you, now, an account of the house and accommodation.

On the ground-floor there is one large and very pleasant room, which is made the dining-parlour. The king and royal family also breakfast in it, by themselves, except the lady-in-waiting, Lady Weymouth. They sup there also, in the same manner. The gentlemen only dine with them, I find. They are to breakfast with us, to drink tea where they will, and to sup–where they can; and I rather fancy, from what I have yet seen, it will be commonly with good Duke Humphrey.

A small, but very neat dressing-room for his majesty is on the other side of the hall, and my little parlour is the third and only other room on the ground-floor: so you will not think our monarch, his consort and offspring, take up too much of the land called their own !

Over this eating- parlour, on the first floor, is the queen's drawing-room, in which she is also obliged to dress and to un-

dress for she has no toilette apartment! Who, after that, can repine at any inconvenience here for the household? Here, after breakfast, she sits, with her daughters and her lady and Lady Courtown, who, with her lord, is lodged in the town of Cheltenham. And here they drink tea, and live till suppertime.

Over the king's dressing-room is his bed-room, and over my store-room is the bed-room of the princess-royal. And here ends the first floor.

The second is divided and sub-divided into bed-rooms, which are thus occupied:– Princess Augusta and Princess Elizabeth sleep in two beds, in the largest room. Lady Weymouth occupies that next in size. Miss Planta and myself have two little rooms, built over the king's bed-room and Mrs. Sandys and Miss Macentomb, and Lady Weymouth's maid, have the rest.

This is the whole house! Not a man but the king sleeps In it.

A house is taken in the town for Mr. Fairly and Colonel Gwynn, and there lodge several of the servants, and among them Columb. The pages sleep in outhouses. Even the house-maids lodge in the town, a quarter of a mile or more from the house!

Lord Courtown, as comptroller of the household, acts here for the king, in distributing his royal bounty to the Wells, rooms, library, and elsewhere. He has sent around very magnificently.

We are surrounded by pleasant meadows, in which I mean to walk a great deal. They are so quiet and so safe, I can go quite alone; and when I have not a first-rate companion, my second best is- -none at all! But I expect, very soon, my poor Miss Port, and I shall have her with me almost constantly.

AT THE WELLS.

Monday, July 14-This morning I was again up at five o'clock, Miss Planta having asked me to accompany her to the wells. The queen herself went this morning, at six o'clock, with his majesty. It is distant about a quarter of a mile from Lord Fauconberg's. I tasted the water, for once; I shall spare myself any such future regale, for it is not prescribed to me, and I think it very unpleasant.

This place and air seem very healthy; but the very early

hours, and no maid! I almost doubt how this will do. The fatigue is very great indeed.

We were too soon for the company, except the royals. We met them all, and were spoken to most graciously by every one. We all came back to breakfast much at the same time, and it was very cheerful.

I spent all the rest of the day in hard fagging, at work and business, and attendance; but the evening amply recompensed it all. Lord Courtown, Mr. Fairly, Colonel Gwynn, and Miss Planta, came to tea. My Lord and Colonel Gwynn retired after it, to go to the rooms; Mr. Fairly said he Would wait to make his bow to his majesty, and see if there were any commands for him.

CONVERSATION AND FLIRTATION WITH COLONEL FAIRLY. And then we had another very long conversation, and if I did not write in so much haste, my dear friends would like to read it.

Our subject to-night–his subject, rather–was, the necessity of participation, to every species of happiness. "His" subject, you may easily believe; for to him should I never have dared touch on one so near and so tender to him. Fredy, however, could join With him more feelingly–though he kept perfectly clear of all that was personal, to which I Would not have led for a thousand worlds. He seems born with the tenderest social affections; and, though religiously resigned to his loss–which, I have been told, the hopeless sufferings of Lady - rendered, at last, even a release to be desired–he thinks life itself, single and unshared, a mere melancholy burthen, and the wish to have done with it appears the only wish he indulges. I could not perceive this without the deepest commiseration, but I did what was possible to conceal it; as it is much more easy, both to the hearer and the speaker, to lead the discourse to matters more lively, under an appearance of being ignorant of the state of a sad heart, than with a betrayed consciousness.

We talked of books, and not a little I astonished him by the discovery I was fain to make, of the number of authors I have never yet read. Particularly he instanced Akenside, and quoted from him some passages I have heard selected by Mr, Locke.

Then we talked of the country, of landscapes, of walking, and then, again, came back the favourite proposition,–participation! That, he said, could make an interest in anything,–everything; and O, how did I agree with him! There is sympathy enough, heaven knows, in our opinions on this subject

But not in what followed. I am neither good nor yet miserable enough to join with him in what he added, -that life, taken all in all, was of so little worth and value, it could afford its thinking possessor but one steady wish,–that its duration might be short!

Alas! thought I, that a man so good should be so unhappy!

We then came back again to books, and he asked us if we had read a little poem called the "Shipwreck"?(279) Neither of us had even heard of it. He said it was somewhat too long, and somewhat too technical, but that it contained many beautiful passages. He had it with him, he said, and proposed sending Columb for it, to his house, if we should like to read it. We thanked him, and off marched Columb. It is in a very small duodecimo volume, and he said he would leave it with me.

Soon after, Miss Planta said she would stroll round the house for a little exercise. When she was gone, he took up the book, and said, "Shall I read some passages to you? I most gladly assented, and got my work,–of which I have no small store, believe me!– morning caps, robins, etc., all to prepare from day to day; which, with my three constant and long attendances, and other official company ceremonies, is no small matter.

The passages he selected were really beautiful: they were chiefly from an episode, of Palemon and Anna, excessively delicate, yet tender in the extreme, and most touchingly melancholy.

One line he came to, that he read with an emotion extremely affecting– 'tis a sweet line–

"He felt the chastity of silent woe."

He stopped upon it, and sighed so deeply that his sadness quite infected me.

Then he read various characters of the ship's company,

which are given with much energy and discrimination. I could not but admire every passage he chose, and I was sensible each of them owed much obligation to his reading, which was full of feeling and effect.

How unwillingly did I interrupt him, to go upstairs and wait my night's summons! But the queen has no bell for me, except to my bed-room.

He hastily took the hint, and rose to go. "Shall I leave the poem," he cried, "or take it with me, in case there should be any leisure to go on with it to-morrow?"

"Which you please," cried I, a little stupidly, for I did not, at the moment, comprehend his meaning which, however, he immediately explained by answering, "Let me take it, then;–let me make a little interest in it to myself, by reading it with you."

And then he put it in his pocket, and went to his home in the town, and up stairs went I to my little cell, not a little internally simpering to see a trait so like what so often I have done myself,–carrying off a favourite book, when I have begun it with my Susanna, that we might finish it together, without leaving her the temptation to peep beforehand,

MISS BURNEY MEETS AN OLD FRIEND.

Tuesday, July 15–While the royals were upon the walks, Miss Planta and I strolled in the meadows, and who should I meet there–but Mr. Seward! This was a great pleasure to me. I had never seen him since the first day of my coming to St. jades's, when he handed me into my father's coach, in my sacque and long ruffles. You may think how much we had to talk over. He had a gentleman with him, fortunately, who was acquainted with Miss Planta's brother, so that we formed two parties, without difficulty. All my aim was to inquire about Mrs. Piozzi,–I must, at last, call her by her now real name!–and of her we conversed incessantly. He told me Mr. Baretti's late attack upon her, which I heard with great concern.(280) It seems he has broken off all intercourse with her, and

not from his own desire, but by her evident wish to drop him. This is very surprising ; but many others of her former friends, once highest in her favour, make the same complaint.

We strolled so long, talking over this ever- interesting subject, that the royals were returned before us, and we found Mr. Fairly waiting in my parlour. The rest soon joined. Mr. Seward had expected to be invited; but it is impossible for me to invite any body while at Cheltenham, as there is neither exit nor entrance but by passing the king's rooms, and as I have no place but this little common parlour in which I can sit, except my own room.

Neither could I see Mr. Seward anywhere else, as my dear friends will easily imagine, when they recollect all that has passed, on the subject of my visitors, with her majesty and with Mr. Smelt. He told me he had strolled in those meadows every day, to watch if I were of the party.

COLONEL FAIRLY AGAIN.

Mr. Fairly again out-stayed them all. Lord Courtown generally is summoned to the royal party after tea, and Colonel Gwynn goes to the town in quest of acquaintance and amusement. Mr. Fairly has not spirit for such researches ; I question, indeed, if he ever had taste for them.

When Miss Planta, went off for her exercise, he again proposed a little reading, which again I thankfully accepted. He took out the little poem, and read on the mournful tale of Anna, with a sensibility that gave pathos to every word.

How unexpected an indulgence–a luxury, I may say, to me, are these evenings now becoming! While I listen to such reading and such a reader, all my work goes on with an alacrity that renders it all pleasure to me. I have had no regale like this for many and many a grievous long evening ! never since I left Norbury park,-never since my dear Fredy there read Madame de S6vign6. And how little could I expect, in a royal residence, a relief of this sort! Indeed, I much question if there is one other person, in the whole establishment, that, in an equal degree, could afford it. Miss Planta, though extremely friendly, is almost wholly absorbed in the cares of her royal duties, and the solicitude

of her ill-health : she takes little interest in anything else, whether for conversation or action. We do together perfectly well, for she is good, and sensible, and prudent, and ready for any kind office: but the powers of giving pleasure are not widely bestowed: we have no right to repine that they are wanting where the character that misses them has intrinsic worth but, also, we have no remedy against weariness, where that worth is united with nothing attractive.

I was forced again, before ten o'clock, to interrupt his interesting narrative, that I might go to my room. He now said he would leave me the book to look over and finish at my leisure, upon one condition, which he begged me to observe: this was, that I would read with a pen or pencil In my hand, and mark the passages that pleased me most as I went on. I readily promised this.

He then gave it me, but desired I would keep it to myself, frankly acknowledging that he did not wish to have it seen by any other, at least not as belonging to him. There was nothing, he said of which he had less ambition than a character for bookism and pedantry, and he knew if it was spread that he was guilty of carrying a book from one house to another, it would be a circumstance sufficient for branding him with these epithets.

I could not possibly help laughing a little at this caution, but again gave him my ready promise.

A VISIT TO MISS PALMER.

Wednesday, July 16.-This morning we had the usual breakfast, and just as it was over I received a note from Miss Palmer, saying she was uncertain whether or not I was at Cheltenham, by not meeting me on the walks or at the play, but wrote to mention that she was with Lady D'Oyley, and hoped, if I was one of the royal suite, my friends might have some chance to see me here, though wholly denied it in town. I sent for answer that I would call upon her; and as no objection was made by her majesty, I went to Sir John D'Oyley's as soon as the royal party rode out.

I found Miss Palmer quite thoroughly enraged. We had never met since I left the paternal home, though I am always much indebted to her warm zeal. Sir John and Lady D'Oyley are a mighty gentle pair. Miss Palmer could make them no better present than a little of her vivacity. Miss Elizabeth

Johnson, her cousin, is of their party : She is pretty, soft, and pleasing; but, unhappily, as deaf as her uncle, Sir Joshua which, in a young female, is a real misfortune. To quiet Miss Palmer as much as I was able, I agreed tonight that I would join her on the walks. Accordingly, at the usual time I set out with Miss Planta, whom I was to introduce to the D'Oyleys. Just as we set out we perceived the king and his three gentlemen, for Lord Courtown is a constant attendant every evening. We were backing on as well as we Could, but his majesty perceived us, and called to ask whither we were going. We met Mr. Seward, who joined us.

There is nothing to describe in the walks : they are straight, clay, and sided by common trees, without any rich foliage, or one beautiful opening. The meadows, and all the country around, are far preferable: yet here everybody meets. All the D'Oyley party came, and Miss Planta slipped away.

The king and queen walked in the same state as on the Terrace at Windsor, followed by the three princesses and their attendants. Everybody stopped and stood up as they passed, or as they stopped themselves to speak to any of the company.

In one of these stoppings, Lord Courtown backed a little from the suite to talk with us, and he said he saw what benefit I reaped from the waters! I told him I Supposed I might be the better for the excursion, according to the definition of a water-drinking person by Mr. Walpole, who says people go to those places well, and then return cured! Mr. Fairly afterwards also joined us a little while, and Miss Palmer said she longed to know him more, there was something so fine in his countenance.

They invited me much to go home with them to tea, but I was engaged. We left the walks soon after the royal family, and they carried me near the house in Sir John D'Oyley's coach. I walked, however, quietly in by myself; and in my little parlour I found Mr. Fairly. The others were gone off to the play without tea, and the moment it was over Miss Planta hurried to her own stroll.

"ORIGINAL LOVE LETTERS."

This whole evening I spent t'ete-'a-t'ete with Mr. Fairly. There is something singular in the perfect trust he seems to have in my discretion, for he speaks to me when we are alone with a frankness unequalled and something very flattering in the

Page 171 apparent relief he seems to find in dedicating what time he has to dispose of to my little parlour. In the long conference of this evening I found him gifted with the justest way of thinking and the most classical taste. I speak that word only as I may presume 'to judge it by English literature.

"I have another little book," he said, "here, which I am sure you would like, but it has a title so very silly that nobody reads or names it: 'Original Love-Letters;(281)– from which you might expect mere nonsense and romance, though, on the contrary, you would find in them nothing but good sense, moral reflections, and refined ideas, clothed in the most expressive and elegant language."

How I longed to read a book that had such a character!–yet, laughable and prudish as it may seem to you, I could not bring myself to accept the half-offer, or make any other reply than to exclaim against the injudiciousness of the title-page.

Yet, whatever were our subjects, books, life, or persons, all concluded with the same melancholy burthen–speed to his existence here, and welcome to that he is awaiting! I fear he has been unfortunate from his first setting out.'

THE FOUNDER OF SUNDAY SCHOOLS CRITICIZED. July 19.–The breakfast missed its best regale Mr. Fairly was ill, and confined to his room all day.

The royal party went to Lord Bathurst's, at Cirencester, and the queen commanded Miss Planta and me to take an airing to Gloucester, and amuse ourselves as well as we could. Miss Planta had a previous slight acquaintance with Mr. Raikes and to his house, therefore, we drove.

Mr. Raikes(282) was the original founder of the Sunday-school, an institution so admirable, so fraught, I hope, with future good and mercy to generations yet unborn, that I saw almost with reverence the man who had first suggested it. He lives at

Gloucester with his wife and a large family. They all received us with open arms. I was quite amazed, but soon found some of the pages had been with them already, and announced our design; and as we followed the pages, perhaps they concluded we also were messengers, or avant-courieres, of what else might be expected. Mr. Raikes is not a man that, without a previous disposition towards approbation, I should greatly have admired. He is somewhat too flourishing, somewhat too forward, somewhat too voluble ; but he is worthy, benevolent, good-natured, and good-hearted, and therefore the overflowing of successful spirits and delighted vanity must meet with some allowance. His wife is a quiet and unpretending woman: his daughters common sort of country misses. They seem to live with great hospitality, plenty, and good cheer. They gave us a grand breakfast, and then did the honours of their city to us with great patriotism. They carried us to their fine old cathedral, where we saw the tomb of poor Edward II., and many more ancient. Several of the Saxon princes were buried in the original cathedral, and their monuments are preserved. Various of the ancient nobility, whose names and families were extinct from the Wars of the Roses, have here left their worldly honours and deposited their last remains. It was all interesting to see, though I will not detail it, for any "Gloucester guide" would beat me hollow at that work. Next they carried us to the jail, to show in how small a space, I suppose, human beings can live, as well as die or be dead. This jail is admirably constructed for its proper purposes– confinement and punishment. Every culprit is to have a separate cell; every cell is clean, neat, and small, looking towards a wide expanse of country, and, far more fitted to his speculation, a wide expanse of the heavens. Air, cleanliness, and health seem all considered, but no other indulgence. A total seclusion of all commerce from accident, and an absolute impossibility of all intercourse between themselves, must needs render the captivity secure from all temptation to further guilt, and all Stimulus to hardihood in past crimes, and makes the solitude become so desperate that it not only seems to leave no opening, for any comfort save in repentance, but to make that almost unavoidable.

After this they carried us to the Infirmary, where I was yet more pleased, for the sick and the destitute awaken an interest far less painful than the wicked and contemned. We went

entirely over the house, and then over the city, which has little else to catch notice. The pin manufactory we did not see, as they discouraged us by an account of its dirt.

Mr. Raikes is a very principal man in all these benevolent institutions; and while I poured forth my satisfaction in them very copiously and warmly, he hinted a question whether I could name them to the queen. "Beyond doubt," I answered; "for these were precisely the things which most interested her majesty's humanity." The joy with which he heard this was nothing short of rapture.

ON THE WALKS.

Sunday, July 20-Colonel Gwynn again brought but a bad account of his companion, who was now under the care of the Cheltenham apothecary, Mr. Clerke.

I had appointed in the evening to go on the walks with Miss Palmer. I scarce ever passed so prodigious a crowd as was assembled before the house when I went out. The people of the whole county seemed gathered together to see their majesties; and so quiet, so decent, so silent, that it was only by the eye they could be discovered, though so immense a multitude. How unlike a London mob!

The king, kindly to gratify their zealous and respectful curiosity, came to his window, and seeing me go out, he called me to speak to him, and give an account of my intentions. The people, observing this graciousness, made way for me on every side, so that I passed through them with as much facility as if the meadows had been empty.

The D'Oyleys and Miss Johnson and Miss Palmer made the walking party, and Mr. Seward joined us. Mr. Raikes and all his family were come from Gloucester to see the royal family on the walks, which were very much crowded, but with the same respectful multitude, who never came forward, but gazed and admired at the most humble distance,

Mr. Raikes introduced me to the Bishop of Gloucester, Dr. Halifax, and afterwards, much more to my satisfaction, to the Dean of Gloucester, Dr. Tucker, the famous author of "Cui bono."(283) I was very glad to see him: he is past eighty, and has a most shrewd and keen old face.

I went afterwards to tea with the D'Oyleys and Miss Palmer, and Mr. Seward again accompanied us. Miss Palmer brought me home in Sir John's carriage, making it drive as near as possible to the house.

But just before we quitted the walks I was run after by a quick female step :–"Miss Burney, don't you know me? have you forgot Spotty?"–and I saw Miss Ogle. She told me she had longed to come and see me, but did not know if she might. She is here with her mother and two younger sisters. I promised to wait on them. Mrs. Oake was daughter to the late Bishop of Winchester, who was a preceptor of the king's: I knew, therefore, I might promise with approbation.

AN UNEXPECTED VISITOR.

Monday, July 21.-I was very much disappointed this morning to see Colonel Gwynn come again alone to breakfast, and to hear from him that his poor colleague was still confined.

The royal party all went at ten o'clock to Tewkesbury. About noon, while I was writing a folio letter to my dear father, of our proceedings, Mr. Alberts, the queen's page, came into my little parlour, and said "If you are at leisure, ma'am, Mr. Fairly begs leave to ask you how you do."

I was all amazement, for I had concluded his confinement irremediable for the present. I was quite happy to receive him; he looked very ill, and his face is still violently swelled. He had a handkerchief held to it, and was muffled up in a great coat; and indeed he seemed unfit enough for coming out.

He apologised for interrupting me. I assured him I should have ample time for my letter.

"What a letter!" cried he, looking at its size, "it is just such a one as I should like to receive, and not–"

"Read," cried I.

"No, no !–and not answer!"

He then sat down, and I saw by his manner he came with design to make a sociable visit to me. He was serious almost to sadness, but with a gentleness that could not but raise in whomsoever he had addressed an implicit sympathy. He led almost immediately to those subjects on which he loves to

dwell–Death and Immortality, and the assured misery of all stations and all seasons in this vain and restless world.

I ventured not to contradict him with my happier sentiments, lest I should awaken some fresh pain. I heard him, therefore, in quiet and meditative silence, or made but such general answers as could hazard no allusions. Yet, should I ever see him in better spirits, I shall not scruple to discuss, in such a way as I can, this point, and to vindicate as well as I am able my opposite opinion.

He told me he had heard a fifth week was to be now added to this excursion, and he confessed a most anxious solicitude to be gone before that time. He dropped something, unexplained, yet very striking, of a peculiar wish to be away ere some approaching period.

I felt his meaning, though I had no key to it; I felt that he coveted to spend in quiet the anniversary of the day on which he lost his lady. You may believe I could say nothing to it; the idea was too tender for discussion; nor can I divine whether or not he wishes to open more on this subject, or is better pleased by my constant silence to his own allusions. I know not, indeed, whether he thinks I even understand them.

COURTS AND COURT LIFE.

We then talked over Cheltenham and our way of life, and then ran into discourse upon Courts and Court life in general. I frankly said I liked them not, and that, if I had the direction of any young person's destination, I would never risk them into such a mode of living; for, though Vices may be as well avoided there as anywhere 'and in this Court particularly, there were mischiefs of a smaller kind, extremely pernicious to all nobleness of character, to which this Court, with all its really bright examples, was as liable as any other,–the mischiefs of jealousy, narrowness, and selfishness.

He did not see, he said, when there was a place of settled income and appropriated business why it might not be filled both with integrity and content in a Court as well as elsewhere. Ambition, the desire of rising, those, he said, were the motives that envy which set such little passions in motion. One situation, however, there was, he said, which he looked upon as truly dangerous, and as almost certain to pervert the fairest disposition- it was one in which he would not place any person for whom he had the smallest regard, as he looked upon it to

be the greatest hazard a character could run. This was, being maid of honour.

THE VINDICTIVE BARETTI.

Tuesday, July 22-To-day, at noon, I had a surprise with which I was very well pleased. His majesty opened the door of my little parlour, called out, "Come, Come in - ," and was followed by Major Price. He was just arrived from his little farm in Herefordshire, and will stay here some days. It is particularly fortunate just now, when another gentleman was really required to assist in attendance upon the royal party.

Mr. Seward, with a good-humoured note, sent me the magazine with Baretti's strictures on Mrs. Thrale. Good heaven, how abusive! It can hardly hurt her–it is so palpably meant to do it. I could not have suspected him, with all his violence, of a bitterness of invective so cruel, so ferocious!

I well remember his saying to me, when first I saw him after the discovery of "Evelina" I see what it is you can do, you little witch–it is, that you can hang us all up for laughing- stocks; but hear me this one thing–don't meddle with me. I see what they are, your powers; but remember, when you provoke an Italian you run a dagger into your own breast!"

I half shuddered at the fearful caution from him, because the dagger was a word of unfortunate recollection:(284) but, good heaven! it could only be a half Shudder when the caution was against an offence I could sooner die than commit, and which, I may truly say, if personal attack was what he meant, never even in sport entered my mind, and was ever, in earnest, a thing I have held in the deepest abhorrence.

I must do, however, the justice to his candour to add, that upon a newer acquaintance with me, which immediately followed, he never repeated his admonition; and when "Cecilia" came out, and he hastened to me with every species of extravagant encomium, he never hinted at any similar idea, and it seemed evident he concluded me, by that time, incapable

meriting such a suspicion; though, to judge by his own conduct, a proceeding of this sort may to him appear in a very different light. He thinks, at least, a spirit of revenge may authorize any attack, any insult. How unhappy and how strange! to join to so much real good nature as this man possesses when pleased, a disposition so savagely vindictive when offended.

SPECULATIONS UPON COLONEL FAIRLY'S RE-MARRYING. Thursday, July 24–"Pray, Miss Burney," cried Colonel Gwynn, "do you think Mr. Fairly will ever marry again?"

"I think it very doubtful," I answered, "but I hope he will, for, whether he is happy or not in marrying, I am sure he will be wretched in singleness; the whole turn of his mind is so social and domestic. He is by no means formed for going always abroad for the relief of society; he requires it more at hand."

"And what do you think of Miss Fuzilier?"

"That he is wholly disengaged with her and with everybody."

"Well, I think it will be, for I know they correspond ; and what should he correspond with her for else?"

"Because, I suppose, he has done it long before this could be suggested as the motive. And, indeed, the very quickness of the report makes me discredit it; 'tis so utterly impossible for a man whose feelings are so delicate to have taken any steps towards a second connexion at so early a period."

"Why, I know he's very romantic,–but I should like to know your opinion."

"I have given it you," cried I, "very exactly."

COLONEL FAIRLY AGAIN PRESENTS HIMSELF.

Not long after, when all the party was broke up from my little parlour, though not yet set out for Gloucester, who should again surprise me by entering but Mr. Fairly! I was quite rejoiced by his sight. He was better, though not well. His face is almost reduced to its natural size. He had a letter for her majesty from Lord Aylesbury, and had determined to venture bringing it himself.

He said he would carry it in to the queen, and then return to my parlour, if I would give him some breakfast.

You may suppose I answered "No!" But, afterwards, fearing he might

be detained and fatigued, he asked me to present it for him, and only say he was waiting in my room for commands. I was forced to say "Yes," though I had rather not.

Her majesty was much surprised to hear he was again out so unexpectedly, and asked if he thought of going to Gloucester?

"No," I said, "I believed he was not equal to that."

She bid me tell him she would see him before she went.

I returned with this message, and would then have ordered him fresh breakfast; but he declared if I was fidgety he should have no comfort, and insisted on my sitting quietly down, while he drew a chair by my side, and made his own cold tea, and drank it weak and vapid, and eat up all the miserable scraps, without suffering me to call for plate, knife, bread, butter, or anything for replenishment. And when he had done, and I would have made some apology, he affected me for him a good deal by gravely saying, "Believe me, this is the pleasantest breakfast I have made these six days."

He then went on speaking of his late confinement, and its comfortless circumstances, in very strong terms, dwelling on its solitude and its uselessness, as if those only formed its disagreeability, and the pain went for nothing. Social and kind is his heart, and finely touched to the most exquisite sensations of sympathy; and, as I told Colonel Gwynn, I must needs wish he may yet find some second gentle partner fitted to alleviate his sorrows, by giving to him an object whose happiness would become his first study.

He brought me back the few books I had procured him but I had no fresh supply. He spoke again of the favourite "Letters," and said he felt so sure I should be pleased with them, that he was desirous I should look at them, adding There is no person into whose hands I would not put them not even my daughter's."

It was now impossible to avoid saying I should be glad to see them: it would seem else to doubt either his taste or his delicacy, while I have the highest opinion of both. In talking them over he told me he believed them to be genuine; "But the woman," he said, "throughout the whole correspondence, is too much the superior. She leaves the man far behind. She is so collected, so composed, so constantly mistress of herself, so unbiased by her passions, so rational, and so dignified, that I would even recommend her as an example to any young woman in similar circumstances to follow."

Page 179 He was summoned to her majesty, in the dining-parlour. But when they were all set out on the Gloucester expedition, he returned to my little parlour, and stayed with me a considerable time.

Grave he came back–grave quite to solemnity, and almost wholly immersed in deep and sad reflections, He spoke little, and that little with a voice so melancholy, yet so gentle, that it filled me with commiseration.

At length, after much silence and many pauses, which I never attempted to interrupt or to dissipate, continuing my work as if not heeding him, he led himself distantly, yet intelligibly–to open upon the immediate state of his mind.

I now found that the king's staying on at Cheltenham a fifth week was scarcely supportable to him; that the 16th of next month was the mournful anniversary of his loss, and that he had planned to dedicate it in some peculiar manner to her memory, with his four children. Nothing of this was positively said; for

"He feels the chastity of silent woe."

But all of it was indubitably comprised in the various short but pointed sentences which fell from him.

THE COLONEL AND THE "ORIGINAL LOVE LETTERS."

Friday, July 25.-Again, to a very late breakfast came Mr. Fairly, which again he made for himself, when the rest were dispersed, of all the odd remnants, eatable and drinkable. He was much better, and less melancholy. He said he should be well enough to join the royal party to-morrow, who were to dine and spend the whole day at Lord Coventry's at Coombe. . . .

In the afternoon, while Miss Planta and myself were Sitting over our dessert, a gentle rap at the parlour-door preceded Mr. Fairly. How we both started! He was muffled up in a great coat, and said he came quite incog., as he was not well enough to dine anywhere but in his private apartment, nor to attend the royals to the walks, whither they go every evening. He had only strolled out for a walk by himself.

I could not persuade him to sit down; he said he must be gone immediately, lest he should be seen, and the king, not aware of his unfitness, should order his attendance.

Miss Planta, presently, was obliged to go to the princesses,

and wait with them till the promenade took place. Quietly, then, he drew a chair to the table, and I saw he had something to say; but, after a little general talk he rose and was going : when, hearing by the dogs the royal family were just in motion, he pulled off his great coat and seated himself again.

And then, he took from his pocket a small volume, which he said he had taken this opportunity to bring me. You Will be sure it was the "Original Letters.;"

I took them, and thanked him: he charged me with a very grave air to keep them safe, and I put them into my work-box–my dear Fredy's work-box–which here is my universal repository of small goods and chattels, and useful past all thanks.

By the time they Were set off, however, we were entered into conversation, and he said he would venture to stay tea; "though, as I tell you," he added, "what I do not tell everybody, I must confess I have upon me some certain symptoms that make me a little suspect these Cheltenham waters are going to bring me to a fit of the gout."

And then he told me that that dreadful disorder had been frequently and dangerously in his family, though he had himself never had it but once, which was after a very bad fall from his horse when hunting with the king.

Miss Planta now joined us, looking not a little surprised to find Mr. Fairly still here, and I ordered tea. After it was over, she went to take her usual evening exercise; and then Mr. Fairly, pointing to my work-box, said, "Shall I read a little to you?"

Certainly, I said, if it would not too much fatigue him; and then, with the greatest pleasure in renewing again a mode in which I had taken so much delight, I got my work and gave him his book. Unluckily, however, it was the second volume; the first, having read, he had left in town. "It is quite, however," he said, "immaterial whether You begin with the first volume or the second; the story is nothing; the language and the sentiments are all you can care for."

I did not quite agree in this, but would not say so, lest he should think of me as Colonel Gwynn does of him, "that I am very romantic which, however, I am not, though I never like to anticipate an end ere I know a beginning.

Indeed, he had not praised them too highly, nor raised my expectations beyond what could answer them, They are full

of beauties-moral, elegant, feeling, and rational. He seemed most unusually grati-fied by seeing me so much pleased with them. I am so glad," he cried, "You like them, for I thought you would!" But we began so late that he could only, get through two letters, when the time of my retiring arrived. I was sorry also to have him out so late after his long confinement; but he wrapped himself up in his great coat, and did not seem to think he should suffer from it.

Miss Planta came to my room upstairs, to Inquire how long Mr. Fairly had stayed, and I was quite happy to appease her astonishment that he should come without sending in to the king, by assuring her he was only nursing for the next day, when he meant to attend the Coombe party.

I thought it so absolutely right to mention his visit to the queen, lest, hearing of it from the princesses through Miss Planta, she Should wonder yet more, that I put aside the disagreeable feel of exciting that wonder myself, and told her he had drank tea here, when I attended her at night. She seemed much more surprised than pleased, till I added that he was preparing and hardening himself for the Coombe expedition the next day, and then she was quite satisfied.(285)

THE GOUT AND THE LOVE LETTERS, AGAIN.

Saturday, July 26.-The royal party were to be Out the whole day, and I had her majesty's permission to go to the play at night with Miss Port and her friends, and to introduce MISS Planta to them for the same purpose. The breakfast was at seven o'clock ; we were all up at half after five. How sorry was I to see Colonel Gwynn enter alone, and to hear that Mr. Fairly was again ill

Soon after the king came into the room and said, "So, no Mr. Fairly again?"

"No, sir; he's very bad this morning."

"What's the matter? His face?"

"No, sir; he has got the gout. These waters., he thinks, have brought it on."

"What, in his foot?"

"Yes, sir; he is quite lame, his foot is swelled prodigiously."

"So he's quite knocked up! Can't he come out?"

"No, sir; he's obliged to order a gouty shoe and stay at home and nurse."

The king declared the Cheltenham waters were admirable friends to the constitution, by bringing disorders out of the habit. Mr. Fairly, he said, had not been well some time, and a smart fit of the gout might set him all to rights again. Alas, thought I, a smart fit of the gout in a lonely lodging at a water-drinking place!

They all presently set off; and so fatigued was my poor little frame, I was glad to go and lie down; but I never can sleep when I try for it in the daytime; the moment I cease all employment, my thoughts take such an ascendance over my morphetic faculty, that the attempt always ends in a deep and most Wakeful meditation.

About twelve o'clock I was reading In my private loan book, when, hearing the step of Miss Planta on the stairs, I put it back in my work-box, and Was just taking thence some other employment, when her voice struck my ear almost in a scream "Is it possible? Mr. Fairly!"

My own with difficulty refrained echoing it when I heard his voice answer her, and in a few minutes they parted, and he rapped at the door and entered my little parlour. He came in hobbling, leaning on a stick, and with a large cloth shoe over one of his feet, which was double the size of the other.

We sat down together, and he soon inquired what I had done with his little book. I had only, I answered, read two more letters.

"Have you read two?" he cried, in a voice rather disappointed; and I found he was actually come to devote the morning, which he knew to be unappropriated on my part, to reading it on to me himself. Then he took up the book and read on from the fifth letter. But he read at first with evident uneasiness, throwing down the book at every noise, and stopping to listen at every sound. At last he asked me if anybody was likely to come?

Not a soul, I said, that I knew or expected.

He laughed a little at his question and apparent anxiety but with an openness that singularly marks his character, he frankly added, I must put the book away, pure as it is, if any one comes or, without knowing a word of the contents, they will run away with the title alone, exclaiming, 'Mr. Fairly

reading love letters to Miss Burney!' A fine story that would make!"

'Pon honour, thought I, I would not hear such a tale for the world. However, he now pursued his reading more at his ease.

I will not tell you what we said of them in talking them over. Our praise I have chiefly given—our criticism must wait till you have read them yourselves. They are well worth your seeking. I am greatly mistaken if you do not read them with delight.

in the course of the discussion he glided, I know not how, upon the writings of another person, saying he never yet had talked them over with me.

"It is much kinder not," cried I hastily. . . .

"Well, but," cried he laughing, "may I find a fault? Will you hear a criticism, if nothing of another sort?" I was forced to accede to this.

He told me, then, there was one thing he wholly disallowed and wished to dispute, which was, Cecilia's refusing to be married on account of the anonymous prohibition to the ceremony. He could not, he said, think such an implied distrust of Delvile, after consenting to be his, was fair or generous.

"To that," cried I, "I cannot judge what a man may think, but I will own it is what most precisely and indubitably I could not have resisted doing myself. An interruption so mysterious and so shocking I could never have had the courage to pass over."

This answer rather silenced him from politeness than convinced him from reason, for I found he thought the woman who had given her promise was already married, and ought to run every risk rather than show the smallest want of confidence in the man of her choice.

Columb now soon came in to inquire what time I should dine, but a ghost could not have made him stare more than Mr. Fairly, whose confinement with the gout had been spread all over the house by Colonel Gwynn.

I ordered an early dinner on account of the play."

"Will you invite me," cried Mr. Fairly, laughing, "to dine with you?"

"Oh yes!" I cried, "with the greatest pleasure." and he said he would go to his home and dress, and return to my hour.

A DINNER WITH COLONEL FAIRLY AND MISS PLANTA, As he was at leisure, I had bespoke the queen's hairdresser, on account of the play; but Miss Planta came to inform me that she could not be of that party, as she had received a letter from Lady Charlotte Finch, concerning Princess Mary, that she must stay to deliver herself.

I told her she would have a beau at dinner. "Well," she exclaimed, "'tis the oddest thing in the world He should come so when the king and queen are away! I am sure, if I was you, I would not mention it."

"Oh yes, I shall," cried I; "I receive no visitors in private; and I am sure if I did, Mr. Fairly is the last who would condescend to make one of them." Such was my proud, but true speech, for him and for myself.

At dinner we all three met; Mr. Fairly in much better spirits than I have yet seen him at Cheltenham. He attacks Miss Planta upon all her little prejudices, and rallies her into a defence of them, in a manner so sportive 'tis impossible to hurt her, yet so nearly sarcastic that she is frequently perplexed whether to take it in good or ill part. But his intentions are so decidedly averse to giving pain, that even when she is most alarmed at finding the laugh raised against her, some suddenly good-humoured or obliging turn sets all to rights, and secures any sting from remaining, even where the bee has been most menacing to fix itself.

I believe Mr. Fairly to possess from nature high animal spirits, though now curbed by misfortune - and a fine vein of satire, though constantly kept in order by genuine benevolence. He is still, in mixed company, gay, shrewd, and arch ; foremost in badinage, and readiest for whatever may promote general entertainment. But in chosen society his spirits do not rise above cheerfulness; he delights in moral discourse, on grave and instructive subjects, and though always ready to be led to the politics or business of the day, in which he is constantly well versed and informing I never observe him to lead but to themes of religion, literature, or moral life.

When dinner and a very sociable dessert were over, we proposed going to the king's dining-parlour, while the servants removed the things, etc., against tea. But the weather was so very fine we were tempted by the open door to go out into the air.

Miss Planta said she would take a walk; Mr. Fairly could not, but all without was so beautiful he would not go into the

parlour, and rather risked the fatigue of standing, as he leant against the porch, to losing the lovely prospect of sweet air.

And here, for near two hours, on the steps of Fauconberg Hall, we remained; and they were two hours of such pure serenity, without and within, as I think, except in Norbury park, with its loved inhabitants and my Susan, I scarce ever remember to have spent. Higher gaiety and greater happiness many and many periods of my life have at different times afforded me; but a tranquillity more perfect has only, I think, been lent to me in Norbury park, where, added to all else that could soothe and attract, every affection of my heart could be expanded and indulged. But what have I to do with a comparison no longer cherished but by memory

The time I have mentioned being past, Miss Planta returned from her walk, and we adjourned to the little parlour, where I made tea, and then I equipped myself for the play.

The sweet Miss Port received me with her usual kind joy, and introduced me to her friends, who are Mr. Delabere, the master of the house, and chief magistrate of Cheltenham, and his family.

We all proceeded to the play-house, which is a very pretty little theatre. Mrs. Jordan played the "Country Girl," most admirably; but the play is so disagreeable in Its whole plot and tendency, that all the merit of her performance was insufficient to ward off disgust.(286) My principal end, however, was wholly answered, in spending the evening with my poor M——. . . .

Lady Harcourt is come to take the place of Lady Weymouth, whose waiting is over; and Lord Harcourt will lodge in the town of Cheltenham. We have no room here for double accommodations.

ROYAL CONCERN FOR THE COLONEL's GOUT.

Sunday, July 27.-This morning in my first attendance I seized a moment to tell her majesty of yesterday's dinner.

"So I hear!" she cried; and I was sorry any one had anticipated my information, nor can I imagine who it might be.

"But pray, ma'am," very gravely, how did it happen ? I understood
Mr. Fairly was confined by the gout."

"He grew better, ma'am, and hoped by exercise to prevent a serious fit."

She said no more, but did not seem pleased. The fatigues of a Court attendance are so little comprehended, that persons known to be able to quit their room and their bed are Instantly concluded to be qualified for all the duties of their office.

We were again very early, as their majesties meant to go to the cathedral at Glouces-ter, where the Bishop of Gloucester, Dr. Halifax, was to Preach to them. But I -was particularly glad, before our breakfast, was over, to see Mr. Fairly enter my little parlour. He was Still In his gouty Shoe, and assisted by a stick, but he had not suffered from his yesterday's exertion.

Before the things were removed, a page opened the door, and all the royal family–king, queen, and three princesses–came into the room to see Mr. Fairly and Inquire how he did. I hardly know with which of the five he is most in favour, or by which most respected, and they all expressed their concern for this second attack, in the kindest terms.

The king, however, who has a flow of spirits at this time quite unequalled, would fain have turned the whole into ridicule, and have persuaded him he was only fanciful.

"Fanciful, Sir?" he repeated, a little displeased; and the good king perceiving it, graciously and good-humouredly drew back his words, by saying "Why I should wonder indeed if you were to be that!"

When they all decamped I prepared for church. I had appointed to go with Miss Port, and to meet her on the road. Mr. Fairly said, if I would give him leave, he would stay and write letters in my little parlour. I supplied him with materials, and emptied my queen's writing-box for a desk, as we possess nothing here but a low dining-table. So away went journals, letters, memorandums, etc., into the red portfolio given me by my dear father.

As soon as I presented him with this, not at all aware of the goods and chattels removed for the occasion, he said it was so very comfortable he should now write all his letters here, for at his lodgings he had such a miserable low table he had been forced to prop it up by brick-bats!

Mr. Fairly sealed and made up his dispatches, and then said he would stroll a little out to put his foot in motion. "And what," he asked, "shall you do?"

I had a great mind to say, Why, stroll with you; for that, I think, was the meaning OF his question; but I feared it might prevent my being dressed against the return Of the queen, and I do not think she would have thought it an adequate excuse.

YOUNG REPUBLICANS CONVERTED.

Monday, July 28.–Miss Ogle acquainted me that this was the last day of her remaining at Cheltenham, and I promised to drink tea with her in the afternoon; and the queen honoured me with a commission to bring Mrs. Ogle on the walks, as his majesty wished again to see her. . . .

I found Mrs. Ogle and her daughters all civility and good humour. Poor Mrs. Ogle has lately (by what means I do not know) wholly lost her eye-sight; but she is perfectly resigned to this calamity, and from motives just such as suit a bishop's daughter. When I told her who desired her to be on the walks, she was extremely gratified. Spotty is a complete rebel, according to the principles of her republican father, and protested it would only be a folly and fuss to go, for their notice. The younger sisters are bred rebels too; but the thought of guiding their mother, when such royal distinction was intended her, flattered and fluctuated them. There was another lady with them, who told me that Dr. Warton, of Winchester, had desired her to make acquaintance with me; but I have forgotten her name, and have no time to refresh my memory with it.

To the walks we went, the good and pious Mrs. Ogle between her two young daughters, and Spotty and I together. Spotty begged me to go to the ball with her, but I had neither licence nor inclination.

The queen immediately espied Mrs. Ogle, by seeing me, as I heard her say to the king; and they approached the spot where we stood, in the most gracious manner. The king spoke with such kindness to Mrs. Ogle, and with such great regard

of her late father, that the good lady was most deeply affected with pleasure. I believe they stayed half an hour with her, talking over old scenes and circumstances.

Spotty kept pulling me all the time, to decamp; but I kept "invincible,"–not quite like Mr. Pitt, yet "invincible." At last the king spoke to her: this confused her so much, between the pleasure of the notice, and the shame of feeling that pleasure, that she knew not what she either did or said, answered everything wrong, and got out of the line, and stood with her back to the queen, and turned about she knew not why, and behaved like one who had lost her wits.

When they left us, Mrs. Ogle expressed her grateful sense of the honour done her, almost with tears ; the two young ones said, they had never conceived the king and queen could be such sweet people and poor Spotty was so affected and so constrained in denying them praise, and persisting that she thought it "all a bore," that I saw the republican heart was gone, though the tongue held its ground.

A second time, after a few more turns, the same gracious party approached, with fresh recollections and fresh questions concerning interesting family matters. This was more than could be withstood; Mrs. Ogle was almost overpowered by their condescension; the young ones protested they should never bear to hear anything but praise of them all their lives to come and poor Spotty was quite dumb! She could not, for shame, join the chorus of praise, and to resist it she had no longer any power.

We did not, however, stop here; for still a third time they advanced, and another conference ensued, in which Mrs. Ogle's sons were inquired for, and their way of life, and designs and characters. This ended and completed the whole; Mrs. Ogle no longer restrained the tears of pleasure from flowing; her little daughters declared, aloud, the king and queen were the two most sweet persons in the whole world, and they would say so as long as they lived; and poor Spotty, colouring and conscious, said– "But I hope I did not behave so bad this time as the first?" Nay, so wholly was she conquered, that, losing her stubbornness more and more by reflection, she would not let me take leave till she obliged me to promise I would either call the next morning, before their departure, or write her a little note, to say if they found out or mentioned her ungraciousness.

I was too well pleased in the convert to refuse her this satis-

action; and so full was her mind of her new loyalty, that when she found me steady in declining to go with her to the ball, she gave it up herself, and said she would go home with her mother and sisters, to talk matters over.

THE PRINCES' ANIMAL SPIRITS.

July 31.—Miss Planta said the Duke of York was expected the next day. This led to much discourse on the princes, in which Mr. Fairly, with his usual but Most uncommon openness, protested there was something in the violence of their animal spirits that Would make him accept no post and no pay to live with them. Their very voices, he said, had a loudness and force that wore him.

Immediately after he made a little attack–a gentle one, Indeed– upon me, for the contrary extreme, of hardly speaking, among strangers at least, so as to be heard. "And why," cried he, "do you speak so low? I used formerly not to catch above a word in a sentence from you." In talking about the princes, he asked me how I managed with them.

Not at all, I said, for since I had resided under the royal roof they were rarely there, and I had merely seen them two or three times.

He congratulated me that I had not been in the family in earlier days, when they all lived together; and Miss Planta enumerated various of their riots, and the distresses and difficulties they caused in the household.

I was very glad, I said, to be out of the way, though I did not doubt but I might have kept clear of them had I been even then a resident.

"O no, no," cried Mr. Fairly; "they would have come to you, I promise you; and what could you have done–what would have become of you?–with Prince William in particular? Do you not think, Miss Planta, the Prince of Wales and Prince William would have been quite enough for Miss Burney? Why she would have been quite subdued."

I assured him I had not a fear but I might always have avoided them.

"Impossible! They would have come to your tea-room."

"I would have given up tea."

"Then they would have followed you–called for you–sent for you–the Prince of Wales would have called about him, 'Here ! where's Miss Burney?'"

"O, no, no, no!" cried I; "I would have kept wholly out of the way, and then they would never have thought about me."

"O, ho!" cried he, laughing, "never think of seeing Miss Burney Prince William, too! what say you to that, Miss Planta?

She agreed there was no probability of such escape. I was only the more glad to have arrived in later times.

Here a page came to call Mr. Fairly to backgammon with his majesty.

THE DUKE OF YORK: ROYAL VISIT TO THE THEATRE. Friday, Aug. 1.-This was a very busy day; the Duke of York was expected, and his fond father had caused a portable wooden house to be moved from the further end of Cheltenham town up to join to Fauconber, Hall. The task had employed twenty or thirty men almost ever since our arrival, and so laborious, slow, difficult, and all but impracticable had it proved, that it was barely accomplished before it was wanted. There was no room, however, in the king's actual dwelling, and he could not endure not to accommodate his son immediately next himself.

His joy upon his arrival was such joy as I have only seen here when he arrived first from Germany; I do not mean it was equally violent, or, alas! equally unmixed, but yet it was next and nearest to that which had been most perfect.

Mr. Bunbury attended his royal highness. We had all dispersed from breakfast, but the king came in, and desired me to make him some. Mr. Fairly had brought him to my little parlour, and, having called Columb, and assisted in arranging a new breakfast, he left us, glad, I suppose, of a morning to himself, for his majesty was wholly engrossed by the duke.

We talked over his usual theme–plays and players–and he languished to go to the theatre and see Mrs. Jordan. Nor did he languish in vain: his royal master, the duke, imbibed his wishes, and conveyed them to the king; and no sooner were they known than an order was hastily sent to the play-house, to prepare a royal box. The queen was so gracious as to order Miss Planta and myself to have the same entertainment.

The delight of the people that their king and queen should visit this country theatre was the most disinterested I ever witnessed; for though they had not even a glance of their royal countenances, they shouted, huzzaed, and clapped, for

many minutes. The managers had prepared the front boxes for their reception, and therefore the galleries were over them. They made a very full and respectable appearance in this village theatre. The king, queen, Duke of York, and three princesses, were all accommodated with front seats ; Lord Harcourt stood behind the king, Lady Harcourt and Mr. Fairly behind the queen; Lord and Lady Courtown and Lady Pembroke behind the princesses; and at the back, Colonel Gwynn and Mr. Bunbury; Mr. Boulby and Lady Mary were also in the back group.

I was somewhat taken up in observing a lady who sat opposite to me, Miss W—. My Susanna will remember that extraordinary young lady at Bath, whose conduct and conversation I have either written or repeated to her.(287)

I could not see her again without being much struck by another recollection, of more recent and vexatious date. Mrs. Thrale, in one of the letters she has published, and which was written just after I had communicated to her my singular rencontre with this lady, says to Dr. Johnson, "Burney has picked up an infidel, and recommended to her to read 'Rasselas.'

This has a strange sound, but when its circumstances are known, its strangeness ceases; it meant Miss W— and I greatly fear, from the date and the book, she cannot but know the "infidel" and herself are one. I was truly Concerned in reading it, and I now felt almost ashamed as well as concerned in facing her, though her infidelity at that time, was of her own public avowal. Mr. Bunbury is particularly intimate with her, and admires her beyond all women.

AN UN-COURTLY VISITOR.

Miss Planta and myself, by the queen's direction, went in a chaise to see Tewkesbury. We were carried to several very beautiful points of view, all terminating with the noble hills of Malvern; and we visited the cathedral. . . . The pews seem the most unsafe, strange, and irregular that were ever constructed; they are mounted up, story after story, without any order, now large, now small, now projecting out wide, now almost indented in back, nearly to the very roof of the building. They look as if, ready-made, they had been thrown up, and stuck wherever they could, entirely by chance.

We returned home just in time to be hastily dressed before

the royals came back. I was a little, however, distressed on being told, as I descended to dinner, that Mr. Richard Burney(288) was in my parlour. The strict discipline observed here, in receiving no visits, made this a very awkward circumstance, for I as much feared hurting him by such a hint, as concurring in an impropriety by detaining him. Miss Planta suffers not a soul to approach her to this house ; and Lady Harcourt has herself told me she thinks it would be wrong to receive even her sisters, Miss Vernons, so much all-together is now the house and household!

My difficulty was still increased, when, upon entering the parlour, I found him in boots, a riding dress, and hair wholly without curl or dressing. Innocently, and very naturally, he had called upon me in his travelling garb, never suspecting that in visiting me he was at all in danger of seeing or being seen by any one else. Had that indeed been the case, I should have been very glad to see him; but I knew, now, his appearance must prove every way to his disadvantage, and I felt an added anxiety to acquaint him with my situation.

Miss Planta looked all amazement; but he was himself all ease and sprightly unconsciousness.

We were obliged to sit down to dinner; he had dined. I was quite in a panic the whole time, lest any of the royals should come in before I could speak - but, after he had partaken of our dessert, as much en badinage as I could, I asked him if he felt stout enough to meet the king? and then explained to him, as concisely as I had power, that I had here no room whatsoever at my own disposal, in such a manner as to enable my having the happiness to receive any of my private friends even Miss Port, though known to all the royal family,, I could never venture to invite, except when they were abroad: such being, at present, the universal practice and forbearance of all the attendants in this tour.

He heard me with much surprise, and much laughter at his own elegant equipment for such encounters as those to which he now found himself liable; but he immediately proposed decamping, and I could not object, Yet, to soften this disagreeable explanation, I kept him a few minutes longer, settling concerning our further meeting at the concerts- at Worcester, and, in this little interval, we were startled by a rap at my door. He laughed, and started back; and I, alarmed,

also retreated. Miss Planta opened the door, and called out "'Tis Mr. Fairly."

I saw him in amaze at sight of a gentleman; and he was himself immediately retiring, concluding, I suppose, that nothing less than business very urgent could have induced me to break through rules so rigidly observed by himself and all others. I would not, however, let him go . but as I continued talking with Richard about the music meeting and my cousins, he walked up to the window with Miss Planta. I now kept Richard as long as I well could, to help off his own embarrassment at this interruption; at length he went.

MR. FAIRLY READS "AKENSIDE" TO MISS BURNEY. Hearing now the barking of the dogs, I knew the royals must be going forth to their promenade; but I found Mr. Fairly either did not hear or did not heed them. While I expected him every moment to recollect himself, and hasten to the walks, he quietly said, "They are all gone but me. I shall venture, to-night, to shirk;–though the king will soon miss me. But what will follow? He will say–'Fairly is tired! How shabby!' Well! let him say so; I am tired!" Miss Planta went off, soon after, to her walk. He then said, "Have you done with my little book?"

"O yes!" I cried, "and this morning I have sent home the map of Gloucester you were so good as to send us. Though, I believe, I have kept both so long, You will not again be in any haste to lend me either a map of the land, or a poem of the sea." I then gave him back "The Shipwreck."

"Shall I tell you," cried I, "a design I have been forming upon you?"

"A design upon me?"

"Yes; and I may as well own it, for I shall be quite as near success as if I disguise it." I then went to my little drawer and took out Akenside."

"Here," I cried, "I intended to have had this fall in your way, by pure accident, on the evening you were called to the conjurer, and I have planned the same ingenious project every evening since, but it has never taken, and so now I produce it fairly!"

"That," cried he, taking it, with a very pleased smile, "is the only way in all things!"

He then began reading "The Pleasures of the Imagination," and I took some work, for which I was much in haste, and my imagination was amply gratified. He only looked out for favourite passages, as he has the poem almost by heart, and he read them with a feeling and energy that showed his whole soul penetrated with their force and merit.

After the first hour, however, he grew uneasy'; he asked me when I expected the king and queen from their walk, and whether they were likely to come into my room?

"All," I said, "was uncertain."

"Can nobody," he cried, "let you know when they are coming?"

"Nobody," I answered, "would know till they were actually arrived."

"But," cried he, "can you not bid somebody watch?"

'Twas rather an awkward commission, but I felt it would be an awkwardness still less pleasant to me to decline it, and therefore I called Columb, and desired he would let me know when the queen returned.

He was then easier, and laughed a little, while he explained himself, "Should they come in and find me reading here before I could put away my book, they would say we were two blue stockings!"

At tea Miss Planta again joined us, and instantly behind him went the book. He was very right; for nobody would have thought it more odd–or more blue.

During this repast they returned home, but all went straight upstairs, the duke wholly occupying the king - and Mr. Bunbury went to the play. When Miss Planta, therefore, took her evening stroll, "Akenside" again came forth, and with more security.

"There is one ode here," he cried, "that I wish to read to you, and now I think I can."

I told him I did not in general like Akenside's odes, at least what I had chanced to read, for I thought they were too inflated, and filled with "liberty cant."

"But this, however," cried he, "I must read to you, it is so pretty, though it is upon love!"

'Tis addressed to Olympia: I dare say my dearest Fredy recollects it.(289) It is, indeed, most feelingly written; but we

had only got through the first stanza when the door Suddenly opened, and enter Mr. Bunbury.

After all the precautions taken, to have him thus appear at the very worst moment! Vexed as I was, I could really have laughed; but Mr. Fairly was ill disposed to take it so merrily. He started, threw the book forcibly behind him, and instantly took up his hat, as if decamping. I really believe he was afraid Mr. Bunbury would caricature us "The sentimental readers!" or what would he have called us? Luckily this confusion passed unnoticed. Mr. Bunbury had run away from the play to see after the horses, etc., for his duke, and was fearful of coming too late.

plays and players now took up all the discourse, with Miss W–, till the duke was ready to go. They then left me together, Mr. Fairly smiling drolly enough in departing, and looking at "Akenside" with a very arch shrug, as who should say "What a scrape you had nearly drawn me into, Mr. Akenside!"

THE DOCTOR's EMBARRASSMENT.

Sunday, Aug. 3.-This morning I was so violently oppressed by a cold, which turns out to be the influenza, it was with the utmost difficulty I could dress myself. I did indeed now want some assistant most wofully.

The princess royal has already been some days disturbed with this influenza. When the queen perceived it in me she told his majesty, who came into the room just as she was going to breakfast. Without making any answer, he himself went immediately to call Mr. Clerk, the apothecary, who was then with the princess royal.

"Now, Mr. Clerk," cried he, "here's another patient for you."

Mr. Clerk, a modest, sensible man, concluded, by the king himself having called him, that it was the queen he had

now to attend, and he stood bowing profoundly before her but soon observing she did not notice him, he turned in some confusion to the Princess Augusta, who was now in the group.

"No, no! it's not me, Mr. Clerk, thank God!" cried the gay
Princess Augusta.

Still more confused, the poor man advanced to Princess Elizabeth.

"No, no; it's not her!" cried the king.

I had held back, having scarce power to open my eyes, from a vehement head-ache, and not, indeed, wishing to go through my examination till there were fewer witnesses. But his majesty now drew me out.

"Here, Mr. Clerk," he cried, "this is your new patient!"

He then came bowing up to me, the king standing close by, and the rest pretty near.

"You–you are not well, ma'am?" he cried in the greatest embarrassment,

"No, sir, not quite," I answered in ditto.

"O, Mr. Clerk will cure you!" cried the king.

"Are-are you feverish, ma'am?"

"Yes, sir, a little."

"I–I will send you a saline draught, ma'am."

"If you please."

And then he bowed and decamped.

Did you ever hear a more perfectly satisfactory examination? The poor modest man was overpowered by such royal listeners and spectators, and I could not possibly relieve him, for I was little better myself.

I went down to breakfast, but was so exceedingly oppressed I could not hold up my head, and as soon as I could escape I went to my own room, and laid down till my noon attendance, which I performed with so much difficulty I was obliged to return to the same indulgence the moment I was at liberty.

FROM GRAVE TO GAY.

Down at last I went, slow and wrapped up. I found Mr. Fairly alone in the parlour, reading letters with such intentness that he did not raise his head, and with an air of the deepest dejection. I remained wholly unnoticed a considerable time; but at last he looked up, and with some surprise, but a voice OF of extreme sadness, he said, "Is that Miss Burney? I thought it had been Miss Planta."

I begged him to read on, and not mind me; and I called for tea. When we had done tea, "See, ma'am," he cried, "I have brought You 'Carr,' and here is a sermon upon the text I mean, when I preach, to choose 'Keep innocency, and take heed to the thing that is right; for that will bring a man peace at the last.'"

Sincerely I commended his choice ; and we had a most solemn discussion of happiness, not such as coincides with gaiety here, but hope of salvation hereafter. His mind has so religious a propensity, that it seems to me, whenever he leaves it to its natural bent, to incline immediately and instinctively to subjects of that holy nature.

Humility, he said, in conclusion, humility was all in all for tranquillity of mind; with that, little was expected and much was borne, and the smallest good was a call for gratitude and content. How could this man be a soldier? Might one not think he was bred in the cloisters?

"Well," cried he, again taking up the volume of "Carr," "I will just sit and read this sermon, and then quietly go home."

He did so, feelingly, forcibly, solemnly; it is an excellent sermon; yet so read–he so sad, and myself so ill–it was almost too much for me, and I had some difficulty to behave with proper propriety. To him subjects of this sort, ill or well, bring nothing, I believe, but strength as well as comfort. The voice of dejection with which he began changed to one of firmness ere he had read three pages.

Something he saw of unusual sinking, notwithstanding what I hid; and, with a very kind concern, when he had finished the sermon, he said, "Is there anything upon your spirits?"

"No," I assured him, "but I was not well; and mind and body seemed to go together sometimes, when they did not."

"But they do go together," cried he, "and will."

However, he took no further- notice: he is like me, for myself, in that–that whatever he thinks only bodily is little worth attention; and I did not care to risk explaining to his strong and virtuous mind the many fears and mixed sensations of mine, when brought to a close disquisition of awaiting eternity.

I never, but with Mrs. Delany and Dr. Johnson, have entered so fully and so frequently upon this awful subject as

Page 198 with Mr. Fairly. My dear and most revered Mrs. Delany dwelt upon it continually, with joy, and pure, yet humble hope. My ever-honoured Dr. Johnson recurred to it perpetually, with a veneration compounded of diffidence and terror, and an incessant, yet unavailing plan, of amending all errors, and rising into perfection. Mr. Fairly leans upon it as the staff of his strength–the trust, the hope, the rest of his soul–too big for satisfaction in aught this world has given, or can reserve for him. '

He did not, however, "go quietly home," when he had finished the sermon; on the contrary, he revived in his spirits, and animated in his discourse, and stayed on.

In speaking of the king he suddenly recollected some very fine lines of Churchill, made on his accession to the throne. I wish I could transcribe them, they are so applicable to that good king, from that moment of promise to the present of performance. But I know not in what part of Churchill's works they may be found.

Finding me unacquainted with his poems he then repeated several passages, all admirably chosen ; but among them his memory called forth some that were written upon Lord H–, which were of the bitterest severity I ever heard:–whether deserved or not, Heaven knows; but Mr. Fairly said he would repeat them, for the merit of the composition. There was no examining his opinion of their veracity, and he made no comments; but this: Lord H– was the famous man so often in the House of Commons accused of expending, or retaining, unaccounted millions

Having run through all he could immediately recollect, he said, with a very droll smile, "Come, now I'll finish our ode," and went to my drawer for "Akenside."

His fears of surprise, however, again came upon him so strongly while reading it, that he flung away the book in the utmost commotion at every sound, lest any one was entering, always saying in excuse, "We must not be called two blue stockings;" and, "They are so glad to laugh; the world is so always on the watch for ridicule." . . .

I know not by what means, but after this we talked over Mr. Hastings's trial. I find he is very much acquainted with Mr. Windham, and I surprised him not a little, I saw, by what I told him of part Of My conferences with that gentleman.

This matter having led us from our serious subjects, he took up "Akenside" once more, and read to me the first book throughout, What a very, very charming poem is the "Pleasures of the Imagination!" He stayed to the last moment, and left me all the better for the time he thus rescued from feverish lassitude and suffering.

A VISIT TO WORCESTER.

Tuesday, Aug. 5-The journey to Worcester was very pleasant, and the country through which we passed extremely luxuriant and pretty. We did not go in by the Barborne road ; but all the road, and all avenues leading to it, were lined with people, and when we arrived at the city we could see nothing but faces ; they lined the windows from top to bottom, and the pavement from end to end.

We drove all through the city to come to the palace of Bishop Hurd, at which we were to reside. Upon stopping there, the king had an huzza that seemed to vibrate through the whole town ; the princess royal's carriage had a second, and the equerries a third; the mob then, as ours drew on in succession, seemed to deliberate whether or not we also should have a cheer: but one of them soon decided the matter by calling out, "These are the maids of honour!" and immediately they gave us an huzza that made us quite ashamed, considering its vicinity.

Mr. Fairly and Colonel Goldsworthy having performed the royal attendance, waited to hand us out of the carriage ; and then the former said he believed he should not be wanted, and would go and make a visit in the town. I should have much liked walking off also, and going to my cousins at Barborne Lodge; but I was no free agent, and obliged to wait for commands.

The house is old and large; part of it looks to the Severn but the celebrated "Fair Sabrina" was so thick and muddy, that at this time her vicinity added but little to the beauty of the situation.

My bed-room is pleasant, with a view of the distant country and the Severn beneath it; but it is through that of the princess royal; which is an inconvenience her royal

highness submits to with a grace that would make me ashamed to call it one to myself. The parlour for our eating is large and dark, and old-fashioned. I made tea in it to-night for Lord Courtown and the two colonels, and Miss Planta, and was so much the
better for my journey, that I felt the influenza nearly conquered.

Wednesday, Aug. 6.-I had the pleasure to arrange going to the music meeting with my own family. Notes were immediately interchanged from and to Barborne Lodge, and the queen was very well pleased that I should have this opportunity of joining my friends. Mr. and Mrs. Hawkins and Betsy called for me at the bishop's.

I was heartily glad to see Betsy and Mrs. Hawkins I introduced Miss Planta to them, who was of our party. We sat in what are called the steward's places, immediately under their majesties. The performance was very long, and tolerably tedious, consisting of Handel's gravest pieces and fullest choruses, and concluding with a sermon concerning the institution of the charity, preached by Dr. Langhorne. I was, however, so glad to be with my cousins, that the morning was very comfortable and pleasant to me. Richard and James joined us occasionally.; the rest of the family are at Shrewsbury.

It was over very late, and we then went about the church, to see King John's tomb, etc, They were very earnest with me to go to Barborne but it was impossible. I promised, however, to accompany them to the concert at night, and be of their party to all the morning meetings at the cathedral. '

My parlour at the bishop's afforded me a good deal of entertainment, from observing the prodigious concourse of people from all the tops of houses, and looking over the walls to watch his majesty's entrance into the court-yard. Poor Lord Courtown, on account of his star, was continually taken for the king, and received so many huzzas and shouts, that he hardly dared show himself except when in attendance.

THE QUEEN AND MR. FAIRLY.

Saturday, Aug. 9.-Her majesty this morning a little surprised me by gravely asking me what were Mr. Fairly's designs with regard to his going away ? I could not tell her I did not know what I was really acquainted with; yet I feared it might seem odd to her that I should be better informed than herself, and it was truly unpleasant to me to relate anything he had told me without his leave. Her question, therefore, gave me a painful sensation; but it was spoken with an air so strongly denoting a belief that I had power to answer it, that I felt no choice in making a plain reply. Simply, then, "I understand,

ma'am," I said, "that he means to go to-morrow morning early."

"Will he stay on to-night, then, at Worcester?"

"N-o, ma'am, I believe not."

"I thought he meant to leave us to-day? He said so."

"He intended it, ma'am,–he would else not have said it."

"I know I understood so, though he has not spoke to me of his designs this great while."

I saw an air bordering upon displeasure as this was said and how sorry I felt!–and how ashamed of being concluded the person better informed! Yet, as he had really related to me his plan, and I knew it to be what he had thought most respectful to herself, I concluded it best, thus catechised, to speak it all, and therefore, after some hesitation uninterrupted by her, I said, "I believe, ma'am, Mr. Fairly had intended fully to begin his journey to-day, but, as Your majesty is to go to the play to-night, he thinks it his duty to defer setting out till to-morrow, that he may have the honour to attend your majesty as usual."

This, which was the exact truth, evidently pleased her.

Here the inquiry dropped; but I was very uneasy to relate it to Mr. Fairly, that the sacrifice I knew he meant to make of another day might not lose all its grace by wanting to be properly revealed.

MR. FAIRLY MORALIZES.

Our journey back to Cheltenham was much more quiet than it had been to Worcester, for the royal party too], another route to see Malvern hills, and we went straight forward.

Miss Planta having now caught the influenza, suffered very much all the way, and I persuaded her immediately to lie down when we got to Fauconberg Hall. She could not come down to dinner, which I had alone. The Princess Elizabeth came to me after it, with her majesty's permission that I might go to the play with my usual party ; but I declined it, that I might make some tea for poor Miss Planta, as she had no maid, nor any creature to help her. The princess told me they were all going first upon the walks, to promener till the play time.

I sat down to make my solitary tea, and had just sent up a basin to Miss Planta, when, to my equal surprise and pleasure, Mr. Fairly entered the room. "I come now," he said, "to take my leave."

They were all, he added, gone to the walks, whither he must

in a few minutes follow them, and thence attend to the play, and the next morning, by five o'clock, be ready for his post-chaise. Seeing me, however, already making tea, with his Usual and invariable sociability he said he would venture to stay and partake, though he was only come, he gravely repeated, to take his leave.

"And I must not say," cried I, "that I am sorry you are going, because I know so well you wish to be gone that it makes me wish it for you myself."

"No," answered he, "you must not be sorry; when our friends are going to any joy. We must think of them, and be glad to part with them."

Readily entering the same tone, with similar plainness of truth I answered, No, I will not be sorry you go, though miss you at Cheltenham I certainly must."

"Yes," was his unreserved assent, "you will miss me here, because I have spent my evenings with you; but You Will not long remain at Cheltenham."

Oim'e!" thought I, you little think how much Worse will be the quitting it. He owned that the bustle and fatigue of this life was too much both for his health and his spirits.

I told him I Wished it might be a gratification to him, in his toils, to hear how the queen always spoke of him; With what evident and constant complacency and distinction. "And you may credit her sincerity," I added, "Since it is to so little a person as me she does this, and when no one else is present."

He was not insensible to this, though he passed it over without much answer. He showed me a letter from his second son, very affectionate and natural. I congratulated him, most sincerely, on his approaching happiness in collecting them all together.

"Yes he answered, "my group will increase, like a snow-ball, as I roll along, and they will soon all four be as happy as four little things know how to be."

This drew him on into some reflections upon affection and upon happiness. "There is no happiness," he said, "without participation; no participation without affection. There is, indeed, in affection a charm that leaves all things behind it, and renders even every calamity that does not interfere with it inconsequential and there is no difficulty, no toil, no labour, no exertion, that will not be endured where there is a view of reaping it."

He ruminated some time, and then told me of a sermon he had heard preached some months ago, sensibly demonstrating

the total vanity and insufficiency, even for this world, of all our best affections, and proving their fallibility from our most infirm humanity.

My concurrence did not here continue: I cannot hold this doctrine to be right, and I am most sure it is not desirable. our best affections, I must and do believe, were given us for the best purposes, for every stimulation to good, and every solace in evil.

But this was not a time for argument. I said nothing, while he, melancholy and moralizing, continued in this style as long as he could venture to stay. He then rose and took his hat, saying, " Well, so much for the day; what may come to-morrow I know not; but, be it what it may, I stand prepared."

I hoped, I told him, that his little snowball would be all he could wish it, and I was heartily glad he would so soon collect it.

"We will say," cried he, "nothing of any regrets," and bowed, and was hastening off.

The "we," however, had an openness and simplicity that drew from me an equally open and simple reply. "No," I cried, "but I will say-for that you will have pleasure in hearing that you have lightened my time here in a manner that no one else could have done, of this party."

To be sure this was rather a circumscribed compliment, those he left considered - but it was strict and exact truth, and therefore like his own dealing. He said not a word of answer, but bowed, and went away, leaving me firmly impressed with a belief that I shall find in him a true, an honourable, and even an affectionate friend, for life.

MAJOR PRICE IS TIRED OF RETIREMENT.

Sunday, Aug. 10.-Major Price was of the breakfast party this morning, to my great contentment. I heartily wish he was again in the king's household, he is so truly attached to his majesty, and he so earnestly himself wishes for a restoration, not to the equerryship, which is too laborious an office, but to any attendance upon the king's person of less fatigue.

He opened to me very much upon his situation and wishes. he has settled himself in a small farm near the house of his eldest brother, but I could see too plainly he has not found there the contentment that satisfies him. He sighs for society ; he owns books are insufficient for everything, and his evenings

Page 204 begin already to grow wearisome. He does not wish it to be talked of publicly, but he is solicitous to return to the king, in any place attached to his person, of but mild duty. Not only the king, he said, he loved, but all his society, and the way of life in general; and he had no tie whatsoever to Herefordshire that would make him hesitate a moment in quitting it, if another place could be made adequate to his fortune. His income was quite too small for any absence from his home of more than a few weeks, in its present plight; and therefore it could alone be by some post under government that he must flatter himself with ever returning to the scenes he had left.

How rarely does a plan of retirement answer the expectations upon which it is raised! He fears having this suspected, and therefore keeps the matter to himself; but I believe he so much opened it to me, in the hope I might have an opportunity to make it known where it might be efficacious; for he told me, at the same time, he apprehended his majesty had a notion his fondness for Herefordshire, not his inability to continue equerry, had occasioned his resignation.

I shall certainly make it my business to hint this to the queen. So faithful and attached a servant ought not to be thrown aside, and, after nine years' service, left unrewarded, and seem considered as if superannuated.

MR. FAIRLY'S LITTLE NOTE.

When I came from her majesty, just before she went down to dinner, I was met by a servant who delivered me a letter, which he told me was just come by express. I took it in some alarm, fearing that ill news alone could bring it by such haste, but, before I could open it, he said, "'Tis from Mr. Fairly, ma'am."

I hastened to read, and will now copy it:-

"Northleach, Aug. 10, 1788. "Her majesty may possibly not have heard that Mr. Edmund Waller died on Thursday night. He was master of St. Catherine's, which is in her majesty's gift. It may be useful to her to have this early intelligence of this circumstance, and you will have the goodness to mention it to her. Mr. W. was at a house upon his own estate within a mile and a half of this place, Very truly and sincerely yours, "S. Fairly." "Miss Burney, Fauconberg Hall."

How to communicate this news, however, was a real distress to me. I know her majesty is rather scrupulous that all messages immediately to herself should be conveyed by the highest channels, and I feared she would think this ought to have been sent through her lady then in waiting, Lady Harcourt. Mr. Fairly, too, however superior to such small matters for himself, is most punctiliously attentive to them for her. I could attribute this only to haste. But my difficulty was not alone to have received the intelligence-the conclusion of the note I was sure would surprise her. The rest, as a message to herself, being without any beginning, would not strike her; but the words "very truly and sincerely yours," come out with such an abrupt plainness, and to her, who knows not with what intimacy of intercourse we have lived together so much during this last month, I felt quite ashamed to show them.

While wavering how to manage, a fortunate circumstance seemed to come to my relief; the Princess Elizabeth ran up hastily to her room, which is just opposite to mine, before she followed the queen down to dinner; I flew after her, and told her I had just heard of the death of Mr. Waller, the Master of St. Catherine's, and I begged her to communicate it to her majesty.

She undertook it, with her usual readiness to oblige, and I was quite delighted to have been so speedy without producing my note, which I determined now not even to mention unless called upon, and even then not to produce; for now, as I should not have the first telling, it might easily be evaded by not having it in my pocket.

The moment, however, that the dinner was over, Princess Elizabeth came to summon me to the queen. This was very unexpected, as I thought I should not see her till night; but I locked up my note and followed.

She was only with the princesses. I found the place was of importance, by the interest she took about it. She asked me several questions relative to Mr. Waller. I answered her all I could collect from my note, for further never did I hear; but the moment I was obliged to stop she said, "Pray have you known him long?"

"I never knew him at all, ma'am."

"No? Why, then, how came you to receive the news about his death?"

Was not this agreeable? I was forced to say, "I heard of it only from Mr. Fairly, ma'am."

Page 206 Nothing Could exceed the surprise with which she now lifted up her eyes to look at me. "From Mr. Fairly?–Why did he not tell it me?"

O, worse and worse! I was now compelled to answer, "He did not know It when he was here, ma'am; he heard it at Northleach, and, thinking it might be of use to your majesty to have the account immediately, he sent it over express."

A dead silence so uncomfortable ensued, that I thought it best presently to go on further, though unasked. "Mr. Fairly, ma'am, wrote the news to me, on such small paper, and in such haste, that it is hardly fit to he shown to your majesty; but I have the note upstairs."

No answer; again all silent; and then Princess Augusta said,
"Mamma, Miss Burney says she has the note upstairs."

"If your majesty pleases to see it"–

She looked up again, much more pleasantly, and said, "I shall be glad to see it," with a little bow.

Out I went for it, half regretting I had not burned it, to make the producing it impossible. When I brought it to her, she received it with the most gracious smile, and immediately read it aloud, with great complacency, till she came to the end and then, with a lowered and somewhat altered tone, the "very truly and sincerely yours," which she seemed to look at for a moment with some doubt if it were not a mistake, but in returning it she bowed again, and simply said, "I am very much obliged to Mr. Fairly."

You will be sure how much I was pleased during this last week to hear that the place of the Master of St. Catherine's was given by her majesty to Mr. Fairly. It is reckoned the best in her gift, as a sinecure. What is the income I know not: reports differ from 400 to 500 per annum.

THE RETURN TO WINDSOR.

Saturday, Aug. 16.-We left Cheltenham early this morning. Major Price breakfasted with us, and was so melancholy at the king's departure he could hardly speak a word. All Cheltenham was drawn out into the High-street, the gentles on one side and the commons on the other, and a band, and "God save the king," playing and singing.

My dear Port, with all her friends, was there for a last look, and a sorrowful one we interchanged; Mr. Seward also, whom again I am not likely to meet for another two years at least.

The journey was quite without accident or adventure.

And thus ends the Cheltenham episode. May I not justly call it so, different as it is to all the mode of life I have hitherto lived here, or alas I am in a way to live henceforward?

melancholy–most melancholy-was the return to Windsor destitute of all that could solace, compose, or delight ; replete with whatever could fatigue, harass, and depress! Ease, leisure, elegant society, and interesting communication, were now to give place to arrogant manners, contentious disputation, and arbitrary ignorance! Oh, heaven! my dearest friends, what scales could have held and have weighed the heart of your F.B. as she drove past the door of her revered, lost comforter, to enter the apartment inhabited by such qualities!

But before I quit this journey let me tell one very pleasant anecdote. When we stopped to change horses at Burford I alighted and went into the inn, to meet Mrs. Gast, to whom I had sent by Mrs. Frodsham a request to be there as we passed through the town. I rejoiced indeed to see again the sister of our first and wisest friend. My Susanna, who knows her too enthusiastic character, will easily suppose my reception. I was folded in her arms, and bathed in her tears all my little stay, and my own, from reflected tenderness for her ever-honoured, loved, and lamented brother, would not be kept quite back; 'twas a species of sorrowful joy–painful, yet pleasing–that seemed like a fresh tribute to his memory and my affection, and made the meeting excite an emotion that occupied my mind and reflections almost all the rest of my journey.

She inquired most kindly after my dear father and my Susanna, and separately and with interest of all the rest of the family; but her surprise to see me now, by this most un expected journey, when she had concluded me inevitably shut up from her sight for the remainder of her life, joined to the natural warmth of her disposition, seemed almost to suffocate her. I was very sorry to leave her, but my time was unavoidably short and hurried. I inquired after Chesington, and heard very good accounts.

AT WINDSOR AGAIN THE CANON AND MRS. SCHWELLENBERG. Windsor, Sunday, Aug. 17.-This day, after our arrival, began precisely the same as every day preceding our journey. The Sleeping Beauty in the Wood could not awake more completely to the same scene; yet I neither have been asleep, nor Page 208 am quite a beauty! O! I wish I were as near to the latter as the former at this minute!

We had all the set assembled to congratulate his majesty on his return–generals and colonels without end. I was very glad while the large party lasted, its diminution into a solitary pair ending in worse than piquet–a tête-à-tête!–and such a one, too! after being so spoiled!

Monday, Aug. 18.-Well, now I have a new personage to introduce to you, and no small one; ask else the stars, moon and planets! While I was surrounded with band-boxes, and unpacking, Dr. Shepherd was announced. Eager to make his compliments on the safe return, he forced a passage through the back avenues and stairs, for he told me he did not like being seen coming to me at the front door, as it might create some jealousies amongst the other canons! A very commendable circumspection! but whether for my sake or his own he did not particularize.

M. de Lalande, he said, the famous astronomer,(290) was just arrived in England, and now at Windsor, and he had expressed a desire to be introduced to me.

Well, while he was talking this over, and I was wondering and evading, entered Mr. Turbulent. What a surprise at sight of the reverend canon! The reverend canon, also, was interrupted and confused, fearing, possibly, the high honour he did me might now transpire amongst his brethren, notwithstanding his generous efforts to spare them its knowledge.

Mr. Turbulent, who looked big with heroics, was quite provoked to see he had no chance of giving them vent. They each outstayed the patience of the other, and at last both went off together.

Some hours after, however, while I was dressing, the canon returned. I could not admit him, and bid Goter tell him at the door I was not visible. He desired he might wait till I was ready, as he had business of importance. I would not let him into the next room, but said he might stay in the eating-parlour.

When I was dressed I sent Goter to bring him in. She came back, grinning and colouring,; she had not found him, she said, but only Mrs. Schwellenberg, who was there alone, and had

called her in to know what she wanted. She answered she came to seek for a gentleman.

"There's no gentleman," she cried, "to come into my parlour. it is not permit. When he comes I will have it locked up."

O, ho, my poor careful canon! thought I. However, soon after a tap again at my door introduced him. He said he had been waiting below in the passage, as he saw Madame Schwellenberg in the parlour, and did not care to have her know him; but his business was to settle bringing M. de Lalande to see me in the evening. I told him I was much honoured, and so forth, but that I received no evening company, as I was officially engaged.

He had made the appointment, he said, and could not break it without affronting him; besides, he gave me to understand it would be an honour to me for ever to be visited by so great an astronomer. I agreed as to that, and was forced, moreover, to agree to all the rest, no resource remaining

I mentioned to her majesty the state of the case. She thought the canon very officious, and disapproved the arrangement, but saw it was unavoidable.

But when the dinner came I was asked by the présidente, "What for send you gentlemen to my parlour?"

" I was dressing, ma'am, and could not possibly receive company in mine, and thought the other empty."

"Empty or full is the same! I won't have it. I will lock up the room when it is done so. No, no, I won't have no gentlemen here; it is not permit, perticklere when they Nvon't not speak to me!"

I then heard that "a large man, what you call," had entered that sacred domain, and seeing there a lady, had quitted it "bob short!"

I immediately explained all that had passed, for I had no other way to save myself from an imputation of favouring the visits and indiscretion of this most gallant canon.

"Vell, when he comes so often he might like you. For what won't you not marry him?"

This was coming to the point, and so seriously, I found myself obliged to be serious in answer, to avoid misconstruction, and to assure her, that were he Archbishop of Canterbury, and actually at my feet, I would not become archbishopess.

"Vell, you been right when you don't not like him; I don't not like the men neither: not one from them!"

So this settled us very amicably till tea-time, and in the midst of that, with a room full of people, I was called out by Westerhaults to Dr. Shepherd!

Mrs. Schwellenberg herself actually te-he'd at this, and I could not possibly help laughing myself, but I hurried into the next room, where I found him with his friend, M. de Lalande. What a reception awaited me! how unexpected a one from a famed and great astronomer.

COMPLIMENTS FROM A FAMOUS FOREIGN ASTRONOMER. M. de Lalande advanced to meet me—I will not be quite positive it was on tiptoe, but certainly with a mixture of jerk and strut that could not be quite flat-footed. He kissed my hand with the air of a petit-maître, and then broke forth into such an harangue of éloges, so solemn with regard to its own weight and importance, and so fade(291) with respect to the little personage addressed, that I could not help thinking it lucky for the planets, stars, and sun, they were not bound to hear his comments, though obliged to undergo his calculations.

On my part sundry profound reverences, with now and then an "O, monsieur!" or "c'est trop d'honneur," acquitted me so well, that the first harangue being finished, on the score of general and grand reputation, éloge the second began, on the excellency with which "cette célèbre demoiselle" spoke French!

This may surprise you, my dear friends; but You must consider M. de Lalande is a great discoverer.

Well, but had you seen Dr. Shepherd! he looked lost in sleek delight and wonder, that a person to whom he had introduced M. de Lalande should be an object for such fine speeches.

This gentleman's figure, meanwhile, corresponds no better with his discourse than his scientific profession, for he is an ugly little wrinkled old man, with a fine showy waistcoat, rich lace ruffles, and the grimaces of a dentist. I believe he chose to display that a Frenchman of science could be also a man of gallantry.

I was seated between them, but the good doctor made no greater interruption to the florid professor than I did myself; he only grinned applause, with placid, but ineffable satisfaction.

Nothing therefore intervening, éloge the third followed, after a pause no longer than might be necessary for due admiration

of éloge the second. This had for sujet the fair female sex; how the ladies were now all improved; how they could write, and read, and spell; how a man now-a-days might talk with them and be understood, and how delightful it was to see such pretty creatures turned rational!

And all this, of course, interspersed with particular observations and most pointed applications; nor was there in the whole string of compliments which made up the three bouquets, one single one amongst them that might have disgraced any petit maître to utter, or any petite maîtresse to hear.

The third being ended, a rather longer pause ensued. I believe he was dry, but I offered him no tea. I would not voluntarily be accessory to detaining such great personages from higher avocations. I wished him next to go and study the stars: from the moon he seemed so lately arrived there was little occasion for another journey.

I flatter myself he was of the same opinion, for the fourth éloge was all upon his unhappiness in tearing himself away from so much merit, and ended in as many bows as had accompanied his entrance.

I suppose, in going, he said, with a shrug, to the canon, "M. le docteur, c'est bien gênant, mais il faut dire des jolies choses aux dames!"(293)

He was going the next day to see Dr. Maskelyne's observatory.

Well! I have had him first in mine!

I was obliged on my return to the tea-room to undergo much dull raillery from my fair companion, and Much of wonder that "since the canon had such good preferment" I did not "marry him at once," for he "would not come so often if he did not want it."

THE PRINCE EYES MISS BURNEY CURIOUSLY.

Tuesday, Aug. 18.–The Duke of York's birthday was kept this day, instead of Saturday, that Sunday morning might not interfere with the ball.

The Prince of Wales arrived early, while I was yet with the queen. He kissed her hand, and she sent for the princesses. Only Princess Elizabeth and Princess Sophia were dressed. Her majesty went into the next room with Mrs. Sandys, to have her shoes put on, with which she always finishes. The prince and princesses then chatted away most fluently. Page 212

Princess Elizabeth frequently addressed me with great sweetness but the prince only with curious eyes. Do not, however, understand that his looks were either haughty or impertinent far from it ; they were curious, however, in the extreme.

COLONEL MANNERS'S BEATING.

Colonel Manners made me laugh as If I had been at a farce, by his history of the late Westminster election, in which Lord John Townshend conquered Lord Hood. Colonel Manners is a most eager and active partisan on the side of the government, but so indiscreet, that he almost regularly gets his head broke at every contested election; and he relates it as a thing of course. I inquired if he pursued his musical studies, so happily begun with Colonel Wellbred? "Why," answered he, "not much, because of the election; but the thing is, to get an ear: however, I think I have got one, because I know a tune when I hear it, if it's one that I've heard before a good many times so I think that's a proof. but I can never get asked to a concert, and that keeps me a little behind."

"Perhaps," cried I, "your friends conclude you have music enough in your three months' waiting to satisfy you for all the year?"

"O, ma'am, as to that, I'd just as lief hear so many pots and pans rattled together; one noise is just as well as another to me."

I asked him whether his electioneering with so much activity did not make his mother, Lady Robert, a little uneasy?–N.B. She is a methodist.

"O, it does her a great deal of good," cried he;"for I could never get her to meddle before ; but when I'd had my head broke, it provoked her so, she went about herself canvassing among the good people,–and she got us twenty votes."

"So then," cried Colonel Goldsworthy, "there are twenty good people in the world? That's your calculation, is it?"

Mr. Fisher, who just then came in, and knew nothing of what had passed, starting the election, said to Colonel Manners, "So, sir, you have been beat, I hear!"

He meant only his party ; but his person having shared the same fate, occasioned a violent shout among the rest at this innocent speech, and its innocent answer - for Colonel Man-

Page 213 ners, looking only a little surprised, simply said, "Yes, I was beat, a little."

"A little, sir?" exclaimed Mr. Fisher, "no, a great deal you were shamefully beat– thrashed thoroughly." In the midst of a violent second shout, Colonel Manners only said, "Well, I always hated all that party, and now I hate them worse than ever."

"Ay, that I'll be bound for you," cried Colonel Goldsworthy.

"Yes for having been so drubbed by them," cried Mr. Fisher.

As I now, through all his good humour, saw Colonel Manners colour a little, I said in a low voice to Mr. Fisher, "Pray is it in innocence, or in malice, that you use these terms."

I saw his innocence by his surprise, and I whispered him the literal state of all he said; he was quite shocked, and coloured in his turn, apologising instantly to Colonel Manners, and protesting he had never heard of his personal ill usage, but only meant the defeat of his party.

MR. FAIRLY IS DISCUSSED BY HIS BROTHER EQUERRIES. Everybody was full of Mr. Fairly's appointment, and spoke of it with pleasure. General Budé had seen him in town, where he had remained some days, to take the oaths, I believe, necessary for his place. General Budé has long been intimate with him, and spoke of his character exactly as it has appeared to me; and Colonel Goldsworthy, who was at Westminster with him, declared he believed a better man did not exist. "This, in particular," cried General Budé, "I must say of Fairly: whatever he thinks right he pursues straightforward and I believe there is not a sacrifice upon earth that he would not make, rather than turn a moment out of the path that he had an opinion it was his duty to keep in."

They talked a good deal of his late lady; none of them knew her but very slightly, as she was remarkably reserved. "More than reserved," cried General Budé, "she was quite cold. Yet she loved London and public life, and Fairly never had any taste for them; in that they were very mal assortis, but in all other things very happy."

"Yes," cried Colonel Goldsworthy, "and how shall we give praise enough to a man that would be happy himself, and make

his wife so too, for all that difference of opinion ? for it was all his management, and good address, and good temper. I hardly know such another man."

General Budé then related many circumstances of his most exemplary conduct during the illness of his poor suffering wife, and after her loss; everybody, indeed, upon the occasion of this new appointment, has broke forth to do justice to his deserving it. Mrs. Ariana Egerton, who came twice to drink tea with me on my being sensa Cerbera, told me that her brother-in-law, Colonel Masters, who had served with him at Gibraltar, protested there was not an officer in the army of a nobler and higher character, both professional and personal.

She asked me a thousand questions of what I thought about Miss Fuzilier? She dislikes her so very much, she cannot bear to think of her becoming Mrs. Fairly. She has met with some marks of contempt from her in their official meetings at St. James's, that cannot be pardoned. Miss Fuziller, indeed, seemed to me formerly, when I used to meet her in company, to have an uncertainty of disposition that made her like two persons; now haughty, silent, and supercilious–and then gentle, composed, and interesting. She Is, however, very little liked, the worst being always what most spreads abroad.

BARON TRENCK: MR. TURBULENT"S RAILLERY.

Sept. 1.-Peace to the manes of the poor slaughtered partridges!

I finished this morning the "Memoirs of Baron Trenck," which have given me a great deal of entertainment; I mean in the first volume, the second containing not more matter than might fill four pages. But the singular hardiness, gallantry, ferocity, and ingenuity of this copy of the knights of ancient times, who has happened to be born since his proper epoch, have wonderfully drawn me on, and I could not rest without finishing his adventures. They are reported to be chiefly of his own invention; but I really find an air of self-belief in his relations, that inclines me to think he has but narrated what he had persuaded himself was true. His ill-usage is such as to raise the utmost indignation in every reader and if it really affected his memory and imagination, and became thence the parent of some few embellishments and episodes, I can neither wonder nor feel the interest of his narrative diminished.

Sept. 2.-Mr. Turbulent was in high rage that I was utterly

Page 215 invisible since my return from Cheltenham; he protested he had called seven times at my door without gaining admission, and never was able to get in but when " Dr. Shepherd had led the way.

He next began a mysterious attack upon the proceedings of Cheltenham. He had heard, he said, strange stories of flirtations there. I could not doubt what he meant, but I would not seem to understand him: first, because I know not from whom he has been picking up this food for his busy spirit, since no one there appeared collecting it for him ; and secondly, because I would not degrade an acquaintance which I must hope will prove as permanent as it is honourable, by conceiving the word flirtation to be possibly connected with it.

By every opportunity, in the course of the day, he renewed this obscure raillery; but I never would second it, either by question or retort, and therefore it cannot but die away unmeaningly as it was born. Some effect, however, it seems to have had upon him, who has withdrawn all his own heroics, while endeavouring to develop what I have received elsewhere.

AMIABLE MRS. SCHWELLENBERG AGAIN.

Sept. 4.-To-day there was a Drawing-room, and I had the blessing of my dearest father while it lasted; but not solus; he was accompanied by my mother; and my dear Esther and her little innocent Sophy spent part of the time with us. I am to be god-mother to the two little ones, Esther's and James's. Heaven bless them!

We returned to Kew to a late dinner; and, indeed, I had one of the severest evenings I ever passed, where my heart took no share in unkindness and injustice. I was wearied in the extreme, as I always am on these drawing-room days, which begin with full hair-dressing at six o'clock in the morning, and hardly ever allow any breakfast time, and certainly only standing, except while frizzing, till the drawing-room commences; and then two journeys in that decked condition–and then another dressing, with three dressing attendances–and a dinner at near seven o'clock.

Yet, not having power to be very amusing after all this, I was sternly asked by Mrs. Schwellenberg, "For what I did not talk?"

I answered simply, "Because I was tired."

"You tired!–what have you done? when I used to do so much more- -you tired! what have you to do but to be happy:

–have you the laces to buy? have you the wardrobe to part? have you–you tired? Vell, what will become next, when you have every happiness!–you might not be tired. No, I can't bear It."

This, and so much more than it would be possible to write, all uttered with a haughtiness and contempt that the lowest servant could not have brooked receiving, awoke me pretty completely, though before I was scarce able to keep my eyelids a moment open; but so sick I turned, that indeed it was neither patience nor effort that enabled me to hear her; I had literally hardly strength, mental or bodily, to have answered her. Every happiness mine!–O gracious heaven! thought I, and is this the companion of my leisure–the associate of my life! Ah, my dear friends, I will not now go on–I turn sick again.

A ROYAL JOKE.

Sept. 29.-The birth-day of our lovely eldest princess. It happens to be also the birth-day of Miss Goldsworthy; and her majesty, in a sportive humour, bid me, as soon as she was dressed, go and bring down the two "Michaelmas geese." I told the message to the Princess Augusta, who repeated It in its proper words. I attended them to the queen's dressing- room, and there had the pleasure to see the cadeaux presentations. The birth-days in this house are made extremely interesting at the moment, by the reciprocations of presents and congratulations in this affectionate family. Were they but attended with less of toil (I hate to add ette, for I am sure it is not little toil), I should like them amazingly.

COLONEL GOLDSWORTHY'S BREACH OF ETIQUETTE. Mrs. Schwellenberg has become both colder and fiercer. I cannot now even meet her eyes-they are almost terrifying. Nothing upon earth having passed between us, nor the most remote subject of offence having occurred, I have only one thing on which to rest my conjectures, for the cause of this newly-awakened evil spirit, and this is from the gentlemen. They had all of late been so wearied that they could not submit even for a quarter of an hour to her society : they had swallowed a dish of tea and quitted the room all in five minutes, and Colonel Goldsworthy in particular, when without any companion in his waiting, had actually always fallen asleep,

even during that short interval, or at least shut his eyes, to save himself the toil of speaking.

This she brooked very ill, but I was esteemed innocent, and therefore made, occasionally, the confidant of her complaints. But lately, that she has been ill, and kept upstairs every night, she has always desired me to come to her as soon as tea was over, which, she observed, "need not keep me five minutes." On the contrary, however, the tea is now at least an hour, and often more.

I have been constantly received with reproaches for not coming sooner, and compelled to declare I had not been sooner at liberty. This has occasioned a deep and visible resentment, all against them, yet vented upon me, not in acknowledged displeasure–pride there interfered–but in constant ill-humour, ill-breeding, and ill-will.

At length, however, she has broken out into one inquiry, which, if favourably answered, might have appeased all; but truth was too strongly in the way. A few evenings after her confinement she very gravely said, "Colonel Goldsworthy always sleeps with me! sleeps he with you the same?"

In the midst of all my irksome discomfort, it was with difficulty I could keep my countenance at this question, which I was forced to negative.

The next evening she repeated it. "Vell, sleeps he yet with you--Colonel Goldsworthy?"

"Not yet, ma'am," I hesitatingly answered.

"O! ver vell! he will sleep with nobody but me! O, i von't come down."

And a little after she added, "I believe he vill marry you."

"I believe not, ma'am," I answered.

And then, very gravely,, she proposed him to me, saying he only wanted a little encouragement, for he was always declaring he wished for a wife, and yet wanted no fortune-" so for what won't you not have him?"

I assured her we were both perfectly well satisfied apart, and equally free from any thoughts of each other.

"Then for what," she cried, "won't you have Dr. Shepherd?" She Is now in the utmost haste to dispose of me! And then she added she had been told that Dr. Shepherd would marry me!

She is an amazing woman ! Alas, I might have told her I knew too well what it was to be tied to a companion ill-assorted and unbeloved, where I could not help myself, to

make any such experiment as a volunteer!

If she asks me any more about Colonel Goldsworthy and his sleeping, I think I will answer I am too near-sighted to be sure if he is awake or not!

However, I cannot but take this stroke concerning the table extremely ill; for though amongst things of the very least consequence in itself, it is more openly designed as an affront than any step that has been taken with me yet.

I have given the colonel a hint, however,-that he may keep awake in future. . . .

ILLNESS OF MRS. SCHWELLENBERG.

Oct. 2.-Mrs. Schwellenberg, very ill indeed, took leave of the queen at St. James's, to set off for Weymouth, in company with Mrs. Hastings. I was really very sorry for her; she was truly in a situation Of suffering, from bodily pain, the most pitiable. I thought, as I looked at her, that if the ill-humours I so often experience could relieve her, I would consent to bear them unrepining, in preference to seeing or knowing her so ill. But it is just the contrary; spleen and ill-temper only aggravate disease, and while they involve others in temporary participation of their misery, twine it around themselves in bandages almost stationary. She was civil, too, poor woman. I suppose when absent she could not well tell why she had ever been otherwise.

GENERAL GRENVILLE'S REGIMENT AT DRILL.

Oct. 9.-I go on now pretty well; and I am so much acquainted with my party, that when no strangers are added, I begin to mind nothing but the first entree of my male visitants. My royal mistress is all sweetness to me; Miss Planta is most kind and friendly; General Budé is ever the same, and ever what I do not wish to alter; Colonel Goldsworthy seems coming round to good-humour; and even General Grenville begins to grow sociable. He has quitted the corner into which he used to cast his long figure, merely to yawn and lounge ; and though yawn and lounge he does still, and must, I believe, to the end of the chapter, he yet does it in society, and mixes between it loud sudden laughter at what is occasionally said, and even here and there a question relative to what is going forward. Nay-yesterday he even seated himself at the tea

table, and amused himself by playing with my work-box, and making sundry inquiries about its contents.

Oct. 10.-This evening, most unwittingly, I put my new neighbour's good-humour somewhat to the test. He asked me whether I had walked out in the morning? Yes, I answered, I always walked. "And in the Little park?" cried he. Yes, I said, and to Old Windsor, and round the park wall, and along the banks of the Thames, and almost to Beaumont Lodge, and in the avenue of the Great park, and in short, in all the vicinage of Windsor. "But in the Little park?" he cried.

Still I did not understand him, but plainly answered, "Yes, this morning,; and indeed many mornings."

"But did you see nothing–remark nothing there?

No, not that I recollect, except some soldiers drilling." You never heard such a laugh as now broke forth from all for, alas for my poor eyes, there had been in the Little park General Grenville's whole regiment, with all his officers, and himself at their head! Fortunately it is reckoned one of the finest in the king's service : this I mentioned, adding that else I could never again appear before him.

He affected to be vehemently affronted, but hardly knew how, even in joke, to appear so ; and all the rest helped the matter on, by saying that they should know now how to distinguish his regiment, which henceforth must always be called " the drill."

The truth is, as soon as I perceived a few red-coats I had turned another way, to avoid being marched at, and therefore their number and splendour had all been thrown away upon me.

(278) "Cerbera" was Fanny's not inappropriate name for Mrs. Schwellenberg.-ED.

(279) By William Falconer, born at Edinburgh in 1730. His poem, "The Ship-wreck," was suggested by his own experience at sea, and was first published in 1762. Falconer sailed for Bengal in 1769, the vessel touched at the Cape in December, and was never heard of more.-ED.

(280) In the "European Magazine" for May 1788, appeared an article from the pen of Baretti, headed "On Signora Piozzi's publication of Dr. Johnson's Letters, Stricture the First." It is filled with coarse, personal abuse of the lady, whom the author terms "the frontless female, who goes now by the mean appellation of Piozzi." "Stricture the Second," in the same tone, appeared the following month, and the "Third," which

closed the series, in August of the same year. In the last number Baretti comments, with excessive bitterness, on Mrs. Piozzi's second marriage.-ED.

(281) "Original Love-letters between a Lady of Quality and a Person of Inferior Station." Dublin, 1784. Though by no means devoid of "nonsense and romance," the little book is not altogether undeserving of Colonel Digby's encomium. The story is very slight, and concludes, quite unnecessarily and rather unexpectedly, with the death of the gentleman, just as his good fortune seems assured.-ED.

(282) Robert Raikes, who was born at Gloucester in 1735, was a printer and the son of a printer. His father was proprietor of the "Gloucester journal." In conjunction with the Rev. Mr. Stocks, Raikes founded the institution of Sunday Schools in 1781. He died at Gloucester in 1811.-ED.

(283) "Cui Bono? or, an Inquiry what Benefits can arise either to the English or the Americans, the French, Spaniards, or Dutch, from the greatest victories, or successes, in the present War, being a Series of Letters, addressed to Monsieur Necker, late Controller- General of the Finances of France," By Josiah Tucker, D.D., published at Gloucester, 1781. The pamphlet was written in the advocacy of a general peace, and attracted much attention. The third edition appeared in 1782.-ED,

(284) Fanny alludes to an old adventure of Baretti's. He was accosted in the Haymarket by a prostitute, October 6, 1769. The woman was importunate, and the irritable Italian struck her on the hand; upon which three men came up and attacked him. He then drew a dagger in self defence, and mortally wounded one of his assailants. Baretti was tried at the Old Bailey for murder, October 20, and acquitted; Johnson, Burke, and Garrick appearing as witnesses to his character.-ED.

(285) With all Fanny's partiality for the "sweet queen," the evidences of that sweet creature's selfishness keep turning up in a very disagreeable manner-ED.

(286)) "The Country Girl," Which is still occasionally performed, is an adaptation by Garrick of one of the most brilliant, and most indecent, of Restoration comedies–Wycherley's "Country Wife." Mrs. Jordan played the part of "Peggy," the "Margery Punchwife" of Wycherley's play. It was in this part that she made her first appearance in London, at Drury Lane, October 18, 1785. She was one of the most admired actresses of her time. Genest, who saw her, writes of her, "As an actress she never had a superior in her proper line Mrs. Jordan's Country Girl, Romp, Miss Hoyden, and all characters of that description were exquisite–in breeches parts no actress can be put in competition with her but Mrs. Woffington, and to Mrs. Woffington she was as superior in point of voice as Mrs. Woffington was superior to her in beauty" (viii. p. 430). Mrs. Jordan died at St. Cloud, July 5, 1816, aged fifty. There is an admirable portrait of her by Romney in the character of the "Country Girl."-ED.

(287) See ante, vol. i., p. 151.-ED.

(288) Fanny's cousin, the son of Dr. Burney's brother, Richard Burney of Worcester.-ED.

(289) The poem in question is the "Ode to the Evening Star," the fifteenth of the first hook of Odes. Mr. Akenside, having paid his tear on fair Olympia's virgin tomb, roams in quest of Philomela's bower, and desires the evening star to send its golden ray to guide him. it is pretty, however. The first stanza runs as follows:–

"To night retired, the queen of heaven
With young Endymion strays;
And now to Hesper it is given
Awhile to rule the vacant sky,
Till she shall to her lamp supply
A stream of lighter rays."-ED.

(290) Joseph jérome le Français de Lalande, one of the most distinguished of French astronomers. He was born in 1732, and died in 1807.-ED.

(291) Silly: insipid.

(292) 'Tis too much honour."

(293) "'Tis very troublesome, but one must say pretty things to ladies."

SECTION 14

(1788-9.)

THE KING'S ILLNESS.

About the commencement of November, 1788, there was no longer any doubt as to the serious nature of the king's malady. At the meeting of Parliament the prime minister, Mr. Pitt, Moved that a committee be appointed to examine the physicians attendant upon his majesty. This motion was agreed to, and on the 10th of December the report of the committee was laid upon the table of the House. The physicians agreed that his Majesty was then totally incapable of attending to public business. They agreed also in holding Out strong hopes of his ultimate recovery, but none of them would venture to give any opinion as to the probable duration of his derangement. Upon this, Mr. Pitt

moved for a committee to examine and report upon such precedents as might be found of proceedings in cases of the interruption, from any cause, of the personal exercise of the royal authority. The motion was strenuously resisted by the opposition, headed by Mr. Fox, who argued that whenever the sovereign was incapacitated from performing the functions of his office, the heir-apparent, if of full age and capacity, had an inalienable right to act as his substitute. This doctrine seems certainly inconsistent with the liberal principles professed by the opposition, but it will be remembered that at this time the Prince of Wales was politically in alliance with that party, and that he was on terms of friendship with Mr. Fox himself. On the other hand, Pitt protested that in such circumstances the heir-apparent had no more claim to exercise, as a matter of right, the royal functions, than any other Subject of the crown ; and that it belonged only to the two Houses of Parliament to make such provision for supplying the deficiency in the government as they should think proper. As to the person of the Regent there was no dispute ; the question was, simply, whether the Prince of Wales should assume the Regency in his own right, or by the authority of Parliament.

Pitt's motion being carried, the committee was accordingly appointed, and proceeded at once to make their examination and report. The prime minister then (December 16) moved two resolutions, declaring, firstly, that the king was incapable of performing the functions of his office, and, secondly, that it was the duty of Parliament to provide for the exercise of those functions. In spite of Fox's opposition both resolutions were carried, and a third resolution was moved by Pitt, and passed (December

23), empowering the lord chancellor to affix the great seal to the intended Regency Bill.

Early in January, 1789, a fresh examination of the physicians Was voted, but gave no more definite hopes of an early recovery. Pitt now wrote to the Prince of Wales, informing him of the plan intended to be pursued : that the prince should be invested with the authority of Regent, under certain restrictions, regarding especially the granting of peerages, offices, or pensions ; and that the care of the king's person and the control of the royal household should remain with the queen. The prince, in reply, expressed his readiness to accept the Regency, while protesting strongly against the proposed limitations of his authority ; and on the 16th of January, a bill, in which the prime ministers scheme was embodied, was introduced into the House. The question was actively debated in both Houses, until, in the latter part of February, the king's recovery put a stop to further proceedings.-ED.]

UNCERTAIN STATE OF THE KING's HEALTH.

Kew, Friday, Oct. 17.-Our return to Windsor is postponed till to- morrow. The king is not well; he has not been quite well some time, yet nothing I hope alarming, though there is an uncertainty as to his complaint not very satisfactory; so precious, too, is his health.

Oct. 18.-The king was this morning better. My royal mistress told me Sir George Baker(294) was to settle whether we returned to Windsor to-day or to-morrow.

Sunday, Oct. 19.-The Windsor journey is again postponed, and the king is but very indifferent. Heaven preserve him! there is something unspeakably alarming in his smallest indisposition. I am very much with the queen, who, I see, is very uneasy, but she talks not of it.

We are to stay here some time longer, and so unprepared were we for more than a day or two, that our distresses are prodigious, even for clothes to wear; and as to books, there are not three amongst us; and for company only Mr. de Luc and Miss Planta; and so, in mere desperation for employment, I have just begun a tragedy.(295) We are now in so spiritless a situation that my mind would bend to nothing less sad, even in fiction. But I am very glad something of this kind has occurred to me; it may while away the tediousness of this unsettled, unoccupied, unpleasant period.

Oct. 20.-The king was taken very ill in the night, and we have all been cruelly frightened - but it went off, and, thank heaven! he is now better.

I had all my morning devoted to receiving inquiring visits. Lady Effingham, Sir George Howard, Lady Frances Howard, all came from Stoke to obtain news of the king; his least illness spreads in a moment. Lady Frances Douglas came also. She is wife of the Archibald Douglas who caused the famous Hamilton trial in the House of Peers, for his claim to the Douglas name.(296) She is fat, and dunch, and heavy, and ugly; otherwise, they say, agreeable enough.

Mr. Turbulent has been sent for, and he enlivens the scene somewhat. He is now all he should be, and so altered ! scarce a flight left.

Oct. 21.-The good and excellent king is again better, and we expect to remove to Windsor in a day or two.

Oct. 23.-The king continues to mend, thank God! Saturday we hope to return to Windsor. Had not this composition fit seized me, societyless, and bookless, and viewless as I am, I know not how I could have whiled away my being; but my tragedy goes on, and fills up all vacancies.

Oct. 25.-Yesterday was so much the same, I have not marked it; not so to-day. The king was so much better that our Windsor journey at length took place, with permission of Sir George Baker, the only physician his majesty will admit. Miss Cambridge was with me to the last moment.

I have been hanging up a darling remembrance of my revered, incomparable Mrs. Delany. Her "Sacharissa" is now over my chimney. I could not at first bear it, but now I look at it, and call her back to my eye's mind perpetually. This, like the tragedy I have set about, suits the turn of things in this habitation.

I had a sort of conference with his Majesty, or rather I was the object to whom he spoke, with a manner so uncommon, that a high fever alone could account for it, a rapidity, a hoarseness of voice, a volubility, an earnestness–a vehemence, rather–it startled me inexpressibly; yet with a graciousness exceeding even all I ever met with before–it was almost kindness!

Heaven–Heaven preserve him! The queen grows more and more uneasy. She alarms me sometimes for herself, at other times she has a sedateness that wonders me still more.

Sunday, Oct. 26-The king was prevailed upon not to go to chapel this morning. I met him in the passage from the queen's room; he stopped me, and conversed upon his health near half-an-hour, still with that extreme quickness of Speech and manner that belongs to fever; and he hardly sleeps, he tells me, one minute all night; indeed, if he recovers not his rest, a most delirious fever seems to threaten him. He is all agitation, all emotion, yet all benevolence and goodness, even to a degree that makes it touching to hear him speak. He assures everybody of his health; he seems only fearful to give uneasiness to others, yet certainly he is better than last night. Nobody speaks of his illness, nor what they think of it.

Oct. 29.-The dear and good king again gains ground, and the queen becomes easier.

To-day Miss Planta told me she heard Mr. Fairly was confined at Sir R- F-'s, and therefore she would now lay any wager he was to marry Miss F-.(297)

In the evening I inquired what news of him of General Bude: he told me he was still confined at a friend's house, but avoided naming where–probably from suggesting that, however little truth there may yet have been in the report, more may belong to it from this particular intercourse.

THE KING COMPLAINS OF WANT OF SLEEP.

Nov. 1.-Our king does not advance in amendment; he grows so weak that he walks like a gouty man, yet has such spirits that he has talked away his voice, and is so hoarse it is painful to hear him. The queen is evidently in great uneasiness. God send him better!

She read to me to-day a lecture of Hunter's. During the reading, twice, at pathetic passages, my poor queen shed tears. "How nervous I am?" she cried; "I am quite a fool! Don't you think so?"

No, ma'am," was all I dared answer.

She revived, however, finished the lecture, and went upstairs and played upon the Princess Augusta's harpsichord.

The king was hunting. Her anxiety for his return was
greater than ever. The moment he arrived he sent a page to desire to have coffee
and take his bark in the queen's dressing- room. She said she would pour it out herself,
and sent to inquire how he drank it.

The king is very sensible of the great change there is in himself, and of her
disturbance at it. It seems, but heaven avert it! a threat of a total breaking up of the
constitution. This, too, seems his own idea. I was present at his first seeing Lady
Effingham on his return to Windsor this last time. "My dear Effy," he cried, "you
see me, all at once, an old man." I was so much affected by this exclamation, that I
wished to run out of the room. Yet I could not but recover when Lady Effingham, in
her well-meaning but literal way, composedly answered, "We must all grow old, sir,-
-I am sure I do."

He then produced a walking-stick which he had just ordered. "He could not," he
said, "get on without it; his strength seemed diminishing hourly."

He took the bark, he said But the queen," he cried, "is my physician, and no man
need have a better; she is my friend, and no Man can have a better."

How the queen commanded herself I cannot conceive; but there was something so
touching in this speech, from his hoarse voice and altered countenance, that it overset
me very much.

Nor can I ever forget him in what passed this night. When I came to the queen's
dressing-room he was still with her. He constantly conducts her to it before he retires
to his own. He was begging her not to speak to him when he got to his room, that he
might fall asleep, as he felt great want of that refreshment. He repeated this desire, I
believe, at least a hundred times, though, far enough from need Ing it, the poor queen
never uttered one syllable! He then applied to me, saying he was really very well,
except in that one particular, that he could not sleep.

The kindness and benevolence of his manner all this time was most penetrating:
he seemed to have no anxiety but to set the queen at rest, and no wish but to quiet
and give pleasure to all around him, To me, he never yet spoke with such excess of
benignity: he appeared even solicitous to satisfy me that he should do well, and to
spare all alarm; but there was a hurry in his manner and voice that indicated sleep to
be
indeed wanted. Nor could I, all night, forbear foreseeing "He sleeps now, or
to-morrow he will be surely delirious!"

Sunday, Nov. 2.-The king was better, and prevailed upon to give up going to the
early prayers. The queen and princesses went. After they were gone, and I was
following towards my room, the king called after me, and he kept me in discourse a
full half hour nearly all the time they were away.

It was all to the same purport; that he was well, but wanted more rest ; yet he said
he had slept the last night like a child. But his manner, still, was so touchingly kind,
so softly gracious, that it doubled my concern to see him so far from well.

DISTRESS OF THE QUEEN.

Nov. 3.–We are all here in a most uneasy state. The king is better and worse so
frequently, and changes so, daily, backwards and forwards, that everything is to be
apprehended, if his nerves are not some way quieted. I dreadfully fear he is on the

eve of some severe fever. The queen is almost overpowered with some secret terror. I am affected beyond all expression in her presence, to see what struggles she makes to support serenity. To-day she gave up the conflict when I was alone with her, and burst into a violent fit of tears. It was very, very terrible to see! How did I wish her a Susan or a Fredy! To unburthen her loaded mind would be to relieve it from all but inevitable affliction. O, may heaven in its mercy never, never drive me to that solitary anguish more!- I have tried what it would do; I speak from bitter recollection of past melancholy experience.

Sometimes she walks up and down the room without uttering a word, but shaking her head frequently, and in evident distress and irresolution. She is often closeted with Miss Goldsworthy, of whom, I believe, she makes inquiry how her brother has found the king, from time to time.

The princes both came to Kew, in several visits to the king. The Duke of York has also been here, and his fond father could hardly bear the pleasure of thinking him anxious for his health. "So good," he says "is Frederick!"

To-night, indeed, at tea-time, I felt a great shock, in hearing, from General Budé, that Dr, Heberden had been called in. It is true more assistance seemed much wanting, yet the king's rooted aversion to physicians makes any new-comer tremen-dous. They said, too, it was merely for counsel, not that his majesty was worse.

Nov. 4.-Passed much the same as the days preceding it, the queen in deep distress, the king in a state almost incomprehensible, and all the house uneasy and alarmed. The Drawing-room was again put off, and a steady residence seemed fixed at Windsor.

Nov. 5.-I found my poor royal mistress, in the morning, sad and sadder still; something horrible seemed impending, and I saw her whole resource was in religion. We had talked lately much upon solemn Subjects, and she appeared already preparing herself to be resigned for whatever might happen.

I was still wholly unsuspicious of the greatness of the cause she had for dread. Illness, a breaking up of the constitution, the payment of sudden infirmity and prema-ture old age for the waste of unguarded health and strength,–these seemed to me the threats awaiting her; and great and grievous enough, yet how short of the fact!

I had given up my walks some days; I was too uneasy to quit the house while the queen remained at home, and she now never left it. Even Lady Effingham, the last two days, could not obtain admission; She Could only hear from a page how the royal family went on.

At noon the king went out in his chaise, with the princess royal, for an airing. I looked from my window to see him; he was all smiling benignity, but gave so many orders to the postilions, and got in and out of the carriage twice, with such agitation, that again my fear of a great fever hanging over him grew more and more powerful. Alas! how little did I imagine I should see him no more for so long–so black a period!

When I went to my poor queen, still worse and worse I found her spirits. She had been greatly offended by some anecdote in a newspaper–the "Morning Herald"– relative to the king's indisposition. She declared the printer should be called to account. She bid me burn the paper, and ruminated upon who could be employed to represent to the editor that he must answer at his peril any further such treasonable paragraphs. I named to her Mr. Fairly, her own servant, and one so peculiarly fitted for any office requiring honour and discretion. "Is he here, then?" she cried. "No," I answered, but he was expected in a few days.

I saw her concurrence with this proposal. The princess royal soon returned. She came in cheerfully, and gave, in

German, a history of the airing, and one that seemed Comforting. Soon after, suddenly arrived the Prince of Wales. He came into the room.- He had just quitted Brighthelmstone. Something passing within seemed to render this meeting awfully distant on both sides. She asked if he should not return to Brighthelmstone? He answered yes, the next day, He desired to speak with her they retired together.

FIRST OUTBURST OF THE KING's DELIRIUM.

I had but just reached my own room, deeply musing on the state of' things, when a chaise stopped at the rails; and I saw Mr. Fairly and his son Charles alight, and enter the house. He walked lamely, and seemed not yet recovered from his late attack. Though most happy to see him at this alarming time, when I knew he could be most useful, as there is no one to whom the queen opens so confidentially upon her affairs, I had yet a fresh stair to see, by his anticipated arrival, though still lame, that he must have been sent for, and hurried hither.

Only Miss Planta dined with me. We were both nearly silent: I was shocked at I scarcely knew what, and she seemed to know too much for speech. She stayed with me till six o'clock, but nothing passed, beyond general solicitude that the king might get better.

Meanwhile, a stillness the most uncommon reigned over the whole house. Nobody stirred ; not a voice was heard - not a step, not a motion. I could do nothing but watch, without knowing for what : there seemed a strangeness in the house most extraordinary.

At seven o'clock Columb came to tell me that the music was all forbid, and the musicians ordered away ! This was the last step to be expected, so fond as his majesty is -of his concert, and I thought it might have rather soothed him: I could not understand the prohibition; all seemed stranger and stranger.

Very late came General Budé. He looked extremely uncomfortable. Later still came Colonel Goldsworthy: his countenance all gloom, and his voice scarce articulating no or yes. General Grenville was gone to town. General Bud asked me if I had seen Mr. Fairly; and last Of all, at length, he also entered. How grave he looked, how shut up in himself! A silent bow was his only salutation Page 229

how changed I thought it,–and how fearful a meeting, SO long expected as a solace!

Colonel Goldsworthy was called away: I heard his voice whispering some time in the passage, but he did not return. Various small speeches now dropped, by which I found the house was all in disturbance, and the king in some strange way worse, and the queen taken ill!

At length, General Budé said he would go and see if any one was in the music-room. Mr. Fairly said he thought he had better not accompany him, for as he had not yet been seen, his appearance might excite fresh emotion. The general agreed, and went.

We were now alone. But I could not speak: neither did Mr. Fairly. I worked—I had begun a hassock for my Fredy. A long and serious pause made me almost turn sick with anxious wonder and fear, and an inward trembling totally disabled me from asking the actual situation of things; if I had not had my work, to employ my eyes and hands, I must have left the room to quiet myself.

I fancy he penetrated into all this, though, at first, he had concluded me informed of everything; but he now, finding me silent, began an inquiry whether I was yet acquainted how bad all was become, and how ill the king? I really had no utterance for very alarm, but my look was probably sufficient; he kindly saved me any questions, and related to me the whole of the mysterious horror!

O my dear friends, what a history! The king, at dinner, had broken forth into positive delirium, which long had been menacing all who saw him most closely; and the queen was so overpowered as to fall into violent hysterics. All the princesses were in misery, and the Prince of Wales had burst into tears. No one knew what was to follow– no one could conjecture the event.

He spoke of the poor queen, in terms of the most tender compassion; he pitied her, he said, from the bottom of his soul; and all her sweet daughters, the lovely princesses–there was no knowing to what we might look forward for them all!

I was an almost silent listener ; but, having expressed himself very warmly for all the principal sufferers, he kindly, and with interest, examined me. "How," he cried, "are You? Are you strong? are you stout? can you go through such scenes as these? you do not look much fitted for them."

Page 230 "I shall do very well," I cried, "for, at a time such as this, I shall surely forget myself utterly. The queen will be all to me. I shall hardly, I think, feel myself at liberty to be unhappy!" . . .

AN ANXIOUS NIGHT.

Mr. Fairly stayed with me all the evening, during which we heard no voice, no sound! all was deadly still!

At ten o'clock I said, " I must go to my own room, to be in waiting." He determined upon remaining downstairs, in the equerries' apartment, there to wait some intelligence. We parted in mutual expectation of dreadful tidings. In separating, he took my hand, and earnestly recommended me to keep myself stout and firm.

If this beginning of the night was affecting, what did it not grow afterwards Two long hours I waited-alone, in silence, in ignorance, in dread! I thought they would never be over; at twelve o'clock I seemed to have spent two whole days in waiting. I then opened my door, to listen, in the passage, if anything seemed stirring. Not a sound could I hear. My apartment seemed wholly separated from life and motion. Whoever was in the house kept at the other end, and not even a servant crossed the stairs or passage by my rooms.

I would fain have crept on myself, anywhere in the world, for some inquiry, or to see but a face, and hear a voice, but I did not dare risk losing a sudden summons. I re-entered my room and there passed another endless hour, in conjectures too horrible to relate.

A little after one, I heard a step–my door opened–and a page said I must come to the queen. I could hardly get along–hardly force myself into the room. dizzy I felt, almost to falling. But, the first shock passed, I became more collected. Useful, indeed, proved the previous lesson of the evening : it had stilled, If not fortified my mind, which had else, in a scene Such is this, been all tumult and emotion.

My poor royal mistress! never can I forget her countenance–pale, ghastly pale she looked; she was seated to be undressed, and attended by Lady Elizabeth Waldegrave and Miss Goldsworthy ; her whole frame was disordered, yet she was still and quiet. These two ladies assisted me to undress her, or rather I assisted them, for they were firmer, from being

longer present; my shaking hands and blinded eyes could scarce be of any use. I gave her some camphor julep, which had been ordered her by Sir George Baker. "How cold I am!" she cried, and put her hand on mine; marble it felt! and went to my heart's core!

The king, at the instance of Sir George Baker, had consented to sleep in the next apartment, as the queen was ill. For himself, he would listen to nothing. Accordingly, a bed was put up for him, by his own order, in the queen's second dressing-room, immediately adjoining to the bed-room. He would not be further removed. Miss Goldsworthy was to sit up with her, by the king's direction.

I would fain have remained in the little dressing-room, on the other side the bed-room, but she would not permit it. She ordered Sandys, her wardrobe-woman, in the place of Mrs. Thielky, to sit up there. Lady Elizabeth also pressed to stay; but we were desired to go to our own rooms.

How reluctantly did I come away ! how hardly to myself leave her! Yet I went to bed, determined to preserve my strength to the utmost of my ability, for the service of my unhappy mistress. I could not, however, sleep. I do not suppose an eye was closed in the house all night.

Nov. 6.-I rose at six, dressed in haste by candle-light, and unable to wait for my summons in a suspense so awful, I stole along the passage in the dark, a thick fog intercepting all faint light, to see if I could meet with Sandys, or any one, to tell me how the night had passed.

When I came to the little dressing-room, I stopped, irresolute what to do. I heard men's voices; I was seized with the most cruel alarm at such a sound in her majesty's dressing-room. I waited some time, and then the door opened, and I saw Colonel Goldsworthy and Mr. Batterscomb.(298) I was relieved from my first apprehension, yet shocked enough to see them there at this early hour. They had both sat up there all night, as well as Sandys. Every page, both of the king and queen, had also sat up, dispersed in the passages and ante-rooms! and O what horror in every face I met! I waited here, amongst them, till Sandys was ordered by the queen to carry her a pair of gloves. I could not resist

the opportunity to venture myself before her. I glided into the room, but stopped at the door: she was in bed, sitting up; Miss Goldsworthy was on a stool by her side! I feared approaching without permission, yet could not prevail with myself to retreat. She was looking down, and did not see me. Miss Goldsworthy, turning round, said, "'Tis Miss Burney, ma'am."

She leaned her head forward, and in a most soft manner, said,
"Miss Burney, how are you?"

Deeply affected, I hastened up to her, but, in trying to speak, burst into an irresistible torrent of tears.

My dearest friends, I do it at this moment again, and can hardly write for them; yet I wish you to know all this piercing history right.

She looked like death–colourless and wan; but nature is infectious; the tears gushed from her own eyes, and a perfect agony of weeping ensued, which, once begun, she could not stop; she did not, indeed, try; for when it subsided, and she wiped her eyes, she said, "I thank you, Miss Burney–you have made me cry– it is a great relief to me–I had not been able to cry before, all this night long." O, what a scene followed! what a scene was related! The king, in the middle of the night, had insisted upon seeing if his queen was not removed from the house and he had come into her room, with a candle in his hand, opened the bed- curtains, and satisfied himself she was there, and Miss Goldsworthy by her side. This observance of his directions had much soothed him; but he stayed a full half hour, and the depth of terror during that time no words can paint. The fear of such another entrance was now so strongly upon the nerves of the poor queen, that she could hardly support herself.

THE KING'S DELIRIOUS CONDITION.

The king-the royal sufferer-was still in the next room, attended by Sir George Baker and Dr. Heberden, and his pages, with Colonel Goldsworthy occasionally, and as he called for him. He kept talking unceasingly; his voice was so lost in hoarseness and weakness, it was rendered almost inarticulate; but its tone was still all benevolence–all kindness–all touching graciousness.

It was thought advisable the queen should not rise, lest the king should be offended that she did not go to him; at present

he was content, because he conceived her to be nursing for her illness.

But what a situation for her! She would not let me leave her now; she made me remain In the room, and ordered me to sit down. I was too trembling to refuse. Lady Elizabeth soon joined us. We all three stayed with her; she frequently bid me listen, to hear what the king was saying or doing. I did, and carried the best accounts I could manage, without deviating from truth, except by some omissions. Nothing could be so afflicting as this task; even now, it brings fresh to my ear his poor exhausted voice. "I am nervous," he cried; "I am not ill, but I am nervous: if you would know what is the matter with me, I am nervous. But I love you both very well; if you would tell me truth: I love Dr. Heberden best, for he has not told me a lie: Sir George has told me a lie–a white lie, he says, but I hate a white lie. If you will tell me a lie, let it be a black lie!"

This was what he kept saying almost constantly, mixed in with other matter, but always returning, and in a voice that truly will never cease vibrating in my recollection.

The queen permitted me to make her breakfast and attend her, and was so affectingly kind and gentle in her distress, that I felt a tenderness of sorrow for her that almost devoted my whole mind to her alone! Miss Goldsworthy was a fixture at her side; I, therefore, provided her breakfast also.

Lady Elizabeth was sent out on inquiries of Colonel Goldsworthy, and Mr. Batter-scomb, and the pages, every ten minutes; while I, at the same intervals, was ordered to listen to what passed in the room, and give warning if anything seemed to threaten another entrance. . . .

The queen bid me bring the prayer book and read the morning service to her. I could hardly do it, the poor voice from the next room was so perpetually in my ears.

When I came to my room, about twelve o'clock, for some breakfast, I found a letter from Lady Carmarthen. It was an answer to my congratulation upon her marriage, and written with honest happiness and delight. She frankly calls herself the luckiest of all God's creatures ; and this, if not elegant, is sincere, and I hope will be permanently her opinion.

While swallowing my breakfast, standing and in haste, and the door ajar, I heard Mr. Fairly's voice, saying, "Is Miss Burney there? is she alone?" and then he sent in Columb, to inquire if he might come and ask me how I did.

Page 234 I received him with as much gladness as I could then feel, but it was a melancholy reception. I consulted with him upon many points in which I wanted counsel : he is quick and deep at once in expedients where anything, is to be done, and simple and clear in explaining himself where he thinks it is best to do nothing. Miss Goldsworthy herself had once stolen out to Consult with him. He became, indeed, for all who belonged to the queen, from this moment the oracle.

THE KING REFUSES TO SEE DR. WARREN.

Dr. Warren(299) had been sent for express, in the middle of the night, at the desire of Sir George Baker, because he had been taken ill himself, and felt unequal to the whole toll.

I returned speedily to the room of woe. The arrival of the physicians was there grievously awaited, for Dr. Heberden and Sir George would now decide upon nothing till Dr. Warren came. The poor queen wanted something very positive to pass, relative to her keeping away, which seemed thought essential at this time, though the courage to assert it was wanting In everybody.

The princesses sent to ask leave to come to their mother. She burst into tears, and declared she could neither see them, nor pray, while in this dreadful situation, expecting every moment to be broken in upon, and quite uncertain in what manner, yet determined not to desert her apartment, except by express direction from the physicians. Who could tell to what height the delirium might rise? There was no constraint, no power: all feared the worst, yet none dared take any measures for security.

The princes also sent word they were at her majesty's command, but she shrunk still more from this Interview: it filled her with a thousand dreadful sensations, too obvious to be wholly hid.

At length news was brought that Dr. Warren was arrived. I never felt so rejoiced: I could have run out to welcome him with rapture. With what cruel impatience did we then wait to hear his sentence! An impatience how fruitless! It ended in information that he had not seen the king, who refused him admittance.

This was terrible. But the king was never so despotic; no one dared oppose him. He would not listen to a word, though, when unopposed, he was still all gentleness and benignity to every one around him. Dr. Warren was then planted where he could hear his voice, and all that passed, and receive Intelligence concerning his pulse, etc., from Sir George Baker.

THE QUEEN'S ANXIETY TO HEAR DR. WARREN'S OPINION. We now expected every moment Dr. Warren would bring her majesty his opinion ; but he neither came nor sent. She waited in dread incessant. She sent for Sir George–he would not speak alone: she sent for Mr. Hawkins, the household surgeon; but all referred to Dr. Warren.

Lady Elizabeth and Miss Goldsworthy earnestly pressed her to remove to a more distant apartment, where he might not hear the unceasing voice of the unhappy king ; but she would only rise and go to the 'little dressing-room, there to wait in her night-clothes Dr. Warren's determination what step she should take.

At length Lady Elizabeth learnt among the pages that Dr. Warren had quitted his post of watching. The poor queen now, in a torrent of tears, prepared herself for seeing him.

He came not.

All astonished and impatient, Lady Elizabeth was sent out on inquiries. She returned, and said Dr. Warren was gone.

"Run! stop him!" was the queen's next order. "Let him but let me know what I am to do."

Poor, poor queen! how I wept to hear those words!

Abashed and distressed, poor Lady Elizabeth returned. She had seen Colonel Goldsworthy, and heard Dr. Warren, -with the other two physicians, had left the house too far to be recalled they were gone over to the Castle, to the Prince of Wales.

I think a deeper blow I have never witnessed. Already to become but second, even for the king! The tears were now wiped; indignation arose, with pain, the severest pain, of every species.

THE QUEEN REMOVES TO MORE DISTANT APARTMENTS. In about a quarter of an hour Colonel Goldsworthy sent in to beg an audience. It was granted, a long cloak only being thrown over the queen. He now brought the opinion of all the physicians in consultation, " That her majesty would re- Page 236

move to a more distant apartment, since the king would undoubtedly be worse from the agitation of seeing her, and there Could be no possibility to prevent it while she remained so near."

She instantly agreed, but with what bitter anguish! Lady Elizabeth, Miss Goldsworthy, and myself attended her; she went to an apartment in the same row, but to which there Was no entrance except by its own door. It consisted of only two rooms, a bedchamber and a dressing-room. They are appropriated to the lady-in-waiting, when she is here.

At the entrance into this new habitation the poor wretched queen once more gave way to a perfect agony of grief and affliction; while the words "What will become of me! What will become of me ! " uttered with the most piercing lamentation, struck deep and hard into all our hearts. Never can I forget their desponding sound ; they implied such complicated apprehensions.

Instantly now the princesses were sent for. The three elder hastened down. O, what a meeting! They all, from a habit that has become a second nature, struggling to repress all outward grief, though the queen herself, wholly overcome, wept even aloud. They all went into the bedroom, and the queen made a slight dressing, but only wore a close gauze cap, and her long dressing gown, which is a dimity chemise.

I was then sent back to the little dressing-room, for something that was left; as I opened the door, I almost ran against a gentleman close to it in the passage.

"Is the queen here?" he cried, and I then saw the Prince of Wales.

"Yes," I answered, shuddering at this new scene for her "should I tell her majesty your royal highness is here?"

This I said lest he should surprise her. But he did not intend that: he was profoundly respectful, and consented to wait at the door while I went in, but called me back, as I turned away, to add, "You will be so good to say I am come by her orders."

She wept a deluge of tears when I delivered my commission, but instantly admitted him. I then retreated. The other two ladies went to Lady Elizabeth's room, which is next the queen's new apartments.

In the passage I was again stopped; it was by Mr. Fairly. I would have hurried on, scarce able to speak, but he desired to know how the queen did. "Very bad," was all I could say,

Page 237 and on I hastened to my own room, which, the next minute, I would as eagerly have hastened to quit, from its distance from all that was going forward ; but now once the prince had entered the queen's rooms, I could go thither no more unsummoned.

Miserable, lonely, and filled with dreadful conjectures, I remained here till a very late dinner brought Miss Planta to the dining-parlour, where I joined her. After a short and dismal meal we immediately parted : she to wait in the apartments of the princesses above-stairs, in case of being wanted; I to my own solitary parlour.

The Prince of Wales and Duke of York stayed here all the day, and were so often in and out of the queen's rooms that no one could enter them but by order. The same etiquette is observed when the princes are with the queen as when the king is there-no interruption whatever is made. I now, therefore, lost my only consolation at this calamitous time, that of attending my poor royal mistress.

A VISIT FROM MR. FAIRLY.

Alone wholly, without seeing a human being, or gathering any, the smallest intelligence of what was going forwards, I remained till tea-time. Impatient then for information, I planted myself in the eating-parlour; but no one came. Every minute seemed an hour. I grew as anxious for the tea society as heretofore I had been anxious to escape it; but so late it grew, and so hopeless, that Columb came to propose bringing in the water.

No; for I could swallow nothing voluntarily.

In a few minutes he came again, and with the compliments of Mr. Fairly, who desired him to tell me he would wait Upon me to tea whenever I pleased.

A little surprised at this single message, but most truly rejoiced, I returned my compliments, with an assurance that all time was the same to me. He came directly, and indeed his very sight, at this season of still horror and silent suspense, was a repose to my poor aching eyes.

"You will see," he said, "nobody else. The physicians being now here, Colonel Goldsworthy thought it right to order tea for the whole party in the music-room, which we have now agreed to make the general waiting-room for us all. It is near the king, and we ought always to be at hand." Page 238

Our tea was very sad. He gave me no hope Of a short seizure ; he saw it, in perspective, as long as it was dreadful : perhaps even worse than long, he thought it–but that he said not. He related to me the whole of the day's transactions, but my most dear and most honourable friends will be the first to forgive me when I promise that I shall commit nothing to paper on this terrible event that is told me in confidence.

He did not stay long–he did not think it right to leave his waiting friends for any time, nor could I wish it, valued as I know he is by them all, and much as they need his able counsel. He left me plunged in a deep gloom, yet he was not gloomy himself; he sees evils as things of course, and bears them, therefore, as things expected. But he was tenderly touched for the poor queen and the princesses.

THE KING'S NIGHT WATCHERS.

Not till one in the morning did I see another face, and then I attended my poor unhappy queen. She was now fixed in her new apartments, bed-room and dressing-room, and stirred not a step but from one to the other. Fortunately all are upon the ground-floor, both for king and queen; so are the two Lady Waldegraves' and mine; the princesses and Miss Planta, as usual, are upstairs, and the gentlemen lodge above them.

Miss Goldsworthy had now a bed put up in the queen's new bed-room. She had by no means health to go on sitting up, and it had been the poor king's own direction that she should remain with the queen. It was settled that Mrs. Sandys and Mrs. Macenton should alternately sit up in the dressing-room.

The queen would not permit me to take that office, though most gladly I would have taken any that would have kept me about her. But she does; not think my strength sufficient. She allowed me however to stay with her till she was in bed, which I had never done till now; I never, indeed, had even seen her in her bed-room till the day before. She has always had the kindness and delicacy, to dismiss me from her dressing-room as soon as I have assisted her with her night-clothes; the wardrobe-woman then was summoned, and I regularly made my courtesy. it was a satisfaction to me, however, now to leave her the last, and to come to her the first.

Her present dressing-room is also her dining-room, her drawing-room, her sitting-room; she has nothing else but her bed-room!

I left her with my fervent prayers for better times, and saw her nearer to composure than I had believed possible in such a calamity. She called to her aid her religion, and without it what, indeed, must have become of her? It was near two in the morning when I quitted her.

In passing through the dressing-room to come away, I found Miss Goldsworthy in some distress how to execute a commission of the queen's: it was to her brother, who was to sit up in a room adjoining to the king's ; and she was undressed, and knew not how to go to him, as the princes were to and fro everywhere. I offered to call him to her she thankfully accepted the proposal. I cared not, just then, whom I encountered, so I could make myself of any use.

When I gently opened the door of the apartment to which I was directed, I found it was quite filled with gentlemen and attendants, arranged round it on chairs and sofas in dead silence. It was a dreadful start, with which I retreated; for anything more alarming and shocking could not be conceived! the poor king within another door, unconscious any one was near him, and thus watched, by dread necessity, at such an hour of the night! I pronounced the words "Colonel Goldsworthy," however, before I drew back, though I could not distinguish one gentleman from another, except the two princes, by their stars.

I waited in the next room; but instead of Colonel Goldsworthy, my call was answered by Mr. Fairly. I acquainted him with my errand. He told me he had himself insisted that Colonel Goldsworthy should go to bed, as he had sat up all the preceding night and he had undertaken to supply his place.

I went back to Miss Goldsworthy with this account. She begged me to entreat Mr. Fairly would come to her, as she must now make the commission devolve on him, and could less than ever appear, herself, as they were all assembled in such a party.

Mr. Fairly, most considerately, had remained in this quiet room to see if anything more might be wanted, which spared me the distress of again intruding into the public room. I begged him to follow, and we were proceeding to the dressing-room, when I was stopped by a gentleman, who said, "Does the queen want anybody?"

It was the Prince of Wales. "Not the queen, sir," I answered, " but Miss Goldsworthy, has desired to see Mr. Fairly."

He let me pass, but stopped Mr. Fairly; and, as he seemed inclined to detain him some time, I only told Miss Goldsworthy what had retarded him, and made off to my own room, and soon after two o'clock, I believe, I was in bed.

A CHANGE IN MISS BURNEYs DUTIES.

Friday, Nov. 7.-I was now arrived at a sort of settled regularity of life more melancholy than can possibly be described. I rose at six, dressed, and hastened to the queen's apartments, uncalled, and there waited in silence and in the dark till I heard her move or speak with Miss Goldsworthy, and then presented myself to the sad bedside of the unhappy queen. She sent Miss Goldsworthy early every morning, to make inquiry what sort of night his majesty had passed; and in the middle of the night she commonly Also sent for news by the wardrobe-woman, or Miss Macenton, whichever sat up.

She dismissed Miss Goldsworthy, on my arrival, to dress herself. Lady Elizabeth Waldegrave accommodated her with her own room for that purpose. I had then a long conference with this most patient sufferer - and equal forbearance and quietness during a period of suspensive unhappiness never have I seen, never could I have imagined.

At noon now I never saw her, which I greatly regretted but she kept on her dressing-gown all day, and the princes were continually about the passages, so that no one unsummoned dared approach the queen's apartments. It was only therefore at night and morning I could see her - but my heart was with her the livelong day. And how long, good heaven! how long that day became! Endless I used to think it, for nothing could I do—to wait and to watch—starting at every sound, yet revived by every noise.

MR. FAIRLY SUCCEEDS IN SOOTHING THE KING.

While I was yet with my poor royal sufferer this morning the Prince of Wales came hastily into the room. He apologized for his intrusion, and then gave a very energetic history of the preceding night. It had been indeed most affectingly dreadful ! The king had risen in the middle of the night, and would take no denial to walking into the next room. There he saw the large congress I have mentioned : amazed and in consternation, he demanded what they did there–Much followed that I have heard since, particularly the warmest éloge on his dear son Frederick–his favourite, his friend. "Yes," he cried, "Frederick is my friend!" and this son was then present amongst the rest, but not seen!

Sir George Baker was there, and was privately exhorted by the gentlemen

to lead the king back to his room; but he had not courage: he attempted only to speak, and the king penned him in a corner, told him he was a mere old woman–that he wondered he had ever followed his advice, for he knew nothing of his complaint, which was only nervous!

The Prince of Wales, by signs and whispers, would have urged others to have drawn him away, but no one dared approach him, and he remained there a considerable time. "Nor do I know when he would have been got back," continued the prince, "if at last Mr. Fairly had not undertaken him. I am extremely obliged to Mr. Fairly indeed. He came boldly up to him, and took him by the arm, and begged him to go to bed, and then drew him along, and said he must go. Then he said he would not, and cried 'Who are you?' 'I am Mr. Fairly, sir,' he answered, 'and your majesty has been very good to me often, and now I am going to be very good to you, for you must come to bed, sir: it is necessary to your life.' And then he was so surprised, that he let himself be drawn along just like a child; and so they got him to bed. I believe else he would have stayed all night.

Mr. Fairly has had some melancholy experience in a case of this sort, with a very near connexion of his own. How fortunate he was present!

NEW ARRANGEMENTS.

At noon I had the most sad pleasure of receiving Mr. and Mrs. Smelt. They had heard in York of the illness of the king, and had travelled -post to Windsor. Poor worthy, excellent couple!–Ill and infirm, what did they not suffer from an attack like this–so wonderfully unexpected upon a patron so adored!

They wished the queen to be acquainted with their arrival, yet would not let me risk meeting the princes in carrying the news. Mr. Smelt I saw languished to see his king: he was

persuaded he might now repay a part of former benefits, and he wished to be made his page during his illness, that he might watch and attend him hourly.

I had had a message in the morning by Mr. Gorton, the clerk of the kitchen, to tell me the Prince of Wales wished our dining-parlour to be appropriated to the physicians, both for their dinner and their consultations. I was therefore obliged to order dinner for Miss Planta, and myself in my own Sitting-parlour, which was now unmaterial, as the equerries did not come to tea, but continued +altogether in the music-room.

In the evening, of course, came Mr. Fairly, but then it was only to let me know it would be of course no longer. He then rang the bell for my tea-urn, finding I had waited, though he 0 declined drinking tea with me; but he sat down, and staved half an hour, telling me the long story he had promised which Was a full detail of the terrible preceding night. The transactions of the day also he related to me, and the designs for the future. How alarming were they all! yet many particulars, he said, he omitted, merely because they were yet more affecting, and could be dwelt upon to no purpose.

THE PRINCESS AUGUSTA'S BIRTHDAY.

Saturday, Nov. 8-This was, if possible, the saddest day yet passed: it was the birthday of Princess Augusta, and Mrs. Siddons had been invited to read a play, and a large party of company to form the audience. What a contrast from such an intention was the event!

When I went, before seven o'clock in the morning, to my most unhappy royal mistress, the princes were both in the room. I retreated to the next apartment till they had finished their conference. The Prince of Wales upon these occasions has always been extremely well-bred and condescending in his manner, which, in a situation such as mine, is no immaterial circumstance.

The poor queen then spoke to me of the birthday present she had designed for her most amiable daughter. She hesitated a little whether or not to produce it, but at length meekly said, "Yes, go to Miss Planta and bring it. Do you think there can be any harm in giving it now?"

"O, no!" I said, happy to encourage whatever was a little less gloomy, and upstairs I flew. I was met by all the poor princesses and the Duke of York, who inquired if he might go

again to the queen. I begged leave first to execute my commission. I did; but so engrossed was my mind with the whole of this living tragedy, that I so little noticed what it was I carried as to be now unable to recollect it. I gave it, however, to the queen, who then sent for the princesses, and carried her gift to her daughter, weeping, who received it with a silent courtesy, kissing and wetting with her gentle tears the hand of her afflicted mother.

STRANGE BEHAVIOUR OF THE FIRST GENTLEMAN IN EUROPE. During my mournful breakfast poor Mr. Smelt arrived from Kew, where he had now settled himself. Mr. de Luc also joined us, and they could neither prevail upon themselves to go away all the morning. Mr. Smelt had some thoughts of taking up his abode in Windsor till the state of things should be more decisive. The accounts of the preceding night had been most cruel, and to quit the spot was scarce supportable to him. Yet he feared the princes might disapprove his stay, and he well knew his influence and welcome at Court was all confined to the sick-room: thence, there could now issue no mandate.

Yet I encouraged him to stay; so did Mr. de Luc; and while he was still wavering he saw Dr. Warren in the courtyard, and again hastened to speak with him. Before he returned the Prince of Wales went out and met him; and you may imagine how much I was pleased to observe from the window that he took him by the arm, and walked up and down with him.

When he came to us he said the prince had told him he had better stay, that he might see the queen. He determined, therefore, to send off an express to Mrs. Smelt, and go and secure an apartment at the inn. This was very soothing to me, who so much needed just such consolation as he could bestow - and I begged he would come back to dinner, and spend the whole day in my room, during his stay.

What, however, was my concern and amaze, when, soon after, hastily returning, he desired to speak to me alone, and, as Mr. de Luc moved off, told me he was going back immediately to Kew! He spoke with a tremor that alarmed me. I entreated to know why such a change? He then informed me that the porter, Mr. Humphreys, had refused him re-entrance, and sent him his great coat ! He had resented this

impertinence, and was told it was by the express order of the prince! In utter astonishment he then only desired admittance for one moment to my room, and having acquainted me with this circumstance, he hurried off, in a state of distress, and indignation that left me penetrated with both.

From this time, as the poor king grew worse, general hope seemed universally to abate; and the Prince of Wales now took the government of the house into his own hands. Nothing was done but by his orders, and he was applied to in every difficulty. The queen interfered not in anything - she lived entirely in her two new rooms, and spent the whole day in patient sorrow and retirement with her daughters.

STRINGENT NEW REGULATIONS.

The next news that reached me, through Mr. de Luc, was, that the prince had sent his commands to the porter, to admit only four persons into the house on any pretence whatever these were Mr. Majendie, Mr. Turbulent, General Harcourt, and Mr. de Luc himself; and these were ordered to repair immediately to the equerry-room below stairs, while no one whatsoever was to be allowed to go to any other apartment.

From this time commenced a total banishment from all intercourse out of the house, and an unremitting confinement within its walls.

Poor Mr. de Luc, however, could not forego coming to my room. He determined to risk that, since he was upon the list of those who might enter the house. I was glad, because he is a truly good man, and our sentiments upon this whole melancholy business were the same. But otherwise, the weariness of a great length of visit daily from a person so slow and methodical in discourse, so explanatory of everything and of nothing, at this agitating period, was truly painful to endure. He has often talked to me till my poor burthened head has seemed lost to all understanding.

I had now, all tea-meetings being over, no means of gaining any particulars of what was passing, which added so much to the horror of the situation, that by the evening I was almost petrified. Imagine, then, alike my surprise and satisfaction at a visit from Mr. Fairly. He had never come to me so unexpectedly. I eagerly begged an account of what was going on, and, with his usual readiness and accuracy, he gave it me in full detail. And nothing could be more tragic than all the

particulars every species of evil seemed now hanging over this unhappy family.

He had had his son with him in his room upstairs; "And I had a good mind," he said, "to have brought him to visit YOU."

I assured him he would have been a very welcome guest; and when he added that he could no longer have him at the Equerry table to dinner, as the Prince of Wales now presided there, I invited him for the next day to mine.

He not only instantly accepted the proposal, but cried, with great vivacity, "I wish you would invite me too."

I thought he was laughing, but said, "Certainly, if such a thing might be allowed;" and then, to my almost speechless surprise, he declared, If I would give him permission, he would dine with me next day. He then proceeded to say that the hurry, and fatigue, and violent animal spirits of the other table quite overpowered him, and a respite of such a quiet sort would be of essential service to him. Yet he paused a little afterwards, upon the propriety of leaving the Prince of Wales's table, and said "He would first consult with General Budé, and hear his opinion." Sunday, Nov. 9.-No one went to church - not a creature now quits the house: but I believe devotion never less required the aid and influence of public worship. For me, I know, I spent almost my whole time between prayer and watching. Even my melancholy resource, my tragedy, was now thrown aside ; misery so actual, living, and present, was knit too closely around me to allow my depressed imagination to fancy any woe beyond what my heart felt.

In coming early from the queen's apartment this morning I was addressed by a gentleman who inquired how I did, by my name; but my bewilderment made him obliged to tell his own before I could recollect him. It was Dr. Warren.

I eagerly expressed my hopes and satisfaction in his attendance upon the poor king, but he would not enter upon that subject. I suppose he feared, from my zeal, some indiscreet questions concerning his opinion of the case; for he passed by all I could start, to answer only with speeches relative to myself-of his disappointment in never meeting me, though residing under the same roof, his surprise in not dining with me when told he was to dine in my room, and the strangeness of never seeing me when so frequently he heard my name.

I could not bring myself to ask him to my apartment, when
I saw, by his whole manner, e held it imprudent to speak with me about the only subject on which I wished to talk—the king; and just then seeing the Duke of York advancing, I hastily retreated.

While I was dressing, Mr. Fairly rapped at my door. I sent out Goter, who brought me his compliments, and, if it would not be inconvenient to me, he and his son would have the pleasure of dining with me.

I answered, I should be very glad of their company, as would Miss Planta. Miss Goldsworthy had now arranged herself with the Lady Waldegraves.

Our dinner was as pleasant as a dinner at such a season could be. Mr. Fairly holds cheerfulness as a duty in the midst of every affliction that can admit it; and, therefore,, whenever his animal spirits have a tendency to rise, he encourages and sustains them, So fond, too, is he of his son, that his very sight is a cordial to him - and that mild, feeling, amiable boy quite idolizes his father, looking up to him, hanging on his arm, and watching his eye to smile and be smiled upon, with a fondness like that of an infant to its maternal nurse.

Repeatedly Mr. Fairly exclaimed, "What a relief is this, to dine thus quietly!"

What a relief should I, too, have found it, but for a little circumstance, which I will soon relate,

MRS. SCHWELLENBERG IS BACK AGAIN.

We were still at table, with the dessert, when Columb entered and announced the sudden return from Weymouth of Mrs. Schwellenberg.

Up we all started; Miss Planta flew out to receive her, and state the situation of the house; Mr. Fairly, expecting, I believe, she was coming into my room, hastily made his exit without a word; his son eagerly scampered after him, and I followed Miss Planta upstairs. My reception, however, was such as to make me deem it most proper to again return to my room. What an addition this to the gloom of all ! and to begin at once with harshness and rudeness! I could hardly tell how to bear it.

Nov. 10.-This was a most dismal day. The dear and most suffering king was extremely ill, the queen very wretched, poor Mrs. Schwellenberg all spasm and horror, Miss Planta all restlessness, the house all mystery, and my only informant and comforter distanced. Not a word, the whole day through, did I hear of what was passing or intending. Our dinner was worse than an almost famished fasting; we parted after it, and met no more. Mrs. Schwellenberg, who never drinks tea herself, hearing the general party was given up, and never surmising there had ever been any particular one, neither desired me to come to her, nor proposed returning to me. She took possession of the poor queen's former dressing-room, and between that and the adjoining apartments she spent all the day, except during dinner.

Nov. 11.-This day passed like the preceding; I only saw her majesty in the morning, and not another human being from that hour till Mrs. Schwellenberg and Miss Planta came to dinner. Nor could I then gather any information of the present state of things, as Mrs. Schwellenberg announced that nothing must be talked of.

To give any idea of the dismal horror of passing so many hours in utter ignorance, where every interest of the mind was sighing for intelligence, would not be easy: the experiment alone could give it its full force; and from that, Heaven ever guard my loved readers!

Nov. 12.-To-day a little brightened upon us some change appeared in the loved royal sufferer, and though it was not actually for the better in itself, yet any change was pronounced to be salutary, as, for some days pas" there had been a monotonous continuation of the same bad symptoms, that had doubly depressed us all. My spirits rose immediately ; indeed, I thank God, I never desponded, though many times I stood nearly alone in my hopes.

In the passage, in the morning, I encountered Colonel Gwynn. I had but just time to inform him I yet thought all would do well, ere the princes appeared. All the equerries are now here except Major Garth, who is ill; and they have all ample employment in watching and waiting. From time to time they have all interviews; but it is only because the poor king will not be denied seeing them: it is not thought light. But I must enter into nothing of this sort-it is all too closely connected with private domestic concerns for paper. After dinner, my chief guest, la Présidente, told me, " If my room was not so warm, she would stay a little with me." I felt this would be rather too superlative an obligation; and therefore I simply answered that "I was too chilly to sit in a

cold room;" and I confess I took no pains to temper it according to this hint.

PUBLIC PRAYERS FOR THE KING DECIDED UPON.

Finding there was now no danger Of disagreeable interviews, Mr. Fairly renewed his visits as usual. He came early this evening, and narrated the state of things; and then, with a laugh, he Inquired What I had done With my head companion, and how I got rid of her? I fairly told him my malice about the temperature.

He could not help laughing, though he instantly remonstrated against an expedient that might prove prejudicial to my health. "You had better not," he cried, "try any experiments of this sort: if you hurt Your nerves, it may prove a permanent evil; this other can only be temporary."

He took up the "Task" again; but he opened, by ill luck, upon nothing striking or good; and soon, with distaste, flung the book down, and committed himself wholly to conversation.

He told me he wished much he had been able to consult with me on the preceding morning, when he had the queen's orders to write, in her majesty's name, to the Archbishop of Canterbury, to issue out public prayers for the poor king, for all the churches.

I assured him I fancied it might do very well without my aid. There was to be a privy council summoned, in consequence of the letter, to settle the mode of compliance.

How right a step in my ever-right royal mistress is this! If you hear less of her now, my dearest friends, and of the internal transactions, it is only because I now rarely saw her but alone, and all that passed, therefore, was in promised confidence. And, for the rest, the whole of my information concerning the princes, and the plans and the proceedings of the house, was told me in perfect reliance on my secrecy and honour.

I know this is saying enough to the most honourable of all confidants and friends to whom I am writing. All that passes with regard to myself is laid completely before them.

Nov. 13- This was the fairest day we have passed since the first seizure of the most beloved of monarchs. He was considerably better. O what a ray of joy lightened us, and how mildly did my poor queen receive it

Nov. 14–Still all was greatly amended, and better spirits reigned throughout the house.

Mr. Fairly–I can write of no one else, for no one else did I see–called early, to tell me he had received an answer relative to the prayer for his majesty's recovery, in consequence of which he had the queen's commands for going to town the next day, to see the archbishop. This was an employment so suited to the religious cast of his character, that I rejoiced to see it fall into his hands.

He came again in the evening, and said he had now got the prayer. He did not entirely approve it, nor think it sufficiently warm and animated. I petitioned to hear it, and he readily complied, and read it with great reverence, but very unaffectedly and quietly. I was very, very much touched by It ; yet not, I own, quite so much as once before by another, which was read to me by Mr. Cambridge, and composed by his son, for the sufferings of his excellent daughter Catherine. It was at once so devout, yet so concise–so fervent, yet so simple, and the many tender relations concerned in it–father, brother, sister,–so powerfully affected me, that I had no command over the feelings then excited, even though Mr. Cambridge almost reproved me for want of fortitude; but there was something so tender in a prayer of a brother for a sister.

Here, however, I was under better control - for though my whole heart was filled with the calamitous state of this unhappy monarch, and with deepest affliction for all his family, I yet knew so well my reader was one to severely censure all failure in calmness and firmness, that I struggled, and not ineffectually, to hear him with a steadiness like his own. But, fortunately for the relief of this force, he left the room for a few minutes to see if he was wanted, and I made use of his absence to give a little vent to those tears which I had painfully restrained in his presence.

When he returned we had one of the best (on his part) conversations in which I have ever been engaged, upon the highest and most solemn of all subjects, prayers and supplications to heaven. He asked my opinion with earnestness, and gave his own with unbounded openness.

Nov. 15-This morning my poor royal mistress herself presented me with one of the prayers for the king. I shall always keep it – how–how fervently did I use it!

Whilst I was at breakfast Mr. Fairly once more called before he set off for town and he brought me also a copy of the

prayer. He had received a large packet of them from the archbishop, Dr. Moore, to distribute in the house.

The whole day the king continued amended.

Sunday, Nov. 16.-This morning I ventured out to church. I did not like to appear abroad, but yet I had a most irresistible earnestness to join the public congregation in the prayer for the king. Indeed nothing could be more deeply moving: the very sound of the cathedral service, performed in his own chapel, overset me at once; and every prayer in the service in which he was mentioned brought torrents of tears from all the suppliants that joined in them. I could scarcely keep my place, scarce command my voice from audible sobs. To come to the House of prayer from such a house of woe! I ran away when the service was over, to avoid inquiries. Mrs. Kennedy ran after me, with swollen eyes; I could not refuse her a hasty answer, but I ran the faster after it, to avoid any more.

The king was worse. His night had been very bad ; all the fair promise of amendment was shaken; he had now some symptoms even dangerous to his life. O good heaven, what a day did this prove! I saw not a human face, save at dinner and then, what faces! gloom and despair in all, and silence to every species of intelligence. . . .

It was melancholy to see the crowds of former welcome visitors who were now denied access. The prince reiterated his former orders; and I perceived from my window those who had ventured to the door returning back in deluges of tears. Amongst them to-day I perceived poor Lady Effingham, the Duchess of Ancaster, and Mr. Bryant ; the last sent me In, afterwards, a mournful little letter, to which he desired no answer. Indeed I was not at liberty to write a word.

SIR LuCAS PEPYS ON THE KING's CONDITION.

Nov. 19.-The account of the dear king this morning was rather better.

Sir Lucas Pepys was now called in, and added to Dr. Warren, Dr. Heberden, and Sir George Baker. I earnestly wished to see him, and I found my poor royal mistress was secretly anxious to know his opinion. I sent to beg to speak with him, as soon as the consultation was over; determined, however, to make that request no more if he was as shy of giving information as Dr. Warren,

poor Mr. de Luc was with me wen he came ; but it was necessary I should see Sir Lucas alone, that I might have a better claim upon his discretion : nevertheless I feared he would have left me, without the smallest intelligence, before I was able to make my worthy, but most slow companion comprehend the necessity of his absence.

The moment we were alone, Sir Lucas opened upon the subject in the most comfortable manner. He assured me there was nothing desponding in the case, and that his royal patient would certainly recover, though not immediately.

Whilst I was in the midst of the almost speechless joy with which I heard this said, and ready to kiss the very feet of Sir Lucas for words of such delight, a rap at my door made me open it to Mr. Fairly, who entered, saying, "I must come to ask you how you do, though I have no good news to bring you; but–"

He then, with the utmost amaze, perceived Sir Lucas. In so very many visits he had constantly found me alone, that I really believe he had hardly thought it possible he should see me in any other way.

They then talked over the poor king's situation, and Sir Lucas was very open and comforting. How many sad meetings have I had with him heretofore ; first in the alarming attacks of poor Mr. Thrale, and next in the agonizing fluctuations of his unhappy widow!

Sir Lucas wished to speak with me alone, as he had something he wanted, through me, to communicate to the queen; but as he saw Mr. Fairly not disposed to retire first, by his manner of saying "Sir Lucas, you will find all the breakfast ready below stairs," he made his bow, and said he would see me again.

Mr. Fairly then informed me he was quite uneasy at the recluse life led by the queen and the princesses, and that he was anxious to prevail with them to take a little air, which must be absolutely necessary to their health. He was projecting a scheme for this purpose, which required the assistance of the Duke of York, and he left me, to confer upon it with his royal highness, promising to return and tell its success.

Sir Lucas soon came back, and then gave me such unequivocal assurances of the king's recovery, that the moment he left me I flew to demand a private audience of the queen, that I might relate such delightful prognostics.

The Duke of York was with her, I waited in the passage,

where I met Lady Charlotte Finch, and tried what I could to instil into her mind the hopes I entertained: this, however, was not possible; a general despondency prevailed throughout the house, and Lady Charlotte was infected by it very deeply.

At length I gained admission and gave my account, which was most meekly received by the most patient of sorrowers.

At night came Mr. Fairly again; but, before he entered into any narrations he asked "DO you expect Sir Lucas?"

"No," I said, "he had been already."

"I saw him rise early from table," he added, "and I thought he was coming to YOU."

He has taken no fancy to poor Sir Lucas, and would rather, apparently, avoid meeting him. However, it is to me so essential a comfort to hear his opinions, that I have earnestly entreated to see him by every opportunity.

FURTHER CHANGES AT THE LODGE.

The equerries now had their own table as usual, to which the physicians were regularly invited, downstairs, and our eating-party was restored. The princes established a table of their own at the Castle, to which they gave daily invitations to such as they chose, from time to time, to select from the Lodge.

The noise of so large a party just under the apartment of the queen occasioned this new regulation, which took place by her majesty's own direction.

Nov. 20.-Poor Miss Goldsworthy was now quite ill, and forced to retire and nurse. No wonder, for she had suffered the worst sort of fatigue, that of fearing to sleep, from the apprehension the queen might speak, and want her. Lady Elizabeth Waldegrave now took her place Of sleeping in the queen's room, but the office of going for early intelligence how his majesty had passed the night devolved upon me.

Exactly at seven o'clock I now went to the queen's apartment - Lady Elizabeth then rose and went to her own room to dress, and I received the queen's commands for my inquiries. I could not, however, go myself into the room where they assembled, which Miss Goldsworthy, who always applied to her brother, had very properly done : I sent in a message to beg to speak with General Bud, or whoever could bring an account.

Mr. Charles Hawkins came; he had sat up. O, how terrible a narrative did he drily give of the night!–short, abrupt,

peremptorily bad, and indubitably hopeless! I did not dare alter, but I greatly softened this relation, in giving it to my poor queen. I had been, indeed, too much shocked by the hard way in which I had been told it, to deliver it in the same manner; neither did I, in my own heart, despair.

I saw Sir Lucas afterwards, who encouraged all my more sanguine opinions. He told me many new regulations had been made. His majesty was to be kept as quiet as possible, and see only physicians, except for a short and stated period in every day, during which he might summon such among his gentlemen as he pleased.

Mr. Fairly came also early, and wrote and read letters of great consequence relative to the situation of affairs ; and he told me he was then to go to the king, who had refused his assent to the new plan, and insisted upon seeing him when he came in from his ride, which, to keep him a little longer quiet, they had made him believe he was then taking. The gentlemen had agreed to be within call alternately, and he meant to have his own turn always in the forenoon, that his evenings might have some chance for quiet, The rest of the day was comfortless; my coadjutrix was now grown so fretful and affronting that, though we only met at dinner, it was hard to support her most unprovoked harshness.

MR. FAIRLY AND THE LEARNED LADIES.

At night, while I was just sealing a short note to my dear Miss Cambridge, who had an anxiety like that of my own Susan and Fredy lest I should suffer from my present fatigues, I heard the softest tap at my door, which, before I could either put down my letter or speak, was suddenly but most gently opened.

I turned about and saw a figure wrapped up in a great, coat, with boots and a hat on, who cautiously entered, and instantly closed the door. I stared, and looked very hard, but the face was much hid by the muffling of the high collar to the great coat. I wondered, and could not conceive who it could be. The figure then took off his hat and bowed, but he did not advance, and the light was away from him. I courtsied, and wondered more, and then a surprised voice exclaimed, "Don't you know me?" and I found it was Mr. Fairly.

"I cannot," he said, "stop now, but I will come again; however, you know it, perhaps, already?

"Know what?"

"Why–the–news."

"What news?"

"Why–that the king is much better, and–"

"Yes, Sir Lucas said so, but I have seen nobody since."

"No? And have you heard nothing more?"

"Nothing at all; I cannot guess what you mean."

"What, then, have not you heard–how Much the king has talked? And–and have not you heard the charge."

"No; I have heard not a word of any charge."

"Why, then, I'll tell you."

A long preamble, uttered very rapidly, of "how much the king had been talking," seemed less necessary to introduce his intelligence than to give him time to arrange it; and I was so much struck with this, that I could not even listen to him, from impatience to have him proceed.

Suddenly, however, breaking off, evidently from not knowing how to go on, he exclaimed, "Well, I shall tell it you all by and by; you come in for your share!"

Almost breathless now with amaze, I could hardly cry,

"Do I?"

"Yes, I'll tell you," cried he; but again he stopped, and, hesitatingly, said, "You–you won't be angry?"

"No," I answered, still more amazed, and even almost terrified, at what I had now to expect.

"Well, then," cried he, instantly resuming his first gay and rapid manner, "the king has been calling them all to order for staying so long away from him. 'All the equerries and gentlemen here,' he said, 'lost their whole time at the table, by drinking so much wine and sitting so long over their bottle, which constantly made them all so slow in returning to their waiting, that when he wanted them in the afternoon they were never ready; and-and-and Mr. Fairly,' says he, 'is as bad as any of them; not that he stays so long at table, or is so fond of wine, but he's just as late as the rest; for he's so fond of the company of learned ladies, that he gets to the tea-table with Miss Burney, and there he stays and spends his whole time.'"

He spoke all this like the velocity of lightning- but, had it been with the most prosing slowness, I had surely never interrupted him, so vexed I was, so surprised, so completely disconcerted. Finding me silent, he began again, and as rapidly as ever; "I know exactly," he cried, "what it all means–what

Page 255 the king has in his head–exactly what has given rise to the idea–'tis Miss Fuzilier."

Now, indeed, I stared afresh, little expecting to hear her named by him. He went on in too much hurry for me to recollect his precise words, but he spoke of her very highly, and mentioned her learning, her education, and her acquirements, with great praise, yet with that sort of general commendation that disclaims all peculiar interest; and then, with some degree of displeasure mixed in his voice, mentioned the report that had been spread concerning- them, and its having reached the ears of the king before his Illness. He then lightly added something I could not completely hear, of its utter falsehood, in a way that seemed to hold even a disavowal too important for it, and then concluded with saying, "And this in the present confused state of his mind is altogether, I know, what he means by the learned ladies."

When he had done he looked earnestly for my answer, but finding I made none, he said, with some concern, "You won't think any more of it?"

"No," I answered, rather faintly.

In a lighter manner then, as if to treat the whole as too light for a thought, he said, as he was leaving the room to change his dress, "Well, since I have now got the character of being so fond of such company, I shall certainly"—he stopped short, evidently at a loss how to go on; but quickly after, with a laugh, he hastily added, "come and drink tea with you very often;" and then, with another laugh, which he had all to himself, he hurried away.

He left me, however, enough to think upon and the predominant thought was an immediate doubt whether or not, since his visits had reached the king, his majesty's observation upon them ought to stop their continuance?

Upon the whole, however, when I summed up all, I found not cause sufficient for any change of system. No raillery had passed upon me; and, for him, he had stoutly evinced a determined contempt of it. Nothing of flirtation had been mentioned for either; I had merely been called a learned lady, and he had merely been accused Of liking such company. I had no other social comfort left me but Mr. Fairly, and I had discomforts past all description or suggestion. Should I drive him from me, what would pay me, and how had he deserved it? and which way could it be worth while? His friendship offered me a solace without hazard; it was held out to me Page 256

when all else was denied me; banished from every friend, confined almost to a state of captivity, harrowed to the very soul with surrounding afflictions, and without a glimpse of light as to when or how all might terminate, it seemed to me, in this situation, that providence had benignly sent in my way a character of so much worth and excellence, to soften the rigour of my condition, by kind sympathy and most honourable confidence.

This idea was sufficient; and I thence determined to follow as he led, in disdaining any further notice, or even remembrance, if possible, of this learned accusation.

Nov. 21.-All went better and better to-day, and I received from the king's room a more cheering account to carry to my poor queen. We had now hopes of a speedy restoration :

the king held long conferences with all his gentlemen, and, though far from composed, was so frequently rational as to- make any resistance to his will nearly impossible. Innumerable difficulties attended this state, but the general promise it gave of a complete recovery recompensed them all.

Sir Lucas Pepys came to me in the morning and acquainted me with the rising hopes of amendment. But he disapproved the admission of so many gentlemen, and would have limited the license to only the equerry in waiting, Colonel Goldsworthy, and Mr. Fairly, who was now principal throughout the house, in universal trust for his superior judgment.

The king, Sir Lucas said, now talked of everybody and everything he could recollect or suggest.

So I have heard, thought I.

And, presently after, he added, "No one escapes; you will have your turn."

Frightened lest he knew I had had it, I eagerly exclaimed, "O, no; I hope not."

"And why?" cried he, good-humouredly; "what need you care? He can say no harm of you."

I ventured then to ask if yet I had been named? He believed not yet.

This doubled my curiosity to know to whom the "learned ladies" had been mentioned, and whether to Mr. Fairly himself, or to someone who related it; I think the latter, but there is no way to inquire.

Very early in the evening I heard a rap at my door. I was in my inner room, and called out, "Who's there?" The door opened and Mr, Fairly appeared.

He had been so long in attendance this morning with our poor sick monarch, that he was too much fatigued to join the dinner-party. He had stood five hours running, besides the concomitant circumstances of attention. He had instantly laid down when he procured his dismission, and had only risen to eat some cold chicken before he came to my room. During that repast he had again been demanded, but he charged the gentleman to make his excuse, as he could go through nothing further.

I hope the king did not conclude him again with the learned; This was the most serene, and even cheerful evening,, I had passed since the poor king's first seizure.

REPORTS ON THE KING'S CONDITION.

Nov. 22.-When I went for my morning inquiries, Colonel Manners came out to me. He could give me no precise account, as the sitters-up had not yet left the king, but he feared the night had been bad. We mutually bewailed the mournful state of the house. He is a very good creature at heart, though as unformed as if he had just left Eton or Westminster. But he loves his master with a true and faithful heart, and is almost as ready to die as to live for him, if any service of that risk was proposed to him.

While the queen's hair was dressing, though only for a close cap, I was sent again. Colonel Manners came out to me, and begged I would enter the music-room, as Mr. Keate, the surgeon, had now just left the king, and was waiting to give me an account before he laid down.

I found him in his night-cap: he took me up to a window, and gave me but a dismal history : the night had been very unfavourable, and the late amendment very transient. I heard nothing further till the evening, when my constant companion came to me. All, he said, was bad: he had been summoned and detained nearly all the morning, and had then rode to St. Leonard's to get a little rest, as he would not return till after dinner.

He had but just begun his tea when his name was called aloud in the passage: up he started, seized his hat, and with a hasty bow, decamped. I fancy it was one of the princes; and the more, as he did not come back.

Sunday, Nov. 23.-A sad day this! I was sent as usual for

the night account, which I had given to me by Mr. Fairly, and a very dismal one indeed. Yet I never, upon this point, yield implicitly to his opinion, as I see him frequently of the despairing side, and as for myself, I thank God, my hopes never wholly fall. A certain faith in his final recovery has uniformly supported my spirits from the beginning. . .

In the evening, a small tap at my door, with, "Here I am again," ushered in Mr. Fairly. He seemcd much hurried and disturbed, and innately uncomfortable; and very soon he entered into a detail of the situation of affairs that saddened me in the extreme. The poor king was very ill indeed, and so little aware of his own condition, that he would submit to no rule, and chose to have company with him from morning till night, sending out for the gentlemen one after another without intermission, and chiefly for Mr. Fairly, who, conscious it was hurtful to his majesty, and nearly worn out himself, had now no chance of respite or escape but by leaving the house and riding out. . . .

I have never seen him so wearied, or so vexed, I know not which. "How shall I rejoice," he cried, "when all this is over, and I can turn my back to this scene!"

I should rejoice, I said, for him when he could make his escape; but his use here, in the whole round, is infinite; almost nothing is done without consulting him.

"I wish," he cried, while he was making some memorandums, "I could live without sleep; I know not now how to spare my night." He then explained to me various miscellaneous matters of occupation, and confessed himself forced to break from the confused scene of action as much as possible, where the tumult and bustle were as overpowering, as the affliction, in the more quiet apartments, was dejecting. Then, by implication, what credit did he not give to my Poor still room, which he made me understand was his only refuge and consolation in this miserable house!

MR. FAIRLY THINKS THE KING NEEDS STRICTER MANAGEMENT. Nov. 24.-Very bad again was the night's account, which I received at seven o'clock this morning from Mr. DUndas. I returned with it to my Poor royal mistress, who heard it with her usual patience.

While I was still with her, Lady Elizabeth came with a request from Mr. Fairly, for an audience before her majesty's breakfast. As soon as she was ready she ordered me to tell Lady Elizabeth to bring him. . . .

Soon after,–with a hasty rap, came Mr. Fairly. He brought his writing to my table, where I was trying to take off impressions of plants. I Saw he meant to read me his letter; but before he had finished it Lady Charlotte Finch came in search of him. It was not for the queen, but herself; she wished to speak and consult with him upon the king's seeing his children, which was now his vehement demand.

He was writing for one of the king's messengers, and could not stop till he had done. Poor Lady Charlotte, overcome with tenderness and compassion, wept the whole time he was at his pen; and when he had put it down, earnestly remonstrated on the cruelty of the present regulations, which debarred his majesty the sight of the princesses. I joined with her, though more firmly, believe me; my tears I suppress for my solitude. I have enough of that to give them vent, and, with all my suppression, my poor aching eyes can frequently scarce see one object from another.

When Mr. Fairly left off writing he entered very deeply into argument with Lady Charlotte. He was averse to her request; he explained the absolute necessity of strong measures, and of the denial of dangerous indulgences, while the poor king was in this wretched state. The disease, he said, was augmented by every agitation, and the discipline of forced quiet was necessary till he was capable of some reflection. At present he spoke everything that occurred to him, and in a manner so wild, unreasonable, and dangerous, with regard to future constructions, that there could be no kindness so great to him as to suffer him only to see those who were his requisite attendants.

He then enumerated many instances very forcibly, in which he showed how much more properly his majesty might have been treated, by greater strength of steadiness in his management. He told various facts which neither of us had heard, and, at last, in speaking of the most recent occurrences, he fell into a narrative relating to himself.

The king, he said, had almost continually demanded him of late, and with the most extreme agitation; he had been as much with him as it was possible for his health to bear. "Five hours,,,, continued he, "I spent with him on Friday, and four

on Saturday, and three and a half yesterday; yet the moment I went to him last night, he accused me of never coming near him. He said I gave him up entirely; that I was always going out, always dining out, always going to Mrs. Harcourt's—riding to St. Leonard's; but he knew why—'twas to meet Miss Fuzilier." . . .

Poor Lady Charlotte was answered, and, looking extremely sorry, went away.

He then read me his messenger's letter. 'Twas upon a very delicate affair, relative to the Prince of Wales, in whose service, he told me, he first began his Court preferment.

When he had made up his packet he returned to the subject of the king's rage, with still greater openness. He had attacked him, he said, more violently than ever about Miss Fuzilier which, certainly, as there had been such a report, was very unpleasant. "And when I seriously assured him," he added, "that there was nothing in it, he said 'I had made him the happiest of men.'"

Nov. 25.—My morning account was from General Bud, and a very despairing one. He has not a ray of hope for better days.

My poor queen was so much pleased with a sort of hymn for the king, which she had been reading In the newspapers, that I scrupled not to tell her of one in manuscript, which, of course, she desired to read; but I stipulated for its return, though I could not possibly stay in the room while she looked at it.

MR. FAIRLY WANTS A CHANGE.

In the evening Mr. Fairly came, entering with a most gently civil exclamation of "How long it is since I have seen you!"

I could not answer, it was only one evening missed; for, in truth, a day at this time seems liberally a week, and a very slow one too. He had been to town, suddenly sent by the queen last night, and had returned only at noon.

he gave me a full account of all that was passing and projecting; and awfully critical everything seemed. "He should now soon," he said, "quit the tragic scene, and go to relax and recruit, with his children, in the country. He regarded his service here as nearly over, since an entirely new regulation was planning, in which the poor king was no longer to be allowed the sight of any of his gentlemen. His continual long conversations with them were judged utterly improper, and

Page 261 he was only to be attended by the medical people and his pages."

He then gave into my hands the office of hinting to the queen his intention, if he could be dispensed with by her majesty, to go into the Country on the 12th of next month (December), with his boy Charles, who then left Eton for the Christmas holidays. I knew this would be unwelcome intelligence, but I wished to forward his departure, and would not refuse the commission. When this was settled he said he would go and take a circuit, and see how matters stood; and then, if he could get away after showing himself, return–if I would give him leave to drink his tea with me.

He had not been gone ten minutes before Lady Charlotte came in search of him. She had been told, she said, that he was with me. I laughed, but could not forbear asking if I passed for his keeper, since whenever he was missing I was always called to account for him. Again, however, he came and drank his tea, and stayed an hour, in most confidential discourse.

When the new regulation is established, only one gentleman is to remain–which will be the equerry in waiting. This is now Colonel Goldsworthy. The rest will disperse.

REMOVAL OF THE KING To KEW DETERMINED UPON. Nov. 26.-I found we were all speedily to remove to Kew. This was to be kept profoundly secret till almost the moment of departure. The king will never consent to quit Windsor and to allure him away by some stratagem occupies all the physicians, who have proposed and enforced this measure. Mr. Fairly is averse to it: the king's repugnance he thinks insurmountable, and that it ought not to be opposed. But the princes take part with the physicians.

He left me to ride out, but more cordial and with greater simplicity of kindness than ever, he smilingly said in going, "Well, good bye, and God bless you."

"Amen," quoth I, after he had shut the door.

Nov. 27.-This morning and whole day were dreadful My early account was given me by Mr. Charles Hawkins, and with such determined decision of incurability, that I left him quite in horror. All that I dared, I softened to my poor queen, who was now harassed to death with state affairs, and impending storms of state dissensions, I would have given

Page 262 the world to have spent the whole day by her side, and poured in what balm of hope I could, since it appeared but too Visibly she scarce received a ray from any other.

Universal despondence now pervaded the whole house. Sir Lucas, indeed, sustained his original good opinion, but he was nearly overpowered by standing alone, and was forced to let the stream take its course with but little opposition. Even poor Mr. de Luc was silenced ; Miss Planta easily yields to fear; and Mrs. Schwellenberg–who thinks it treason to say the king is ever at all indisposed–not being able to say all was quite well, forbade a single word being uttered upon the subject The dinners, therefore, became a time of extremest pain; all was ignorance, mystery, and trembling expectation of evil.

In the evening, thank heaven! came again my sole relief, Mr. Fairly. He brought his son. and they entered with such serene aspects, that I soon shook off a little of my gloom; and I heard there was no new cause, for though all was bad, nothing was worse. We talked over everything; and that always opens the mind, and softens the bitterness of sorrow.

The prospect before us, with respect to Kew, is indeed terrible. There is to be a total seclusion from all but those within the walls, and those are to be contracted to merely necessary attendants. Mr. Fairly disapproved the scheme, though a gainer by it of leisure and liberty. Only the equerry in waiting Is to have a room in the house;

the rest of the gentlemen are to take their leave. He meant, therefore, himself, to go into the country with all speed.

Nov. 28.-How woful-how bitter a day, in every part, was this!

My early account was from the king's page, Mr. Stillingfleet, and the night had been extremely bad. I dared not sink the truth to my poor queen, though I mixed in it whatever I Could devise of cheer and hope; and she bore it with the most wonderful calmness.

Dr. Addington was now called in: a very old physician, but peculiarly experienced in disorders such as afflicted our poor king, though not professedly a practitioner in them.

Sir Lucas made me a visit, and informed me of all the medical proceedings; and told me, in confidence, we were to go to Kew to-morrow, though the queen herself had not yet concurred in the measure; but the physicians joined to desire

Page 263 it, and they were supported by the princes. The difficulty how to get the king away from his favourite abode was all that rested. If they even attempted force, they had not a doubt but his smallest resistance would call up the whole country to his fancied rescue! Yet how, at such a time, prevail by persuasion?

He moved me even to tears, by telling me that none of their own lives would be safe if the king did not recover so Prodigiously high ran the tide of affection and loyalty. All the physicians received threatening letters daily to answer for the safety of their monarch with their lives! Sir George Baker had already been Stopped in his carriage by the mob to give an account of the king; and when he said it Was a bad one, they had furiously exclaimed, "The more shame for you!"

A PRIVY COUNCIL HELD.

After he left me, a privy council was held at the Castle, with the Prince of Wales; the chancellor,(300) Mr. Pitt, and all the officers of state were summoned, to sign a Permission for the king's removal. The poor queen gave an audience to the chancellor– it was necessary to sanctify their proceedings. The princess royal and Lady Courtown attended her. It was a tragedy the most dismal!

The queen's knowledge of the king's aversion to Kew made her consent to this measure with the extremest reluctance yet it was not to be opposed: It Was stated as much the best for him, on account of the garden: as here there is none but what Is Public to spectators from the terrace or tops of houses. I believe they were perfectly right though the removal was so tremendous. The physicians were summoned to the privy Council, to give their Opinions, upon oath, that this step was necessary.

Inexpressible was the alarm of everyone, lest the king, if he recovered, should bear a lasting resentment against the authors and promoters of this Journey. To give it, therefore, every possible sanction it was decreed that he should be seen, both by the chancellor and Mr. Pitt.

The chancellor went in to his presence with a tremor such as, before, he had been only accustomed to inspire; and when he came out, he was so extremely affected by the state in which he

saw his royal master and patron that the tears ran down his cheeks, and his feet had difficulty to support him. Mr. Pitt was more composed, but expressed his grief with so much respect and attachment, that it added new weight to the universal admiration with which he is here beheld.

All these circumstances, with various others, of equal sadness which I must not relate, came to my knowledge from Sir Lucas, Mr. de Luc, and my noon attendance upon her majesty, who was compelled to dress for her audience of the chancellor. And, altogether, with the horror of the next day's removal, an([the gloom of the ensuing Kew residence, I was so powerfully depressed, that when Mr. Fairly came in the evening, not all my earnestness to support my firmness could re-animate me, and I gave him a most solemn reception, and made the tea directly, and almost in silence.

He endeavoured, at first, to revive me by enlivening discourse, but finding that fail, he had recourse to more serious means. He began his former favourite topic-the miseries of life-the inherent miseries, he thinks them, to which we are so universally born and bred, that it was as much consonant with our reason to expect as with our duty to support them.

I heard him with that respect his subject and his character alike merited; but I could not answer–my heart was sunk–my spirits were all exhausted: I knew not what to expect next, nor how I might be enabled to wade through the dreadful winter. . . .

He had not, I saw, one ray of hope to offer me of better times, yet he recommended me to cheer myself; but not by more sanguine expectations–simply and solely by religion. To submit, he said, to pray and to submit, were all we had to do. . . .

The voice of the Prince of Wales, in the passage, carried him away. They remained together, in deep conference, all the rest of the evening, consulting upon measures for facilitating the king's removal, and obtaining his consent.

I went very late to the queen, and found her in deep sorrow but nothing confidential passed: I found her not alone, nor alone did I leave her. But I knew what was passing in her mind–the removing the king!-Its difficulty and danger at present, and the dread of his permanent indignation hereafter.

THE REMOVAL To KEW.

Nov. 29.-Shall I ever forget the varied emotions of this dreadful day! I rose with the heaviest of hearts, and found my poor royal mistress in the deepest dejection: she told me now of our intended expedition to Kew. Lady Elizabeth hastened away to dress, and I was alone with her for some time. Her mind, she said, quite misgave her about Kew: the king's dislike was terrible to think of, and she could not foresee in what it might end. She would have resisted the measure herself, hut that she had determined not to have upon her own mind any opposition to the opinion of the physicians.

The account of the night was still more and more discouraging: it was related to me by one of the pages, Mr. Brawan; and though a little I softened or omitted particulars, I yet most sorrowfully conveyed it to the queen.

Terrible was the morning!–uninterruptedly terrible! all spent in hasty packing up, preparing for we knew not what, nor for how long, nor with what circumstances, nor scarcely with what view! We seemed preparing for captivity, without having committed any offence; and for banishment, without the least conjecture when we might be recalled from it.

The poor queen was to get off in private: the plan settled, between the princes and the physicians, was, that her majesty and the princesses should go away quietly, and then that the king should be told that they were gone, which was the sole method they could devise to prevail with him to follow. He was then to be allured by a promise of seeing them at Kew again, as they knew he would doubt their assertion, he was to go through the rooms and examine the house himself.

I believe it was about ten o'clock when her majesty departed drowned in tears, she glided along the passage, and got softly into her carriage, with two weeping princesses, and Lady Courtown, who was to be her lady-in-waiting during this dreadful residence. Then followed the third princess, With Lady Charlotte Finch. They went off without any state or parade, and a more melancholy Scene cannot be imagined. There was not a dry eye in the house. The footmen, the house-maids, the porter, the sentinels–all cried even bitterly as they looked on.

The three younger princesses were to wait till the event was known. Lady Elizabeth Waldegrave and Miss Goldsworthy had their royal highnesses in charge,

Page 266 It was settled the king was to be attended by three of his gentlemen, in the carriage, and to be followed by the physicians, and preceded by his pages. But all were to depart on his arrival at Kew, except his own equerry-in-waiting. It Was not very pleasant to these gentlemen to attend his majesty at such a time, and upon such a plan, so adverse to his inclination, without any power of assistance : however, they would rather have died than refused, and it was certain the king would no other way travel but by compulsion, which no human being dared even mention. Miss Planta and I were to go as soon as the packages could be ready, with some of the queen's things. Mrs. Schwellenberg was to remain behind, for one day, in order to make arrangements about the jewels.

In what a confusion was the house! Princes, equerries, physicians, pages–all conferring, whispering, plotting, and caballing, how to induce the king to set off!

At length we found an opportunity to glide through the passage to the coach; Miss Planta and myself, with her maid and Goter. But the heaviness of heart with which we began this journey, and the dreadful prognostics of the duration of misery to which it led us–who can tell?

We were almost wholly silent all the way. When we arrived at Kew, we found the suspense with which the king was awaited truly terrible. Her majesty had determined to return to Windsor at night, if he came not. We were all to forbear unpacking in the mean while.

The house was all now regulated by express order of the Prince of Wales, who rode over first, and arranged all the apartments, and writ, with chalk, the names of the destined inhabitants on each door. My own room he had given to Lady Courtown ; and for me, he had fixed on one immediately adjoining to Mrs. Schwellenberg's; a very pleasant room, looking into the garden, but by everybody avoided, because the partition is so thin of the next apartment, that not a word can be spoken in either that is not heard in both.

A MYSTERIOUS VISITOR.

While I was surveying this new habitation, the princess royal came into it, and, with a cheered countenance, told me that the queen had just received intelligence that the king was rather better, and would come directly, and therefore I was

Page 267,

commissioned to issue orders to Columb to keep out of sight, and to see that none of the servants were in the way when the king passed.

Eagerly, and enlivened, downstairs I hastened, to speak to Columb. I flew to the parlour to ring the bell for him, as In my new room I had no bell for either man or maid; but judge my surprise, when, upon opening the door, and almost rushing in, I perceived a Windsor uniform! I was retreating with equal haste, when the figure before me started, in so theatric an attitude of astonishment, that it forced me to look again. The arms were then wide opened, while the figure fell back, in tragic paces.

Much at a loss, and unable to distinguish the face, I was again retiring, when the figure advanced, but in such measured steps as might have suited a march upon a stage. I now suspected it was Mr. Fairly; yet so unlikely I thought it, I could not believe it without speech. "Surely," I cried, " it is not–it is not–" I stopped, afraid to make a mistake.

With arms yet more sublimed, he only advanced, in silence and dumb heroics. I now ventured to look more steadily at the face, and then to exclaim-" "Is it Mr. Fairly?"

The laugh now betrayed him: he could hardly believe I had really not known him. I explained that my very little expectation of seeing him at Kew had assisted my near-sightedness to perplex me.

But I was glad to see him so sportive, which I found was Owing to the good spirits of bringing good news; he had mounted his horse as soon as he had heard the king had consented to the journey, and he had galloped to Kew, to acquaint her majesty with the welcome tidings.

I rang and gave my orders to Columb and he then begged me not to hurry away, and to give him leave to wait, in this parlour, the king's arrival. He then explained to me the whole of the intended proceedings and arrangements, with details innumerable and most interesting.

He meant to go almost immediately into the country–all was settled with the queen. I told him I was most cordially glad his recruit was so near at hand.

"I shall, however," he said, "be in town a few days longer, and come hither constantly to pay you all a little visit."

Miss Planta then appeared. A more general conversation now took place, though in its course Mr. Fairly had the malice to give me a start I little expected from him. We were talk-

Page 268 ing of our poor king, and wondering at the delay of his arrival, when Mr. Fairly said, "The king now, Miss Planta, mentions everybody and everything that he knows or has heard mentioned in his whole life. Pray does he know any Of your secrets? he'll surely tell them if he does!"

"So I hear," cried she, "but I'm sure he can't tell anything of Me! But I wonder what he says of everybody?"

"Why, everything," cried he. "Have you not heard of yourself?"

"Dear, no! Dear me, Mr. Fairly!"

"And, dear Miss Planta! why should not you have your share? Have you not heard he spares nobody?"

"Yes, I have; but I can't think what he says of them!"

Fearful of anything more, I arose and looked at the Window to see if any sign of approach appeared, but he dropped the subject without coming any nearer, and Miss Planta dropped it too.

I believe he wished to discover if she had heard of his learned ladies!

THE KING's ARRIVAL.

Dinner went on, and still no king. We now began to grow very anxious, when Miss Planta exclaimed that she thought she heard a carriage. We all listened. "I hope!" I cried. "I see you do!" cried he, "you have a very face of hope at this moment!"–and it was not disappointed. The sound came nearer, and presently a carriage drove into the front court. I could see nothing, it was so dark; but I presently heard the much-respected voice of the dear unhappy king, speaking rapidly to the porter, as he alighted from the coach. Mr. Fairly flew instantly upstairs, to acquaint the queen with the welcome tidings.

The poor king had been prevailed upon to quit Windsor with the utmost difficulty: he was accompanied by General Harcourt, his aide-de-camp, and Colonels Goldsworthy and Wellbred–no one else! He had passed all the rest with apparent composure, to come to his carriage, for they lined the passage, eager to see him once more! and almost all Windsor was collected round the rails, etc. to witness the mournful spectacle of his departure, which left them in the deepest despondence, with scarce a ray of hope ever to see him again.

The bribery, however, which brought, was denied him!–he was by no means to see the queen

When I went to her at night, she was all graciousness, and kept me till very late. I had not seen her alone so long, except for a few minutes in the morning, that I had a thousand things I wished to say to her. You may be sure they were all, as far as they went, consolatory.

Princess Augusta had a small tent-bed put up in the queen's bed-chamber: I called her royal highness when the queen dismissed me. She undressed in an adjoining apartment.

THE ARRANGEMENTS AT KEW PALACE.

I must now tell you how the house is disposed. The whole of the ground-floor that looks towards the 'garden is appropriated to the king, though he is not indulged with its range. In the side wing is a room for the physicians, destined to their consultations; adjoining to that is the equerry's dining-room. Mrs. Schwellenberg's parlours, which are in the front of the house, one for dining, the other for coffee and tea, are still allowed us. The other front rooms below are for the pages to dine, and the rest of the more detached buildings are for the servants of various sorts.

All the rooms immediately over those which are actually occupied by the king are locked up; her majesty relinquishes them, that he may never be tantalized by footsteps overhead. She has retained only the bed-room, the drawing-room, which joins to it, and the gallery, in which she eats. Beyond this gallery are the apartments of the three elder princesses, in one .of which rooms Miss Planta sleeps. There is nothing more on the first floor.

On the second a very large room for Mrs. Schwellenberg, and a very pleasant one for myself, are over the queen's rooms. Farther on are three bed-rooms, one for the surgeon or apothecary in waiting, the next for the equerry, and the third, lately mine, for the queen's lady–all written thus with chalk by the prince.

Then follows a very long dark passage, with little bed-rooms on each side, for the maids, and one of the pages. These look like so many little cells of a convent.

Mrs. Sandys has a room nearer the queen's, and Goter has one nearer to mine. At the end of this passage there is a larger room, formerly appropriated to Mr. de Luc, but now

chalked "The physicians'." One physician, one equerry, and one surgeon or apothecary, are regularly to sleep in the house. This is the general arrangement.

The prince very properly has also ordered that one of his majesty's grooms of' the bedchamber should be in constant waiting; he is to reside in the prince's house, over the way, which is also fitting up for some others. This gentleman is to receive all inquiries about the king's health. The same regulation had taken place at Windsor, in the Castle, where the gentlemen waited in turn. Though, as the physicians send their account to St. James's, this is now become an almost useless ceremony, for everybody goes thither to read the bulletin.

The three young princesses are to be in a house belonging to the king on Kew green, commonly called Princess Elizabeth's, as her royal highness has long inhabited it in her illness. There will lodge Miss Goldsworthy, Mlle. Montmoulin, and Miss Gomme. Lady Charlotte Finch is to be at the Prince of Wales's.

I could not sleep all night—-I thought I heard the poor king. He was under the same range of apartments, though far distant, but his indignant disappointment haunted me. The queen, too, was very angry at having promises made in her name which could not be kept. What a day altogether was this!

A REGENCY HINTED AT.

Sunday, Nov. 30.-Here, in all its dread colours, dark as its darkest prognostics, began the Kew campaign. I went to my poor queen at seven o'clock: the Princess Augusta arose and went away to dress, and I received her majesty's commands to go down for inquiries. She had herself passed a wretched night, and already lamented leaving Windsor.

I waited very long in the cold dark passages below, before I could find any one of whom to ask intelligence. The parlours were without fires, and washing. I gave directions afterwards, to have a fire in one of them by seven o'clock every morning.

At length I procured the speech of one of the pages, and heard that the night had been the most violently bad of any yet passed!–and no wonder!

I hardly knew how to creep upstairs, frozen both within and without, to tell such news; but it was not received as if unexpected, and I omitted whatever was not essential to be known.

Afterwards arrived Mrs: Schwellenberg, so oppressed between her spasms and the house's horrors, that the oppression she inflicted ought perhaps to be pardoned. It was, however, difficult enough to bear! Harshness, tyranny, dissension, and even insult, seemed personified. I cut short details upon this subject-they would but make you sick. . . .

My dear Miss Cambridge sent to me immediately. I saw she had a secret hope she might come and sit with me now and then in this confinement. It would have been my greatest possible solace in this dreary abode: but I hastened to acquaint her of the absolute seclusion, and even to beg she would not send her servant to the house - for I found it was much desired to keep off all who might carry away any intelligence.

She is ever most reasonable, and never thenceforward hinted upon the subject. But she wrote continually long letters, and filled with news and anecdotes of much interest, relating to anything she could gather of "out-house proceedings," which now became very important–the length of the malady threatening a regency!– a Word which I have not yet been able to articulate.

MR. FAIRLY'S KIND OFFICES.

Kew, Monday, Dec. 1.-Mournful was the opening of the month! My account of the night from Gezewell, the page, was very alarming, and my poor royal mistress began to sink more than I had ever yet seen. No wonder; the length of the malady so uncertain, the steps which seemed now requisite so shocking: for new advice, and such as suited only disorders that physicians in general relinquish, was now proposed, and compliance or refusal were almost equally tremendous.

In sadness I returned from her, and, moping and unoccupied, I was walking up and down my room, when Columb came to say Mr. Fairly desired to know if I could see him.

Certainly, I said, I would come to him in the parlour. He was not at all well, nor did he seem at all comfortable. He had undertaken, by his own desire, to purchase small carpets for the princesses, for the house is in a state of cold and discomfort past all imagination. It has never been a winter residence, and there was nothing prepared for its becoming one. He could not, he told me, look at the rooms of their royal highnesses without shuddering for them; and he longed, he said, to cover all the naked, cold boards, to render them

more habitable. He had obtained permission to execute this as a commission: for so miserable is the house at present that no general orders to the proper people are either given Or thought about; and every one is so absorbed in the general calamity, that they would individually sooner perish than offer up complaint or petition. I Should never end were I to explain the reasons there are for both.

What he must next, he said, effect, was supplying them with sand-bags for windows and doors, which he intended to fill and to place himself. The wind which blew in upon those lovely princesses, he declared, was enough to destroy them.

When he had informed me of these kind offices, he began an inquiry into how I was lodged. Well enough, I said; but he would not accept so general an answer. He insisted upon knowing what was my furniture, and in particular if I had any carpet; and when I owned I had none, he smiled, and said he would bring six, though his commission only extended to three.

He did not at all like the parlour, which, indeed, is wretchedly cold and miserable: he wished to bring it a carpet, and new fit it up with warm winter accommodations. He reminded me of my dearest Fredy, when she brought me a decanter of barley-water and a bright tin saucepan, under her hoop. I Could not tell him that history in detail, but I rewarded his good-nature by hinting at the resemblance it bore, in its active zeal, to my sweet Mrs. Locke. . . .

The queen afterwards presented me with a very pretty little new carpet; only a bed-side slip, but very warm. She knew not how much I was acquainted with its history, but I found she had settled for them all six. She gave another to Mrs. Schwellenberg.

MRS. SCHWELLENBERG'S PARLOUR.

Dec. 3.-Worse again to-day was the poor king: the little fair gleam, how soon did it pass away!

I was beginning to grow ill myself, from the added fatigue of disturbance in the night, unavoidably occasioned by the neighbourhood to an invalid who summoned her maids at all hours; and my royal mistress issued orders for a removal to take place.

My new apartment is at the end of the long dark passage mentioned, with bed-room cells on each side it. It is a

very comfortable room, carpeted all over, with one window looking- to the front of the house and two into a court-yard. It is the most distant from the queen, but in all other respects is very desirable.

I must now relate briefly a new piece of cruelty. I happened to mention to la première présidente my waiting for a page to bring the morning accounts.

"And where do you wait?"

"In the parlour, ma'am."

"In my parlour? Oh, ver well! I will see to that!"

"There is no other place, ma'am, but the cold passages, which, at that time in the morning, are commonly wet as well as dark."

"O, ver well! When everybody goes to my room I might keep an inn--what you call hotel."

All good humour now again vanished; and this morning, when I made my seven o'clock inquiry, I found the parlour doors both locked! I returned so shivering to my queen, that she demanded the cause, which I simply related; foreseeing inevitable destruction from continuing to run such a hazard. She instantly protested there should be a new arrangement.

Dec. 4.-No opportunity offered yesterday for my better security, and therefore I was again exposed this morning to the cold dark damp of the miserable passage. The account was tolerable, but a threat of sore-throat accelerated the reform.

It was now settled that the dining-parlour should be made over for the officers of state who came upon business to the house, and who hitherto had waited in the hall; and the room which was next to Mrs. Schwellenberg's, and which had first been mine, was now made our salle à manger. By this means, the parlour being taken away for other people, and by command relinquished, I obtained once again the freedom of entering it, to 'gather my account for her majesty. But the excess of ill-will awakened by my obtaining this little privilege, which was actually necessary to my very life, was so great, that more of personal offence and harshness could not have been shown to the most guilty of culprits.

One of the pages acquainted me his majesty was not worse, and the night had been as usual. As usual, too, was my day sad and solitary all the morning--not solitary but worse during dinner and coffee.

just after it, however, came the good and sweet Mr. Smelt.

The Prince of Wales sent for him, and condescended to apologise for the Windsor transaction, and to order he might regain admission.

How this was brought about I am not clear: I only know it is agreed by all parties that the prince has the faculty of making his peace, where he wishes it, with the most captivating grace In the world.

A NEW PHYSICIAN SUMMONED.

Mr. Fairly told me this evening that Dr. Willis, a physician of Lincoln, of peculiar skill and practice in intellectual maladies, had been sent for by express. The poor queen had most painfully concurred in a measure which seemed to fix the nature of the king's attack in the face of the world; but the necessity and strong advice had prevailed over her repugnance.

Dec. 6.-Mr. Fairly came to me, to borrow pen and ink for a few memorandums. Notwithstanding much haste. he could not, he said, go till he had acquainted me with the opening of Dr. Willis with his royal patient. I told him there was nothing I more anxiously wished to hear.

He then gave me the full narration, interesting, curious, extraordinary; full of promise and hope. He is extremely pleased both with the doctor and his son, Dr. John, he says they are fine, lively, natural, independent characters.

Sunday, Dec. 7.-Very bad Was this morning's account. Lady Charlotte Finch read prayers to the queen and princess, and Lady Courtown, and the rest for themselves. M r. Fairly wishes her majesty would summon a chaplain, and let the house join in congregation. I think he is right, as far as the house extends to those who are still admitted into her majesty's presence.

Dec. 8.-The accounts began mending considerably, and hope broke in upon all.

Dec. 9.—All gets now into a better channel, and the dear royal invalid gives every symptom of amendment. God be praised!

Dec. 11.-To-day We have had the fairest hopes: the king took his first walk in Kew garden! There have been impediments to this trial hitherto, that have been thought insurmountable, though, in fact, they were most frivolous. The walk seemed to do him good, and we are all in better
spirits about him than for this many and many a long day past.

MRS. SCHWELLENBERG'S OPINION OF MR. FAIRLY. Dec. 12.-This day passed in much the same manner. Late in the evening, after Mr. Smelt was gone, Mrs. Schwellenberg began talking about Mr. Fairly, and giving free vent to all her strong innate aversion to him. She went back to the old history of the "newseepaper," and gave to his naming it every unheard motive of spite, disloyalty, and calumny! three qualities which I believe equally and utterly unknown to him. He was also, she said, "very onfeeling, for she had heard him laugh prodigious with the Lady Waldegraves, Perticleer with lady Carlisle, what you call Lady Elizabeth her sister, and this in the king's illness." And, in fine, she could not bear him.

Such gross injustice I could not hear quietly. I began a warm defence, protesting I knew no one whose heart was more feelingly devoted to the royal family, except, perhaps, Mr. Smelt; and that as to his laughing, it must have been at something of passing and accidental amusement, since he was grave even to melancholy, except when he exerted his spirits for the relief or entertainment of others.

Equally amazed and provoked, she disdainfully asked me what I knew of him?

I made no answer. I was not quite prepared for the interrogatory, and feared she might next inquire when and where I had seen him?

My silence was regarded as self-conviction of error, and she added, "I know you can't not know him; I know he had never seen you two year and half ago; when you came here he had not heard your name."

"Two years and a half," I answered coolly, "I did not regard as a short time for forming a judgment of any one's character."

"When you don't not see them ? You have never seen him, I am sure, but once, or what you call twice."

I did not dare let this pass, it was so very wide from the truth; but calmly said I had seen him much oftener than once or twice. "And where? when have you seen him?"

"Many times; and at Cheltenham constantly; but never to observe in him anything but honour and goodness."

"O ver well! you don't not know him like me, you can't

Page 276 not know him; he is not from your acquaintance—I know that ver well!"

She presently went on by herself. "You could not know such a person—he told me the same himself: he told me he had not never seen you when you first came. You might see him at Cheltenham, that is true; but nothing others, I am sure. At Windsor there was no tea, not wonce, so you can't not have seen him, only at Cheltenham."

I hardly knew whether to laugh or be frightened at this width of error; nor, indeed, whether it was not all some artifice to draw me out, from pique, into some recital: at all events I thought it best to say nothing, for she was too affronting to deserve to be set right.

She went on to the same purpose some time, more than insinuating that a person such as Mr. Fairly could never let him self down to be acquainted with me; till finding me too much offended to think her assertions worth answering, she started, at last, another subject. I then forced myself to talk much as usual. But how did I rejoice when the clock struck ten—how wish it had been twelve!

THE KING'S VARYING CONDITION.

Dec. 15.-This whole day was passed in great internal agitation throughout the house, as the great and important business of the Regency was to be discussed to-morrow in Parliament. All is now too painful and intricate for writing a word. I begin to confine my memorandums almost wholly to my own personal proceedings.

Dec. 16.-Whatsoever might pass in the House on this momentous subject, it sat so late that no news could arrive. Sweeter and better news, however, was immediately at hand than any the whole senate could transmit; the account from the pages was truly cheering. With what joy did I hasten with it to the queen, who immediately ordered me to be its welcome messenger to the three princesses. And when Mr. Smelt came to my breakfast, with what rapture did he receive it! seizing and kissing my hand, while his eyes ran over, and joy seemed quite to bewitch him. He flew away in a very few minutes, to share his happiness with his faithful partner.

After breakfast I had a long conference in the parlour with Sir Lucas Pepys, who justly gloried in the advancement of his

original prediction; but there had been much dissension
Page 277

amongst the physicians, concerning the bulletin to go to St. James's, no two agreeing in the degree of better to be announced to the world.

Dr. Willis came in while we were conversing, but instantly retreated, to leave us undisturbed. He looks a very fine old man. I wish to be introduced to him. Mr. Smelt and Mr. Fairly are both quite enchanted with all the family; for another son now, a clergyman, Mr. Thomas Willis, has joined their forces.

Dec. 17.-MY account this morning was most afflictive once more: it was given by Mr. Hawkins, and was cruelly subversive of all our rising hopes. I carried it to the queen in trembling but she bore it most mildly. What resignation is hers!

Dec. 22.-With what joy did I carry, this morning, an exceeding good account of the king to my royal mistress! It was trebly welcome., as much might depend upon it in the resolutions of the House concerning the Regency, which was of to-day's discussion.

Mr. Fairly took leave, for a week, he said, wishing me my health, while I expressed my own wishes for his good journey But, in looking forward to a friendship the most permanent, saw the eligibility of rendering it the most open. I therefore went back to Mrs. Schwellenberg; and the moment I received a reproach for staying so long, I calmly answered, "Mr. Fairly had made me a visit, to take leave before he went into the country."

Amazement was perhaps never more indignant. Mr. Fairly to take leave of me! while not once he even called upon her! This offence swallowed up all other comments upon the communication. I seemed not to understand it; but we had a terrible two hours and a-half. Yet to such, now, I may look forward without any mixture, any alleviation, for evening after evening in this sad abode.

N.B. My own separate adventures for this month, and year, concluded upon this day.

The king went on now better, now worse, in a most fearful manner; but Sir Lucas Pepys never lost sight of hope, and the management of Dr. Willis and his two sons was most wonderfully acute and successful. Yet so much were they perplexed and tormented by the interruptions given to their plans and methods, that they were frequently almost tempted to resign the undertaking from anger and confusion.

DR. WILLIS AND His SON.

Kew Palace, Thursday, Jan. 1, 1789.-The year opened with an account the most promising of our beloved king. I saw Dr, Willis, and he told me the night had been very tranquil and he sent for his son, Dr. John Willis, to give me a history of the morning. Dr. John's narration was in many parts very affecting: the dear and excellent king had been praying for his own restoration! Both the doctors told me that such strong symptoms of true piety had scarce ever been discernible through so dreadful a malady.

How I hastened to my queen!–and with what alacrity I besought permission to run next to the princesses! It was so sweet, so soothing, to open a new year with the solace of anticipated good!

Jan. 3.-I have the great pleasure, now, of a change in my morning's historiographers; I have made acquaintance with Dr. Willis and his son, and they have desired me to summon one of them constantly for my information. I am extremely struck with both these physicians. Dr. Willis is a man of ten thousand; open, holiest, dauntless, lighthearted, innocent, and high minded: I see him impressed with the most animated reverence and affection for his royal patient; but it is wholly for his character,–not a whit for his rank.

Dr. John, his eldest son, is extremely handsome, and inherits, in a milder degree, all the qualities of his father; but living more in the general world, and having his fame and fortune still to settle, he has not yet acquired the same courage, nor is he, by nature, quite so sanguine in his opinions. The manners of both are extremely pleasing, and they both proceed completely their own way, not merely unacquainted with court etiquette, but wholly, and most artlessly, unambitious to form any such acquaintance.

Jan. 11.-This morning Dr. John gave me but a bad account of the poor king. His amendment is not progressive; it fails, and goes back, and disappoints most grievously; yet it would be nothing were the case and its circumstances less discussed, and were expectation more reasonable.

Jan. 12.-A melancholy day: news bad both at home and abroad. At home the dear unhappy king still worse–abroad new examinations voted of the physicians! Good heaven! what an insult does this seem from parliamentary power, to investigate and bring forth to the world every circumstance Of

Page 279 such a malady as is ever held sacred to secrecy in the most private families! How indignant we all feel here no words can say.

LEARNING IN WOMEN.

Jan. 13.-The two younger Willises, Dr. John and Mr. Thomas, came upstairs in the afternoon, to make a visit to Mrs. Schwellenberg.
I took the opportunity to decamp to my own room, where I found
Mr. Fairly in waiting.

In the course of conversation that followed, Mrs. Carter was named: Mr. Smelt is seriously of opinion her ode is the best in our language.(301) I spoke of her very highly, for indeed I reverence her.

Learning in women was then Our theme. I rather wished to hear than to declaim upon this subject, yet I never seek to disguise that I think it has no recommendation of sufficient value to compensate its evil excitement of envy and satire.

He spoke with very uncommon liberality on the female powers and intellects, and protested he had never, in his commerce with the world, been able to discern any other inferiority in their parts than what resulted from their Pursuits -and yet, with all this, he doubted much whether he had ever seen any woman who might not have been rather better without than with the learned languages, one only excepted.

He was some time silent, and I could not but suppose he meant his correspondent, Miss Fuzilier; but, with a very tender sigh, he said, "And she was my mother,–who neglected nothing else, while she cultivated Latin, and who knew it very well, and would have known it very superiorly, but that her brother disliked her studying, and one day burnt all her books!"

This anecdote led to one in return, from myself. I told him, briefly the history of Dr. Johnson's most kind condescension, in desiring to make me his pupil, and beginning to give me regular lessons of the Latin language, and i proceeded to the speedy conclusion–my great apprehension,– conviction rather,–that what I learnt of so great a man could never be private, and that he himself would contemn concealment, if any

progress should be made; which to Me was sufficient motive for relinquishing the scheme, and declining the honour, highly as I valued it, of obtaining Such a master– "and this," I added, "though difficult to be done without offending, was yet the better effected, as my father himself likes and approves all accomplishments for women better than the dead languages."

THE QUEEN AND MR. FAIRLY'S VISITS.

Jan. 14.-I must now mention a rather singular conversation. I had no opportunity last night to name, as usual, my visitor; but I have done it so often, so constantly indeed, that I was not uneasy In the omission.

But this morning, while her hair was dressing, my royal Mistress suddenly said, "Did you see any body yesterday?" I could not but be sure of her meaning, and though vexed to be anticipated in my avowal, which had but waited the departure of the wardrobe-woman, Sandys, I instantly answered, "Yes, ma'am; Mr, Smelt in the morning and Mr. Fairly in the evening."

"O! Mr. Fairly was here, then?"

I was now doubly sorry she should know this only from me! He had Mentioned being just come from town, but I had concluded Lady Charlotte Finch, as usual, knew of his arrival, and had made it known to her Majesty. A little while after,–"Did he go away from you early?" she said.

"No, ma'am," I Immediately answered, "not early: he drank tea with Me, as he generally does, I believe, when he is here for the night."

"Perhaps," cried she after a pause, "the gentlemen below do not drink tea."

"I cannot tell, ma'am, I never heard him say; I only know he asked me if I would give him some, and I told him yes, with great pleasure."

Never did I feel so happy in unblushing consciousness of internal liberty as in this little catechism! However, I soon found I had Mistaken the Motive of the catechism: it was not on account of Mr. Fairly and his visit; it was all for Mrs. Schwellenberg and her no visits; for she soon dropped something of "poor Mrs. Schwellenberg" and her Miserable state, that opened her whole meaning.

A MELANCHOLY BIRTHDAY.

Sunday, Jan. 18.-The public birthday of my poor royal mistress. How sadly did she pass it; and how was I filled With sorrow for her reflections upon this its first anniversary for these last twenty-eight years in which the king and the nation have not united in its celebration! All now was passed over in silence and obscurity; all observance of the day was prohibited, both abroad and at home.

The poor king whose attention to times and dates is unremittingly exact, knew the day, and insisted upon seeing the queen and three of the princesses; but–it was not a good day.

MR. FAIRLY ON FANS.

Jan. 21.-I came to my room; and there, in my own corner, sat poor Mr. Fairly, looking a little forlorn, and telling me he had been there near an hour. I made every apology that could mark in the strongest manner how little I thought his patience worth such exertion. . . .

He was going to spend the next day at St. Leonard's, where he was to meet his son; and he portrayed to me the character of Mrs. Harcourt so fairly and favourably, that her flightiness sunk away on the rise of her good qualities. He spoke of his chapel of St. Catherine's, its emoluments, chaplain, brothers, sisters, and full establishment.

Finding I entered into nothing, he took up a fan which lay on my table, and began playing off various imitative airs with it, exclaiming, "How thoroughly useless a toy!"

"No," I said; "on the contrary, taken as an ornament, it was the most useful ornament of any belonging to full dress, occupying the hands, giving the eyes something to look at, and taking away stiffness and formality from the figure and deportment."

"Men have no fans," cried he, "and how do they do?"

"Worse," quoth I, plumply.

He laughed quite out, saying, "That's ingenuous, however; and, indeed, I must confess they are reduced, from time to time, to shift their hands from one pocket to another."

"Not, to speak of lounging about in their chairs from one side to another."

"But the real use of a fan," cried he, "if there is any, is it not–to hide a particular blush that ought not to appear?"

"O, no; it Would rather make it the sooner noticed." "Not at all; it may be done under pretence of absence–rubbing the cheek, or nose–putting it up accidentally to the eye–in a thousand ways."

He went through all these evolutions comically enough, and then, putting aside his toy, came back to graver matters.

MR. FAIRLY CONTINUES HIS VISITS: THE QUEEN AGAIN REMARKS UPON THEM.

Jan. 26.-In the evening Mr. Fairly came to tea. He was grave, and my reception did not make him gayer. General discourse took place till Mrs. Dickenson happened to be named. He knew her very well as Miss Hamilton. Her conjugal conduct, in displaying her Superior power over her husband, was our particular theme, till in the midst of it he exclaimed, "How well you will be trained in by Mrs. Schwellenberg–if you come to trial!"

Ah! thought I, the more I suffer through her, the less and less do I feel disposed to run any new and more lasting risk, But I said not this. I only protested I was much less her humble servant than might be supposed.

"How can that be," cried he, "when you never contest any one point with her?"

Not, I said, in positive wrangling, which could never answer its horrible pain; but still I refused undue obedience when exacted with indignity, and always hastened to retire when offended and affronted.

He took up Mrs. Smith's "Emmeline,"(302) which is just lent me by the queen; but he found it not piquant and putting it down, begged me to choose him a Rambler." I had a good deal of difficulty In my decision, as he had already seen almost all I could particularly wish to recommend; and, when he saw me turn over leaf after leaf with some hesitation, he began a serious reproach to me of inflexible reserve. And then away he went.

I hastened immediately to Mrs. Schwellenberg; and found all in a tumult. She had been, she said, alone all the evening, and was going to have sent for me, but found I had my company. She sent for Mlle. Montmoulin but she had a cold; for Miss Gomme, but she could not come because of the snow;

for Miss Planta but she was ill with a fever, "what you call head-ache:" she had then "sent to princess royal, who had been to her, and pitied her ver moch, for princess royal was really sensible."

And all this was communicated with a look of accusation, and a tone of menace, that might have suited an attack upon some hardened felon. . . .

I made no sort of apology nor any other answer than that I had had the honour of Mr. Fairly's company to tea, which was always a pleasure to me.

I believe something like consciousness whispered her here, that it might really be possible his society was as pleasant as I had found hers, for she then dropped her lamentation, and said she thanked God she wanted nobody, not one; she could always amuse herself, and was glad enough to be alone.

Were it but true!

I offered cards: she refused, because it was too late, though we yet remained together near two hours.

If this a little disordered me, You will not think what followed was matter of composure. While the queen's hair was rolling up, by the wardrobe woman, at night, Mrs. Schwellenberg happened to leave the room, and almost instantly her majesty, in a rather abrupt manner, said "Is Mr. Fairly here to-night?"

"Yes, ma'am."

"When did he come back?"

I could not recollect.

"I did not know he was here."

This thunderstruck me; that he should come again, or stay, at least, without apprising his royal mistress, startled me inwardly, and distressed me outwardly.

"I knew, indeed," she then added, "he was here in the morning, but I understood he went away afterwards."

The idea of connivance now struck me with a real disdain, that brought back my courage and recollection in full force, and I answered, "I remember, ma'am, he told me he had rode over to Richmond park at noon, and returned here to dinner with Colonel Wellbred, and in the evening he drank tea with me, and said he should sup with General Harcourt."

All this, spoken with an openness that rather invited than shunned further investigation, seemed to give an immediate satisfaction ; the tone of voice changed to its usual com-

Page 284 placency, and she inquired various things concerning the Stuart family, and then spoke upon more common topics.

I concluded it now all over; but soon after Mrs. Sandys went away, and then, very unexpectedly, the queen renewed the subject. "The reason," she said, "that I asked about Mr. Fairly was that the Schwellenberg sent to ask Miss Planta to come to her, because Mr. Fairly was—no, not with her—he never goes to her."

She stopped; but I was wholly silent. I felt instantly with how little propriety I could undertake either to defend or to excuse Mr. Fairly, whom I determined to consider as a visitor,, over whom, having no particular influence, I could be charged with no particular responsibility.

After waiting a few minutes,-"With you," she said, "Mr. Fairly was and the Schwellenberg was alone."

My spirits quite panted at this moment to make a full Confession of the usage I had endured from the person thus compassionated; but I had so frequently resolved, in moments Of cool deliberation, not even to risk doing mischief to a favourite old servant, that I withstood the impulse ; but the inward conflict silenced me from saying anything else.

I believe she was surprised but she added, after a long pause, "I believe–he comes to you every evening when here."

"I do not know, ma'am, always, when he is here or away; but I am always very glad to see him, for indeed his visits make all the little variety that–"

I hastily stopped, lest she should think me discontented with this strict confinement during this dreadful season ; and that I can never be, when it is not accompanied by tyranny and injustice.

She immediately took up the word, but without the slightest displeasure. "Why here there might be more variety than anywhere, from the nearness to town, except for–"

" The present situation of things." I eagerly interrupted her to say, and went on: "Indeed, ma'am, I have scarce a wish to break into the present arrangement, by seeing anybody while the house is in this state; nor have I, from last October, seen one human being that does not live here, except Mr. Smelt, Mr. Fairly, and Sir Lucas Pepys; and they all come upon their own calls, and not for me."

"The only objection," she gently answered, "to seeing anybody, is that every one who comes carries some sort of information away with them."

I assured her I was perfectly content to wait for better times, Here the matter dropped ; she appeared satisfied with what I said, and became soft and serene as before the little attack.

Jan. 27.-The intelligence this morning was not very pleasant. I had a conference afterwards with Sir Lucas Pepys, who keeps up undiminished hope. We held our council in the physicians' room, which chanced to be empty; but before it broke up Colonel Wellbred entered. It was a pleasure to me to see him, though somewhat an embarrassment to hear him immediately lament that we never met, and add that he knew not in what manner to procure himself that pleasure. I joined in the lamentation, and its cause, which confined us all to our cells. Sir Lucas declared my confinement menaced my health, and charged me to walk out, and take air and exercise very sedulously, if I would avoid an illness.

Colonel Wellbred instantly offered me a key of Richmond gardens, which opened into them by a nearer door than what was used in common. I accepted his kindness, and took an hour's walk,-for the first time since last October; ten minutes in Kew gardens are all I have spent without doors since the middle of that month.

THE SEARCH FOR MR. FAIRLY.

Jan. 30.-To-day my poor royal mistress received the address of the Lords and Commons, of condolence, etc., upon his majesty's illness. What a painful, but necessary ceremony! It was most properly presented by but few members, and those almost all chosen from the household: a great propriety.

Not long after came Mr. Fairly, looking harassed. "May I," he cried, "come in?–and-for an hour? Can you allow me entrance and room for that time?"

Much Surprised, for already it was three o'clock, I assented: he then told me he had something to copy for her majesty, which was of the highest importance, and said he could find no quiet room in the house but mine for such a business. I gave him every accommodation in my power. When he had written a few lines, he asked if I was very busy, or could help him ? Most readily I offered my services, and then I read to him the original, sentence by sentence, to facilitate his copying; receiving his assurances of my "great assistance" every two lines. In the midst of this occupation,

a tap at my door made me precipitately put down the paper to receive-lady Charlotte Finch!

"Can you," she cried, "have the goodness to tell me any thing of
Mr. Fairly?"

The screen had hidden him; but, gently,–though, I believe ill enough pleased,–he called out himself, "Here is Mr. Fairly."

She flew up to him, crying, "O, Mr. Fairly, what a search has there been for you, by the queen's orders ! She has wanted you extremely, and no one knew where to find you. They have been to the waiting-room, to the equerries', all over the garden, to the prince's house, in your own room, and could find you nowhere, and at last they thought you were gone back to town."

He calmly answered, while he still wrote on, he was sorry they had had so much trouble, for he had only been executing her majesty's commands.

She then hesitated a little, almost to stammering, in adding
"So–at last–I said–that perhaps–you might be here!"

He now raised his head from the paper, and bowing it towards me, "Yes," he cried, "Miss Burney is so good as to give me leave, and there is no other room in the house in Which I can be at rest."

"So I told her majesty," answered Lady Charlotte, "though she said she was sure you could not be here ; but I said there was really no room of quiet here for any business, and so then I came to see."

"Miss Burney," he rejoined, "has the goodness also to help me– she has taken the trouble to read as I go on, which forwards me very much."

Lady Charlotte stared, and I felt sorry at this confession of a confidence she could not but think too much, and I believe he half repented it, for he added, "This, however, you need not perhaps mention, though I know where I trust!"

He proceeded again with his writing, and she then recollected her errand. She told him that what he was copying was to be carried to town by Lord Aylesbury, but the queen desired to see it first. She then returned to her majesty.

She soon, however, returned again. She brought the queen's seal, and leave that he might make up the packet, and give it to Lord Aylesbury, without showing it first to her majesty, who was just gone to dinner. With her customary good-humour

and good-breeding, she then chatted with me some time, and again departed.

We then went to work with all our might, reading and copying. The original was extremely curious–I am sorry I must make it equally secret.

Miss BURNEY's ALARM ON BEING CHASED BY THE KING. Kew Palace, Monday, Feb. 2.-What an adventure had I this morning! one that has occasioned me the severest personal terror I ever experienced in my life.

Sir Lucas Pepys still persisting that exercise and air were absolutely necessary to save me from illness, I have continued my walks, varying my gardens from Richmond to Kew, according to the accounts I received of the movements of the king. For this I had her majesty's permission, on the representation of Sir Lucas. This morning, when I received my intelligence of the king from Dr. John Willis, I begged to know where I might walk in safety? "In Kew gardens," he said, "as the king would be in Richmond."

"Should any unfortunate circumstance," I cried, "at any time, occasion my being seen by his majesty, do not mention my name, but let me run off without call or notice." This he promised. Everybody, indeed, is ordered to keep out of sight. Taking, therefore, the time I had most at command, I strolled into the gardens. I had proceeded, in my quick way, nearly half the round, when I suddenly perceived, through some trees, two or three figures. Relying on the instructions of Dr. John, I concluded them to be workmen and gardeners; yet tried to look sharp, and in so doing, as they were less shaded, I thought I saw the person of his majesty!

Alarmed past all possible expression, I waited not to know more, but turning back, ran off with all my might. But what was my terror to hear myself pursued!–to hear the voice of the king himself loudly and hoarsely calling after me, "MISS Burney! Miss Burney!

I protest I was ready to die. I knew not in what state he might be at the time; I only knew the orders to keep out of his way were universal; that the queen would highly disapprove any unauthorized meeting, and that the very action of my running away might deeply, in his present irritable state, offend him. Nevertheless, on I ran, too terrified to stop, and Page 288

In search Of some short passage, for the g)arden is full of labyrinths, by which I might escape.

The steps still pursued me, and Still the poor hoarse and altered voice rang in my ears:–more and more footsteps sounded frightfully behind me,–the attendants all running to catch their eager master, and the voices of the two Doctor Willises loudly exhorting him not to heat himself so unmercifully.

Heavens, how I ran! I do not think I should have felt the hot lava from Vesuvius–at least not the hot cinders–hadd I so run during its eruption. My feet were not sensible that they even touched the ground.

Soon after, I heard other voices, shriller, though less nervous, call out "Stop! stop! stop!"

I could by no means consent: I knew not what was purposed, but I recollected fully my agreement with Dr. John that very morning, that I should decamp if Surprised, and not b named. My own fears and repugnance, also, after a flight and disobedience like this, were doubled in the thought of not escaping; I knew not to what I might be exposed, should the malady be then high, and take the turn of resentment. Still, therefore, on I flew; and such was my speed, so almost incredible to relate or recollect, that I fairly believe no one of the whole party could have overtaken me, if these words, from one of the attendants, had not reached me, "Doctor Willis begs you to stop!"

"I cannot! I cannot!" I answered, still flying on, when he called out, "You must, ma'am; it hurts the king to run."

Then, indeed, I stopped—in a state of fear really amounting to agony. I turned round, I saw the two doctors had got the king between them, and three attendants of Dr. Willis's were hovering about. They all slackened their pace, as they saw me stand still; but such was the excess of my alarm, that I was wholly insensible to the effects of a race which, at any other time, would have required an hour's recruit.

As they approached, some little presence of mind happily came to my command it occurred to me that, to appease the wrath of my flight, I must now show some confidence: I therefore faced them as undauntedly as I was able, only charging the nearest of the attendants to stand by my side.

When they were within a few yards of me, the king called out, "Why did you run away?"

Shocked at a question impossible to answer, yet a little

assured by the mild tone of his voice, I instantly forced myself forward, to meet him, though the internal sensation which satisfied me this was a step the most proper, to appease his suspicions and displeasure, was so violently combated by the tremor of my nerves, that I fairly think I may reckon it the greatest effort of personal courage-I have ever made.

A ROYAL SALUTE AND ROYAL CONFIDENCES.

The effort answered : I looked up, and met all his wonted benignity of countenance, though something still of wildness in his eyes. Think, however, of my surprise, to feel him put both his hands round my two shoulders, and then kiss my cheek ! * I wonder I did not really sink, so exquisite was my affright when I saw him spread out his arms! Involuntarily, I concluded he meant to crush me: but the Willises, who have never seen him till this fatal illness, not knowing how very extraordinary an action this was from him, simply smiled and looked pleased, supposing, perhaps, it was his customary salutation!

I believe, however, it was but the joy of a heart unbridled, now, by the forms and proprieties of established custom and sober reason. To see any of his household thus by accident, seemed such a near approach to liberty and recovery, that who can wonder it should serve rather to elate than lessen what yet remains of his disorder!

He now spoke in such terms of his pleasure in seeing me, that I soon lost the whole of my terror; astonishment to find him so nearly well, and gratification to see him so pleased, removed every uneasy feeling, and the joy that succeeded, in my conviction of his recovery, made me ready to throw myself at his feet to express it.

What conversation followed! When he saw me fearless, he grew more and more alive, and made me walk close by his side, away from the attendants, and even the

Willises themselves, who, to indulge him, retreated. I own myself not completely composed, but alarm I could entertain no more.

Everything that came uppermost in his mind he mentioned; he seemed to have just such remains of his flightiness as heated his imagination without deranging his reason, and robbed him of all control over his speech, though nearly in his perfect state Of mind as to his opinions. What did he not say !–He opened his whole heart to me,–expounded all his sentiments, and acquainted me with all his intentions.

The heads of his discourse I must give you briefly, as I am sure you will be highly curious to hear them, and as no accident can render of much consequence what a man says in such a state of physical intoxication. He assured me he was quite well–as well as he had ever been in his life ; and then inquired how I did, and how I went on? and whether I was more comfortable? If these questions, in their implications, surprised me, imagine how that surprise must increase when he proceeded to explain them! He asked after the coadjutrix, laughing, and saying "Never mind her!–don't be oppressed–I am your friend! don't let her cast you down!–I know you have a hard time of it–but don't mind her!"

Almost thunderstruck with astonishment, I merely curtsied to his kind "I am your friend," and said nothing. Then presently he added, "Stick to your father–stick to your own family–let them be your objects."

How readily I assented! Again he repeated all I have just written, nearly in the same words, but ended it more seriously: He suddenly stopped, and held me to stop too, and putting his hand on his breast. in the most solemn manner, he gravely and slowly said, "I will protect you!– I promise you that–and therefore depend upon me!"

I thanked him ; and the Willises, thinking him rather too elevated, came to propose my walking on. "No, no, no!" he cried, a hundred times in a breath and their good humour prevailed, and they let him again walk on with his new Companion.

He then gave me a history of his pages, animating almost into a rage, as he related his subjects of displeasure with them, particularly with Mr. Ernst, who he told me had been brought up by himself. I hope his ideas upon these men are the result of the mistakes of his malady.

Then he asked me some questions that very greatly stressed me, relating to information given him in his illness, from various motives, but which he suspected to be false, and which I knew he had reason to suspect: yet was It most dangerous to set anything right, as I was not aware what might be the views of their having been stated wrong. I was as discreet as I knew how to be, and I hope I did no mischief; but this was the worst part of the dialogue.

He next talked to me a great deal of my dear father, and made a thousand inquiries concerning his "History of Music." This brought him to his favourite theme, Handel; and he told me innumerable anecdotes of him, and particularly that celebrated tale of Handel's saying of himself, when a boy, "While that boy lives, my music will never want a protector." And this, he said, I might relate to my father. Then he ran over most of his oratorios, attempting to sing the subjects of several airs and choruses, but so dreadfully hoarse that the sound was terrible.

Dr. Willis, quite alarmed at this exertion, feared he would do himself harm, and again proposed a separation. " "No! no! no!" he exclaimed, "not yet; I have something I must just mention first."

Dr. Willis, delighted to comply, even when uneasy at compliance, again gave way. The good king then greatly affected me. He began upon my revered old friend, Mrs. Delany and he spoke of her with such warmth–such kindness! "She was my friend!" he cried, "and I loved her as a friend! I have made a memorandum when I lost her–I will show it YOU."

He pulled out a pocket-book, and rummaged some time, but to no purpose. The tears stood in his eyes–he wiped them, and Dr. Willis again became very anxious. "Come, sir," he cried, "now do you come in and let the lady go on her walk,-come, now you have talked a long while,-so we'll go in,–if your majesty pleases."

"No, no!" he cried, "I want to ask her a few questions ; –I have lived so long out of the world, I know nothing!"

This touched me to the heart. We walked on together, and he inquired after various persons, particularly Mrs. Boscawen, because she was Mrs. Delany's friend! Then, for the same reason, after Mr. Frederick Montagu,(303) of whom he kindly said, "I know he has a great regard for me, for all he joined the opposition." Lord Grey de Wilton, Sir Watkin Wynn, the Duke of Beaufort, and various others, followed. He then told me he was very much dissatisfied with several of his state officers, and meant to form an entire new establishment. He took a paper out of his pocket-book, and showed me his new list.

This was the wildest thing that passed ; and Dr. John Willis now seriously urged our separating; but he would not consent he had only three more words to say, he declared, and again he conquered.

He now spoke of my father, with still more kindness, and told me he ought to have had the post of master of the band, and not that little poor musician Parsons, who was not fit for it: "But Lord Salisbury," he cried, "used your father vary ill in that business, and so he did me! However, I have dashed out his name, and I shall put your father's in,–as soon as I get loose again!"

This again–how affecting was this!

"And what," cried he,"has your father got, at last? nothing but that poor thing at Chelsea?(304) O fie! fie! fie! But never mind! I will take care of him. I will do it myself!" Then presently he added, "As to Lord Salisbury, he is out already, as this memorandum will Show you, and so are many more. I shall be much better served and when once I get away, I shall rule with a rod of iron!"

This was very unlike himself, and startled the two good doctors, who could not bear to cross him, and were exulting at seeing his great amendment, but yet grew quite uneasy at his earnestness and volubility. Finding we now must part, he stopped to take leave, and renewed again his charges about the coadjutrix. "Never mind her!" he cried, "depend upon me! I will be your friend as long as I live–I here pledge myself to be your friend!" And then he saluted me again just as at the meeting, and suffered me to go on.

What a scene! how variously was I affected by it! but, upon the whole, how inexpressibly thankful to see him so nearly himself– so little removed from recovery!

CURIOSITY REGARDING Miss BURNEY'S MEETING WITH THE KING.

I went very soon after to the queen to whom I was most eager to avow the meeting, and how little I could help it. Her astonishment, and her earnestness to hear every particular, were very great. I told her almost all. Some few things relating to the distressing questions I could not repeat nor Page 293

many things said of Mrs. Schwellenberg, which would much, very needlessly, have hurt her.

This interview, and the circumstances belonging to it, excited general curiosity, and all the house watched for opportunities to beg a relation of it. How delighted was I to tell them all my happy prognostics!

But the first to hasten to hear of it was Mr. Smelt; eager and enchanted was the countenance and attention of that truly loyal and most affectionate adherent to his old master. He wished me to see Lady Harcourt and the general, and to make them a brief relation of this extraordinary rencounter but for that I had not effort enough left.

I did what I Could, however, to gratify the curiosity of Colonel Wellbred, which I never saw equally excited. I was passing him on the stairs, and he followed me, to say he had heard what had happened–I imagine from the Willises. I told him, with the highest satisfaction, the general effect produced upon my mind by the accident, that the king seemed so nearly, himself, that patience itself could have but little longer trial. He wanted to hear more particulars: I fancy the Willises had vaguely related some: "Did he not," he cried, "promise to do something for you?" I only laughed, and answered, "O yes! if you want any thing, apply to me;–now is my time!"

Feb. 3.–I had the great happiness to be assured this morning, by both the Dr. Willises, that his majesty was by no means the worse for our long conference. Those good men are inexpressibly happy themselves in the delightful conviction given me, and by me spread about, of the near recovery of their royal patient.

While I was dressing came Mr. Fairly: I could not admit him, but he said he would try again in the evening. I heard by the tone of his voice a peculiar eagerness, and doubted not he was apprized of my adventure.

He came early, before I could leave my fair companion, and sent on Goter. I found him reading a new pamphlet of Horne Tooke: "How long," he cried, "it is since I have been here!"

I was not flippantly disposed, or I would have said I had thought the time he spent away always short, by his avowed eagerness to decamp.

He made so many inquiries of how I had gone on and what I had done since I saw him, that I was soon satisfied he was

Page 294 not uninformed of yesterday's transaction. I told him so; he could not deny it, but wished to hear the whole from myself.

I most readily complied. He listened with the most eager, nay, anxious attention, scarce breathing: he repeatedly ex claimed, when I had finished, "How I wish I had been there! how I should have liked to have seen you!"

I assured him he would not wish that, if he knew the terror I had suffered. He was quite elated with the charges against Cerberic tyranny, and expressed himself gratified by the promises of favour and protection.

THE REGENCY BILL.

Feb. 6.-These last three days have been spent very unpleasantly indeed: all goes hardly and difficultly with my poor royal mistress.

Yet his majesty is now, thank heaven, so much better, that he generally sees his gentlemen in some part of the evening; and Mr. Fairly, having no particular taste for being kept in waiting whole hours for this satisfaction of a few minutes, yet finding himself, if in the house, indispensably required to attend with the rest, has changed his Kew visits from nights to mornings.

He brought me the "Regency Bill!"–I shuddered to hear it named. It was just printed, and he read it to me, with comments and explanations, which took up all our time, and in a manner, at present, the most deeply interesting in which it could be occupied.

'Tis indeed a dread event!–and how it may terminate who can say? My poor royal mistress is much disturbed. Her daughters behave like angels - they seem content to reside in this gloomy solitude for ever, if it prove of comfort to their mother, or mark their duteous affection for their father.

INFINITELY LICENTIOUS!

Feb. 9.-I now walk on the road-side, along the park-wall, every fair morning, as I shall venture no more into either of the gardens. In returning this morning, I was overtaken by Mr. Fairly, who rode up to me, and, dismounting, gave his horse to his groom, to walk on with me.

About two hours after I was, however, surprised by a visit from him in my own room, He came, he said, only to ask

Page 295 me a second time how I did, as he should be here now less and less, the king's amendment rendering his services of smaller and smaller importance.

He brought me a new political parody of Pope's "Eloisa to Abelard," from Mr. Eden to Lord Hawkesbury. It is a most daring, though very clever imitation. It introduces many of the present household. Mrs. Schwellenberg is now in eternal abuse from all these scribblers; Lady Harcourt, and many others, less notorious to their attacks, are here brought forward. How infinitely licentious!

MISS BURNEY IS TAXED WITH VISITING GENTLEMEN.

Feb. 10.-The amendment of the king is progressive, and without any reasonable fear, though not without some few drawbacks. The Willis family were surely sent by heaven to restore peace, and health, and prosperity to this miserable house

Lady Charlotte Finch called upon me two days ago, almost purposely, to inquire concerning the report of my young friend's marriage; and she made me promise to acquaint her when I received any further news: at noon, therefore, I went to her apartment at the Prince of Wales's, with this information. Mr. Fairly, I knew, was with the equerries in our lodge. Lady Charlotte had the Duchess of Beaufort and all the Fieldings with her, and therefore I only left a message, by no means, feeling spirits for encountering any stranger.

At noon, when I attended her majesty, she inquired if I had walked?–Yes.–Where?– In Richmond gardens.–And nowhere else?– No. She looked thoughtful,–and presently I recollected my intended visit to Lady Charlotte, and mentioned it. She cleared up, and said, "O!–you. went to Lady Charlotte?"

"Yes, ma'am," I answered, thinking her very absent,–which I thought with sorrow, as that is so small a part of her character, that I know not I ever saw any symptom of it before. Nor, in fact, as I found afterwards, did I see it now. It was soon explained. Miss Gomme, Mlle. Montmoulin, and Miss Planta, all dined with Mrs. Schwellenberg to-day. The moment I joined them, Mrs. Schwellenberg called out,–"Pray, Miss Berner, for what visit you the gentlemen?"

"Me?"

"Yes, you,–and for what, I say?"

Amazed, I declared I did not know what she meant.

"O," cried she, scoffingly, "that won't not do!–we all saw you,–princess royal the same,–so don't not say that."

I stared,–and Miss Gomme burst out in laughter, and then Mrs. Schwellenberg added,–"For what go you over to the Prince of Wales his house?–nobody lives there but the gentlemen,–nobody others."

I laughed too, now, and told her the fact.

"O," cried she, "Lady Charlotte!–ver true. I had forgot Lady Charlotte!"

"O, very well, imagine," cried I,–"so only the gentlemen were remembered!"

I then found this had been related to the queen; and Mlle. Montmoulin said she supposed the visit had been to General Gordon!–He is the groom now in waiting.

Then followed an open raillery from Mlle. Montmoulin of Mr. Fairly's visits; but I stood it very well, assuring her I should never seek to get rid of my two prison-visitors, Mr. Smelt and Mr. Fairly, till I Could replace them by better, or go abroad for others

IMPROVEMENT IN THE KING'S, HEALTH.

Feb. 14.-The king is infinitely better. O that there were patience in the land ! and this Regency Bill postponed Two of the princesses regularly, and in turn, attend their royal mother in her evening visits to the king. Some of those who stay behind now and then spend the time in Mrs. Schwellenberg's room. They all long for their turn of going to the king, and count the hours till it returns. Their dutiful affection is truly beautiful to behold.

This evening the Princesses Elizabeth and Mary came into Mrs. Schwellenberg's room while I was yet there. They sang songs in two parts all the evening, and vary prettily in point of voice. Their good humour, however, and inherent condescension and sweetness of manners, would make a much worse performance pleasing.

Feb. 16-All well, and the king is preparing for an interview with the chancellor Dr. Willis now confides in me all his schemes and notions; we are growing the best of friends and his son Dr. John is nearly as trusty. Excellent people! how I love and honour them all!

I had a visit at noon from Mr. Fairly. He hastened to tell me the joyful news that the king and queen were just gone out, to walk in Richmond gardens, arm in arm.–what a delight to all the house!

When I came to tea, I found Mr. Fairly waiting in my room. He had left Kew for Richmond park, but only dined there. We had much discussion of state business. The king is SO much himself, that he is soon to be informed of the general situation of the kingdom. O what an information!–how we all tremble in looking forward to it., Mr. Fairly thinks Mr. Smelt the fittest man for this office; Mr. Smelt thinks the same of Mr. Fairly: both have told me this.

MR. FAIRLY AND MR. WINDHAM.

Mr. Fairly began soon to look at his watch, complaining very much of the new ceremony imposed, of this attendance of handing the Queen, which, he said, broke into his whole evening. Yet he does as little as possible. "The rest of them," he said, " think it necessary to wait in an adjoining apartment during the whole interview, to be ready to show themselves when it is over!

He now sat with his watch in his hand, dreading to pass his time, but determined not to anticipate its occupation, till half past nine o'clock, when he drew on his white gloves, ready for action. But then, stopping short, he desired me to guess whom, amongst my acquaintance, he had met in London this last time of his going thither. I could not guess whom he meant–but I saw it was no common person, by his manner. He then continued–"A tall, thin, meagre, sallow, black-eyed, penetrating, keen-looking figure."

I could still not guess,-and he named Mr. Windham.

"Mr. Windham!" I exclaimed, "no, indeed,–you do not describe him fairly,-he merits better colouring."

He accuses me of being very partial to him: however, I am angry enough with him just now, though firmly persuaded still, that whatever has fallen from him, that is wrong and unfeeling on the subject of the Regency, has been the effect of his enthusiastic friendship for Mr. Burke: for he has never risen, on this cruel business, but in Support of that most misguided of Vehement and wild orators. This I have observed in the debates, and felt that Mr. Burke was not more run away with by violence of temper, and passion, than Mr. Windham by excess of friendship and admiration.

Page 298 Mr. Fairly has, I fancy, been very intimate with him, for he told me he observed he was passing him, in Queen Anne Street, and stopped his horse, to call out, "O ho, Windham! so I see you will not know me with this servant!" He was on business of the queen's, and had one of the royal grooms with him.

Mr. Windham laughed, and said he was very glad to see who it was, for, on looking at the royal servant, he had just been going to make his lowest bow.

"O, I thank you!" returned Mr. Fairly, "you took me, then, for the Duke of Cumberĺand,"

THE KING CONTINUES TO IMPROVE.

Feb. 17.-The times are now most interesting and critical. Dr. Willis confided to me this morning that to-day the king is to see the chancellor. How important will be the result of his appearance!–the whole national fate depends upon it!

Feb. 18.-I had this morning the highest gratification, the purest feelings of delight, I have been regaled with for many months: I saw, from the road, the king and queen, accompanied by Dr. Willis, walking in Richmond gardens, near the farm, arm in arm!– It was a pleasure that quite melted me, after a separation so bitter, scenes so distressful-to witness such harmony and security! Heaven bless and preserve them was all I could incessantly say while I kept in their sight. I was in the carriage with

Mrs. Schwellenberg at the time. They saw us also, as I heard afterwards from the queen.

In the evening Mrs. Arline, Mrs. Schwellenberg's maid, came into Mrs. Schwellenberg's room, after coffee, and said to me, "If you please, ma'am, somebody wants you." I concluded this somebody my shoemaker, or the like; but in my room I saw Mr. Fairly. He was in high spirits. He had seen his majesty; Dr. Willis had carried him in. He was received with open arms, and embraced; he found nothing now remaining of the disorder, but too in much hurry of spirits. When he had related the particulars of the interview, he suddenly exclaimed, "How amazingly well you have borne all this!"

I made some short answers, and would have taken-refuge in some other topic: but he seemed bent upon pursuing his own, and started various questions and surmises, to draw me on, In vain, however; I gave but general, or evasive answers,

THE KING'S HEALTH IS COMPLETELY RESTORED. This was a sweet, and will prove a most memorable day: Regency was put off, in the House of Lords, by a motion from the chancellor!–huzza! huzza! And this evening, for the first time, the king came upstairs, to drink tea with the queen and princesses in the drawing-room! My heart was so full of joy and thankfulness, I could hardly breathe! Heaven–heaven be praised! What a different house is this house become!–sadness and terror, that wholly occupied it so lately, are now flown away, or rather are now driven out ; and though anxiety still forcibly prevails, 'tis in so small a proportion to joy and thankfulness, that it is borne as if scarce an ill!

Feb. 23.-This morning opened wofully to me, though gaily to the house; for as my news of his majesty was perfectly comfortable, I ventured, in direct words, to ask leave to receive my dear friends Mr. and Mrs. Locke, who were now in town:–in understood sentences, and open looks, I had already failed again and again. My answer was-" I have no particular objection, only you'll keep them to your room." Heavens!–did they ever, unsummoned, quit it? or have they any wish to enlarge their range of visit? I was silent, and then heard a history of some imprudence in Lady Effingham, who had received some of her friends. My resolution, upon this, I need not mention: I preferred the most lengthened absence to such a permission. But I felt it acutely! and I hoped, at least, that by taking no steps, something more favourable might soon pass.
. . .

The king I have seen again in the queen's dressing-room. On opening the door, there he stood! He smiled at my start, and saying he had waited on purpose to see me, added, "I am quite well now,–I was nearly so when I saw you before, but I could overtake you better now." And then he left the room. I was quite melted with joy and thankfulness at this so entire restoration.

End of February, 1789. Dieu merci!

(294) Physician-in-ordinary to the king-ED.

(295) Her tragedy of "Edwy and Elgiva," which was produced at Drury Lane in 1795. See note ante, vol. i., p. xlv.–ED.

(296) The "Douglas cause" was one of the causes celebres of its tine. Its history is briefly as follows. In 1746 Lady Jane Douglas married Sir John Stewart. At Paris, in July, 1748, she gave birth to twins, Archibald and Sholto, of whom the latter died an infant. Lady Jane herself died in 1753. The surviving child, Archibald, was always

recognized as their son by Lady Jane and Sir John. In 1760 the Duke of Douglas, the brother of Lady Jane, being childless, recognised his sister's son as his heir, and bequeathed to him by will the whole of the Douglas estates, revoking, for that purpose, a previous testament which he had made in favour of the Hamilton family. The Duke died in 1761, and Archibald, who had assumed his mother's, name of Douglas, duly succeeded to the estates. His right, however, Was disputed at law by the Duke of Hamilton, on the pretence, which he sought to establish, that Archibald Douglas was not in fact the son of his reputed mother. The Lords of Session in Scotland decided in favour of the Duke of Hamilton, whereupon Mr. Douglas appealed to the House of Lords, which reversed the decision of the Scottish court (February 2-, 1769), 1, "thereby confirming to Mr. Douglas his Filiation and his Fortune."-ED.

(297) "Miss Fuzilier," the Diary-name for Miss Gunning, whom Colonel Digby did subsequently marry. "Sir R- F-" is her father, Sir Robert Gunning.-ED,

(298) One of the apothecaries to the royal household.-ED.

(299) Dr. Richard Warren, one of the physicians in ordinary to the king and the Prince of Wales.-ED.

(300) The Lord chancellor Thurlow.-ED.

(301) Mrs. Elizabeth Carter's "Ode to Wisdom," printed in "Clarissa Harlowe" (vol. ii., letter x.), with a musical setting, given as the composition of Clarisa herself. The Ode is by no means without merit of a modest kind, but can scarcely be ranked the production of a genuine poet.-ED.

(302) "Emmeline, the Orphan of the Castle," a novel in four volumes, by Charlotte Smith. Published 1788.-ED.

(303) Mr. Frederick Montagu was not only a member of the opposition but One of the managers of the impeachment of Warren Hastings.-ED.

(304) Burke's last act before quitting office at the close of 1783, had been to procure for Dr. Burney the post of organist to Chelsea hospital, to which was attached a salary of fifty pounds a year.-ED.

SECTION 15. (1789-)
THE KING'S RECOVERY:
ROYAL VISIT To WEYMOUTH.
THE KING'S REAPPEARANCE.
Kew Palace, Sunday, March 1.-What a pleasure was mine this morning! how solemn, but how grateful! The queen gave me the "Prayer of Thanksgiving" upon the king's recovery. It was this morning read in all the churches throughout the metropolis, and by this day week it will reach every church in the kingdom. It kept me in tears all the morning,–that such a moment should actually arrive! after fears so dreadful, scenes so terrible.

The queen gave me a dozen to distribute among the female servants: but I reserved one of them for dear Mr. Smelt, who took it from me in speechless extacy–his fine and feeling eyes swimming in tears of joy. There is no describing–and I will not attempt it–the fullness, the almost overwhelming fullness of this morning's thankful feelings!

I had the great gratification to see the honoured object of this joy, for a few minutes, in the queen's dressing-room. He was all calmness and benevolent graciousness. I fancied my strong emotion had disfigured me; or perhaps the whole of this long confinement and most affecting winter may have somewhat marked my countenance; for the king presently said to me, "Pray, are you quite well to-day?"

" I think not quite, sir," I answered,

"She does not look well," said he to the queen; "she looks a little yellow, I think." How kind, to think of anybody and their looks, at this first moment of reappearance!

AN AIRING AND ITS CONSEQUENCES.

Wednesday, March 4.-A message from Mrs. Schwellenberg this morning, to ask me to air with her, received my most reluctant acquiescence; for the frost is so severe that any air, without exercise, is terrible to me; though, were her atmosphere milder, the rigour of the season I might not regard.

When we came to the passage the carriage was not ready. She murmured most vehemently; and so bitterly cold was I, I could heartily have joined, had it answered any purpose. In this cold passage we waited in this miserable manner a full quarter of an hour; Mrs. Schwellenberg all the time scolding the servants, threatening them With exile, sending message after message, repining, thwarting, and contentious.

Now we were to go, and wait in the king's rooms–now in the gentlemen's–now in Dr. Willis's–her own–and this, in the end, took place.

In our way we encountered Mr. Fairly. He asked where we were going. "To my own parlour!" she answered.

He accompanied us in; and, to cheer the gloom, seized some of the stores of Dr. Willis,–sandwiches, wine and water, and other refreshments,–and brought them to us, one after another in a sportive manner, recommending to us to break through common rules, on such an occasion, and eat and drink to warm ourselves. Mrs. Schwellenberg stood in stately silence, and bolt upright, scarce deigning to speak even a refusal; till, upon his saying, while he held a glass of wine in his hand, "Come, ma'am, do something eccentric for once–it will warm you," she angrily answered, "You been reely–what you call–too much hospital!"

Neither of us could help laughing. "Yes," cried he, "with the goods of others;–that makes a wide difference in hospitality!" Then he rattled away upon the honours the room had lately received, of having had Mr. Pitt, the Chancellor, Archbishop of Canterbury, etc., to wait in it. This she resented highly, as seeming to think it more honoured in her absence than presence.

At length we took our miserable airing, in which I was treated with as much fierce harshness as if I was being conveyed to some place of confinement for the punishment Of some dreadful offence!

She would have the glass down on my side; the piercing wind cut my face; I put my muff up to it: this incensed her so much, that she vehemently declared "she never, no never would trobble any won to air with her again but go always selfs."–And who will repine at that? thought I.

Yet by night I had caught a violent cold, which flew to my face, and occasioned me dreadful pain.

March 10.-I have been in too much pain to write these last five days; and I became very feverish, and universally ill, affected with the fury of the cold.

My royal mistress, who could not but observe me very unwell, though I have never omitted my daily three attendances, which I have performed with a difficulty all but insurmountable, concluded I had been guilty of some imprudence: I told the simple fact of the glass,–but quite simply, and without one circumstance. She instantly said she was surprised I could catch cold in an airing, as it never appeared that it disagreed with me when I took it with Mrs. Delany.

"No, ma'am," I immediately answered, "nor with Mrs, Locke; nor formerly with Mrs. Thrale:–but they left me the regulation of the glass on my own side to myself; or, if they interfered, it was to draw it up for me."

This I could not resist. I can be silent; but when challenged to speak at all, it must be plain truth.

I had no answer. Illness here–till of late–has been so unknown, that it is commonly supposed it must be wilful, and therefore meets little notice, till accompanied by danger, or incapacity of duty. This is by no means from hardness of heart-far otherwise ; there is no hardness of heart in any one of them ; but it is prejudice and want of personal experience.

ILLUMINATIONS ON THE KING's RECOVERY.

March 10.-This was a day of happiness indeed!—a day of such heartfelt public delight as Could not but suppress all private disturbance. The general illumination of all London proved the universal joy of a thankful and most affectionate people, who have shown so largely, on this trying occasion, how well they merited the monarch thus benignantly preserved.

Page 303 The queen, from the privy purse, gave private orders for a Splendid illumination at this palace.(305) The King– Providence–Health–and Britannia, were displayed with elegant devices; the queen and princesses, all but the youngest, went to town to see the illumination there; and Mr. Smelt was to conduct the surprise.–It was magnificently beautiful.

When it was lighted and prepared, the Princess Amelia went to lead her papa to the front window: but first she dropped on -her knees, and presented him a paper with these lines-which, at the queen's desire, I had scribbled in her name, for the happy occasion:–

TO THE KING.

Amid a rapt'rous nation's praise
That sees Thee to their prayers restor'd,
Turn gently from the gen'ral blaze,–
Thy Charlotte woos her bosom's lord.

Turn and behold where, bright and clear,
Depictur'd with transparent art,
The emblems of her thoughts appear,
The tribute of a grateful heart.

O! small the tribute, were it weigh'd
With all she feels–or half she owes!
But noble minds are best repaid
From the pure spring whence bounty flows.

PS. The little bearer begs a kiss From dear papa for bringing this.

I need not, I think, tell you, the little bearer begged not in vain. The king was extremely pleased. He came into a room belonging to the princesses, in which we had a party to look at the illuminations, and there he stayed above an hour; cheerful, composed, and gracious! all that could merit the great national testimony to his worth this day paid him.

MR FAIRLY ON MISS BURNEY's DUTIES.

Windsor, March 18.-A little rap announced Mr. Fairly, who came in, saying, "I am escaped for a little while, to have some quiet conversation with you, before the general assemblage and storm of company." He then gravely said, "Tomorrow I shall take leave of you–for a long time

He intended setting off to-morrow morning for town, by the opportunity of the equerries' coach, which would convey him to Kew, where his majesty was to receive an address.

He told me, with a good deal of humour, that he suspected me of being rather absent in my official occupation, from little natural care about toilettes and such things. I could not possibly deny this,–on the contrary, I owned I had, at first, found my attention unattainable, partly from flutter and embarrassment, and partly from the reasons he so discerningly assigned. "I have even," I added, "and not seldom, handed her fan before her gown, and her gloves before her cap but I am better in all that now!"

"I should think all that very likely," cried he, smiling; "yet it is not very trifling with her majesty, who is so exact and precise, such things seem to her of moment."

This is truth itself.

I said, "No,–she is more gracious, more kind, indeed, to me than ever: she scarce speaks, scarce turns to me without a smile."

" Well," cried he, extremely pleased, "this must much soften your employment and confinement. And, indeed, it was most natural to expect this time of distress should prove a cement."

A VISIT FROM MISS FUZILIER.

I think I need not mention meeting my beloved Fredy in town, on our delightful excursion thither for the grand restoration Drawing-room, in which the queen received the compliments and congratulations of almost all the Court part of the nation. Miss Cambridge worked me, upon this occasion, a suit, in silks upon tiffany, most excessively delicate and pretty, and much admired by her majesty.

All I shall mention of this town visit is, that, the day after the great Drawing-room, Miss Fuzilier, for the first time since I have been in office, called upon me to inquire after the queen. Miss Tryon, and Mrs. Tracey, and Mrs. Fielding were with her.

She looked serious, sensible, interesting. I thought instantly of the report concerning Mr. Fairly, and of his disavowal : but it was singular that the only time she opened her mouth to speak was to name him! Miss Tryon, who chatted incessantly, had spoken of the great confusion at the Drawing-room, from the crowd: "It was intended to be better regulated," said Miss

F., "Mr. Fairly told me." She dropped her eye the moment she had spoken his name. After this, as before it, she said nothing. . . .

Mr. George Villiers, a younger brother of Lord Clarendon, was now here as groom of the bedchamber. He is very clever, somewhat caustigue, but so loyal and vehement in the king's cause, that he has the appellation, from his party, of "The Tiger."

He would not obtain it for his person, which is remarkably slim, slight, and delicate.

A COMMAND FROM HER MAJESTY.

Kew, April, 1789. My dearest friends, - I have her majesty's commands to inquire–whether you have any of a certain breed of poultry?

N.B. What breed I do not remember.

And to say she has just received a small group of the same herself.

N.B. The quantity I have forgotten.

And to add, she is assured they are something very rare and scarce, and extraordinary and curious.

N.B. By whom she was assured I have not heard.

And to subjoin, that you must send word if you have any of the same sort.

N.B. How you are to find that out, I cannot tell.

And to mention, as a corollary, that, if you have none of them, and should like to have some, she has a cock and a hen she can spare, and will appropriate them to Mr. Locke and my dearest Fredy.

This conclusive stroke so pleased and exhilarated me, that forthwith I said you would both be enchanted, and so forgot all the preceding particulars. And I said, moreover, that I knew you would rear them, and cheer them, and fondle them like your children.

So now-pray write a very fair answer fairly, in fair hand, and to her fair purpose.

COLONEL MANNERS MYSTIFIES MRS. SCHWELLENBERG.

Queen's Lodge, Windsor, April.-Mrs. Schwellenberg is softened into nothing but civility and courtesy to me. To what the change is owing I cannot conjecture; but I do all that in me lies Page 306

to support it, preferring the entire sacrifice of every moment, from our dinner to twelve at night, to her harshness and horrors. Nevertheless, a lassitude of existence creeps sensibly upon me.

Colonel Manners, however, for the short half-hour of tea-time, is irresistibly diverting. He continues my constant friend and neighbour, and, while he affects to play off the coadjutrix to advantage, he nods at me, to draw forth my laughter or approbation, with the most alarming undisguise. I often fear her being affronted ; but naturally she admires him very much for his uncommon share of beauty, and makes much allowance for his levity. However, the never-quite-comprehended affair of the leather bed-cover,(306) has in some degree intimidated her ever since, as she constantly apprehends that, if he were provoked, he would play her some trick.

He had been at White's ball, given in town upon his majesty's recovery. We begged some account of it: he ranted away with great fluency, uttering little queer sarcasms at Mrs, Schwellenberg by every opportunity, and colouring when he had done, with private fear of enraging her. This, however, she suspected not, or all his aim had been lost; for to alarm her is his delight.

"I liked it all," he said, in summing up his relation, "very well, except the music, and I like any caw-caw-caw, better than that sort of noise,–only you must not tell the king I say that, ma'am, because the king likes it."

She objected to the words " must not," and protested she would not be directed by no one, and would tell it, if she pleased.

Upon this, he began a most boisterous threatening of the evil consequences which would accrue to herself, though in so ludicrous a manner, that how she could suppose him serious was my wonder. "Take care of yourself, ma'am," he cried, holding up his finger as if menacing a child; "take care of yourself! I am not to be provoked twice!"

This, after a proud resistance, conquered her - and, really frightened at she knew not what, she fretfully exclaimed, "Ver well, sir!–I wish I had not come down! I won't no more! you might have your tea when you can get It."

Returning to his account, he owned he had been rather a little musical himself for once, which was when they all sang "God save the king," after the supper; for then he joined in

Page 307 the chorus, as well and as loud as any of them, "though some of the company," he added, "took the liberty to ask me not to be so loud, because they pretended I was out of tune; but it was In such a good cause that I did not mind that."

She was no sooner recovered than the attack became personal again; and so it has continued ever since: he seems bent upon "playing her off" in all manners; he braves her, then compliments her, assents to her opinion, and the next moment contradicts her; pretends uncommon friendship for her, and then laughs in her face. But his worst manoeuvre is a perpetual application to me, by looks and sly glances, which fill me with terror of passing for an accomplice; and the more, as I find it utterly impossible to keep grave during these absurdities. And yet, the most extraordinary part of the story is that she really likes him! though at times she is so angry, she makes vows to keep to her own room.

Mr. George Villiers, with far deeper aim, sneers out his own more artful satire, but is never understood ; while Colonel Manners domineers with so high a hand, he carries all before him; and whenever Mrs. Schwellenberg, to lessen her mortification, draws me into the question, he instantly turns off whatever she begins into some high-flown compliment, so worded also as to convey some comparative reproach. This offends more than all.

When she complains to me of him, in his absence, I answer he is a mere schoolboy, for mischief, without serious design of displeasing: but she tells me she sees he means to do her some harm, and she will let the king know, if he goes on at that rate, for she does not choose such sort of familiarness.

Once she apologised suddenly for her English, and Colonel Manners said, "O, don't mind that, ma'am, for I take no particular notice as to your language."

"But," says she, "Miss Berner might tell me, when I speak it sometimes not quite right, what you call."

"O dear no, ma'am!" exclaimed he; "Miss Burney is of too mild a disposition for that: she could not correct you strong enough to do you good."

"Oh!-ver well, sir!" she cried, confounded by his effrontery.

One day she lamented she had been absent when there was so much agreeable company in the house; "And now," she

Page 308 added, "now that I am comm back, here is nobody.–not one!–no society!"

.

He protested this was not to be endured, and told her that to reckon all us nobody was so bad, he should resent it.

"What will you do, my good colonel?" she cried.

"O ma'am, do?–I will tell Dr. Davis."

"And who bin he?"

"Why, he's the master of Eton school, ma'am," with a thundering bawl in her ears, that made her stop them.

"No, sir!" she cried, indignantly, "I thank you for that, I won't have no Dr. schoolmaster, what you call! I bin too old for that."

"But, ma'am, he shall bring you a Latin oration upon this subject, and you must hear it!"

"O, 'tis all the same! I shan't not understand it, so I won't not hear it."

"But you must, ma'am. If I write it, I shan't let you off so:– you must hear it!"

"No, I won't!–Miss Berner might,–give it her."

"Does Miss Burney know Latin?" cried Mr. G. Villiers.

"Not one word," quoth I.

"I believe that cried she "but she might hear it the sam!"

THE SAILOR PRINCE.

On the 2nd of May I met Colonel Manners, waiting at the corner of a passage leading towards the queen's apartments. "Is the king, ma'am," he cried, "there? because Prince William(307) is come."

I had heard he was arrived in town,-and with much concern, since it was without leave of the king. It was in the illness, indeed, of the king he sailed to England, and when he had probably all the excuse of believing his royal father incapable of further governance. How did I grieve for the feelings of that royal father, in this idea! yet it certainly offers for Prince William his best apology.

In the evening, while Mrs. Schwellenberg, Mrs. Zachary and myself were sitting in the eating parlour, the door was suddenly opened by Mr. Alberts, the queen's page, and "prince William" was announced.

He came to see Mrs. Schwellenberg. He is handsome, as are all the royal family, though he is not of a height to be called a good figure. He looked very hard at the two strangers, but made us all sit, very civilly, and drew a chair for himself, and began to discourse with the most unbounded openness and careless ease, of everything that Occurred to him.

Mrs. Schwellenberg said she had pitied him for the grief he must have felt at the news of the king's illness : "Yes," cried he, "I was very sorry, for his majesty, very sorry indeed, -no man loves the king better ; of that be assured. but all sailors love their king. And I felt for the queen, too,–I did, faith. I was horridly agitated when I saw the king first. I could hardly stand."

Then Mrs. Schwellenberg suddenly said, "Miss Berner, now you might see his royal highness; you wanted it so moch, and now you might do it. Your royal highness, that is Miss Berner."

He rose very civilly, and bowed, to this strange freak of an introduction; and, of course, I rose and Curtsied low, and waited his commands to sit again; which were given instantly, with great courtesy.

"Ma'am," cried he, "you have a brother in the service?" "Yes, sir," I answered, much pleased with this professional attention. He had not, he civilly said, the pleasure to know him, but he had heard of him.

Then, turning suddenly to Mrs. Schwellenberg, "Pray," cried he, " what is become of Mrs.–Mrs.–Mrs. Hogentot?"

"O, your royal highness!" cried she, stifling much offence, "do you mean the poor Haggerdorn?–O your royal highness! have you forgot her?"

"i have, upon my word!" cried he, plumply "upon my soul, I have!"

Then turning again to me, "I am very happy, ma'am," he cried, "to see you here; it gives me great pleasure the queen should appoint the sister of a sea-officer to so eligible a situation. As long as she has a brother in the service, ma'am,, cried he to Mrs. Schwellenberg, "I look upon her as one of us. O, faith I do! I do indeed! she is one of the corps."

Then he said he had been making acquaintance with a new princess, one he did not know nor remember-Princess Amelia. "Mary, too,"– he said, "I had quite forgot; and they did not tell me who she was; so I went up to her, and, without in the least recollecting her, she's so monstrously grown, I said, 'Pray, ma'am, are you one of the attendants?'"

Princess Sophia is his professed favourite. "I have had the

honour," he cried, "of about an hour's conversation with that young lady, in the old style; though I have given up my mad frolics now. To be sure, I had a few in that style formerly; upon my word I am almost ashamed;–Ha! ha! ha!"

Then, recollecting particulars, he laughed vehemently; but Mrs. Schwellenberg eagerly interrupted his communications. I fancy some of them might have related to our own sacred person!

"Augusta," he said "looks very well,–a good face and countenance,–she looks interesting,–she looks as if she knew more than she Would say; and I like that character."

He stayed a full hour, chatting in this good-humoured and familiar manner.

LOYAL RECEPTION OF THE KING IN THE NEW FOREST.

Thursday, June 25.-This morning I was called before five o'clock, though various packages and business had kept me up till near three.

The day was rainy, but the road was beautiful; Windsor great park, in particular, is charming. The crowds increased as we advanced, and at Winchester the town was one head. I saw Dr. Warton, but could not stop the carriage. The king was everywhere received with acclamation. His popularity is greater than ever. Compassion for his late sufferings seems to have endeared him now to all conditions of men.

At Romsey, on the steps of the town-hall, an orchestra was formed, and a band of musicians, in common brown coarse cloth and red neckcloths, and even in carters' loose gowns, made a chorus of "God save the king," In which the countless multitude joined, in such loud acclamation, that their loyalty and heartiness, and natural joy, almost surprised me into a sob before I knew myself at all affected by them.

The New Forest Is all beauty, and when we approached Lyndhurst the crowds wore as picturesque an appearance as the landscapes ; They were all in decent attire, and, the great space giving them full room, the cool beauty of the verdure between the groups took away all idea of inconvenience, and made their live gaiety a scene to joy beholders.

Carriages of all sorts lined the road-side :-chariots, chaises, landaus, carts, waggons, whiskies, gigs, phatons—mixed and intermixed, filled Within and surrounded without by faces all glee and delight.

Such was the scenery for miles before we reached Lyndhurst. The old law of the forest, that his majesty must be presented with two milk-white greyhounds, peculiarly decorated, upon his entrance into the New Forest, gathered together multitudes to see the show. A party, also, of foresters, habited in green, and each with a bugle-horn, met his majesty at the same time.

Arrived at Lyndhurst, we drove to the Duke of Gloucester's. The royal family were just before us, but the two colonels came and handed us through the crowd. The house, intended for a mere hunting-seat, was built by Charles II., and seems quite unimproved and unrepaired from its first foundation. It is the king's, but lent to the Duke of Gloucester. It is a straggling, inconvenient, old house, but delightfully situated, in a village,—looking, indeed, at present, like a populous town, from the amazing concourse of people that have crowded into it.

The bow-men and archers and bugle-horns are to attend the king while he stays here, in all his rides.

The Duke of Gloucester was ready to receive the royal family, who are all in the highest spirits and delight.

I have a small old bed-chamber, but a large and commodious parlour, in which the gentlemen join Miss Planta and me to breakfast and to drink tea. They dine at the royal table. We are to remain here some days.

During the king's dinner, which was in a parlour looking into the garden, he permitted the people to come to the window; and their delight and rapture in seeing their monarch at table, with the evident hungry feeling it occasioned, made a contrast of admiration and deprivation, truly comic. They crowded, however, so excessively, that this can be permitted them no more. They broke down all the paling, and much of the hedges, and some of the windows, and all by eagerness and multitude, for they were perfectly civil and well-behaved.

In the afternoon the royal party came into my parlour; and the moment the people saw the star, they set up such a shout as made a ring all around the village; for my parlour has the same view with the royal rooms into the garden, where this crowd was assembled, and the new rapture was simply at seeing the king in a new apartment!

They all walked out, about and around the village, in the evening, and the delighted mob accompanied them. The

moment they stepped out of the house, the people, With voice, struck up "God save the king!" I assure you I cried like a child twenty times in the day, at the honest and rapturous effusions of such artless and disinterested loyalty. The king's illness and recovery make me tender, as Count Mannuccia said, upon every recollection.

These good villagers continued singing this loyal song during the whole walk, without any intermission, except to shout "huzza!" at the end of every stanza. They returned so hoarse, that I longed to give them all some lemonade. Probably they longed for something they would have called better! 'Twas well the king could walk no longer; I think, if he had, they would have died singing around him.

June 30.-We continued at Lyndhurst five days and the tranquillity of the life, and the beauty of the country, would have made it very regaling to me indeed, but for the fatigue of having no maid, yet being always in readiness to play the part of an attendant myself.

I went twice to see the house of Sir Phillip Jennings Clerke, my old acquaintance at Streatham. I regretted he was no more; he would so much have prided and rejoiced in shewing his place. His opposition principles would not have interfered with that private act of duty from a subject to a sovereign. How did I call to mind Mrs. Thrale, upon this spot! not that I had seen it with her, or ever before; but that its late owner was one of her sincerest admirers.

Miss Planta and myself drove also to Southampton, by the queen's direction. It is a pretty clean town, and the views from the Southampton water are highly picturesque : but all this I had seen to far greater advantage, with Mr. and Mrs. and Miss Thrale. Ah, Mrs. Thrale!–In thinking her over, as I saw again the same spot, how much did I wish to see with it the same–once so dear– companion!

On the Sunday we all went to the parish church ; and after the service, instead of a psalm, imagine our surprise to hear the whole congregation join in "God save the king!" Misplaced as this was in a church, its intent was so kind, loyal, and affectionate, that I believe there was not a dry eye amongst either singers or hearers. The king's late dreadful illness has rendered this song quite melting to me. This day we quitted Lyndhurst; not without regret, for so private is its situation, I could stroll about in its beautiful neighbourhood quite alone.

THE ROYAL JOURNEY TO WEYMOUTH.

The journey to Weymouth was one scene of festivity and rejoicing. The people were everywhere collected, and everywhere delighted. We passed through Salisbury, where a magnificent arch was erected, of festoons of flowers, for the king's carriage to pass under, and mottoed with "The king restored," and "Long live the king," in three divisions. The green bowmen accompanied the train thus far; and the clothiers and manufacturers here met it, dressed out in white loose frocks, flowers, and ribbons, with sticks or caps emblematically decorated from their several manufactories. And the acclamations with which the king was received amongst them–it was a rapture past description. At Blandford there was nearly the same ceremony.

At every gentleman's seat which we passed, the owners and their families stood at the gate, and their guests Or neighbours were in carriages all round.

At Dorchester the crowd seemed still increased. The city had so antique an air, I longed to investigate its old buildings. The houses have the most ancient appearance of any that are inhabited that I have happened to see: and inhabited they were indeed! every window-sash was removed, for face above face to peep Out, and every old balcony and all the leads of the houses seemed turned into booths for fairs. It seems, also, the most populous town I have seen; I judge by the concourse of the young and middle-aged–those we saw everywhere alike, as they may gather together from all quarters-but from the amazing quantity of indigenous residers; old women and young children. There seemed families of ten or twelve of the latter in every house; and the old women were so numerous, that they gave the whole scene the air of a rural masquerade.

Girls, with chaplets, beautiful young creatures, strewed the entrance of various villages with flowers.

WELCOME TO WEYMOUTH.

Gloucester House, which we now inhabit, at Weymouth, is Situated in front of the sea, and the sands of the bay before it are perfectly smooth and soft. The whole town, and Melcomb Regis, and half the county of Dorset, seemed assembled to welcome their majesties.

I have here a very good parlour, but dull, from its aspect.

Nothing but the sea at Weymouth affords any life Or Spirit. My bed-room is in the attics. Nothing like living at a Court for exaltation. Yet even with this gratification, which extends to Miss Planta, the house will only hold the females of the party. The two adjoining houses are added, for the gentlemen, an(] the pages, and some other of the suite, cooks, etc.–but the footmen are obliged to lodge still farther off.

The bay is very beautiful, after its kind; a peninsula shuts out
Portland island and the broad ocean.

The king, and queen, and princesses, and their suite, walked out in the evening; an immense crowd attended them–sailors bargemen, mechanics, countrymen; and all united with so vociferous a volley of "God save the king," that the noise was stunning.

At near ten o'clock Lord Courtown came into my parlour, as it is called, and said the town was all illuminated, and invited Miss Planta and me to a walk upon the sands. Their majesties were come in to supper. We took a stroll under his escort, and found it singularly beautiful, the night being very fine, and several boats and small vessels lighted up, and in motion upon the sea. The illumination extended through Melcomb Regis and Weymouth. Gloucester-row, in which we live, is properly in Melcomb Regis; but the two towns join each other, and are often confounded.

The preparations of festive loyalty were universal. Not a child could we meet that had not a bandeau round its head, cap, or hat, of "God save the king;" all the bargemen wore it in cockades and even the bathing-women had it in large coarse girdles round their waists. It is printed in golden letters upon most of the bathing-machines, and in various scrolls and devices it adorns every shop and almost every house in the two towns.

THE ROYAL PLUNGE WITH MUSICAL HONOURS. "YOU MUST KNEEL, SIR!"

Gloucester House, Weymouth, Wednesday, July 9.-We are settled here comfortably enough. Miss Planta and I breakfast as well as dine together alone; the gentlemen have a breakfast parlour in the adjoining house, and we meet only at tea, and seldom then. They have all acquaintance here, in this Gloucester-row, and stroll from the terrace or the sands, to visit them during the tea vacation time.

Page 315.'

I like this much: I see them just enough to keep up sociability, without any necessary constraint; for I attend the tea-table only at my own hour, and they come, or not, according to chance or their convenience.

The king bathes, and with great success; a machine follows the royal one into the sea, filled with fiddlers, who play "God save the king," as his majesty takes his plunge!

I am delighted with the soft air and soft footing upon the sands, and stroll up and down them morning, noon, and night. As they are close before the house, I can get to and from them in a moment.

Her majesty has graciously hired a little maid between Miss Planta and me, who comes for the day. We have no accommodation for her sleeping here; but it is an unspeakable relief to our personal fatigues.

Dr. Gisburne is here, to attend his majesty; and the queen has ordered me to invite him to dine at my table. He comes regularly.

(Fanny Burney to Dr. Burney.)

Gloucester Rowe, Weymouth, July 13, 1789.

My dearest padre's kind letter was most truly welcome to me.

When I am so distant, the term of absence or of silence seems always doubly long to me.

The bay here is most beautiful; the sea never rough, generally calm and gentle, and the sands perfectly smooth and pleasant. I have not bathed, for I have had a cold in my head, which I caught at Lyndhurst, and which makes me fear beginning; but I have hopes to be well enough to-morrow, and thenceforward to ail nothing more. It is my intention to cast away all superfluous complaints into the main ocean, which I think quite sufficiently capacious to hold them ; and really my little frame will find enough to carry and manage without them. . . .

His majesty is in delightful health, and much-improved spirits. All agree he never looked better. The loyalty of all this place is excessive; they have dressed out every street with labels of "God save the king:" all the shops have it over the doors: all the children wear it in their caps, all the labourers in their hats, and all the sailors in their voices, for they never approach the house without shouting it aloud, nor see the king, or his shadow, without beginning to huzza, and going on to three cheers.

The bathing-machines make it their motto over the windows; and those bathers that belong to the royal dippers wear it in bandeaus on their bonnets, to go into the sea; and have it again, in large letters, round their waists, to encounter the waves. Flannel dresses, tucked up, and no shoes nor stockings, with bandeaus and girdles, have a most singular appearance, and when first I surveyed these loyal nymphs it was with some difficulty I kept my features in order. Nor is this all. Think but Of the Surprise of his majesty when, the first time of his bathing, he had no sooner popped his royal head under water than a band of music, concealed in a neighbouring machine, struck up "God save great George our king."

One thing, however, was a little unlucky ,–when the mayor and burgesses came with the address, they requested leave to kiss hands: this was graciously accorded; but, the mayor advancing, in a common way, to take the queen's hand, as he might that of any lady mayoress, Colonel Gwynn, who stood by, whispered, "You must kneel, sir!" He found, however, that he took no notice of this hint, but kissed the queen's hand erect. As he passed him, in his way back, the colonel Said, "You should have knelt, Sir!"

"Sir," answered the poor mayor, "I cannot."

"Everybody does, sir."

"Sir,–I have a wooden leg!"

Poor man! 'twas such a surprise! and such an excuse as no one could dispute. But the absurdity of the matter followed–all the rest did the same; taking the same privilege, by the example, without the same or any cause!

ROYAL DOINGS IN AND ABOUT WEYMOUTH.

July 15.-The Magnificent, a man-of-war Of 74 guns, commanded by an old captain of James's (Onslow), is now stationed at the entrance of the bay, for the security at once and pleasure of the king; and a fine frigate, the Southampton, Captain Douglas, is nearer in, and brought for the king to cruise about. Captain Douglas is nephew to Sir Andrew Snape Hammond, who married a cousin of our Mr. Crisp. The king and royal party have been to visit the frigate. Miss Planta and myself went to see the ceremony from a place called the Look-out,–a beautiful spot. But I have not much taste for sea receptions and honours: the firing a salute is SO strange a mode of hospitality and politeness. . . .

Mrs. Gwynn(308) is arrived, and means to spend the royal season here. She lodges at the hotel just by, and we have met several times. She is very soft and pleasing, and still as beautiful as an angel. We have had two or three long tête– têtes and talked over, with great pleasure, anecdotes Of Our former mutual acquaintances–Dr. Johnson, Sir Joshua Reynolds, Mrs. Thrale, Baretti, Miss Reynolds, Miss Palmer, and her old admirer, Dr. Goldsmith, of whom she relates–as who does not?–a thousand ridiculous traits.

The queen is reading Mrs. Piozzi's tour(309) to me, instead of my reading it to her. She loves reading aloud, and in this work finds me an able commentator. How like herself, how characteristic is every line–Wild, entertaining, flighty, inconsistent, and clever!

July 16.-Yesterday we all wen to the theatre. The king has taken the centre front box for himself, family, and attendants. The side boxes are too small. The queen ordered places for Miss Planta and me, which are in the front row of a box next but one to the royals. Thus, in this case, Our want of rank to be in their public suite gives us better seats than those high enough to stand behind them,

Lady Sydney, Lady Courtown's sister, and Miss Townshend, her daughter, are in the intermediate box, and were very sociable. I have met them here occasionally, and like them very well.

'Tis a pretty little theatre: but its entertainment was quite in the barn style a mere medley,–songs, dances, imitations,- and all very bad. But Lord Chesterfield, who is here, and who seems chief director, promises all will be better.

This morning the royal party went to Dorchester, and I strolled upon the sands with Mrs. Gwynn. We overtook a lady, of a very majestic port and demeanour, who solemnly returned Mrs. Gwynn's salutation, and then addressed herself to me with similar gravity. I saw a face I knew, and of very uncommon beauty; but did not immediately recollect it was Mrs. Siddons. She is come here, she says, solely for her health : she has spent some days with Mrs. Gwynn, at General Harcourt's. Her husband was with her, and a sweet child. I wished to have tried if her solemnity would have worn away

by length of conversation ; but I was obliged to hasten home.
But my dearest Fredy's opinion, joined to that of my Sister
Esther, satisfies me I was a loser by this necessary forbearance.

Sunday, July 26.-Yesterday we wen again to the play, and saw "The Midnight Hour" and "The Commissary." The latter from the "Bourgeois Gentilhomme," is comic to convulsion and the burlesque of Quick and Mrs. Wells united made ne laugh quite immoderately.(310)

July 29.-We went to the play, and saw Mrs. Siddons in Rosalind. She looked beautifully, but too large for that shepherd's dress; and her gaiety sits not naturally upon her,–it seems more like disguised gravity. I must own my admiration for her confined to her tragic powers; and there it is raised so high that I feel mortified, in a degree, to see her so much fainter attempts and success in comedy.

A PATIENT AUDIENCE.

Monday, Aug. 3.-The whole royal party went to see Lulworth Castle, intending to be back to dinner, and go to the play at night, which their majesties had ordered, with Mrs. Siddons to play Lady Townly.(311) Dinner-time, however, came and passed, and they arrived not. They went by sea, and the wind proved contrary; and about seven o'clock a hobby groom was despatched thither by land, with intelligence that they had only reached Lulworth Castle at five o'clock. They meant to be certainly back by eight ; but sent their commands that the farce might be performed first, and the play wait them.

The manager repeated this to the audience,–already waiting and wearied but a loud applause testified their agreeability to whatever could be proposed. The farce, however, was much sooner over than the passage from Lulworth Castle. It was ten o'clock when they landed! And all this time the audience–spectators rather–quietly waited!

They landed, just by the theatre, and went to the house of Lady Pembroke, who is now here in attendance upon the queen : and there they Sent home for the king's page, with

a wig, etc.; and the queen's wardrobe woman, with similar decorations; and a message to Miss Planta and me, that we might go at once to the theatre.

We obeyed; and soon after they appeared, and were received with the most violent gusts of joy and huzzas, even from the galleries over their heads, whose patience had not the reward of seeing them at last. Is not this a charming trait of provincial popularity?

Mrs. Siddons, in her looks, and the tragic part, was exquisite.

A FATIGUING BUT PLEASANT DAY.

Aug. 4.-To-day all the royals went to Sherborne Castle. My day being perfectly at liberty, Mrs. Gwynn stayed and spent it with me. The weather was beautiful; the sea-breezes here keep off intense heat in the warmest season. We walked first to see the shrubbery and plantation of a lady, Mrs. B–, who has a very pretty house about a mile and a half out of the town. Here we rested, and regaled ourselves with sweet flowers, and then proceeded to the old castle,-its ruins rather,- which we most completely examined, not leaving one stone' untrod, except such as must have precipitated us into the sea. This castle is built almost in the sea, upon a perpendicular rock, and its situation, therefore, is nobly bold and striking. It is little more now than walls, and a few little winding staircases at its four corners.

I had not imagined my beautiful companion could have taken so much pleasure from an excursion so romantic and ,lonely ; but she enjoyed it very much, clambered about as unaffectedly as if she had lived in rural scenes all her life, and left nothing unexamined.

We then prowled along the sands at the foot of the adjoining rocks, and picked up sea-weeds and shells - but I do not think they were such as to drive Sir Ashton Lever,(312) or the Museum keepers, to despair! We had the queen's two little dogs, Badine and Phillis, for our guards and associates. We returned home to a very late tea, thoroughly tired, but very much pleased. To me it was the only rural excursion I had taken for more than three years.

Page 320 The royal party came not home till past eleven o'clock. The queen was much delighted with Sherborne Castle, which abounds with regal curiosities, honourably acquired by the family.

LULWORTH CASTLE.

Aug. 8.–To-day we went to Lulworth Castle; but not with Mrs. Gwynn. Her majesty ordered our royal coach and four, and directed me to take the two De Lucs.

Lulworth Castle is beautifully situated, with a near and noble view of the sea, It has a spacious and very fine park, and commands a great extent of prospect. It is the property of Mr. Weld, a Roman Catholic, whose eldest brother was first husband of Mrs. Fitzherbert.(313) A singular circumstance, that their majesties should visit a house in which, so few years ago, she might have received them.

There is in it a Roman Catholic chapel that is truly elegant,–a Pantheon in miniature,–and ornamented with immense expense and richness. The altar is all of finest variegated marbles, and precious stones are glittering from every angle. The priests' vestments, which are very superb, and all the sacerdotal array, were shown us as particular favours: and Colonel Goldsworthy comically said he doubted not they had incense and oblations for a week to come, by way of purification for our heretical curiosity.

The castle is built with four turrets. It is not very ancient, and the inside is completely modern, and fitted up with great elegance. It abounds in pictures of priests, saints, monks, and nuns, and is decorated with crosses and Roman Catholic devices without end. They show one room in which two of our kings have slept; Charles II. and poor James II.

We returned home to dinner, and in the evening went to the

Page 321 play. Mrs. Siddons performed Mrs. Oakley.(313) What pity thus to throw away her talents ! but the queen dislikes tragedy, and the honour to play before the royal family blinds her to the little credit acquired by playing comedy.

THE ROYAL PARTY AT THE ASSEMBLY Rooms.

Sunday, Aug 9.-The king had a council yesterday, which brought most of the great officers of state to Weymouth.

In the evening, her majesty desired Miss Planta and me to go to the rooms, whither they commonly go themselves on Sunday evenings, and, after looking round them, and speaking where they choose, they retire to tea in an inner apartment with their own party, but leave the door wide open, both to see and be seen.

The rooms are convenient and spacious : we found them very full. As soon as the royal party came, a circle was formed, and they moved round it, just as before the ball at St. James's, the king one way with his chamberlain, the new-made Marquis of Salisbury, and the queen the other with the princesses, Lady Courtown, etc. The rest of the attendants planted themselves round in the circle.

I had now the pleasure, for the first time, to see Mr. Pitt but his appearance is his least recommendation ; it is neither noble nor expressive. Lord Chatham, the Duke of Richmond, Mr. Villiers, Lord Delawarr, etc., were in the circle, and spoken to a long time each.

A JOURNEY To EXETER AND SALTRAM.

Thursday, Aug. 13.-We began our Western tour. We all went in the same order as we set out from Windsor. We arrived at Exeter to a very late dinner. We were lodged at the Deanery; and Dr. Buller, the dean, desired a conference with me, for we came first, leaving the royals at Sir George Young's. He was very civil, and in highest glee: I had never seen him before; but he told me he introduced himself, by this opportunity, at the express desire of Mrs. Chapone and Mrs. Castle, who were both his relations, as well as of Dr. Warton. I was glad to hear myself yet remembered by them.

The crowds, the rejoicings, the hallooing, and singing, and garlanding, and decorating of all the inhabitants of this old Page 322 city, and of all the country through which we passed, made the journey quite charming : such happy loyalty as beamed from all ranks and descriptions of men carried close to the heart in sympathetic joy.

We passed all the next day at the Deanery, which was insufficient to our party, that not only the gentlemen, one an(l all, lodged at the hotel, but even Lady Courtown and the two Lady Waldegraves. I saw nothing of any of them while we stayed at Exeter. I strolled with Miss Planta about the town, which is populous and busy enough, but close and ugly. The principal parade for company, however, takes in a fine view of the country; and the cathedral is old and curious.

The next morning, Saturday the 15th, we quitted Exeter, in which there had been one constant mob surrounding the Deanery from the moment of our entrance. We proceeded through a country the most fertile, varied, rural, and delightful, in England, till we came to the end of our aim, Saltram. We passed through such beautiful villages, and so animated a concourse of people, that the whole journey proved truly delectable. Arches of flowers were-erected for the royal family to pass under at almost every town, with various loyal devices, expressive of their satisfaction in this circuit. How happy must have been the king!-how deservedly ! The greatest conqueror could never pass through his dominions with fuller acclamations of joy from his devoted subjects than George III. experienced, simply from having won their love by the even tenor of an unspotted life, which, at length, has vanquished all the hearts of all his subjects.

Our entrance at Saltram was, personally to Miss Planta and me, very disagreeable: we followed immediately after the royals and equerries and so many of the neighbouring gentry, the officers, etc., were assembled to receive them, that we had to make our way through a crowd of starers the most tremendous, while the royals all stood at the windows, and the other attendants in the hall.

The house is one of the most magnificent in the kingdom. It accommodated us all, even to every footman, without by any means filling the whole. The state apartments on the ground floor are superb, hung with crimson damask, and ornamented with pictures, some few of the Spanish school, the rest by Sir Joshua Reynolds, Angelica, and some few by other artists.

Its view is noble; it extends to Plymouth, Mount-Edge-

cumbe, and the neighbouring fine country. The sea at times fills up a part of the domain almost close to the house, and then its prospect is Complete.

MAY "ONE" COME IN?

Sunday, Aug. 16.-Lord Courtown brought me a very obliging message from Lady Mount-Edgecumbe, who had been here at noon to kiss hands, on becoming a countess from a baroness. She sent to invite me to see her place, and contrive to dine and spend the day there. Her majesty approves the Mount-Edgecumbe invitation.

Aug. 18.-This morning the royals were all at a grand naval review. I spent the time very serenely in my favourite wood, which abounds in seats of all sorts - and then I took a fountain Pen, and wrote my rough journal for copying to my dear Sorelle.(314)

In the evening, Lord Courtown, opening my parlour door, called out, "May one come in?"

"May one?" exclaimed Colonel Goldsworthy; "may two, may three,–may four?–I like your one, indeed!"

And in they all entered, and remained in sociable conversation till they were all called, late, to cards.

AN EXCURSION To PLYMOUTH DOCKYARD.

Aug. 19.-Again this morning was spent by the royals at Plymouth dock–by me in strolls round the house. The wood here is truly enchanting–the paths on the slant down to the water resemble those of sweet Norbury park.

The tea, also, was too much the same to be worth detailing. I will only mention a speech which could not but divert me, of Mr. Alberts, the queen's page. He said nobody dared represent to the king the danger of his present continual exertion in this hot weather,–"unless it is Mr. Fairly," he added, "who can say anything, in his genteel roundabout way."

Aug. 21.-To-day the royals went to Mount-Edgecumbe, and her majesty had commissioned Lady Courtown to arrange a plan for Miss Planta and me to see Plymouth Dock. According, therefore, to her ladyship's directions, we set off for that place, and, after a dull drive of about five miles, arrived at the house of the commissioner, Admiral La Forey. Here

Page 324 Mrs. La Forey and her daughters were prepared to expect us, and take the trouble of entertaining us for the day.

Three large and populous towns, Plymouth, Stockton, and Dock,(315) nearly join each other. Plymouth is long, dirty, ill built, and wholly unornamented with any edifice worth notice. Stockton is rather neater,-nothing more. Dock runs higher and Is newer, and looks far cleaner and more habitable. The commissioner's is the best-situated house in Dock: it is opposite a handsome quay, on an arm of the sea, with a pretty paved walk, or terrace, before the house, which seems used as a mall by the inhabitants, and is stored with naval offices innumerable.

The two ladies received us very pleasantly. Mrs. La Forey Is well bred, in the formal way ; but her eldest daughter, Mrs. Molloy, is quite free from stiffness, yet perfectly obliging, very easy, very modest, and very engaging, and, when dressed for a ball in the evening, very handsome. She does not become a déshabille, but cannot look otherwise than pleasing and agreeable, from her manners and countenance.

Captain Molloy, her husband, was gone to attend in the naval procession that conducted the royals to Mount-Edgecumbe, where he expected to dine ; but he had left a younger officer, Lieutenant Gregory, to do the honours of the naval show to us.

The commissioner himself is yet more formal than his lady, but equally civil. An unmarried daughter appeared next, who seems sensible and good humoured, but very plain.

We sallied forth to the dockyard, with these two daughters, and Lieutenant Gregory, a very pleasing and well-bred young officer. How often I wished my dear James had happened to be here, in any employment, at this time!

The dockyard you will dispense with my describing. It is a noble and tremendous sight, and we were shown it with every advantage of explanation. It was a sort of sighing satisfaction to see such numerous stores of war's alarms !-ropes, sails, masts, anchors,–and all in the finest symmetry, divided and subdivided, as if placed only for show, The neatness and exactness of all the arrangement of those stores for tempest, filled me with admiration; so did the whole scene–though not with pleasure. All assurances, however well to be depended upon, of safety, are but so many indications of danger.

While we were seeing the anchor business,–which seemed performed by Vulcanic demons, so black they looked, so savage was their howl in striking the red-hot iron, and so coarse and slight their attire,–we were saluted with three cheers, from the accidental entrance of Lord Stopford, Lord Courtown's son, and Mr. Townshend, his nephew, a son of Lord Sydney, just made a lord of the Admiralty. And the sound, in those black regions, where all the light was red-hot fire, had a Very fine demoniac effect. In beating the anchor they all strike at the same instant, giving about three quick strokes to one slow stroke; and were they not to time them with the most perfect conformity, they must inevitably knock out one another's brains. The sight of this apparently continual danger gave to the whole the appearance of some wild rite performed from motives of superstition in some uncivilised country.

While we were yet]it the dockyard we were joined by two sea-captains, Captain Molloy and Captain Duckworth. Captain Molloy is a sensible and agreeable man, but somewhat haughty, and of conscious consequence. Captain Duckworth is both sensible and amiable in his style of conversation, and has a most perfect and kind openness of manner and countenance; but he greatly amused me by letting me see how much I amused him. I never surprised him looking near me, without seeing on his face so irresistible a simper, that I expected him every moment to break forth; never even trying to keep a grave face, except when I looked at him in full front. I found he knew "Burney, of the Bristol," as he called our James, and I named and conversed about him by every opportunity. .

A VISIT TO A SEVENTY-FOUR.

Captain Molloy invited us, when we had exhausted the show on land, to see his ship. I dislike going anywhere beyond the reach of the Humane society, but could not be left without breaking up the party: this was my first water-excursion, though two had been proposed to me at Weymouth, which I had begged leave to decline.

All, however, was smooth and calm, and we had the best possible navigators. We went to the ship in Captain Molloy's large boat, which was very trim and neat, and had all its rowers new dressed and smart for royal attendance, as it followed the king in all his water-excursions.

The Ship is the Bombay Castle, of seventy-four guns. It had the Admiralty flag hoisted, as Lord Chatham had held a board there in the morning. It is a very fine ship, and I was truly edified by the sight of all its accommodations, ingenuity, utility, cleanliness, and contrivances. A man-of-war, fitted out and manned,- is a glorious and a fearful sight!

In going over the ship we came to the midshipmen's mess, and those young officers were at dinner, but we were taken in: they were lighted by a few candles fastened to the wall in sockets. Involuntarily I exclaimed, "Dining by candle-light at noon-day!" A midshipman, starting forward, said, "Yes', ma'am, and Admiral Lord Hood did the same for seven years following!"

I liked his spirit so much that I turned to him, and said I was very glad they looked forward to such an example, for I had a brother in the service, which gave me a warm interest in its prosperity. This made the midshipman so much my friend, that we entered into a detailed discourse upon the accommodations of their cabin, mess, etc., and various other matters. I liked him much, though I know not his name; but my constant Captain Duckworth kept me again wholly to his own cicerone-ing, when I turned out of the cabin.

A little, however, he was mortified to find me a coward upon the water. I assured him he should cure me if he could convince me there was no reason for fear. He would not allow of any, but could not disprove it.

"Tell me," I said, "and honestly,–should we be overturned in the boat while out at sea, what would prevent our being drowned?" He would not suppose such an accident possible.

I pressed him, however, upon the possibility it might happen once in a century, and he could not help laughing, and answered, "O, we should pick you all up!" –I desired to know by what means. "Instruments," he said. I forced him, after a long and comic resistance, to show me them. Good heaven! they were three-pronged iron forks,–very tridents of Neptune!

I exclaimed with great horror, "These!—why, they would tear the body to pieces!"

"O," answered he calmly, "one must not think of legs and arms when life is in danger."

I would not, however, under such protection, refuse sailing round Mount-Edgecumbe, which we did in Captain Molloy's boat, and just at the time when the royals, in sundry garden-

Page 327 chairs, were driving about the place. It was a beautiful view the situation is delightful. But Captain Molloy was not in the best harmony with its owners, as they had disappointed his expectations of an Invitation to dinner.

A DAY AT MOUNT-EDGECUMBE.

Aug. 24.-To-day the royals went to Marystow, Colonel Heywood's, and Miss Planta and myself to Mount-Edgecumbe. The queen had desired me to take Miss Planta, and I had written to prepare Lady Mount-Edgecumbe for a companion.

We went in a chaise to the ferry, and thence in a boat. I did not like this part of the business, for we had no pilot we knew, nor any one to direct us. They would hardly believe, at Mount-Edgecumbe, we had adventured in so unguarded a manner: but our superior is too high to discover difficulties, or know common precautions ; and we fare, therefore, considerably worse in all these excursions, from belonging to crowned heads, than we should do in our own private stations, if visiting at any part of the kingdom.

Safe, however, though not pleasantly, we arrived on the opposite shore ; when we found a gardener and a very commodious garden-chair waiting for us. We drove through a sweet park to the house, at the gate of which stood Lord and Lady Mount-Edgecumbe, who told us that they had just heard an intention of their majesties to sail the next day up the River Tamer, and therefore they thought it their duty to hasten off to a seat they have near its banks, Coteil, with refreshments and accommodations, in case they should be honoured with a visit to see the place, which was very ancient and curious. They should leave Lord Valletort to do the honours, and expressed much civil regret in the circumstance: but the distance was too great to admit of the journey, over bad roads, if they deferred it till after dinner.

We then proceeded, in the chair, to see the place: it is truly noble; but I shall enter into no description from want of time: take a list simply of its particular points. The sea, in some places, shows itself in its whole vast and unlimited expanse; at others, the jutting land renders it merely a beautiful basin or canal: the borders down to the sea are in some parts flourishing with the finest evergreens and most vivid verdure, and in others are barren, rocky, and perilous. In one moment you might suppose yourself cast on a desert island,

and the next find yourself in the most fertile and luxurious country. In different views we were shown Cawsand bay, the Hamoaze, the rocks called "the Maker," etc.,–Dartmoor hills, Plymouth, the dockyard, Saltram, and St. George's channel. Several noble ships, manned and commissioned -were in the Hamoaze amongst them our Weymouth friends' the Magnificent and Southampton.

A very beautiful flower-garden is enclosed in one part of the grounds ; and huts, seats, and ornaments in general, were well adapted to the scenery of the place. A seat is consecrated to Mrs. Damer,(316) with an acrostic on her name by Lord Valletort. It is surprising to see the state of vegetation at this place, so close to the main. Myrtles, pomegranates, everg.reens, and flowering shrubs, all thrive, and stand the cold blast, when planted in a southern aspect, as safely as in an inland country. As it is a peninsula, it has all aspects, and the plantations and dispositions of the ground are admirably and skilfully assorted to them.

The great open view, however, disappointed me : the towns it shows have no prominent features, the country is as flat as it is extensive, and the various branches of the sea which run into it give, upon their retreat, a marshy, muddy, unpleasant appearance. There is, besides, a want of some one striking object to arrest the eye, and fix the attention, which wearies from the general glare. Points, however, there are, both of the sublime and beautiful, that merit all the fame which this noble place has acquired.

In our tour around it we met Lord Stopford, Mr. Townshend, and Captain Douglas ; and heard a tremendous account of the rage of the sea-captains, on being disappointed of a dinner at the royal visit to Mount-Edgecumbe.

We did not quit these fine grounds till near dinner-time. The housekeeper then showed us the house, and a set of apartments newly fitted up for the royals, had they chosen to sleep at Mount-Edgecumbe. The house is old, and seems pleasant and convenient.

In a very pretty circular parlour, which had the appearance of being the chief living room, I saw amongst a small collection of books, "Cecilia." I immediately laid a wager with myself the first volume would open upon Pacchierotti; and I won it very honestly, though I never expect to be paid it. The chapter, "An Opera Rehearsal," was so well read, the leaves always flew apart to display it.

The library is an exceeding good room, and seems charmingly furnished. Here Lord Valletort received us. His lady was confined to her room by indisposition. He is a most neat little beau, and his face has the roses and lilies as finely blended as that of his pretty young wife. He was extremely civil and attentive, and appears to be really amiable in his disposition.

Mr. Brett, a plain, sensible, conversible man, who has an estate in the neighbour-hood, dined with us; and a young Frenchman. The dinner was very cheerful: my lord, at the head of the table, looked only like his lady in a riding-dress. However, he received one mortifying trial of his temper - he had sent to request sailing up the Tamer next day with Sir Richard Bickerton; and he had a blunt refusal, in a note, during our repast. Not an officer in the fleet would accommodate him; their resentment of the dinner slight is quite vehement.

We returned home the same way we came; the good-natured little lord, and Mr. Brett also, quite shocked we had no better guard or care taken of us.

MR. FAIRLY ON A COURT LIFE.

Weymouth, Sunday, Sept. 6.-This evening, the royals and their train all went again to the rooms to drink their tea. Miss Planta and myself were taking ours quietly together, and I was finishing a charming sermon of Blair while she was running over some old newspapers, when, suddenly, but very gently, the room-door was opened, and then I heard, "Will Miss Burney permit me to come in, and give me a dish of tea?" 'Twas Mr. Fairly.

He said we were to go on Monday se'nnight to Lord Bath's, on Wednesday to Lord Aylesbury's, and on Friday to return to Windsor. He was himself to be discharged some days sooner, as he should not be wanted on the road. He said many things relative - to Court lives and situations: with respect, deference, and regard invariable, mentioned the leading individuals ; but said nothing could be so weak as to look there, in such stations, for such impossibilities as sympathy, friendship, or cordiality ! And he finished with saying, "People forget themselves who look for them!"

Such, however, is not my feeling ; and I am satisfied he has met with some unexpected coldness. Miss Planta being present, he explained only in generals.

A BRIEF SOJOURN AT LONGLEAT.

Monday, Sept. 14.-We all left Weymouth. All possible honours were paid the king on his departure; lords, ladies, and sea- officers, lined the way that he passed, the guns of the Magnificent and Southampton fired the parting salute, and the ships were under sail.

We all set out as before, but parted on the road. The royals went to breakfast at Redlinch, the seat of Lord Ilchester, where Mr, Fairly(317) was in waiting for them, and thence proceeded to a collation at Sherborne Castle, whither he was to accompany them, and then resign his present attendance, which has been long and troublesome and irksome, I am sure.

Miss Planta and myself proceeded to Longleat, the seat of the Marquis of Bath, late Lord Weymouth; where we were all to dine, sleep, and spend the following day and night. Longleat was formerly the dwelling of the Earl of Lansdowne, uncle to Mrs. Delany; and here, at this seat, that heartless uncle, to promote some political views, sacrificed his incomparable niece, at the age of seventeen, marrying her to an unwieldly, uncultivated, country esquire, near sixty years of age, and scarce ever sober– his name Pendarves.

With how sad an awe, in recollecting her submissive unhappiness, did I enter these doors!–and with what indignant hatred did I look at the portrait of the unfeeling earl, to whom her gentle repugnance, shown by almost incessant tears, was thrown away, as if she, her person, and her existence were nothing in the scale, where the disposition of a few boroughs opposed them! Yet was this the famous Granville–the poet, the fine gentleman, the statesman, the friend and patron of Pope, of whom he wrote–

"What Muse for Granville can refuse to sing?"

Mine, I am sure, for one.

Lady Bath showed us our rooms, to which we repaired immediately, to dress before the arrival of the royals.

We dined with the gentlemen, all but the marquis, who was admitted, in his own house, to dine with the king and queen, as were all the ladies of his family. Lord Weymouth, the eldest son, was our president; and two of his brothers, Lords George and John, with Lord Courtown and the two colonels, made the party. The Weymouths, Thynnes rather, are silent, and we had but little talk or entertainment.

The house is very magnificent, and of in immense magnitude. It seems much out of repair, and by no means cheerful or comfortable. Gloomy grandeur seems the proper epithet for the building and its fitting-up. It had been designed for a monastery, and as such was nearly completed when Henry VIII. dissolved those seminaries. It was finished as a- dwelling-house in the reign of his son, by one of the Thynnes, who was knighted in a field of battle by the protector Somerset.(318)

Many things in the house, and many queer old portraits, afforded me matter of Speculation, and would have filled up more time than I had to bestow. There are portraits of Jane Shore and Fair Rosamond, which have some marks of originality, being miserable daubs, yet from evidently beautiful subjects. Arabella Stuart is also at full length, and King Charleses and Jameses in abundance, with their queens, brethren, and cousins. There are galleries in this house of the dimensions of college halls.

The state rooms on the ground floor are very handsome but the queer antique little old corners, cells, recesses, "passages that lead to nothing," unexpected openings, and abrupt stoppages, with the quaint devices of various old-fashioned ornaments, amused me the most.

Page 332

My bed-room was furnished with crimson velvet, bed included, yet so high, though only the second story, that it made me giddy to look into the park, and tired to wind up the flight of stairs. It was formerly the favourite room, the housekeeper told me, of Bishop Ken, who put on his shroud in it before he died. Had I fancied I had seen his ghost, I might have screamed my voice away, unheard by any assistant to lay it; for so far was I from the rest of the habitable part of the mansion, that not the lungs of Mr. Bruce could have availed me.(319)

The park is noble and spacious. It was filled with country folks, permitted to enter that they might see their sovereigns, and it looked as gay without as it seemed gloomy within. The people were dressed in their best, as if they came to a fair ; and such shouts and hallooings ensued, whenever the king appeared at a window, that the whole building rang again with the vibration. Nothing upon earth can be more gratifying than the sight of this dear and excellent king thus loved and received by all descriptions of his subjects.

TOTTENHAM COURT: RETURN TO WINDSOR.

Sept. 16.-We set out, amidst the acclamations of a multitude, from Longleat for Tottenham park, the seat of Lord Aylesbury. The park is of great extent and moderate beauty. The house is very well.

We had only our own party, the three gentlemen, at dinner and breakfast. These gentlemen only dine with the king when he keeps house, and keeps it incog. himself. At Tottenham park, only my Lord Aylesbury, as master of the house, was admitted. He and his lady were both extremely desirous to make all their guests comfortable ; and Lady Aylesbury very politely offered me the use of her own collection of books. But I found, at the top of the house, a very large old library, in which there were sundry uncommon and curious old English tracts, that afforded me much entertainment. 'Tis a library of long standing.

Here are many original portraits also, that offer enough for speculation. A "Bloody Mary," by Sir Anthony More, which I saw with much curiosity, and liked better than I expected. The beautiful Duchesses of Cleveland and Portsmouth, I fancy by Kneller; but we had no cicerone. A very fine picture of a lady in black, that I can credit to be Vandyke, but who else can I know not. Several portraits by Sir Peter Lely, extremely soft and pleasing, and of subjects uncommonly beautiful; many by Sir Godfrey Kneller, well enough; and many more by Sir Something Thornhill,(320) very thick and heavy.

The good lord of the mansion put up a new bed for the king and queen that cost him nine hundred pounds.

Two things I heard here with concern-that my godmother, Mrs. Greville, was dead; and that poor Sir Joshua Reynolds had lost the sight of one of his eyes.(321)

Sept. 18.-We left Tottenham Court, and returned to Windsor. The royals hastened to the younger princesses, and I to Mrs. Schwellenberg. I was civilly received, however. But deadly dead sunk my heart as I entered her apartment.

The next day I had a visit from my dear brother Charles full of business, letters, etc. I rejoiced to see him, and to confab over all his affairs, plans, and visions, more at full length than for a long time past. I was forced to introduce him to Mrs. Schwellenberg, and he flourished away successfully enough; but it was very vexatious, as he had matters innumerable for discussion.

(305) The palace of Kew.-ED.

(306) See ante, p. 44.-ED.

(307) The Duke of Clarence, third son of George III.; afterwards William IV.-ED.

(308) The Jessamy Bride." See ante, vol. i, p. 111.-ED.

(309) "Observations and Reflections made in the course of a Journey through France, Italy, and Germany," by published in 1789.

(310) "The Midnight Hour," a comedy by Mrs. Inchbald, well known as the authoress of "A Simple Story," and "Nature and Art," was originally produced at Covent Garden, May 22, 1787. "The Commissary," a comedy by Samuel Foote, partly taken from "Le Bourgeois Gentilhomme," was first performed at the Haymarket in June, 1765. Mr. Quick and Mrs. Wells were popular comedians of the time.-ED.

(311) In "The Provoked Husband," by Vanbrugh and Cibber.-ED.

(312) Sir Ashton Lever was noted for his extensive and valuable collection of objects of natural history. In 1775 he opened a museum in Leicester Square, in which his collection was shown to the public; but ten years later he was compelled to dispose of it. The new proprietor exhibited the collection for some years, but it was finally sold and dispersed.-ED.

(312) Maria Anne Smythe was born in 1756, and married, in 1775, Edward Weld of Lulworth Castle. He died within a year, and she married, in 1778, Thomas Fitzherbert of Swinnerton, Staffordshire, who died in 1781. In December, 1785, Mrs. Fitzherbert was privately married to the Prince of Wales. The marriage was never publicly recognised, and its legality was perhaps disputable: for by the Act of 1772 the marriage of any member of the Royal family under the age of twenty-five without the king's consent, was declared invalid, and at the date of his marriage with the beautiful Mrs Fitzherbert, the Prince was but twenty-three years of age. he always treated her as his wife, however, and she was received in society. She continued to live with him even after his marriage with the Princess Caroline, and finally parted from him in 1803, retiring with an allowance of 6,000 pounds a year to Brighton, where she died in 1837.-ED.

(313) A character in Colman's comedy of "The Jealous Wife."-ED.

(314) Sisters–the Italian word.-ED.

(315) Dock is now called Devonport.-ED.

(316) The lady-sculptor, the Hon. Mrs. Damer, daughter of General Conway and kinswoman of Horace Walpole, who bequeathed to her, for the term of her life, his villa at Strawberry Hill. Her performances in sculpture were of no great merit, but

were prodigiously admired by Horace Walpole, who had a notorious weakness for the works of persons of quality. Mrs. Damer was a staunch whig, and canvassed Westminster on behalf of Charles Fox at the election of 1784, in company with the Duchess of Devonshire and Mrs. Crewe.-ED.

(317) His late wife, it will be remembered, was a daughter of Lord Ilchester.-ED.

(318) Longleat, in Wiltshire, was never intended for a monastery, but Was built from a design, it is said, by John of Padua, for Sir John Thynne, who was knighted by Somerset on the field, after the battle of Pinkie. Sir John's descendant, Thomas Thynne, Esq., of Longleat, the wealthy friend of Monmouth, and the "wise Issachar" of Dryden's "Absalom and Achitophel," was murdered in his coach in Pall-Mall (February 12, 1682), by the contrivance of Count Koenigsmark, who was tried for the murder and acquitted, although his confederates, the actual perpetrators of the crime, were hanged for it. Thomas Thynne was succeeded in his estates by his cousin, Sir Thomas Thynne, who was the same year created Baron Thynne and Viscount Weymouth, titles which have descended in the family, and to which that of Marquis of Bath has since been added." (See "Count Koenigsmark and Tom of Ten Thousand," by H. Vizetelly, London, 1890.)-ED.

(319) James Bruce, the famous African traveller, made the acquaintance of the Burney family in 1775. He was about seven feet in height. In her early letters to Mr. Crisp, Fanny calls him the "man-mountain."-ED.

(320) Sir James Thornhill, the father-in-law of Hogarth.-ED.

(321) "One day, in the month of July, 1789, while finishing the portrait of the Marchioness of Hereford, he felt a sudden decay of sight in his left eye. He laid down the pencil, sat a little while in mute consideration, and never lifted it more. His sight gradually darkened, and within ten weeks of the first attack his left eye was wholly blind." (Allan Cunningham.) For some time after this he attended to his duties as President of the Royal Academy, and he delivered his last address to the students in 1790. Sir Joshua died in his sixty-ninth year, February 23, 1792-ED.

SECTION 16.

(1789-90.)

MR. FAIRLY'S'MARRIAGE: THE HASTINGS TRIAL, RUMOURS OF MR. FAIRLY'S IMPENDING MARRIAGE.

Colonel Gwynn told us, at tea-time, of the wonderful recovery of Colonel Goldsworthy, who has had an almost desperate illness; and then added that he had dined the preceding day with him, and met Mr. Fairly, who was coming to Windsor, and all prepared, when he was suddenly stopped, on the very preceding evening, by a fresh attack of the gout.

I heard this with much concern, and made many inquiries, which were presently interrupted by an exclamation of Major Garth, who was now in waiting: "The gout?" he cried: "nay, then, it is time he should get a nurse; and, indeed, I hear he has one in view." Colonel Gwynn instantly turned short, with a very significant smile of triumph, towards me, that seemed to confirm this assertion, while it exulted in his own prediction at Cheltenham.

The following morning, while I was alone with my royal mistress, she mentioned Mr. Fairly for the first time since we left Weymouth. It was to express much displeasure against him: e had misled Lord Aylesbury about the ensuing Drawing-room, by affirming there would be none this month. After saying how wrong this was, and hearing me venture to answer I could not doubt but he must have had some reason, which, if known, might account for his mistake, she suddenly, and with some severity of accent, said, "He will not come

here! For some reason or other he does not choose it! He cannot bear to come!"

How was I amazed! and silenced pretty effectually

She then added, "He has set his head against coming. I know he has been in town some considerable time, but he has desired it may not be told here. I know, too, that when he has been met in the streets, he has called out, 'For heaven's sake, if you are going to Windsor, do not say you have seen me.'"

Nov. 18.-We were to go to town: but while I was taking my hasty breakfast Miss Planta flew into the room, eagerly exclaiming, "Have you heard the news?" I saw, instantly, by her eyes and manner, what she meant and therefore answered, "I believe so."

"Mr. Fairly is going to be married! I resolved I would tell you."

I heard the rumour," I replied, "the other day, from Colonel Gwynn."

"O, it's true!" she cried; "he has written to ask leave; but for heaven's sake don't say so!"

I gave her my ready promise, for I believed not a syllable of the matter; but I would not tell her that.

A ROYAL VISIT TO THE THEATRE: JAMMED IN THE CROWD.

We went to town not only for the Drawing-room on the next day, but also for the play on this Wednesday night,(322) and the party appointed to sit in the queen's private box, as, on these occasions, the balcony-box opposite to the royals is called, dined with Mrs. Schwellenberg,–namely, Mrs. Stainforth, Miss Planta, Mr. de Luc, and Mr. Thomas Willis,

When we arrived at the playhouse(323) we found the lobby and all the avenues so crowded, that it was with the utmost difficulty we forced our way up the stairs. It was the first appearance of the good king at the theatre since his illness.

When we got up stairs, we were stopped effectually: there was not room for a fly ; and though our box was not only taken and kept, but partitioned off, to get to it was wholly impracticable.

Mr. Willis and Miss Planta protested they would go down

Page 336 again, and remonstrate with Mr. Harris, the manager; and I must own the scene that followed was not unentertaining. Mrs. Stainforth and myself were fast fixed in an angle at the corner of the stairs, and Mr. de Luc stood in the midst of the crowd, where he began offering so many grave arguments, with such deliberation and precision, every now and then going back in his reasoning to correct his own English, representing our right to proceed, and the wrong of not making way for us, that it was irresistibly comic to see the people stare, as they pushed On, and to see his unconscious content in their passing him, so long as he completed his expostulations on their indecorum.

Meanwhile, poor Mrs. Stainforth lost her cloak, and in her loud lamentations, and calls upon all present to witness her distress (to which, for enhancing its importance, she continually added, "Whoever has found it should bring it to the Queen's house"), she occupied the attention of all upon the stairs as completely as it was occupied by Mr. de Luc for all in 'the passages : but, alas! neither the philosophic harangue of the one, nor the royal dignity of the other, prevailed; and while there we stood, expecting an avenue to be formed, either for our eloquence or our consequence, not an inch of ground did we gain, and those who had neither made their way, and got on in multitudes.

Offended, at length, as well as tired, Mrs. Stainforth proposed our going down, and waiting in the lobby, till Mr. Harris arrived. Here we were joined by a gentleman, whose manner of fixing me showed a half-recollection of my face, which I precisely returned him, without being able to recollect where I had seen him before. He spoke to Mrs. Stainforth, who answered as if she knew him, and then he came to me and offered to assist in getting me to my box. I told him the manager had already been sent to. He did not, however, go off, but entered into conversation upon the crowd, play, etc., with the ease of an old acquaintance. I took the first opportunity to inquire of Mrs. Stainforth who he was, and heard–Lord Mountmorres, whom you may remember I met with at the theatre at Cheltenham.

What, however, was ridiculous though was, that, after a considerable length of time, he asked me who Mrs. Stainforth was, and I afterwards heard he had made the same inquiry of herself about me! The difference of a dressed and undressed head had occasioned, I suppose, the doubt. The moment,

however, he had completely satisfied himself in this, he fairly joined me, as if he had naturally belonged to our party. And it turned out very acceptable, for we were involved in all such sort of difficulties as our philosopher was the least adapted to remove.

We now went about, in and out, up and down, but without any power to make way, the crowd every instant thickening. We then were fain to return to our quiet post, behind the side-boxes in the lobby, where we remained till the arrival of the king, and then were somewhat recompensed for missing the sight of his entrance, by hearing the sound of his reception: for so violent an huzzaing commenced, such thundering clapping, knocking with sticks, and shouting, and so universal a chorus of "God save the king," that not all the inconveniences of my situation could keep my heart from beating with joy, nor my eyes from running over with gratitude for its occasion.

Lord Mountmorres, who joined in the stick part of the general plaudit, exclaimed frequently, "What popularity is this! how fine to a man's feelings! yet he Must find it embarrassing." Indeed I should suppose he could with difficulty bear it, 'Twas almost adoration! How much I lament that I lost the sight of his benign countenance, during such glorious moments as the most favoured monarchs can scarce enjoy twice in the longest life!

Miss Planta and Mr. Willis now returned: they had had no success; Mr. Harris said they might as well stem the tide of the ocean as oppose or rule such a crowd. The play now began ; and Lord Mountmorres went away to reconnoitre, but, presently returning, said, "If you will trust yourselves with me I will show you your chance."

And then he conducted me to the foot of the stairs leading to our box, which exhibited such a mass of living creatures, that the insects of an ant-hill could scarce be more compact.

We were passed by Lord Stopford, Captain Douglas, and some other of our acquaintance, who told us of similar distresses; and in this manner passed the first act! The boxkeeper came and told Lord Mountmorres he could now give his lordship one seat: but the humours of the lobby he now preferred, and refused the place: though I repeatedly begged that we might not detain him. But he was determined to see us safe landed before he left us.

Page 338 Mr. Harris now came again, and proposed taking us another way, to try to get up some back-stairs. We then went behind the scenes for this purpose : but here Mr. Harris was called away, and we were left upon the stage. Lord Mountmorres led me to various peep-holes, where I could at least have the satisfaction of seeing the king and royal family, as well as the people, and the whole was a sight most grateful to my eyes.

So civil, however, and so attentive he was, that a new perplexity now occurred to me : he had given up his place, and had taken so much trouble, that I thought, if we at last got to our box, he would certainly expect to be accommodated. in it. And to take any one, without previous permission, into the queen's private box, and immediately facing their majesties, was a liberty I knew not how to risk ; and, in truth, I knew not enough of his present politics to be at all sure if they might not be even peculiarly obnoxious. This consideration, therefore, began now so much to reconcile me to this emigrant evening, that I ceased even to wish for recovering our box.

IN THE MANAGER's Box.

When Mr. Harris came back, he said he had nothing to propose but his own box, which was readily accepted. To this our access was easy, as it was over the king and queen, and consequently not desirable to those who came to see them. I too now preferred it, as it was out of their sight, and enabled me to tell Lord Mountmorres, who led me to it through the crowd with unceasing trouble and attention, that till he could get better accommodated a place was at his service.

He closed instantly with the offer, placing himself behind me ; but said he saw some of his relations in the opposite stage-box, Lady Mornington and her beautiful daughter Lady Ann Wellesley, and, as soon as the act was over, he would go down and persuade them to make room for him.

I was shocked, however, after all this, to hear him own himself glad to sit down, as he was still rather lame, from a dreadful overturn in a carriage, in which his leg had been nearly crushed by being caught within the coach-door, which beat down upon it, and almost demolished it.

This anecdote, however, led to another more pleasant; for it brought on a conversation which showed me his present principles, at least, were all on the government side. The accident had happened during a Journey to Chester, in his way to Ireland, whither he was hastening upon the Regency business, last winter: and he went to the Irish House of Peers the first time he quitted his room, after a confinement of three weeks from this terrible bruise.

"But how," cried I, "could you stand?"

"I did not stand," he answered; "they indulged me with leave to speak sitting."

"What a useful opening, then, my lord," cried I, "did you lose for every new paragraph!" I meant, the cant of "Now I am upon my legs." He understood it instantly, and laughed heartily, protesting it was no small detriment to his oratory.

The play was the "Dramatist,"(324) written with that species of humour in caricature that resembles O'Keefe's performances; full of absurdities, yet laughable in the extreme. We heard very ill, and, missing the beginning, we understood still worse: so that, in fact, I was indebted to my new associate for all the entertainment I received the whole evening.

When the act was over, the place on which he had cast his eye, near Lady Mornington, was seized; he laughed, put down his hat, and composed himself quietly for remaining where he was. He must be a man of a singular character, though of what sort I know not: but in his conversation he showed much information, and a spirited desire of interchanging ideas with those who came in his way.

We talked a great deal of France, and he related to me a variety of anecdotes just fresh imported thence. He was there at the first assembling of the Notables, and he saw, he said impending great events from that assemblage. The two most remarkable things that had struck him, he told me, in this wonderful revolution, were–first, that the French guards should ever give up their king; and secondly, that the chief spirit and capacity hither-to shown amongst individuals had come from the ecclesiastics.

He is very much of the opinion the spirit of the times will come round to this island. In what, I asked, could be its pretence?– The game-laws, he answered, and the tithes. He told me, also, a great deal of Ireland, and enlarged my political knowledge abundantly,–but I shall not be so generous, my dear friends, as to let you into all these state matters.

But I must tell you a good sort of quirk of Mr. Wilkes, who, when the power of the mob and their cruelty were first reciting,

quarrelled with a gentleman for saying the French government was become a democracy and asserted it was rather a mobocracy. The pit, he said, reminded him of a sight he once saw in Westminster Hall,–a floor of faces.

He was a candidate for Westminster at that time, with Charles Fox!–thus do we veer about.

At the end of the farce, "God save the king" was most vociferously called for from all parts of the theatre, and all the singers of the theatre came on the stage to sing it, joined by the whole audience, who kept it up till the sovereign of his people's hearts left the house. It was noble and heart-melting at once to hear and see such loyal rapture, and to feel and know it so deserved.

MR. FAIRLY'S MARRIAGE IMMINENT.

NOV. 20.-Some business sent me to speak with Miss Planta before our journey back to Windsor. When it was executed and I was coming away, she called out, "O! propos–it's all declared, and the princesses wished Miss Fuzilier joy yesterday in the Drawing-room. She looked remarkably well ; but said Mr. Fairly had still a little gout, and could not appear."

Now first my belief followed assertion;–but it was only because it was inevitable, since the princesses could not have proceeded so far without certainty. . . . . .

We returned to Windsor as usual, and there I was, just as usual, obliged to finish every evening with picquet !–and to pass all and every afternoon, from dinner to midnight, in picquet company.

Nov. 28.-The queen, after a very long airing, came * in to dress, and summoned me immediately; and in two minutes the princess royal entered, and said something in German, and then added, "And Mr. Fairly, ma'am, begs he may see you a moment, now, if possible."

This is his first coming to the house since her royal highness's birthday, just two months ago.

"I am very sorry," was answered coolly, "but I am going to dress."

"He won't keep you a moment, mamma, only he wants to get on to St. Leonards to dinner,"

Miss Fuzilier is now there."

"Well, then," she answered, "I'll slip on my powdering-gown, and see him."

I found, however, they had already met, probably in the passage, for the queen added, "How melancholy he looks, does not he, princess royal?"

"Yes, indeed, mamma!"–They then again talked ' German.

The princess then went to call him ; and I hastened into the next room, with some caps just then inspecting.

Mr. Turbulent again dined with us, and said, "I find Mr. Fairly is here to-day? when is he to be married?"

Mrs. Schwellenberg reproved him for talking of "soch things:" she holds it petty treason to speak of it, as they are both in office about the Court; though she confessed it would be in a fortnight.

At tea, when the gentlemen–General Budé, Majors Price and Garth, and Mr. Willis–appeared, she said, "Where be Mr. Fairly?" They all exclaimed, "Is he here?"

"O, certain, if he ben't gone!"

I then said he had gone on to St. Leonards.

They all expressed the utmost surprise that he should come, and go, and see none of them.

When they retired, Mrs. Schwellenberg exclaimed, "For what not stay one night? For what not go to the gentlemen? It looks like when he been ashamed.–O fie! I don't not like soch ting. And for what always say contrarie?–always say to everybody he won't not have her!–There might be something wrong in all that–it looks not well."

I saw a strong desire to have me enter into the merits of the case; but I constantly answer to these exclamations, that these sort of situations are regarded in the world as licensing denials first, and truancy from all others afterwards.

COURT DUTIES DISCUSSED.

December.-Let me now, to enliven you a little, introduce to you a new acquaintance, self-made, that I meet at the chapel, and who always sits next me when there is room,– Mrs. J–, wife to the Bishop of K–: and before the service begins, she enters into small talk, with a pretty tolerable degree of frankness, not much repressed by scruples of delicacy.

Take a specimen. She opened, the other morning, upon my situation and occupation, and made the most plump inquiries into its particulars, with a sort of hearty good humour

that removed all impertinence, whatever it left of inelegance and then began her comments.

"Well; the queen, to be sure, is a great deal better dressed than she used to be; but for all that, I really think it is but an odd thing for you!–Dear! I think it's something so out of the way for you!–I can't think how you set about it. It must have been very droll to you at first. A great deal of honour, to be sure, to serve a queen, and all that: but I dare say a lady's-maid could do it better,–though to be called about a queen, as I say, is a great deal of honour: but, for my part, I should not like it; because to be always obliged to go to a person, whether one was in the humour or not, and to get up in a morning, if one was never so sleepy!–dear! it must be a mighty hurry-skurry life! you don't look at all fit for it, to judge by appearances, for all its great honour, and all that."

Is not this a fit bishop's wife? is not here primitive candour and veracity? I laughed most heartily,–and we have now commenced acquaintance for these occasional meetings.

If this honest dame does not think me fit for this part of my business, there is another person, Mlle. Montmoulin, who, with equal simplicity, expresses her idea of my unfitness for another part.– How you bear it," she cries, "living with Mrs. Schwellenberg!–I like it better living in prison!–'pon m'honneur, I prefer it bread and water; I think her so cross never was. If I you, I won't bear it–poor Miss Burney!–I so sorry!–'pon m'honneur, I think to you oftens!–you so confined, you won't have no pleasures!–"

Miss Gomme, less plaintive, but more solemn, declared the other day, "I am sure you must go to heaven for living this life!"—So, at least, you see, though in a court, I am not an object of envy.

MR. FAIRLY'S STRANGE WEDDING.

January, 1790.-Mr. Fairly was married the 6th–I must wish happiness to smile on that day, and all its anniversaries, it gave a happiness to me unequalled, for it was the birthday of my Susanna!

One evening, about this time, Mr. Fisher, now Doctor, drank tea with us at Windsor, and gave me an account of Mr. Fairly's marriage that much amazed me. He had been called upon to perform the ceremony. It was by special licence, and at the house of Sir R- G-.(325) @

So religious, so strict in all ceremonies, even, of religion, as he always appeared, his marrying out of a church was to me very unexpected. Dr. Fisher was himself surprised, when called upon, and said he supposed it must be to please the lady.

Nothing, he owned, could be less formal or solemn than the whole. Lady C., Mrs. and Miss S., and her father and brother and sister, were present. They all dined together at the usual hour,'and then the ladies, as usual, retired. Some time after, the clerk was sent for, and then, with the gentlemen, joined the ladies, who were in the drawing-room, seated on sofas, just as at any other time, Dr. Fisher says he is not sure they were working, but the air of common employment was such, that he rather thinks it, and everything of that sort was spread about as on any common day—workboxes, netting-cases, etc. Mr. Fairly then asked Dr. Fisher what they were to do? He answered, he could not tell; for he had never married anybody in a room before.

Upon this, they agreed to move a table to the upper end of the room, the ladies still sitting quietly, and then Put on it candles and a prayer-book. Dr. Fisher says he hopes it was not a card-table, and rather believes it was only a Pembroke work-table. The lady and Sir R. then came forward, and Dr. Fisher read the service.

So this, methinks, seems the way to make all things easy!

Yet—with so little solemnity-without even a room prepared and empty—to go through a business of such portentous seriousness!— 'Tis truly amazing from a man who seemed to delight so much in religious regulations and observances. Dr. Fisher himself was dissatisfied, and wondered at his compliance, though he attributed the plan to the lady.

The bride behaved extremely well, he said, and was all smile and complacency. He had never seen her to such advantage, or in such soft looks, before; and perfectly serene, though her sister was so much moved as to go into hysterics.

Afterwards, at seven o'clock, the bride and bride-groom set off for a friend's house in Hertfordshire by themselves, attended by servants with white favours. The rest of the party, father, sister, and priest included, went to the play, which happened to be Benedict.

A VISIT FROM THE BRIDE.

I shall say nothing of the queen's birthday, but that I had a most beautiful trimming worked me for it by Miss Cambridge, who half fatigued herself to death, for the kind pleasure that I should have my decorations from her hands. If in some points my lot has been unenviable, what a constant solace, what sweet and soft amends, do I find and feel in the almost unexampled union of kindness and excellence in my chosen friends!

The day after the birthday produced a curious scene. To soften off, by the air, a violent headache, I determined upon walking to Chelsea to see my dear father. I knew I should thus avoid numerous visitors of the household, who might pay their devoirs to Mrs. Schwellenberg.

I missed my errand, and speedily returned, and found many cards from bed-chamber women and maids of honour; and, while still reading them, I was honoured with a call from the Bishop of Salisbury; and in two minutes my dear father came himself.

A pleasant conversation was commencing, when Columb opened the door, and said, "Colonel Fairly begs leave to ask you how you do." He had been married but a week before he came into the midst of all the Court bustle, which he had regularly attended ever since!

It was a good while before the door opened again - and I heard a buzz of voices in the passage: but when it was thrown open, there appeared—the bride herself—and alone! She looked quite brilliant in smiles and spirits. I never saw a countenance so enlivened. I really believe she has long cherished a passionate regard for Mr. Fairly, and brightens now from its prosperity.

I received her with all' the attention in my power, immediately wishing her joy: she accepted it with a thousand dimples, and I seated her on the sofa, and myself by her side. Nobody followed; and I left the bishop to my father, while we entered into conversation, upon the birthday, her new situation in being exempt from its fatigues, and other matters of the time being.

I apologised to Mrs. Fairly for my inability to return the honour of her visit, but readily undertook to inform her majesty of her inquiries, which she earnestly begged from me,

RENEWAL OF THE HASTINGS TRIAL: A POETICAL IMPROMPTU.

Feb. 16-Mr. Hastings's trial re-commenced; and her majesty graciously presented me with tickets for Mr. Francis, Charlotte, and myself. She acknowledged a very great curiosity to know whether my old friends amongst the managers would renew their intercourse with a Court friend, or include me in the distaste conceived against herself, and drop their visits. I had not once been to the trial the preceding year, nor seen any of the set since the king's illness.

We were there hours before they entered, all spent in a harmony of converse and communication I never for three hours following can have elsewhere: no summons impending–no fear of accidental delay drawing off attention to official solicitude.

At the stated time they entered in the usual form, Mr. Burke first. I felt so grieved a resentment of his late conduct,(326) that I was glad to turn away from his countenance. I looked elsewhere during the whole procession, and their subsequent arrangement, that I might leave totally to themselves and their consciences whether to notice a friend from Court or not. Their consciences said not. No one came; I only heard through Charlotte that Mr. Windham was of the set.

Mr. Anstruther spoke, and all others took gentle naps! I don't believe he found it out. When all was concluded, I saw one of them ascending towards our seats : and presently heard the voice of Mr. Burke.

I wished myself many miles off! 'tis so painful to see with utter disapprobation those faces we have met, with joy and pleasure! He came to speak to some relations of Mr. Anstruther. I was next them, and, when recovered from my first repugnance, I thought it better to turn round, not to seem leading the way myself to any breach. I met his eyes immediately, and curtsied. He only said, "O! is it you?" then asked how I did, said something in praise of Mr. Anstruther, partly to his friends and partly to me–heard from me no reply–and hurried away, coldly, and with a look dissatisfied and uncordial. I was much concerned; and we came away soon after.

Here is an impromptu, said to have been written by Mr.

Hastings during Mr. Grey's speech, which was a panegyric on Mr,

Philip Francis:–

"It hurts me not, that Grey,, as Burke's assessor,

Proclaims me Tyrant, Robber, and Oppressor,

Tho' for abuse alone meant:

For when he call'd himself the bosom friend,

The Friend of Philip Francis,–I con'end

He made me full atonement."

I was called upon, on my return, to relate the day's business. Heavy and lame was the relation - but their majesties were curious, and nothing better suited truth.

AN ILLBRED EARL OF CHESTERFIELD.

Our tea-party was suddenly enlarged by the entrance of the Lords Chesterfield, Bulkley, and Fortescue. Lord Chesterfield brought in the two latter without any ceremony, and never introduced nor named them, but chatted off with them apart, as if they were in a room to themselves: and Colonel Wellbred, to whom all gentlemen here belong, was out of the room]if search of a curious snuff-box that he had promised to show to us. Major Price, who by great chance was seated next me, jumped up as if so many wild beasts had entered, and escaped to the other side of the room, and Mr. Willis was only a sharp looker-on.

This was awkward enough for a thing so immaterial, as I could not even ask them to have any tea, from uncertainty how to address them; and I believe they were entirely ignorant whither Lord Chesterfield was bringing them, as they came In only to wait for a royal summons.

How would that quintessence of high ton, the late Lord Chesterfield, blush to behold his successor! who, with much share of humour, and of good humour also, has as little good breeding as any mail I ever met with.

Take an instance.-Lord Bulkley, who is a handsome man, is immensely tall; the major, who is middle-sized, was standing by his chair, in close conference with him–"Why, Bulkley," cried Lord Chesterfield, "you are just the height sitting that Price is standing."

Disconcerted a little, they slightly laughed; but Lord Bulkley rose, and they walked off to a greater distance. Lord Chesterfield, looking after them, exclaimed, "What a Page 347 walking steeple he is!–why, Bulkley, you ought to cut off your legs to be on a level with society!"

When they were all summoned away, except Mr. Willis, who has never that honour but in private, he lifted up his hands and eyes, and called out, "I shall pity those men when the book comes out!–I would not be in their skins!"

I understood him perfectly,–and answered, truly, that I was never affronted more than a minute with those by whom I could never longer be pleased.

Miss BURNEY IN A NEW CAPACITY.

March 2.- In one of our Windsor excursions at this time, while I was in her majesty's dressing-room, with only Mr. de Luc present, she suddenly said, "Prepare yourself, Miss Burney, with all your spirits, for to-night you must be reader."

She then added that she recollected what she had been told by my honoured Mrs. Delany, of my reading- Shakspeare to her, and was desirous that I should read a play to herself and the princesses; and she had lately heard, from Mrs. Schwellenberg, "nobody could do it better, when I would."

I assured her majesty it was rather when I could, as any reading Mrs. Schwellenberg had heard must wholly have been better or worse according to my spirits, as she had justly seemed to suggest.

The moment coffee was over the Princess Elizabeth came for me. I found her majesty knotting, the princess royal drawing, Princess Augusta spinning, and Lady Courtown I believe in the same employment, but I saw none of them perfectly well.

"Come, Miss Burney," cried the queen, " how are your spirits?–
How is your voice?" '

"She says, ma'am," cried the kind Princess Elizabeth, "she shall do her best!"

This had been said in attending her royal highness back. I could only confirm it, and that cheerfully-to hide fearfully.

I had not the advantage of choosing my play, nor do I know what would have been my decision had it fallen to my lot. Her majesty, had just begun Colman's works, and "Polly Honeycomb" was to open my campaign.

"I think," cried the queen most graciously, "Miss Burney will read the better for drawing a chair and sitting down,".

Page 348 " yes, mamma! I dare say so!" cried Princess Augusta and Princess Elizabeth, both in a moment.

The queen then told me to draw my chair close to her side. I made no scruples. Heaven knows I needed not the addition of standing! but most glad I felt in being placed thus near, as it saved a constant painful effort of loud reading.

"Lady Courtown," cried the queen, "you had better draw nearer, for Miss Burney has the misfortune of reading rather low at first."

Nothing could be more amiable than this opening. Accordingly, I did, as I had promised, my best; and, indifferent as that was, it would rather have surprised you, all things considered, that it was not yet worse. But I exerted all the courage I possess, and, having often read to the queen, I felt how much it behoved me not to let her surmise I had any greater awe to surmount.

It is but a vulgar performance; and I was obliged to omit, as well as I could at sight, several circumstances very unpleasant for reading, and ill enough fitted for such hearers. it went off pretty flat. Nobody is to comment, nobody is to interrupt; and even between one act and another not a moment's pause is expected to be made.

I had been already informed of this etiquette by Mr. Turbulent and Miss Planta; nevertheless, it is not only oppressive to the reader, but loses to the hearers so much spirit and satisfaction, that I determined to endeavour, should I again be called upon, to introduce a little break into this tiresome and unnatural profundity of respectful solemnity. My own embarrassment, however, made it agree with me for the present uncommonly well.

Lady Courtown never uttered one single word the whole time; yet is she one of the most loquacious of our establishment. But such is the settled etiquette.

The queen has a taste for conversation, and the princesses a good-humoured love for it, that doubles the regret of such an annihilation of all nature and all pleasantry. But what will not prejudice and education inculcate? They have been brought up to annex silence to respect and decorum: to talk, therefore, unbid, or to differ from any given opinion even when called upon, are regarded as high improprieties, if not presumptions.

They none of them do justice to their own minds, while they enforce this subjection upon the minds of others. I had not

experienced it before ; for when reading alone with the queen, or listening to her reading to me, I have always frankly spoken almost whatever has occurred to me. But there I had no other examples before me, and therefore I might inoffensively be guided by myself; and her majesty's continuance of the same honour has shown no disapprobation of my proceeding. But here it was not easy to make any decision for myself: to have done what Lady Courtown forbore doing would have been undoubtedly a liberty.

So we all behaved alike - and easily can I now conceive the disappointment and mortification of poor Mr. Garrick when he read "Lethe" to a royal audience. Its tameness must have tamed even him, and I doubt not he never acquitted himself so ill.

THE LONG-FORGOTTEN TRAGEDY: MISS BURNEY AGAIN AS READER.

On Easter Sunday, the 4th of April, when I left my beloved Susan at St. James's, I left with her all spirit for any voluntary employment, and it occurred to me I could best while away the leisure allowed me by returning to my long-forgotten tragedy. This I have done, in those moments as yet given to my journal, and it is well I had so sad a resource, since any merrier I must have aimed at in vain.

It was a year and four months since I had looked at or thought of it. I found nothing but unconnected speeches, and hints, and ideas, though enough in quantity, perhaps, for a whole play. I have now begun planning and methodising, and have written three or four regular scenes. I mention all these particulars of my progress, in answer to certain queries in the comments of my Susan and Fredy, both of old date.

Well (for that is my hack, as "however" is my dear Susanna's), we set off rather late for Windsor,-Mr. de Luc, Miss Planta, and myself; Mrs. Schwellenberg stayed in town. . . .

I invited my old beau, as her majesty calls Mr. Bryant, to dinner, and he made me my best day out of the ten days of our Windsor sojourn. He has insisted upon lending me some more books, all concerning the most distant parts of the earth, or on subjects the most abstruse. His singular simplicity in constantly conceiving that, because to him such books alone are new, they must have the same recommendation to me, is

extremely amusing; and though I do all that is possible to clear up the distinction, he never remembers it.

The king, for which I was very sorry, did not come Into the room. He made it but one visit, indeed, during this week. He then conversed almost wholly with General Grenville upon the affairs of France; and in a manner so unaffected, open and manly, so highly superior to all despotic principles, even while most condemning the unlicensed fury of the Parisian mob, that I wished all the nations of the world to have heard him, that they might have known the real existence of a patriot king.

Another reading took place, and much more comfortably; it was to the queen and princesses, without any lady-in-waiting. The queen, as before, condescended to order me to sit close to her side; and as I had no model before me, I scrupled much less to follow the bent of my own ideas by small occasional comments. And these were of use both to body and mind; they rested the lungs from one invariable exertion, as much as they saved the mind from one strain of attention.

Our play was "The Man of Business," a very good comedy, but too local for long life. And another of Colman's which I read afterwards has the same defect. Half the follies and peculiarities it satirises are wholly at an end and forgotten. Humour springing from mere dress, or habits, or phraseology, is quickly obsolete; when it sinks deeper, and dives into character, it may live for ever.

I dedicated my Wednesday evening to a very comfortable visit to our dear James, whose very good and deserving wife, and fine little fat children, with our Esther and her fair Marianne and Fanny, all cordially conspired to make me happy. We read a good deal of Captain Bligh's interesting narrative,(327)

Page 351

every word Of which James has taken as much to heart as if it were his own production.

I go on, occasionally, with my tragedy. It does not much enliven, but it soothes me.

COLONEL MANNERS IN HIS SENATORIAL CAPACITY.

April 23.–I shall add nothing at present to my Journal but the summary of a conversation I have had with Colonel Manners, who, at our last excursion, was here without any other gentleman.

Knowing he likes to be considered as a senator, I thought the best subject for our discussion would be the House of Commons; I therefore made sundry political inquiries, so foreign to My Usual mode, that you would not a little have smiled to have heard them. I had been informed he had once made an attempt to speak, during the Regency business, last winter ; I begged to know how the matter stood, and he made a most frank display of its whole circumstances. "Why, they were speaking away," he cried, "upon the Regency, and so,—and they were saying if the king could not reign, and recover; and Burke was making some of his eloquence, and talking; and, says he, 'hurled from his throne,'—and so I put out my finger in this manner, as if I was in a great passion, for I felt myself very red, and I was in a monstrous passion I suppose, but I was only going to say 'Hear! Hear!' but I happened to lean one hand down upon my knee, in this way, just as Mr. Pitt does when he wants to speak.- and I stooped forward, just as if I was going to rise up and begin but just then I caught Mr. Pitt's eye, looking at me so pitifully; he thought I was going to speak, and he was frightened to death, for he thought–for the thing was, he got up himself, and he said over all I wanted to say; and the thing is, he almost always does; for just as I have something particular to say, Mr. Pitt begins, and goes through it all, so that he don't leave anything more to be said about it; and so, I suppose, as he looked at me so pitifully, he thought I should say it first, or else that I

should get into some scrape, because I was so warm and looking so red."

Any comment would disgrace this; I will therefore only tell you his opinion, in his own words, of one of our late taxes.

"There's only one tax, ma'am, that ever I voted for against my conscience, for I've always been very particular about that; but that is the bacheldor's tax, and that I hold to be very unconstitutional, and I am very sorry I voted for it, because it's very unfair; for how can a man help being a bacheldor, if nobody will have him? and besides, it's not any fault to be taxed for, because We did not make ourselves bacheldors, for we were made so by God, for nobody was born married, and so I think it's a very unconstitutional tax."

A CONVERSATION WITH MR. WINDHAM AT THE HASTINGS TRIAL.

April 27.-I had the happiness of my dearest Fredy's society in Westminster Hall–if happiness and that place may be named together.

The day was mixed: Evidence and Mr. Anstruther weighing it down, and Mr. Burke speaking from time to time, and lighting it up. O, were his purpose worthy his talents, what an effect would his oratory produce! I always hear him with so much concern, I can scarce rejoice even in being kept awake by him.

The day was nearly passed, and I was eating a biscuit to prevent an absolute doze while Mr. Anstruther was talking, when, raising myself from a listening bend, I turned to the left, and perceived Mr. Windham, who had quietly placed himself by my side without speaking.

My surprise was so great, and so totally had I given up all idea of renewing our conferences, that I could scarce refrain expressing it. Probably it was visible enough, for he said, as if apologising for coming up, that so to do was the only regale their toils allowed them. He then regretted that it was a stupid day, and, with all his old civility about me and my time, declared he was always sorry to see me there when nothing worth attention was going forward.

This soon brought us round to our former intimacy of converse ; and, the moment I was able, I ventured at my usual inquiry about his own speaking, and if it would soon take place.

Page 353 "No," he answered, with a look of great pleasure, "I shall now not speak at all.–I have cleared myself from that task, and never with such satisfaction did I get rid of any!"

Amazed, yet internally glad, I hazarded some further inquiry into the reason of this change of plan.

They were drawing, he said, to a conclusion, and the particular charge which he had engaged himself to open was relinquished.(328) "I have therefore," he cried, "washed my hands of making a speech, yet satisfied my conscience, my honour, my promises, and my intentions; for I have declined undertaking anything new, and no claim therefore remains upon me."

"Well," quoth I, "I am at a loss whether to be glad or sorry."

He comprehended instantly,–glad for Mr. Hastings, or sorry for not hearing him. He laughed, but said something a little reproachful, upon my continued interest for that gentleman. I would not pretend it was diminished; I determined he should find me as frank as heretofore, and abscond, or abide, as his nerves stood the firmness.

"You are never, then" (I said afterwards), "to speak here?"

"Once," he answered, "I said a few words–"

"O when?" I cried; "I am very sorry I did not know it, and hear you,–as you did speak!"

"O," cried he, laughing, "I do not fear this flattery now, as I shall speak no more."

"But what," cried I, "was the occasion that drew you forth?"

"Nothing very material but I saw Burke run hard, and I wished to help him."

"That was just," cried I, "what I should have expected from you– and just what I have not been able not to honour, on some other occasions, even where I have most blamed the matter that has drawn forth the assistance."

This was going pretty far:–he could not but instantly feel I meant the Regency discussions. He neither made me any answer, nor turned his head, even obliquely, my way.

I was not sorry, however. 'Tis always best to be sincere. Finding him quite silent, to soften matters as well as I could with honesty, I began an éloge of Mr. Burke, both warm and true, as far as regards his wonderful abilities. But he soon
distinguished the rigorous precision with which, Involuntarily, I praised the powers without adverting to their Use.

Suddenly then, and with a look of extreme keenness, he turned his eyes upon me, and exclaimed, "Yes,–and he has very highly, also the faculty of being right!" I would the friendship that dictated this assertion were as unwarped as it is animated.

I could not help saying rather faintly, "Has he?"

Not faintly he answered, "He has!–but not the world alone, even his friends, are apt to misjudge him. What he enters upon, however with earnestness, YOU will commonly find turn out as he represents it."

His genius, his mental faculties, and the natural goodness of his heart, I then praised as warmly as Mr. Windham could have praised them himself; but the subject ran me aground a second time, as, quite undesignedly, I concluded my panegyric with declaring that I found it impossible not to admire,–nay, love him, through all his wrong. Ending another total silence and averted head, I started something more general upon the trial.

His openness then returned, with all its customary vivacity, and he expressed himself extremely irritated upon various matters which had been carried against the managers by the judges.

"But, Mr. Windham!" exclaimed I, "the judges!–is it possible you can enter into such a notion as to suppose Mr. Hastings capable of bribing them?"

"O, for capable," cried he, "I don't know–"

"Well, leave that word out, and suppose him even willing–can you imagine all the judges and all the lords–for they must concur– disposed to be bribed?"

"No; but I see them all determined to acquit Mr. Hastings."

"Determined?–nay, that indeed is doing him very little honour."

"O, for honour!–if he is acquitted–" He stopped,–as if that were sufficient.

I ventured to ask why the judges and the lords-should make such a determination.

"From the general knavery and villainy of mankind." was his hard answer, "which always wishes to abet successful guilt."

"Well!" cried I, shaking my head, "you have not,
relinquished your speech from having nothing to say. But I am glad you have relinquished it, for I have always been most afraid of you ; and the reason is, those who know how to hold back will not for nothing come forward. There is one down there, who, if he knew how ever to hold back, would be great indeed!"

He could not deny this, but would not affirm it. Poor Mr. Burke!–so near to being wholly right, while yet wholly wrong!

When Mr. Burke mounted the rostrum, Mr. Windham stopped short, saying, "I won't interrupt you-" and, in a moment, glided back to the managers' box; where he stood behind Mr. Burke, evidently at hand to assist in any difficulty. His affection for him seems to amount to fondness. This is not for me to wonder at. Who was so captivated as myself by that extraordinary man, till he would no longer suffer me to reverence the talents I must still ever admire?

A GLIMPSE OF MRS. PIOZZI.

Sunday, May 2.-This morning, in my way to church, just as I arrived at the iron gate of our courtyard, a well-known voice called out, "Ah, there's Miss Burney!"

I started, and looked round–and saw–Mrs. Piozzi! I hastened up to her; she met my held-out hand with both hers: Mr. Piozzi an Cecilia(329) were with her–all smiling and good-humoured.

"You are going," she cried, "to church?–so, am I. I must run first to the inn: I suppose one–may sit–anywhere one pleases?"

"Yes," I cried, "but you must be quick, or you will sit nowhere, there will be such a throng." This was all;–she hurried on,–so did I.

I received exceeding great satisfaction in this little and unexpected meeting. She had been upon the Terrace, and was going to change her hat, and haste on both sides prevented awkwardness on either.

Yet I saw she had taken in good part my concluding hand- presentation at my dear Mr. Locke's:(330) she met me no more

356 with that fiert'e of defiance: it was not-nor can it ever be with her old cordiality, but it was with some degree of pleasure, and that species of readiness which evinces a consciousness of meeting with a good reception.

CAPTAIN BURNEY WANTS A SHIP AND TO GO TO COURT.

May 6.-This being the last Pantheon, I put in my long intended claim; and it was greatly facilitated by the circumstance of a new singer, Madame Benda, making her first appearance. My dearest father fetched me from the Queen's house. Esther and Marianne kept me places between them. Marianne never looked so pretty; I saw not a face there I thought equally lovely. And, oh, how Pacchierotti sung!–How -with what exquisite feeling, what penetrating pathos! I could almost have cried the whole time, that this one short song was all I should be able to hear !

At the beginning of the second act I was obliged to decamp.

James, who had just found me out, was my esquire. "Well," he cried, in our way to the chair, "will there be war with Spain?"

I assured him I thought not.

"So I am afraid!" answered the true English tar. " "However, if there is, I should be glad of a frigate of thirty-two guns. Now, if you ask for it, don't say a frigate, and get me one of twenty-eight!"

Good heaven!–poor innocent James!–

And just as I reached the chair–"But how shall you feel," he cried, "when I ask you to desire a guard-ship for me, in about two years' time?"

I could make no precise answer to that! He then added that he intended coming to Court! Very much frightened, I besought him first to come and drink tea with me–which he promised.

In my way home, as I went ruminating upon this apparently but just, though really impracticable demand, I weighed well certain thoughts long revolving, and of late nearly bursting forth and the result was this–to try all, while yet there is time. Reproach else may aver, when too late, greater courage Would have had greater success. This idea settled my resolutions, and they all bent to one point, risking all risks.

Page 357 May 10.-This evening, by appointment came our good James and his wife, and soon afterwards, to my great pleasure, Captain Phillips joined us. I take it, therefore, for granted, he will have told all that passed in the business way. I was very anxious to gather more intelligibly the wishes and requests of poor James, and to put a stop to his coming to Court without taking such previous steps as are customary. I prevailed, and promised, in return, to make known his pretensions.

You may believe, my dear friends, this promise was the result of the same wish of experiment, and sense of claim upon me of my family to make it while I may, that I have mentioned. I did– this very evening. I did it gaily, and in relating such anecdotes as were amusingly characteristic of a sailor's honest but singular notions of things: yet I have done it completely; his wishes and his claims are now laid open–Heaven knows to what effect! The Court scheme I have also told; and my royal mistress very graciously informed me, that if presented by some superior officer there could be no objection; but otherwise, unless he had some promotion, it was not quite usual.

CAPTAIN BURNEY AND MR. WINDHAM.

May 11.-This morning my royal mistress had previously arranged for me that I should go to the trial, and had given me a ticket for my little Sarah(331) to accompany me; and late last night, I believe after twelve o'clock, she most graciously gave me another for James. just at this time she could not more have gratified me than by a condescension to my dear brother. Poor Columb was sent with the intelligence, and directions for our meeting at seven o'clock this morning, to Norton-street.

Sarah came early; but James was so late we were obliged to leave word for him to follow us. He did,–two hours afterwards! by way of being our esquire; and then told me he knew it would be in good time, and so he had stopped to breakfast at Sir Joseph Banks's. I suppose the truth is, it saved him a fresh puff of powder for some other day.

We talked over all affairs, naval and national, very comfortably. The trial is my only place for long dialogues! I gave him a new and earnest charge that he would not speak home concerning the prosecution to Mr. Winndham, should he join

358

us. He made me a less reluctant promise than heretofore, for when last with Charlotte at Aylsham he had frequently visited Mr. Windham, and had several battles at draughts or backgammon with him; and there is no Such good security against giving offence as seeing ourselves that our opponents are worth pleasing. Here, too, as I told James, however we might think all the managers in the wrong, they were at least open enemies, and acting a public part, and therefore they must fight it Out, as he would do with the Spaniards, if, after all negotiation, they came to battle.

He allowed this; and promised to leave him to the attacks of the little privateer, without falling foul of him with a broadside.

Soon after the trial began Mr. Windham came up to us, and after a few minutes' chat with me addressed himself to James about the approaching war. "Are you preparing," he cried, "for a campaign?"

"Not such one," cried James, "as we had last summer at Aylsham!"

"But what officers you are!" he cried, "you men of Captain Cook; you rise upon us in every trial! This Captain Bligh,–what feats, what wonders he has performed! What difficulties got through! What dangers defied! And with such cool, manly skill!"

They talked the narrative over as far as Mr. Windham had in Manuscript seen its sketch; but as I had not read it, I could not enter into its detail.

MR. WINDHAM SPEAKS ON A LEGAL POINT.

Mr. Windham took his seat by my elbow, and renewed one of his old style of conversations about the trial ; each of us firmly maintaining our original ground. I believe he has now relinquished his expectation of making me a convert. He surprised me soon by saying, "I begin to fear, after all, that what you have been talking about to me will come to pass."

I found he meant his own speaking upon a new charge, which, when I last saw him, he exultingly told me was given up. He explained the apparent inconsistency by telling me that some new change of plan had taken place, and that Mr. Burke was extremely urgent with him to open the next charge: "And I cannot," he cried emphatically, "leave Burke in the lurch!" I both believed and applauded him so far; but why

)Page 59 are either of them engaged in a prosecution so uncoloured by necessity?

One chance he had still of escaping this tremendous task, he told me, which was that it might devolve upon Grey but Burke, he did not disavow, wished it to be himself. "However," he laughingly added, "I think we may toss up In that case, how I wish he may lose! not only from believing him the abler enemy, but to reserve his name from amongst the active list in such a cause.

He bewailed,—with an arch look that showed his consciousness I should like the lamentation,–that he was now all unprepared,– all fresh to begin in documents and materials, the charge being wholly new and unexpected, and that which he had considered relinquished.

"I am glad, however," cried I, "your original charge is given up; for I well remember what you said of it."

"I might be flattered," cried he, "and enough, that you should remember anything I say–did I not know it was only for the sake of its subject,"–looking down upon Mr. Hastings.

I could not possibly deny this but added that I recollected he had acknowledged his charge was to prove Mr. Hastings mean, pitiful, little, and fraudulent."

The trial this day consisted almost wholly in dispute upon evidence - the managers offered such as the counsel held improper, and the judges and lords at last adjourned to debate the matter in their own chamber. Mr. Burke made a very fine speech upon the rights of the prosecutor to bring forward his accusation, for the benefit of justice, in such mode as appeared most consonant to his own reason and the nature of things, according to their varying appearances as fresh and fresh matter Occurred.

The counsel justly alleged the hardship to the client, if thus liable to new allegations and suggestions, for which he came unprepared, from a reliance that those publicly given were all against which he need arm himself, and that, if those were disproved, he was cleared; while the desultory and shifting charges of the managers put him out in every method of defence, by making it impossible to him to discern where he might be attacked.

In the course of this debate I observed Mr. Windham so agitated and so deeply attentive, that it prepared me for what soon followed : he mounted the rostrum-for the third time only since this trial commenced.

His speech was only to a point Of law respecting evidence he kept close to his subject, with a clearness and perspicuity very uncommon indeed amongst these orators. His voice, however, is greatly in his disfavour ; for he forces it so violently, either from earnestness or a fear of not being heard, that, though it answered the purpose of giving the most perfect distinctness to what he uttered, its sound had an unpleasing and crude quality that amazed and disappointed me. The command of his language and fluency of his delivery, joined to the compact style of his reasoning and conciseness of his arguments, were all that could answer my expectations: but his manner–whether from energy or secret terror–lost all its grace, and by no means seemed to belong to the elegant and high-bred character that had just quitted me.

In brief,–how it may happen I know not,–but he certainly does not do justice to his own powers and talents in public. He was excessively agitated: when he had done and dismounted, I saw his pale face of the most fiery red. Yet he had uttered nothing in a passion. It must have been simply from internal effort.

The counsel answered him, and he mounted to reply. Here, indeed, he did himself honour; his readiness of answer, the vivacity of his objections, and the instantaneous command of all his reasoning faculties, were truly striking. Had what he said not fallen in reply to a speech but that moment made, I must have concluded it the result Of Study, and all harangue learnt by heart. He was heard with the most marked attention.

The second speech, like the first, was wholly upon the laws of evidence, and Mr. Hastings was not named in either. He is certainly practising against his great day. And, in truth, I hold still to my fear of it; for, however little his manner in public speaking may keep pace with its promise in private conversation, his matter was tremendously pointed and severe.

The trial of the day concluded by an adjournment to consult upon the evidence in debate, with the judges, in the House of Lords.

Mr. Windham came up to the seats of the Commons in my neighbourhood, but not to me; he spoke to the Misses Francis,–daughters of Mr. Hastings's worst foe,–and hurried down.

On my return I was called upon to give an account of the

Page 361 trial to their majesties and the princesses, and a formidable business, I assure you, to perform.

AN EMPHATIC PERORATION.

May 18.-This morning I again went to the trial of poor Mr. Hastings. Heavens! who can see him sit there unmoved? not even those who think him guilty,–if they are human.

I took with me Mrs. Bogle. She had long since begged a ticket for her husband, which I could never before Procure. We now went all three. And, indeed, her original speeches and remarks made a great part of my entertainment.

Mr. Hastings and his counsel were this day most victorious. I never saw the prosecutors so dismayed. Yet both Mr. Burke and Mr. Fox spoke, and before the conclusion so did Mr. Windham. They were all in evident embarrassment. Mr. Hastings's counsel finished the day, with a most noble appeal to justice and innocence, protesting that, if his client did not fairly claim the one, by proving the other, he wished himself that the prosecutors–that the lords–that the nation at large–that the hand of God–might fall heavy upon him!

This had a great and sudden effect,– not a word was uttered. The prosecutors looked dismayed and astonished ; and the day closed.

Mr. Windham came up to speak to Misses Francis about a dinner: but he only, bowed to me, and with a look so conscious—so much saying, "'TiS your turn to triumph now!: that I had not the spite to attack him.

But when the counsel had uttered this animated speech, Mrs. Bogle was so much struck, she hastily arose, and, clapping her hands, called out audibly, in a broad Scotch accent, "O, charming!" I could hardly, quiet her till I assured her we should make a paragraph for the newspapers. I had the pleasure to deliver this myself to their majesties, and the princesses–and as I was called upon while it was fresh in my memory, I believe but little of the general energy was forgotten.

It gave me great pleasure to repeat so striking an affirmation of the innocence of so high, so injured I believe, a character. The queen eagerly declared I should go again the next sitting.

Wednesday, May 19.–The real birthday of my royal mistress, to whom may Heaven grant many, many and prosperous! Dressing, and so forth, filled up all the morning

and at night I had a t'ete-'a-t'ete with Charles, till twelve. I got to bed about five in the morning. The sweet princesses had a ball, and I could not lament my fatigue.

AN APTITUDE FOR LOGIC AND FOR GREEK.

May 20.-To-day again to the trial, to which I took MISS Young, her majesty having given me two tickets very late overnight. Miss Young is singularly, as far as I can see, the reverse of her eccentric parents she is moderation personified.

Mr. Windham again spoke in the course of this morning's business, which was chiefly occupied in debating on the admissibility of the evidence brought forward by the prosecutors. The quickness and aptness of his arguments, with the admirable facility and address with which he seized upon those of his opponents, the counsel, were strong marks of that high and penetrating capacity so strikingly his characteristic. The only defect in his speaking is the tone of his voice, which, from exertion, loses all its powers of modulation, and has a crude accent and expression very disagreeable.

During the examination of Mr. Anderson, one of Mr. Hastings's best friends,–a sensible, well-bred, and gentlemanlike man,–Mr. Windham came up to my elbow.

"And can this man," cried he, presently, "this man–so gentle—be guilty?"

I accused him of making a point to destroy all admiration of gentleness in my opinion. "But you are grown very good now!" I added, "No, very bad I mean!" He knew I meant for speaking ; and I then gave him burlesqued, various definitions of good, which had fallen from Mr. Fox in my hearing, the most contradictory, and, taken out of their place, the most ridiculous imaginable.

He laughed very much, but seriously confessed that technical terms and explanations had better have been wholly avoided by them all, as the counsel were sure to out-technicalise them, and they were then exposed to greater embarrassments than by steering clear of the attempt, and resting only upon their common forces.

"There is one praise," I cried, "which I am always sure to meet in the newspapers whenever I meet with your name; and I begin to quite tire of seeing it for you,-your skill in logic!"

"O, I thank you," he cried, earnestly "I am indeed quite ashamed of the incessant misappropriation of that word."

"No, no," cried I; "I only tire of it because they seem to think, when once the word logic and your name are combined, they have completely stated all. However, in what little I have heard, I could have suspected you to have been prepared with a speech ready written, had I not myself heard just before all the arguments which it answered."

I then added that I was the less surprise(! at this facility of language, from having heard my brother declare he knew no man who read Greek with that extraordinary rapidity–no, not Dr. Parr, nor any of the professed Grecians, whose peculiar study it had been through life.

This could be nothing, he said, but partiality.

"Not mine, at least," cried I, laughing, "for Greek excellence is rather Out Of my sphere of panegyric!"
"

Well," cried he, laughing too at my disclaiming, "'Tis' your brother's partiality. However, 'tis one I must try not to lose. I must take to my Greek exercises again."

They will do you a world of good, thought I, if they take you but from your prosecution-exercises.

MORE TALK WITH MR. WINDHAM.

We then talked of Mr. Burke. "How finely," I cried, "he has spoken! with what fullness of intelligence, and what fervour!"

He agreed, with delighted concurrence. "Yet,–so much so long!" I added.

"True!" cried he, ingenuously, yet concerned. "What pity he can never stop!"

And then I enumerated some of the diffuse and unnecessary paragraphs which had weakened his cause, as well as his speech.

He was perfectly candid, though always with some reluctance. "But a man who speaks in public," he said, "should never forget what will do for his auditors: for himself alone, it is not enough to think ; but for what is fitted, and likely to be interesting to them."

"He wants nothing," cried I, "but a flapper."

"Yes, and he takes flapping inimitably."

"You, then," I cried, "should be his flapper."

"And sometimes," said he, smiling, "I am."

"O, I often see," said I, "of what use you are to him. I see you watching him,–reminding, checking him in turn,–at least, I fancy all this as I look into the managers' box, which is no small amusement to me,–when there is any commotion there!"

He bowed; but I never diminished from the frank unfriendliness to the cause with which I began. But I assured him I saw but too well how important and useful he was to them, even without speaking.

"Perhaps," cried he, laughing, "more than with speaking."

"I am not meaning to talk Of that now," said I, "but yet, one thing I will tell you: I hear you more distinctly than any one; the rest I as often miss as catch, except when they turn this way,–a favour Which you never did me!"

"No, no, indeed!" cried he; "to abstract myself from all, is all that enables me to get on." And then, with his native candour, he cast aside prejudice, and very liberally praised several points in this poor persecuted great man.

I had seen, I said, an initiation from Horace, which had manifested, I presumed, his scholarship."

"O, ay," cried he, "an Ode to Mr. Shore, who is one of the next witnesses. Burke was going to allude to it, but I begged him not. I do not like to make their lordships smile in this grave business."

"That is so right!: cried I: "Ah, you know it IS you and your attack I have feared most all along!"

"This flattery"–cried he.

"Do not use that word any more, Mr. Windham," interrupted I; "if you do, I shall be tempted to make a very shocking speech to you–the very reverse of flattery, I assure you." He stared,– and I went on. "I shall say,–that those who think themselves flattered–flatter themselves.!"

"What?–hey?–How?" cried he.

"Nay, they cannot conclude themselves flattered, without concluding they have de quoi to make it worth while!"

"Why, there–there may be something In that but not here!–no, here it must flow simply front general benevolence,–from a wish to give comfort or pleasure."

I disclaimed all and turned his attention again to Mr. Hastings. "See!" I cried, "see but how thin–how ill–looks that poor little uncle of yours!"(332) Again I upbraided him with being unnatural; and lamented Mr. Hastings's

change since I had known him in former days. "And shall I tell you," I added, "something in which you had nearly been involved with him?"

"Me?–with Mr. Hastings?"

"Yes ! and I regret it did not happen ! You may recollect my mentioning my original acquaintance with him, before I lived where I now do." '

"Yes, but where you now .I understand you,–expect ere long you may see him!"

He meant from his acquittal, and reception at the Queen's house.
And I would not contradict him.

But, however," I continued, "my acquaintance and regard began very fairly while I lived at home at my father's and indeed I regret you could not then and so have known him, as I am satisfied you would have been pleased with him, which now you cannot judge. He is so gentle-mannered, so intelligent, so unassuming, yet so full-minded."

I have Understood that," he answered; "yet 'tis amazing how little unison there may be between mariners and characters, and how softly gentle a man may appear without, whose nature within is all ferocity and cruelty. This is a part of mankind of which you cannot judge–of which, indeed, you can scarce form an idea."

After a few comments I continued what I had to say, which, in fact, was nothing but another malice of my own against him. I reminded him of one day in a former year of this trial, when I had the happiness of sitting at it with my dearest Mrs. Locke, in which he had been so obliging, with reiterated offers, as to propose seeing for my servant, etc.-" "Well," I continued, "I was afterwards extremely sorry I had not accepted your kindness; for just as we were going away, who should be passing, and turn back to speak to me, but Mr. Hastings!" 'O!' he cried, 'I must come here to see you, I find!' Now, had you but been with me at that moment! I own it would have been the greatest pleasure to me to have brought you together though I am quite at a loss to know whether I ought, in that case, to have presented you to each other."

He laughed most heartily,-half, probably, with joy at his escape; but he had all his wits about him in his answer. "If you," he cried, "had been between US, we might, for once, have coalesced– in both bowing to the same shrine!"

(322) Wednesday, November 18.-ED.

(323) Covent Garden.-ED.

(324) A comedy by Reynolds, originally produced at Covent Garden, May 15, 1789.-ED.

(325) Sir Robert Gunning, the bride's father.-ED.

(326) Fanny refers to Burke's attitude during the Regency debates, in which, as a member of the opposition, he had supported Mr. Fox.-ED,

(327) "A Narrative of the mutiny on board his majesty's ship Bounty; and the subsequent Voyage of part of the Crew, in the ship's boat, from Tofoa, one of the Friendly Islands, to Timor, a Dutch settlement in the East Indies. Written by Lieutenant William Bligh." London, 1790. Lieutenant (afterwards Admiral) Bligh was appointed to the command of the Bounty in August, 1787. He sailed from England in December, and arrived at Otaheite, October 26, 1788, the object of his voyage being to transplant the bread fruit tree from the South Sea Islands to the British colonies in the West Indies, with a view to its acclimatisation there. A delay of more than five months at Otaheite demoralized the crew, to whom the dolce far mente of life in a Pacific island, and the Charms of the Otaheitan women, offered greater attractions than the toils of sea-faring under a somewhat tyrannical captain. The Bounty left Otaheite April 4, 1789, and on the 28th of the same month a mutiny broke out under the leadership of the mater's mate, Fletcher Christian. Captain Bligh and eighteen of his men were set adrift in the ship's boat, in which they sailed for nearly three months, undergoing terrible privations, and reaching the Dutch settlement at Timor, an island off the east coast of Java, June 14. Bligh arrived in England, March 14, 1790. The mutineers finally settled in Pitcairn's island, where their descendants are still living.-ED.

(328) See note ante 263, p. 102.-ED.

(329) Mrs. Piozzi's youngest daughter, who had accompanied her mother and step-father abroad.-ED. 2 It appears from a note in (330) It appears from a note in the "Memoirs of Dr. Burney" (vol. iii. p. 199), that Fanny had once before met Mrs Piozzi since her marriage, at an assembly at Mrs. Locke's. This meeting must have

taken place Soon after the marriage, as Mrs. Piozzi went abroad with her husband shortly afterwards.-ED.

(331) Fanny's half-sister.-ED.

(332) An allusion to the personal resemblance between Windham and Hastings. See ante, p. 149.-ED.

SECTION 17.

(1790-1)

MISS BURNEY RESIGNS HER PLACE AT COURT.

During the interval which elapsed between the consultation with Dr. Burney and the presentation of the memorial, an incident occurred which occasioned to Fanny much distress and not a little annoyance. Her own narrative of the affair we have not thought it necessary to include in our selection from the "Diary," but here a few words on the subject may be not unacceptable. Fanny's man-servant, a Swiss named Jacob Columb, had fallen dangerously ill in the summer of 1790, and was sent, in August, to St. George's Hospital. He was much attached to his mistress, who, he said, had treated him with greater kindness than father, mother, or any of his relatives, and on leaving Windsor he begged her to hold in trust for him the little money in his possession, amounting to ten guineas. She offered him a receipt for the money, but he refused it, and when she insisted, exclaimed, "No, ma'am, I won't take it! You know what it is, and I know what it is; and if I live I'm sure you won't wrong me: and if I don't, nobody else sha'n't have it!" Moved to tears by the poor fellow's earnestness, Fanny complied with his request. In the following month he died at the hospital, desiring, in his last moments, to leave everything to his sisters in Switzerland. "He certainly meant," writes Fanny, "everything of his wearing apparel, watches, etc., for what money he had left in my hands he would never tell anybody." She was preparing, accordingly, to transmit Columb's effects, including, of course, the ten guineas, to Switzerland, when a claimant appeared in the person of Peter Bayond, a countryman of the deceased. This man produced a will, purporting to be Columb's, by which the property was left to be divided between Bayond himself and James Columb, a cousin of the pretended testator, then in service with Horace Walpole. Fanny's instant conviction was that the will was a forgery, and the appearance and behaviour of Bayond confirmed her in this belief. James Columb, moreover, concurred in her opinion, and she had decided to ignore this new claim, when she received an attorney's letter, desiring her to pay to Bayond the sum in her hands of the late Jacob Columb. She then wrote to Walpole, who offered her his assistance, with many expressions of warm regard. But finally, after much trouble, and threats of a lawsuit, she was advised that her best plan would be to let the will take its course, and to pay over to the claimant the sum in question ; and thus the matter was settled, "in a manner," she writes, "the most mortifying to Mr. Walpole and myself."-ED.)

A MELANCHOLY CONFESSION.

May 25.-The Princess Augusta condescended to bring me a most gracious message from the king, desiring to know if I wished to go to Handel's Commemoration, and if I should like the "Messiah," or prefer any other day?

With my humble acknowledgments for his goodness, I fixed instantly on the "Messiah" and the very amiable princess came smiling back to me, bringing me my ticket from the king. This would not, indeed, much have availed me, but that I fortunately knew my dear father meant to go to the Abbey. I despatched Columb to Chelsea, and he promised to call for me the next morning.

My "Visions" I had meant to produce in a few days; and to know their chance before I left town for the summer.(333) But I thought the present opportunity not to be slighted, for some little opening, that might lighten the task of the exordium upon the day of attempt. He was all himself–all his native self- -kind, gay, open, and full fraught with converse.

Chance favoured me: we found so little room, that we were fain to accept two vacant places at once, though they separated us from my uncle, Mr. Burney, and his brother James, who were all there, and all meant to be of the same party.

I might not, at another time, have rejoiced in this disunion, but it was now most opportune: it gave me three hours' conference with my dearest father–the only conference of that length I have had in four years.

Fortune again was kind ; for my father began relating various anecdotes of attacks made upon him for procuring to sundry strangers some acquaintance with his daughter,(334) particularly with the Duchesse de Biron, and the Mesdames de Boufflers(335) to whom he answered, he had no power; but was somewhat

struck by the question of Madame de B. in return, who exclaimed, "Mais, monsieur, est-ce possible! Mademoiselle votre fille n'a-t- elle point de vacance?"(336)

This led to much interesting discussion, and to many confessions and explanations on my part, never made before; which induced him to enter more fully into the whole of the situation, and its circumstances, than he had ever yet had the leisure or the spirits to do; and he repeated sundry speeches of discontent at my seclusion from the world.

All this encouraged me to much detail: I spoke my high and constant veneration for my royal mistress, her merits, her virtues, her condescension, and her even peculiar kindness towards me. But I owned the species of life distasteful to me; I was lost to all private comfort, dead to all domestic endearment; I was worn with want of rest, and fatigued with laborious watchfulness and attendance. My time was devoted to official duties; and all that in life was dearest to me–my friends, my chosen society, my best affections–lived now in my mind only by recollection, and rested upon that with nothing but bitter regret. With relations the most deservedly dear, with friends of almost unequalled goodness, I lived like an orphan-like one who had no natural ties, and must make her way as she could by those that were factitious. Melancholy was the existence where happiness was excluded, though not a complaint could be made! where the illustrious personages who were served possessed almost all human excellence, yet where those who were their servants, though treated with the most benevolent condescension, could never, in any part of the live-long day, command liberty, or social intercourse, or repose.

The silence of my dearest father now silencing myself, I turned to look at him; but how was I struck to see his honoured head bowed down almost into his bosom with dejection and discomfort!– we were both perfectly still a few moments; but when he raised his head I could hardly keep my seat, to see his eyes filled with tears!–"I have long," he cried, "been uneasy, though I have not spoken; but if you wish to resign, my house, my purse, my arms, shall be open to receive you, back;"

The emotion of my whole heart at this speech-this sweet, this generous speech-O my dear friends, I need not say it

We were mutually forced to break up Our conference. I could only instantly accept his paternal offer, and tell him it was my guardian angel, it was Providence in its own benignity, that inspired him with such goodness. I begged him to love the day in which he had given me such comfort, and assured him it would rest upon my heart with grateful pleasure till it ceased to beat.

He promised to drink tea with me before I left town, and settle all our proceedings. I acknowledged my intention to have ventured to solicit this very permission of resigning.- "But I," cried he, smiling with the sweetest kindness, "have spoken first myself."

What a joy to me, what a relief, this very circumstance! it will always lighten any evil that may, unhappily, follow this proposed step.

CAPTAIN BURNEY's LACONIC LETTER AND INTERVIEW.

June.-I went again to the trial of poor Mr. Hastings : Mrs. Ord received from me my companion ticket, kindly giving up the Duke of Newcastle's box to indulge me with her company.

But I must mention an extraordinary circumstance that happened in the last week. I received in a parcel-No, I will recite it you as I told it to Mr. Windham, who, fortunately, saw and came up to me-fortunately, I say, as the business of the day was very unedifying, and as Mrs. Ord much wished to hear some of his conversation.

He inquired kindly about James and his affairs, and if he had yet a ship; and, to let him see a person might reside in a Court, and yet have no undue influence, I related his proceedings with Lord Chatham, and his laconic letter and interview. The first running thus:-

"My Lord,-I should be glad of an audience; if your Lordship will
be so good to appoint a time, I will wait upon you. I am, my
Lord, your humble servant,
"James Burney."

"And pray," quoth I to James, when he told me this, "did you not say the honour of an audience?"

Page 371 "No," answered he, "I was civil enough without that; I said, If you will be so good-that was very civil-and honour is quite left off now."

How comic! to run away proudly from forms and etiquettes, and then pretend it was only to be more in the last mode. Mr. Windham enjoyed this characteristic trait very much; and he likes James so well that he deserved it, as well as the interview which ensued.

"How do you do, Captain Burney?"

"My lord, I should be glad to be employed."

" You must be sensible, Captain Burney, we have many claimants just now, and more than it is possible to satisfy immediately."

"I am very sensible of that, my lord; but, at the same time, I wish to let your lordship know what I should like to have-a frigate of thirty-two guns."

"I am very glad to know what you wish, sir."

He took out his pocket-book, made a memorandum, and wished James a good morning.

Whether or not it occurred to Mr. Windham, while I told this, that there seemed a shorter way to Lord Chatham, and one more in his own style, I know not: he was too delicate to let such a hint escape, and I would not for the world intrust him with my applications and disappointments.

BURKE'S SPEECH ON THE FRENCH REVOLUTION.

But I have found," cried I afterwards, "another newspaper praise for you now, 'Mr. Windham, with his usual vein of irony.'"

"O, yes," cried he, "I saw that! But what can it mean?–I use no 'vein of irony;'–I dislike it, except for peculiar purposes, keenly handled, and soon passed over."

" Yet this is the favourite panegyric you receive continually,– this, or logic, always attends your name in the newspapers."

"But do I use it?"

"Nay, not to me, I own. As a manner, I never found it out, at least. However, I am less averse now than formerly to the other panegyric–close logic,–for I own the more frequently I come hither the more convinced I find myself that that is no character of commendation to be given universally."

He could say nothing to this; and really the dilatory,

desultory style of these prosecutors in general deserved a much deeper censure.

"If a little closeness of logic and reasoning were observed by one I look at now, what a man would he be, and who could compare with him!" Mr. Burke you are sure was here my object; and his entire, though silent and unwilling, assent was obvious.

"What a speech," I continued, "has he lately made!(337) how noble, how energetic, how enlarged throughout!"

"O," cried he, very unaffectedly, "upon the French Revolution?"

"Yes; and any party might have been proud of it, for liberality, for feeling, for all in one–genius. I, who am only a reader of detached speeches, have read none I have thought its equal."

"Yet, such as you have seen it, it does not do him justice. I was not in the House that day ; but I am assured the actual speech, as he spoke it at the moment, was highly superior to what has since been printed. There was in it a force–there were shades of reflection so fine–allusions so quick and so happy– and strokes of satire and observation so pointed and so apt,– that it had ten times more brilliancy when absolutely extempore than when transmitted to paper."

"Wonderful, wonderful! He is a truly wonderful creature!" And, alas, thought I, as wonderful in inconsistency as in greatness!

In the course of a discussion more detailed upon faculties, I ventured to tell him what impression they had made upon James, who was with me during one of the early long speeches. "I was listening," I said, " with the most fer-

vent attention to such strokes of eloquence as, while I heard them, carried all before them, when my brother pulled me by the sleeve to exclaim, 'When will he come to the point?'"

The justness, notwithstanding his characteristic conciseness, of this criticism, I was glad thus to convey. Mr. Windham however, would not subscribe to it; but, with a significant smile, coolly said, "Yes, 'tis curious to hear a man of war's ideas of rhetoric."

"Well," quoth I, to make a little amends, "shall I tell you a compliment he paid you?"

"Me?"

"Yes. 'He speaks to the purpose,' he cried."

AN AWKWARD MEETING.

Some time after, with a sudden recollection, he eagerly exclaimed, "O, I knew I had something I wished to tell you! I was the other day at a place to see Stuart's Athenian architecture, and whom do you think I met in the room?"

I could not guess.

"Nay, 'tis precisely what you will like–Mr. Hastings!"

"Indeed!" cried I, laughing; "I must own I am extremely glad to hear it. I only wish you could both meet without either knowing the other."

"Well, we behaved extremely well, I assure you ; and looked each as if we had never seen one another before. I determined to let you know it." . . .

A NEW VISIT FROM MRS. FAIRLY.

The day after the birthday I had again a visit from Mrs. Fairly. I was in the midst of packing, and breakfasting, and confusion - for we left town immediately, to return no more till next year, except to St. James's for the Drawing-room. However, I made her as welcome as I was able, and she was more soft and ingratiating in her manners than I ever before observed her. I apologised two or three times for not waiting upon her, representing my confined abilities for visiting.

ONE TRAGEDY FINISHED AND ANOTHER COMMENCED.

August.-As I have only my almanac memorandums for this month, I shall hasten immediately to what I think my dear partial lecturers will find most to their taste in the course of it.

Know then, fair ladies, about the middle of this August, 17 90, the author finished the rough first draft and copy of her first tragedy. What species of a composition it may prove she is very unable to tell; she only knows it was an almost spontaneous work, and soothed the melancholy of imagination for a while, though afterwards it impressed it with a secret sensation of horror, so like real woe, that she believes it contributed to the injury her sleep received about this period.

Nevertheless, whether well or ill, she is pleased to have done something at last, she had so long lived in all ways as nothing.

You will smile, however, at my next trust; but scarce was this completed,-as to design and scenery I mean, for the whole is in its first rough state, and legible only to herself,- scarce, however, had this done with imagination, to be consigned over to correction, when imagination seized upon another subject for another tragedy.

The first therefore I have deposited in my strong-box, in all its imperfections, to attend to the other; I well know correction may always be summoned, Imagination never will come but by choice. I received her, therefore, a welcome guest,–the best adapted for softening weary solitude, where only coveted to avoid irksome exertion.

MISS BURNEY's RESIGNATION MEMORIAL.

October.-I now drew up my memorial, or rather, showed it to my dearest father. He so much approved it, that he told me he would not have a comma of it altered. I will copy it for you. It is as respectful and as grateful as I had words at command to make it, and expressive of strong devotion and attachment; but it fairly and firmly states that my strength is inadequate to the duties of my charge, and, therefore, that I humbly crave permission to resign it and retire into domestic life. It was written in my father's name and my own. I had now that dear father's desire to present it upon the first auspicious moment: and O! with what a mixture of impatience and dread unspeakable did I look forward to such an opportunity!

The war was still undecided : still I inclined to wait its issue, as I perpetually brought in my wishes for poor James, though without avail. Major Garth, our last equerry, was raised to a high post in the West Indies, and the rank of colonel, I recommended James to his notice and regard if

Page 375 they met; and a promise most readily and pleasantly made to seek him out and present him to his brother, the general, if they ever served in the same district, was all, I think, that my Court residence obtained for my marine department of interest!

Meanwhile, one morning at Kew, Miss Cambridge was so much alarmed at my declining state of health that she would take no denial to my seeing and consulting Mr. Dundas. He ordered me the bark, and it strengthened me so much for awhile, that I was too much recruited for presenting my sick memorial, which I therefore cast aside.

Mrs. Ord spent near a week at Windsor in the beginning of this month. I was ill, however, the whole time, and suffered so much from my official duties, that my good Mrs. Ord, day after day, evidently lost something more and more of her partiality to my station, from witnessing fatigues of which she had formed no idea, and difficulties and disagreeabilities in carrying on a week's intercourse, even with so respectable a friend, which I believe she had thought impossible.

Two or three times she burst forth into ejaculations strongly expressive of fears for my health and sorrow at its exhausting calls. I could not but be relieved in my own mind that this much-valued, most maternal friend should thus receive a conviction beyond all powers of representation, that my place was of a sort to require a strength foreign to my make.

She left me in great and visible uneasiness, and wrote to me continually for bills of health, I never yet so much loved her, for, kind as I have always found her, I never yet saw in her so much true tenderness.

MR. WINDHAM INTERVENES.

In this month, also, I first heard of the zealous exertions and chivalrous intentions of Mr. Windham. Charles told me they never met without his demounting the whole thunders of his oratory against the confinement by which he thought my health injured; with his opinion that it must be counteracted speedily by elopement, no other way seeming effectual.

But with Charlotte he came more home to the point. Their vicinity in Norfolk occasions their meeting, though very seldom at the house of Mr. Francis, who resents his prosecution of Mr. Hastings, and never returns his visits; but at assemblies at Aylsham and at Lord Buckingham's dinners they are certain of now and then encountering.

This summer, when Mr. Windham went to Felbrig, his Norfolk seat, they soon met at an assembly, and he immediately opened upon his disapprobation of her sister's monastic life, adding, "I do not venture to speak thus freely upon this subject to everybody, but to you I think I may; at least, I hope it."

Poor dear Charlotte was too full-hearted for disguise, and they presently entered into a confidential cabal, that made her quite disturbed and provoked when hurried away. From this time, whenever they met, they were pretty much of a mind. "I cannot see you," he always cried, "without recurring to that painful subject—your sister's situation." He then broke forth in an animated offer of his own services to induce Dr. Burney to finish such a captivity, if he could flatter himself he might have any influence.

Charlotte eagerly promised him the greatest, and he gave her his promise to go to work.

O What a noble Quixote! How much I feel obliged to him! How happy, when I may thank him!

He then pondered upon ways and means. He had already sounded my father: "but it is resolution," he added, "not inclination, Dr. Burney wants." After some further reflection, he then fixed upon a plan : "I will set the Literary Club(338) upon him!" he cried: "Miss Burney has some very true admirers there, and I am sure they will all eagerly assist. We will present him a petition—an address."

Much more passed: Mr. Windham expressed a degree of interest and kindness so cordial, that Charlotte says she quite longed to shake hands with him; and if any success ever accrues, she certainly must do it.

Frightened, however, after she returned home, she feared our dearest father might unfairly be overpowered, and frankly wrote him a recital of the whole, counselling him to see Mr. Windham in private before a meeting at the club should take place.

AN AMUSING INTERVIEW WITH MR. BOSWELL.

And now for a scene a little surprising.

The beautiful chapel of St. George, repaired and finished by the best artists at an immense expense, which was now opened after a very long shutting up for its preparations, brought in-numerable strangers to Windsor, and, among others, Mr. Boswell.

This I heard, in my way to the chapel, from Mr. Turbulent, who overtook me, and mentioned having met Mr. Boswell at the Bishop of Carlisle's the evening, before. He proposed bringing him to call upon me; but this I declined, certain how little satisfaction would be given here by the entrance of a man so famous for compiling anecdotes. But yet I really wished to see him again, for old acquaintance sake, and unavoidable amusement from his oddity and good humour, as well as respect for the object of his constant admiration, my revered Dr. Johnson. I therefore told Mr. Turbulent I should be extremely glad to speak with him after the service was over.

Accordingly, at the gate of the choir, Mr. Turbulent brought him to me. We saluted With mutual glee: his comic-serious face and manner have lost nothing of their wonted singularity nor yet have his mind and language, as you will soon confess.

"I am extremely glad to see you indeed," he cried, "but very sorry to see you here. My dear ma'am, why do you stay ?–it won't do, ma'am! You must resign!–we can put up with it no longer. I told my good host the bishop so last night; we are all grown quite outrageous!"

Whether I laughed the most, or stared the most, I am at a loss to say, but i hurried away from the cathedral, not to have such treasonable declarations overheard, for We Were surrounded by a multitude.

He accompanied me, however, not losing one moment in continuing his exhortations: "If you do not quit, ma'am, very soon, some violent measures, I assure you, will be taken. We shall address Dr. Burney in a body; I am ready to make the harangue myself. We shall fall upon him all at once."

I stopped him to inquire about Sir Joshua; he said he saw him very often, and that his spirits were very good. I asked about Mr. Burke's book.(339) "O," cried he "it Will come Out next week: 'tis the first book in the World, except my own, and that's coming out also very soon; only I want your help."

"My help?"

"Yes, madam,–you must give me some of your choice little notes of the doctor's; we have seen him long enough upon

Page 378

stilts; I want to show him in a new light. Grave Sam, and great Sam, and solemn Sam, and learned Sam,–all these he has appeared over and over. Now I want to entwine a wreath of the graces across his brow; I want to show him as gay Sam, agreeable Sam, pleasant Sam; so you must help me with some of his beautiful billets to yourself."

I evaded this by declaring I had not any stores at hand. He proposed a thousand curious expedients to get at them, but I was invincible.

Then I was hurrying on, lest I should be too late. He followed eagerly, and again exclaimed, "But, ma'am, as I tell you, this won't do; you must resign off hand! Why, I would farm you out myself for double, treble the money! I wish I had the regulation of such a farm,–yet I am no farmer-general. But I should like to farm you, and so I will tell Dr. Burney. I mean to address him; I have a speech ready for the first opportunity."

He then told me his " Life of Dr. Johnson " was nearly printed, and took a proof-sheet out of his pocket to show me; with crowds passing and repassing, knowing me well, and staring well at him: for we were now at the iron rails of the Queen's lodge.

I stopped; I could not ask him in : I saw he expected it, and was reduced to apologise, and tell him I must attend the queen immediately.

He uttered again stronger and stronger exhortations for my retreat, accompanied by expressions which I was obliged to check in their bud. But finding he had no chance for entering, he stopped me again at the gate, and said he would read me a part of his work.

There was no refusing this: and he began with a letter of Dr. Johnson's to himself. He read it in strong imitation of the doctor's manner, very well, and not caricature. But Mrs. Schwellenberg was at her window, a crowd was gathering to stand round the rails, and the king and queen and royal family now approached from the Terrace.

I made a rather quick apology, and, with a step as quick as my now weakened limbs have left in my power, I hurried to my apartment.

You may suppose I had inquiries enough, from all around, of "Who was the gentleman I was talking to at the rails? And an injunction rather frank not to admit him beyond those limits.

However, I saw him again the next morning, in coming

from early prayers, and he again renewed his remonstrances, and his petition for my letters of Dr. Johnson. I cannot consent to print private letters, even of a man so justly celebrated, when addressed to myself: no, I shall hold sacred those revered and but too scarce testimonies of the high honour his kindness conferred upon me. One letter I have from him that is a masterpiece of elegance and kindness united. 'Twas his last,

ILL, UNSETTLED, AND UNHAPPY.

November.-This month will be very brief of annals; I was so ill, so unsettled, so unhappy during every day, that I kept not a memorandum. All the short benefit I had received from the bark was now at an end : languor, feverish nights, and restless days were incessant. My memorial was always in my mind ; my courage never rose to bringing it from my letter-case. Yet the war was over, the hope of a ship for my brother demolished, and my health required a change of life equally with my spirits and my happiness.

The queen was all graciousness; and her favour and confidence and smiles redoubled my difficulties. I saw she had no suspicion but that I was hers for life ; and, unimportant as I felt myself to her, in any comparison with those for whom I quitted her, I yet knew not how to give her the unpleasant surprise of a resignation for which I saw her wholly unprepared. .

It is true, my depression of spirits and extreme alteration of person might have operated as a preface; for I saw no one, except my royal mistress and Mrs. Schwellen-berg, who noticed not the change, or who failed to pity and question me upon my health and my fatigues; but as they alone saw it not, or mentioned it not, that afforded me no resource. And thus, with daily intention to present my petition and conclude this struggle, night always returned with the effort unmade, and the watchful morning arose fresh to new purposes that seemed only formed for demolition. And the month expired as it began, with a desire the most strenuous of liberty and peace, combated by reluctance unconquerable to give pain, displeasure, or distress to my very gracious royal mistress.

December.-My loss of health was now so notorious, that no part of the house could wholly avoid acknowledging it; yet was the terrible picquet the catastrophe of every evening,

though frequent pains in my side forced me, three or four times in a game, to creep to my own room for hartshorn and for rest. And so weak and faint I was become, that I was compelled to put my head out into the air, at all hours, and in all weathers, from time to time, to recover the power of breathing, which seemed not seldom almost withdrawn.

Her majesty was very kind during this time, and the princesses interested themselves about me with a sweetness very grateful to me; indeed, the whole household showed compassion and regard, and a general opinion that I was falling into a decline ran through the establishment. . . . Thus there seemed about my little person a universal commotion ; and it spread much farther, amongst those I have never or slightly mentioned. There seemed, indeed, but one opinion, that resignation of place or of life was the only remaining alternative.

There seemed now no time to be lost - when I saw my dear father he recommended to me to be speedy,, and my mother was very kind in urgency for immediate measures. I could not, however, summon courage to present my memorial; my heart always failed me, from seeing the queen's entire freedom from such an expectation: for though I was frequently so ill in her presence that I could hardly stand, I saw she concluded me, while life remained, inevitably hers.

A MEDICAL OPINION ON MISS BURNEY'S CONDITION.

Finding my inability unconquerable, I at length determined upon consulting Mr. Francis. I wrote to Charlotte a faithful and Minute account of myself', with all my attacks–cough, pain In the side, weakness, sleeplessness, etc.,–at full length, and begged Mr. Francis's opinion how I must proceed. Very kindly he wrote directly to my father, exhorting instantaneous resignation, as all that stood before me to avert some dangerous malady.

The dear Charlotte at the same time wrote to me conjuring my prompt retreat with the most affecting earnestness.

The uneasiness that preyed upon my spirits in a task so difficult to perform for myself, joined to my daily declension in health, was now so apparent, that, though I could go no farther, I paved the way for an opening, by owning to the queen that Mr. Francis had been consulted upon my health.

The queen now frequently inquired concerning his answer;

but as I knew he had written to my father, I deferred giving the result till I had had a final conference with that dear parent. I told her majesty my father Would show me the letter when I saw him. This I saw raised for the first time a surmise that something was in agitation, though I am certain the suspicion did not exceed an expectation that leave would be requested for a short absence to recruit.

My dearest father, all kindness and goodness, yet all alarm, thought time could never be more favourable; and when next I saw him at Chelsea, I wrote a second memorial to enclose the original one. With a beating heart, and every pulse throbbing, I returned thus armed to the Queen's house.

Mrs. Schwellenberg sent for me to her room. I could hardly articulate a word to her. My agitation was so great that I was compelled to acknowledge something very awful was impending in my affairs, and to beg she would make no present inquiries. I had not meant to employ her in the business, nor to name it to her, but I was too much disturbed for concealment or evasion. She seemed really sorry, and behaved with a humanity I had not had much reason to expect.

I spent a terrible time till I went to the queen at night, spiriting myself up for my task, and yet finding apprehension gain ground every moment. Mrs. Schwellenberg had already been some time with her majesty when I was summoned. I am sure she had already mentioned the little she had gathered. I could hardly perform my customary offices from excess of trepidation. The queen looked at me with the most inquisitive solicitude. When left with her a moment I tried vainly to make an opening: I could not. She was too much impressed herself by my manner to wait long. She soon inquired what answer had arrived from Mr. Francis?

That he could not, I said, prescribe at a distance.

I hoped this would be understood, and said no more. The queen looked much perplexed, but made no answer.

MISS BURNEY BREAKS THE MATTER TO THE QUEEN.

The next morning I was half dead with real illness, excessive nervousness, and the struggle of what I had to force myself to perform. The queen again was struck with my appearance, which I believe indeed to have been shocking. When I was alone with her, she began upon Mr. Francis with more inquiry. I then tried to articulate that I had something of

deep consequence to myself to lay before her majesty; but that I was so unequal in my weakened state to speak it, that I had ventured to commit it to Writing, and entreated Permission to produce it.

She could hardly hear me, yet understood enough to give immediate consent.

I then begged to know if I might present it -myself, or whether I should give it to Mrs. Schwellenberg.

"O, to me! to me!" she cried, with kind eagerness. She added, however, not then; as she was going to breakfast.

This done was already some relief, terrible as was all that remained; but I now knew I must go on, and that all my fears and horrors were powerless to stop me.

This was a Drawing-room day. I saw the king at St. James's, and he made the most gracious inquiries about my health: so did each of the princesses. I found they were now all aware of its failure. The queen proposed to me to see Dr. Gisburne: the king seconded the proposition. There was no refusing; yet, just now, it was distressing to comply.

The next morning, Friday, when again I was alone with the queen, she named the subject, and told me she would rather I should give the paper to the Schwellenberg, who had been lamenting to her my want of confidence in her, and saying I confided and told everything to the queen. "I answered," continued her majesty, "that you were always very good; but that, with regard to confiding, you seemed so happy with all your family, and to live so well together, that there was nothing to say."

I now perceived Mrs. Schwellenberg suspected some dissension at home was the cause of my depression. I was sorry not to deliver my memorial to the Principal person, and yet glad to have it to do where I felt so much less compunction in giving pain.

THE MEMORIAL AND EXPLANATORY NOTE.

I now desired an audience of Mrs. Schwellenberg. With what trembling agitation did I deliver her my paper, requesting her to have the goodness to lay it at the feet of the queen before her majesty left town ! We were then to set out for Windsor before twelve o'clock. Mrs. Schwellenberg herself remained in town.

Here let me copy the memorial.

Most humbly presented to Her Majesty.

"Madam, "With the deepest sense of your Majesty's goodness and condescension, amounting even to sweetness–to kindness who can wonder I should never have been able to say what I know not how to write–that I find my strength and health unequal to my duty?

"Satisfied that I have regularly been spared and favoured by your Majesty's humane consideration to the utmost, I could never bring myself to the painful confession of my secret disquietude ; but I have long felt creeping upon me a languor, a feebleness, that makes, at times, the most common attendance a degree of capital pain to me, and an exertion that I could scarce have made, but for the revived alacrity with which your Majesty's constant graciousness has inspired me, and would still, I believe, inspire me, even to my latest hour, while in your Majesty's immediate presence. I kept this to myself while I thought it might wear away,-or, at least, I only communicated it to obtain some medical advice: but the weakness, though it comes only in fits, has of late so much Increased, that I have hardly known how, many days, to keep myself about–or to rise up in the morning, or to stay up at night.

"At length, however, as my constitution itself seems slowly, yet surely, giving way, my father became alarmed.

"I must not enter, here, upon his mortification and disappointment: the health and preservation of his daughter could alone be more precious to him than your Majesty's protection.

"With my own feelings upon the subject it would ill become me to detain your Majesty, and the less, as I am fully sensible my place, in point of its real business, may easily he far better supplied;–In point of sincere devotion to your majesty, I do not so readily yield. I can only, therefore, most humbly entreat that your Majesty will deign to accept from my father and myself the most dutiful acknowledgments for the uniform benignity so graciously shown to me during the whole of my attendance. My father had originally been apprehensive of my inability, with regard to strength, for sustaining any but the indulgence of a domestic life : but your Majesty's justice and liberality will make every allowance for the flattered feelings of a parent's heart, which could not endure, untried, to relinquish for his daughter so high an honour as a personal office about your Majesty.

I dare not, Madam, presume to hope that Your Majesty's condescension will reach to the smallest degree of concern at parting with me; but permit me, Madam, humbly, earnestly, and fervently, to solicit that I may not be deprived of the mental benevolence of your Majesty, which so thankfully I have experienced, and so gratefully must for ever remember.

That every blessing, every good, may light upon your Majesties here, and await a future and happier period hereafter, will be always amongst the first prayers of,

"Madam, your Majesty's ever devoted, ever grateful, most attached, and most dutiful subject and servant, "Frances Burney."

With this, though written so long ago, I only wrote an explanatory note to accompany it, which I will also copy:–

"Madam, "May I yet humbly presume to entreat your Majesty's patience for a few added lines, to say that the address which I now most respectfully lay at your Majesty's feet was drawn up two months ago, when first I felt so extreme a weakness as to render the smallest exertion a fatigue? While I waited, however, for firmness to present it, I took the bark, and found myself, for some time, so much amended, that I put it aside, and my father, perceiving me better, lost his anxious uneasiness for my trying a new mode of life. But the good effect has, of late, so wholly failed, that an entire change of air and manner of living are strongly recommended as the best chance for restoring my shattered health. We hold it, therefore, a point of that grateful duty we owe to your Majesty's goodness and graciousness, to make this melancholy statement at once, rather than to stay till absolute incapacity might disable me from offering one small but sincere tribute of profound respect to your Majesty,–the only one in my power–that of continuing the high honour of attending your Majesty, till your Majesty's own choice, time, and convenience nominate a successor."

THE KEEPER OF THE ROBES' CONSTERNATION.

Mrs. Schwellenberg took the memorial, and promised me her services, but desired to know its contents. I begged vainly to be excused speaking them. She persisted, and I then was compelled to own they contained my resignation.

How aghast she looked!–how inflamed with wrath!–how

Petrified with astonishment! It was truly a dreadful moment to me. She expostulated on such a step, as if it led to destruction : she offered to save me from it, as if the peace of my life depended on averting it and she menaced me with its bad consequences, as it life itself, removed from these walls, would become an evil.

I plainly recapitulated the suffering state in which I had lived for the last three months; the difficulty with which I had waded through even the most common fatigues of the day; the constraint of attendance, however honourable, to an invalid; and the impracticability of pursuing such a life, when thus enfeebled, with the smallest chance of ever recovering the health and strength which it had demolished.

To all this she began a vehement eulogium on the superior happiness and blessing of my lot, while under such a protection ; and angrily exhorted me not to forfeit what I could never regain.

I then frankly begged her to forbear SO painful a discussion, and told her that the memorial was from my father as well as myself–that I had no right or authority to hesitate in delivering it–that the queen herself was prepared to expect it -and that I had promised my father not to go again to Windsor till it was presented. I entreated her, therefore, to have the goodness to show it at once.

This was unanswerable, and she left me with the paper in her hand, slowly conveying it to its place of destination.

just as she was gone, I was called to Dr. Gisburne or, rather, without being called, I found him in my room, as I returned to it.

Think If my mind, now, wanted not medicine the most I told him, however, my corporeal complaints and he ordered me opium and three glasses of wine in the day, and recommended rest to me, and an application to retire to my friends for some weeks, as freedom from anxiety was as necessary to my restoration as freedom from attendance.

LEAVE OF ABSENCE IS SUGGESTED.

During this consultation I was called to Mrs. Schwellenberg. Do you think I breathed as I went along?–No! She received me, nevertheless, with complacency and smiles;

she began a laboured panegyric of her own friendly zeal and goodness, and then said she had a proposal to make to me, which she con-

sidered as the most fortunate turn my affairs could take, and a,, a proof that I should find her the best friend I had in the world. She then premised that she had shown the paper,–that the queen had read it, and said it was very modest, and nothing improper.

Her proposal was, that I should have leave of absence for six weeks, to go about and change the air, to Chelsea, and Norbury Park, and Capitan Phillips, and Mr. Francis, and Mr. Cambrick, which would get me quite well; and, during that time, she would engage Mlle. Montmoulin to perform my office.

I was much disturbed at this; and though rejoiced and relieved to understand that the queen had read my memorial without displeasure, I was grieved to see it was not regarded as final. I only replied I would communicate her plan to my father. Soon after this we set out for Windsor.

Here the first presenting myself before the queen was a task the heaviest, if possible, of any. Yet I was ill enough, heaven knows, to carry the apology of my retreat in my countenance. However, it was a terrible effort. I could hardly enter her room. She spoke at once, and with infinite softness, asking me how I did after my journey ? "Not well, indeed," I simply answered. "But better?" she cried; "are you not a little better?"

I only shook my head; I believe the rest of my frame shook without my aid.

"What! not a little?–not a little bit better?" she cried, in the most soothing voice.

"To-day, ma'am," I said, "I did indeed not expect to be better." I then muttered something indistinctly enough, of the pain I had suffered in what I had done: she opened, however, upon another subject immediately, and no more was said upon this. But she was kind, and sweet, and gentle, and all consideration with respect to my attendance.

I wrote the proposal to my poor father, I received by return of post, the most truly tender letter he ever wrote me. He returns thanks for the clemency With which my melancholy memorial has been received, and is truly sensible of the high honour shown me In the new proposition; but he sees my health so impaired, my strength so decayed, my whole frame so nearly demolished, that he apprehends anything short of a permanent resignation, that would ensure lasting rest and recruit, might prove fatal. He quotes a letter from Mr. Francis,

containing his opinion that I must even be speedy in my retiring or risk the utmost danger - and he finishes a letter filled with gratitude towards the queen and affection to his daughter, with his decisive opinion that I cannot go on, and his prayers and blessings on my retreat.

The term "speedy," in Mr. Francis's opinion, deterred me from producing this letter, as it seemed indelicate and unfair to hurry the queen, after offering her the fullest time. I therefore waited till Mrs. Schwellenberg came to Windsor before I made any report of my answer.

A scene almost horrible ensued, when I told Cerbera the offer was declined. She was too much enraged for disguise, and uttered the most furious expressions of indignant contempt at our proceedings. I am sure she would gladly have confined us both in the Bastille, had England such a misery, as a fit place to bring us to ourselves, from a daring so outrageous against imperial wishes.

(Fanny Burney to Dr. Burney) January, 1791- I thank heaven, there was much softness in the manner of naming you this morning. I see no ill-will mixed with the reluctance, which much consoles me. I do what is possible to avoid all discussion; I see its danger still so glaring. How could I resist, should the queen condescend to desire, to ask, that I would yet try another year?–and another year would but be uselessly demolishing me; for never could I explain to her that a situation which unavoidably casts all my leisure into the presence of Mrs. Schwellenberg must necessarily be subversive of my health, because incompatible with my peace, my ease, my freedom, my spirits, and my affections.

The queen is probably kept from any suspicion Of the true nature of the case, by the praises of Mrs. Schwellenberg, who, with all her asperity and persecution, is uncommonly partial to my society; because, in order to relieve myself from sullen gloom, or apparent dependency, I generally make my best exertions to appear gay and chatty; for when I can do this, she forbears both rudeness and imperiousness. She then, I have reason to believe, says to the queen, as I know She does to some others, "The Bernan bin reely agribble"; and the queen, not knowing the incitement that forces my elaborate and painful efforts, may suppose I am lively at heart, when she hears I am so in discourse. And there is no developing this without giving the queen the severest embarrassment as well as chagrin.

I would not turn Informer for the world. Mrs. Schwellenberg too, with all her faults, is heart and soul devoted to her roil mistress, with the truest faith and loyalty. I hold, therefore, silence on this subject to be a sacred duty. To return to you, my dearest padre, is the only road that has open for my return to strength and comfort, bodily and mental. I m inexpressibly grateful to the queen, but I burn to be delivered from Mrs. Schwellenberg, and I pine to be again in the arms of my padre.

A ROYAL GIFT TO THE MASTER OF THE HORSE.

What will you give me, fair ladies, for a copy of verse, written between the Queen of Great Britain and your most small little journalist?

The morning of the ball the queen sent for me, and said she had a fine pair of old-fashioned gloves, white, with stiff tops and a deep gold fringe, which she meant to send to her new master of the horse, Lord Harcourt, who was to be at the dance, She wished to convey them in a copy of verses, of which she had composed three lines, but could not get on. She told me her ideas, and I had the honour to help her in the metre and now I have the honour to copy them from her own royal hand:–

"TO THE EARL OF HARCOURT.

"Go, happy gloves, bedeck Earl Harcourt's hand,
And let him know they come from fairy-land,
Where ancient customs still retain their reign;
To modernize them all attempts were vain.
Go, cries Queen Mab, some noble owner seek,
Who has a proper taste for the antique."

Now, no criticising, fair ladies !-the assistant was neither allowed a pen nor a moment, but called upon to help finish, as she might have been to hand a fan. The earl, you may suppose, was sufficiently enchanted.

CONFERENCES WITH THE QUEEN.

April.-In the course of this month I had two conferences with my royal mistress upon my resignation, in which I spoke with all possible openness upon its necessity. She condescended to speak very honourably of my dear father to me,–and, in a long discourse upon my altered health with Mrs. de

Luc, she still further condescended to speak most graciously of his daughter, saying in particular, these strong words, in answer to something kind uttered by that good friend in my favour. "O, as to character, she is what we call in German 'true as gold' and, in point of heart, there is not, all the world over, one better"–and added something further upon sincerity very forcibly. This makes me very happy.

She deigned, also, in one of these conferences, to consult with me openly upon my successor, stating her difficulties, and making me enumerate various requisites. It would be dangerous, she said, to build upon meeting in England with one who would be discreet in point of keeping off friends and acquaintances from frequenting the palace; and she graciously implied much commendation of my discretion, in her statement of what she feared from a new person.

May.-As no notice whatever was taken, all this time, of my successor, or my retirement, after very great harass of suspense, and sundry attempts to conquer it, I had at length again a conference with my royal mistress. She was evidently displeased at again being called upon, but I took the courage to openly remind her that the birthday was her majesty's own time, and that my father conceived it to be the period of my attendance by her especial appointment. And this was a truth which flashed its own conviction on her recollection. She paused, and then, assentingly, said, "Certainly." I then added, that as, after the birthday, their majesties went to Windsor, and the early prayers began immediately, I must needs confess I felt myself wholly unequal to encountering the fatigue of rising for them in my present weakened state. She was now very gracious again, conscious all this was fair and true. She told me her own embarrassments concerning the successor, spoke confidentially of her reasons for not engaging an Englishwoman, and acknowledged a person was fixed upon, though something yet remained unarranged. She gave me, however, to understand that all would be expedited: and foreign letters were despatched, I know, immediately.

MISS BURNEY DETERMINES ON SECLUSION.

From Sunday, May 15 to May 22.-The trial of the poor persecuted Mr. Hastings being now again debating and arranging for continuance, all our house, I found, expected me now to come forth, and my royal mistress and Mrs. Schwellenberg

thought I should find it irresistible. indeed it nearly was so, from my anxious interest in the approaching defence; but when I considered the rumours likely to be raised after my retreat, by those terrifying watchers of Court transactions who inform the public of their conjectures, I dreaded the probable assertion that I must needs be disgusted or discontented, for health could not be the true motive of my resignation, since I was in public just before it took place. I feared, too, that even those who promoted the enterprise might reproach me with my ability to do what I wished. These considerations determined me to run no voluntary risks - especially as I should so ill know how to parry Mr. Windham, should he now attack me upon a subject concerning which he merits thanks so nobly, that I am satisfied my next interview with him must draw them forth from me. Justice, satisfaction in his exertions, and gratitude for their spirited willingness, all call upon me to give him that poor return. The danger of it, however, now, is too great to be tried, if avoidable : and I had far rather avoid seeing him, than either gratify myself by expressing my sense of his kindness, or unjustly withhold from him what I think of it.

These considerations determined me upon relinquishing all public places, and all private visits, for the present.

The trial, however, was delayed, and the Handelian Commemoration came on. My beloved Mr. and Mrs. Locke will have told my Susan my difficulties in this business, and I will now tell all three how they ended.

The queen, unexpectedly, having given me a ticket, and enjoined me to go the first day, that I might have longer time to recruit against the king's birthday, I became, as you will have heard, much distressed what course to pursue.

I took the first moment I was alone with her majesty to express my father's obligation to her for not suffering me to sit up on her own birthday, in this week, and I besought her permission to lay before her my father's motives for hitherto wishing me to keep quiet this spring, as well as my own, adding I was sure her majesty would benignly wish this business to be done as peaceably and unobserved as possible. She looked extremely earnest, and bid me proceed.

I then briefly stated that whoever had the high honour of belonging to their majesties were liable to comments upon all their actions, that, if the comment was only founded in truth, we had nothing to fear, but that, as the world was much less

addicted to veracity, than to mischief, my father and myself had an equal apprehension that, if I should now be seen in public so quickly before the impending change, reports might be spread, as soon as I went home, that it could not be for health I resigned. She listened very attentively and graciously, and instantly, acquiesced.

When the trial actually recommenced, the queen grew anxious for my going to it : she condescended to intimate that my accounts of it were the most faithful and satisfactory she received, and to express much Ill-will to giving them up. The motives I had mentioned, however, were not merely personal she could not but see any comments must involve more than myself, and therefore I abided steadily by her first agreement to my absenting myself from all public places, and only gently joined in her regret, which I forcibly enough felt in this instance, Without venturing any offer of relinquishing the prudential plan previously arranged. She gave me tickets for Charles for every day that the hall was opened, and I collected what I could of information from him for her satisfaction.

THE HASTINGS TRIAL RESUMED: 'THE ACCUSED MAKES HIS DEFENCE.

Queen's House, London, June.-the opening of this month her majesty told me that the next day Mr. Hastings was to make his defence, and warmly added, "I would give the world you could go to it!"

This was an expression so unusual in animation, that I instantly told her I would write to my father, who could not possibly, in that case, hesitate.

"Surely," she cried, "you may wrap up, so as not to catch cold that once?"

I told her majesty that, as my father had never thought going out would be really prejudicial to my health, he had only wished to have his motive laid fairly before her majesty, and then to leave it to her own command. Her majesty accepted this mode of consent, and gave me tickets for Charles and Sarah to accompany me, and gave leave and another ticket for Mr. de Luc to be of the party. Thursday, June 2.-I went once more to Westminster Hall. Charles and Sarah came not to their time, and I left directions and tickets, and set off with only Mr. de Luc, to secure our

own, and keep places for them. The Hall was more crowded than on any day since the trial commenced, except the first. Peers, commoners, and counsel, peeresses, commoneresses, and the numerous indefinites crowded every part, with a just and fair curiosity to hear one day's defence, after seventy-three of accusation.

Unfortunately I sat too high up to hear the opening, and when, afterwards, the departure of some of my obstacles removed me lower, I was just behind some of those unfeeling enemies who have not even the decorum due to themselves, of appearing to listen to what is offered against their own side. I could only make out that this great and persecuted man upon a plan all his own, and at a risk impossible to ascertain) was formally making his own defence, not with retaliating declamation, but by a simple, concise, and most interesting statement of facts, and of the necessities accompanying them in the situation to which the House then impeaching had five times called him. He spoke with most gentlemanly temper of his accusers, his provocation considered, yet with a firmness of disdain of the injustice with which he had been treated in return for his services, that was striking and affecting, though unadorned and manly.

His spirit, however, and the injuries which raised it, rested not quietly upon his particular accusers: he arraigned the late minister, Lord North, of ingratitude and double-dealing, and the present minister, Mr. Pitt, of unjustifiably and unworthily forbearing to Sustain him.

Here Mr. Fox, artfully enough, interrupted to say the king's ministers were not to be arraigned for what passed in the House of Parliament. Mr. Burke arose also' to enter his protest.

But Mr. Hastings then lost his patience and his temper: he would not suffer the interruption; he had never, he said, interrupted their long speeches; and when Mr. Burke again attempted to speak, Mr. Hastings, in an impassioned but affecting manner, extended his arms, and called out loudly, "I throw myself Upon the protection of your lordships:–I am not used to public speaking, and cannot answer them. what I wish to submit to your lordships I have committed to paper; but, if I am punished for what I say, I must insist upon being heard–I call upon you, my lords, to protect me from this violence!"

This animated appeal prevailed; the managers were silenced by an almost universal cry of "Hear, hear, hear!" from the

lords; and by Lord Kenyon, who represented the chancellor, and said, "Mr. Hastings, proceed."

The angry orators, though with a very ill grace, were then silenced. They were little aware what a compliment this intemperate eagerness was paying to Mr. Hastings, who for so many long days manifested that fortitude against attack, and that patience against abuse, which they could not muster, Without any parallel in provocation, even for three short hours. I rejoiced with all my heart to find Mr. Windham was not in their box. He did not enter with them in procession, nor appear as a manager or party concerned, further than as a member of the House of Commons. I could not distinguish him in so large a group, and he either saw not, or knew not, me.

The conclusion of the defence I heard better, as Mr. Hastings spoke considerably louder from this time; the spirit of indignation animated his manner and gave strength to his voice. You will have seen the chief parts of his discourse In the newspapers and you cannot, I think, but grow more and more his friend as you peruse it. He called pathetically and solemnly for instant judgment; but the Lords, after an adjournment decided to hear his defence by evidence, and order, the next sessions. How grievous such continual delay to a man past sixty, and sighing for such a length of time for redress from a prosecution as yet unparalleled in our annals.

When it was over, Colonel Manners came round to speak to -me and talk over the defence. He is warmly for Mr. Hastings. He inquired about Windsor; I should have made him stare a little had I told him I never expected to see him there again.

MR. WINDHAM IS CONGRATULATED ON HIS SILENCE.

When he came down-stairs into the large waiting-hall, Mr. de Luc went in search of William and chairs. Sally then immediately discerned Mr. Windham with some ladies. He looked at me without at first knowing me. . . . Sarah whispered me Mr. Windham was looking harder and harder; and presently he came up to me, and in a tone of very deep concern, and with a look that fully concurred with 'it, he said, "Do I see Miss Burney?"

I could not but feel the extent of the interrogation, and my assent acknowledged my comprehension.

"Indeed," he cried, "I was going to make a speech–not Very gallant!"

, "But it is what I should like better," I cried, " for it is kind if you were going to say I look miserably ill, as that is but a necessary consequence of feeling so,–and miserably ill enough I have felt this long time past."

He would not allow quite that, he said; but I flew from the subject, to tell him I had been made very happy by him. HE gave me one of his starts,–but immediately concluded it was by no good, and therefore would not speak in inquiry.

"Why, I did not see you in the box," I cried, "and I had been very much afraid I should have seen you there. But now my fears are completely over, and you have made me completely happy!"

He protested, with a comic but reproachful smile, he knew not how to be glad, if it was still only in the support of a bad cause, and if still I really supported it. And then he added he had gone amongst the House of Commons instead of joining the managers, because that enabled him to give his place to a friend, who was not a member.

"You must be sure," said I, "you would see me here to-day."

I had always threatened him with giving fairest play to the defence, and always owned I had been most afraid Of his harangue; therefore to find the charges end without his making it saved me certainly a shake,–either for Mr. Hastings or himself,– for one of them must thenceforth have fallen in my estimation. I believe, however, this was a rather delicate point, as he made me no answer, but a grave smile; but I am sure he instantly understood his relinquishing his intended charge was my subject of exultation. And, to make it plainer, I then added, "I am really very generous to be thus made happy, considering how great has been my curiosity."

"But, to have gratified that curiosity," cried he, "would have been no very particular inducement with me; though I have no right to take it for a compliment, as there are two species of curiosity,–yours, therefore, you leave wholly ambiguous."

"O, I am content with that," cried I so long as I am gratified, I give you leave to take it which way you please."

He murmured something I could not distinctly hear, of concern at my continued opinion upon this subject; but I do not think, by his manner, it much surprised him.

"You know," cried I, "why, as well as what, I feared–that fatal candour, of which so long ago you warned me to beware.

to the very last moment And, indeed, I was kept n alarm for at every figure I saw start up, just now,–Mr. Fox, Mr. Burke, Mr. Grey,–I concluded yours would be the next."

"You were prepared, then," cried he, with no little malice, "for a voice issuing from a distant pew."(340)

Miss BURNEY MAKES HER REPORT.

When we came home I was immediately summoned to her majesty, to whom I gave a full and fair account of all I had heard of the defence; and it drew tears from her expressive eyes as I repeated Mr. Hastings's own words, upon the hardship and injustice of the treatment he had sustained.

Afterwards, at night, the king called upon me to repeat my account and I was equally faithful, sparing nothing of what had dropped from the persecuted defendant relative to his majesty's ministers. I thought official accounts might be less detailed there than against the managers, who, as open enemies, excite not so much my "high displeasure" as the friends of government, who so insidiously elected and panegyrised him while they wanted his assistance, and betrayed and deserted him when he was no longer in a capacity to serve them. Such, at least, is the light in which the defence places them.

The king listened with much earnestness and a marked compassion. He had already read the account sent him officially, but he was as eager to hear all I could recollect, as if still uninformed of what had passed. The words may be given to the eye, but the impression they make can only be conveyed by the ear; and I came back so eagerly interested, that my memory was not more stored with the very words than my voice with the intonations of all that had passed.

With regard to My bearing this sole unofficial exertion since my illness, I can only say the fatigue I felt bore not any parallel with that of every Drawing–room day, because I was seated.

PRINCE WILLIAM INSISTS ON THE KING'S HEALTH BEING DRUNK.

June 4.-Let me now come to the 4th, the last birthday of the good, gracious, benevolent king I shall ever, in all human probability, pass under his royal roof.

The thought was affecting to me, in defiance of MY volunteer conduct, and I could scarce speak to the queen when I first went to her, and wished to say something upon a day So interesting. The king was most gracious and kind when he came into the state dressing-room at St. James's, and particularly inquired about my health and strength, and if they would befriend me for the day. I longed again to tell him how hard I would work them, rather than let them, on such a day, drive me from my office; but I found it better suited me to be quiet; It was safer not to trust to any expression of loyalty, with a mind so full, and on a day so critical.

At dinner Mrs. Schwellenberg presided, attired magnificently. Miss Goldsworthy, Mrs. Stainforth, Messrs. de Luc and Stanhope dined with us; and, while we were still eating fruit, the Duke of Clarence entered. He was just risen from the king's table, and waiting for his equipage to go home and prepare for the ball. To give you an idea of the energy of his royal highness's language, I ought to set apart a "general objection to writing, or rather intimating, certain forcible words, and beg leave to show you, in genuine colours, a royal sailor.

We all rose, of course, upon his entrance, and the two gentlemen placed themselves behind their chairs while the footmen left the room ; but he ordered us all to sit down, and called the men back to hand about some wine. He was in exceeding high spirits and in the utmost good humour. He placed himself at the head of the table, next Mrs. Schwellenberg, and looked remarkably well, gay, and full of sport and mischief, yet clever withal as well as comical.

"Well, this is the first day I have ever dined with the king at St. James's on his birthday. Pray, have you all drunk his majesty's health?"

"No, your roy'l highness: your roy'l highness might make dem do dat," said Mrs. Schwellenberg.

"O, by — will I! Here, you (to the footman), bring champagne! I'll drink the king's health again, if I die for it Yet, I have done pretty well already: so has the king, I promise you! I believe his majesty was never taken such good care of before. We have kept his spirits up, I promise you: we have enabled him to go through his fatigues; and I should have done more still, but for the ball and Mary–I have promised to dance with Mary!"

Princess Mary made her first appearance at Court to-day
She looked most interesting and unaffectedly lovely - she is a
Page 397,
Sweet creature, and perhaps, in point of beauty, the first of this truly beautiful race, of which Princess Mary may be called pendant to the Prince of Wales.

Champagne being now brought for the duke, he ordered it all round. When it came to me I whispered to Westerhaults to carry it on: the duke slapped his hand violently on the table, and called out, "O, by —, you shall drink it!"

There was no resisting this. We all stood up, and the duke sonorously gave the royal toast. "And now," cried he, making us all sit down again, "where are my rascals of servants? I sha'n't be in time for the ball; besides, I've got a deuced tailor waiting to fix on my epaulette! Here, you, go and see for my servants! d'ye hear? Scamper off!"

Off ran William.

"Come, let's have the king's health again. De Luc, drink it.
Here, champagne to De Luc!"

I wish you could have seen Mr. de Luc's mixed simper half pleased, half alarmed. However, the wine came and he drank it, the duke taking a bumper for himself at the same time."

Poor Stanhope!" cried he; "Stanhope shall have a glass too. Here, champagne! what are you all about? Why don't YOU give champagne to poor Stanhope?"

Mr. Stanhope, with great pleasure, complied, and the duke again accompanied him.

"Come hither, do you hear?" cried the duke to the servants; and on the approach, slow and submissive, of Mrs. Stainforth's man, he hit him a violent slap on the back, calling out, "Hang you! why don't you see for my rascals?"

Away flew the man, and then he called out to Westerhaults,

"Hark'ee! bring another glass of champagne to Mr. de Luc!"

Mr. de Luc knows these royal youths too well to venture at so vain an experiment as disputing with them, so he only shrugged his shoulders and drank the wine. The duke did the same.

"And now, poor Stanhope," cried the duke, "give another glass to poor Stanhope, d'ye hear?"

"Is not your royal highness afraid," cried Mr. Stanhope, displaying the full circle of his borrowed teeth, "I shall be apt to be rather up in the world, as the folks say, if I tope on at this rate?"

"Not at all! you can't get drunk in a better cause,

I'd get

drunk myself' if it was not for the ball. Here, champagne! another glass for the philosopher! I keep sober for Mary."

"O, your royal highness cried Mr. de Luc, gaining courage as he drank, "you will make me quite droll Of it if you make me go on,–quite droll!"

"So much the better! so much the better! it will do you a monstrous deal of good. Here, another glass of- champagne for the queen's philosopher!"

Mr. de Luc obeyed, and the duke then addressed Mrs. Schwellenberg's George. "Here! you! you! why, where is my carriage? run and see, do you hear?"

Off hurried George, grinning irrepressibly.

"If it was not for that deuced tailor, I would not stir. I shall dine at the Queen's house on Monday, Miss Goldsworthy; I shall come to dine with the princess royal. I find she does not go to Windsor with the queen."

The queen meant to spend one day at Windsor, on account of a review which carried the king that way.

Some talk then ensued upon the duke's new carriage, which they all agreed to be the most beautiful that day, at court. I had not seen it, which, to me, was some impediment against praising it.

THE QUEEN's HEALTH.

He then said it was necessary to drink the queens health. The gentlemen here made no demur, though Mr. de Luc arched his eyebrows in expressive fear of consequences.

"A bumper," cried the duke, "to the queen's gentleman-usher."

They all stood up and drank the queen's health.

"Here are three of us," cried the duke, "all belonging to the queen: the queen's philosopher, the queen's gentlemanusher, and the queen's son; but, thank heaven, I'm the nearest!"

"Sir," cried Mr. Stanhope, a little affronted, "I am not now the queen's gentleman-usher; I am the queen's equerry, sir."

"A glass more of champagne here! What are you all so slow for? Where are all my rascals gone? They've put me in one passion already this morning. Come, a glass of champagne for the queen's gentleman-usher!" laughing heartily.

"No, sir," repeated Mr. Stanhope; "I am equerry, sir."

"And another glass to the queen's philosopher!"

Neither gentleman objected; but Mrs. Schwellenberg, who

Page 399 had sat laughing and happy all this time, now grew alarmed, and said, "Your royal highness, I am afraid for the ball!"

"Hold your potato-jaw, my dear," cried the duke, patting her - but, recollecting himself, he took her hand and pretty abruptly kissed it, and then, flinging it away hastily, laughed aloud, and called out, "There, that will make amends for anything, so now I may say what I will. So here! a glass of champagne for the queen's philosopher and the queen's gentleman-usher! Hang me if it will not do them a monstrous deal of good!"

Here news was brought that the equipage was in order. He started up, calling out, "Now, then, for my deuced tailor."

"O, your royal highness," cried Mr. de Luc, in a tone of expostulation, "now you have made us droll, you go!"

Off! however, he went. And is it not a curious scene? All my amaze is, how any of their heads bore such libations.

THE PROCESSION TO THE BALL-ROOM: ABSENCE OF THE PRINCES.

In the evening I had by no means strength to encounter the ball-room. I gave my tickets to Mrs. and Miss Douglas. Mrs. Stainforth was dying to see the Princess Mary in her Court dress. Mr. Stanhope offered to conduct her to a place of prospect. She went with him. I thought this preferable to an unbroken evening with my fair companion, and Mr. de Luc, thinking the same, we both left Mrs. Schwellenberg to unattire, and followed. But we were rather in a scrape by trusting to Mr. Stanhope after all this champagne: he had carried Mrs. Stainforth to the very door of the ball-room, and there fixed her–in a place which the king, queen, and suite must brush past in order to enter the ball-room. I had followed, however, and the crowds of beef-eaters, officers, and guards that lined all the state-rooms through which we exhibited ourselves, prevented my retreating alone. I stood, therefore, next to Mrs. Stainforth, and saw the ceremony.

The passage was made so narrow by attendants, that they were all forced to go one by one. First, all the king's great state-officers, amongst whom I recognised Lord Courtown, a treasurer of the household; Lord Salisbury carried a candle!– 'tis an odd etiquette.–These being passed, came the king–he saw us and laughed; then the queen's master of the horse, Lord Harcourt, who did ditto; then some more.

The vice-chamberlain carries the queen's candle, that she may have the arm of the lord chamberlain to lean on; accordingly, Lord Aylesbury, receiving that honour, now preceded the queen: she looked amazed at sight of us. The kind princesses one by one acknowledged us. I spoke to sweet Princess Mary, wishing her royal highness joy: she looked in a delight and an alarm nearly equal. She was to dance her first minuet. Then followed the ladies of the bedchamber, and Lady Harcourt was particularly civil. Then the maids of honour, every one of whom knew and spoke to us. I peered vainly for the Duke of Clarence, but none of the princes passed us.(341) What a crowd brought up the rear! I was vexed not to see the Prince of Wales.

Well, God bless the king! and many and many such days may he know!

I was now so tired as to be eager to go back; but the queen's philosopher, the good and most sober and temperate of men, was really a little giddy with all his bumpers, and his eyes, which were quite lustrous, could not fix any object steadily; while the poor gentleman-usher–equerry, I mean–kept his Mouth so wide open with one continued grin,-I suppose from the sparkling beverage,–that I was every minute afraid its pearly ornaments, which never fit their case, would have fallen at our feet. Mrs. Stainforth gave me a significant look of making the same observation, and, catching me fast by the arm, said, "Come, Miss Burney, let's you and I take care of one another"; and then she safely toddled me back to Mrs. Schwellenberg, who greeted us with saying, "Vell! bin you Much amused? Dat Prince Villiam–oders de Duke de Clarrence–bin raelly ver merry–oders vat you call tipsy!"

BOSWELL's LIFE OF JOHNSON.

Mr, Turbulent had been reading, like all the rest of the world, Boswell's "Life of Dr. Johnson," and the preference there expressed of Mrs. Lenox to all other females had filled

him with astonishment, as he had never even heard her name.(342)

These occasional sallies of Dr. Johnson, uttered from local causes and circum-stances, but all retailed verbatim by Mr. Boswell, are filling all sort of readers with amaze, except the small part to whom Dr. Johnson was known, and who, by acquain-tance with the power of the moment over his unguarded conversation, know how little of his solid opinion was- to be gathered from his accidental assertions.

The king, who was now also reading this work, applied to me for explanations without end. Every night at his period he entered the queen's dressing-room, and detained her majesty's proceedings by a length of discourse with me upon this subject. All that flowed from himself was constantly full of the goodness and benevolence of his character - and I was never so happy as in the opportunity thus graciously given me of vindicating, in instances almost innumerable, the serious principles and various excellences of my revered Dr. Johnson from the clouds so frequently involving and darkening them, in narrations so little calculated for any readers who were strangers to his intrinsic worth, and therefore worked upon and struck by what was faulty in his temper and manners.

I regretted not having strength to read this work to her majesty myself. It was an honour I should else have certainly received ; for so much wanted clearing! so little was understood! However, the queen frequently condescended to read over passages and anecdotes which perplexed or offended her; and there were none I had not a fair power to soften or to justify.

THE CLOSE OF MISS BURNEY'S COURT DUTIES.

Her majesty, the day before we left Windsor, gave me to understand my attendance
Would be yet one more fortnight

requisite, though no longer. I heard this with a fearful presentiment I should surely
never go through another fortnight in so weak and languishing and painful a state of
health. However, I could but accede, though I fear with no very Courtly grace. So
melancholy indeed was the state of my mind, from the weakness of my frame, that
I was never alone but to form scenes of "foreign woe," where my own disturbance
did not occupy me wholly. I began—almost whether I would or not—another tragedy!
The other three all unfinished! not one read! and one of them, indeed, only generally
sketched as to plan and character. But I could go on With nothing; I could only suggest
and invent.

The power of composition has to me indeed proved a blessing! When incapable of
all else, that, unsolicited, unthought of, has presented itself to my solitary leisure, and
beguiled me of myself, though it has not of late regaled me with gayer associates.

July.-I come now to write the last week of my royal residence. The queen honoured me with the most uniform graciousness, and though, as the time of separation
approached, her cordiality rather diminished, and traces of internal displeasure appeared sometimes, arising from an opinion I ought rather to have struggled on, live
or die, than to quit her, yet I am sure she saw how poor was my own chance, except
by a change in the mode of life, and at least ceased to wonder, though she could not
approve.

The king was more Courteous, more communicative, more amiable, at very meeting: and he condescended to hold me in conversation with him by every opportunity,
and with an air of such benevolence and goodness, that I never felt such ease and
pleasure in his notice before. He talked over all Mr. Boswell's book, and I related to
him sundry anecdotes of Dr. Johnson, all highly to his honour, and such as I was eager
to make known, He always heard me with the utmost complacency and encouraged
me to proceed in my accounts by every mark of attention and interest.

He told me once, laughing heartily, that, having seen my name in the index, he was
eager to come to what was said of me, but which he found so little, he was surprised
and disappointed.

I ventured to assure him how much I had myself been rejoiced at this very circumstance, and with what satisfaction had reflected upon having very seldom met Mr.
Boswell, as

I

new there was no other security against all manner of risks in his relations.

About this time Mr. Turbulent made me a visit at tea-time when the gentlemen
were at the Castle and the moment William left the room he eagerly said, "Is this true,
Miss Burney, that I hear? Are we going to lose you?"

I was much surprised, but Could not deny the charge. He, very good-naturedly,
declared himself much pleased at a release which he protested he thought necessary
to my life's preservation. I made him tell me the channel through which a business I

had guarded SO scrupulously Myself had reached him; but it Is too full of windings for writing.

With Mr. de Luc I was already in confidence upon my resignation, and with the knowledge of the queen, as he had received the intelligence from Germany, whence my successor was now arriving. I then also begged the indulgence of writing to Mr. Smelt upon the subject, which was accorded me.

My next attack was from Miss Planta. She expressed herself in the deepest concern at my retiring, though she not only acknowledged its necessity, but confessed she had not thought I could have performed my official duty even one year! She broke from me while we talked, leaving me abruptly in a violent passion of tears.

MISS BURNEY'S SUCCESSOR. A PENSION FROM THE QUEEN.

I had soon the pleasure to receive Mlle. jacobi.(343) She brought with her a young German, as her maid, who proved to be her niece, but so poor she could not live when her aunt left Germany! Mr. Best, a messenger of the king's, brought her to Windsor, and Mrs. Best, his wife, accompanied him.

I was extremely pleased with Mlle. Jacobi, who is tall, well made, and nearly handsome, and of a humour so gay, an understanding so lively, and manners so frank and ingenuous, that I felt an immediate regard for her, and we grew mutual good friends. She is the daughter of a dignified clergyman of Hanover, high in theological fame.

They all dined with me, - and, indeed, Mlle. Jacobi, wanting a thousand informations in her new situation, which I was most happy to give her, seldom quitted me an instant.

Tuesday morning I had a conversation, very long and very affecting to me, with her majesty. I cannot pretend to detail

it. I will only tell you she began by speaking of Mlle. Jacobi, whom I had the satisfaction to praise, as far as had appeared, very warmly and then she led me to talk at large upon the nature and requisites and circumstances of the situation I was leaving. I said whatever I could suggest that would tend to render my Successor more comfortable, and had the great happiness to represent with success the consolation and very innocent pleasure she might reap from the society of the young relation she had brought over, if she might be permitted to treat her at once as a companion, and not as a servant. This was heard with the most humane complacency, and I had leave given me to forward the plan in various ways. She then conversed upon sundry Subjects, all of them confidential in their nature, for near an hour; and then, after a pause, said, "Do I owe you anything, my dear Miss Burney?"

I acquainted her with a debt or two amounting to near seventy pounds. She said she would settle it in the afternoon, and then paused again, after which, with a look full of benignity, she very expressively said, "As I don't know your plan, or what you propose, I cannot tell what Would make you comfortable, but you know the size of my family."

I comprehended her, and was immediately interrupting her with assurances of my freedom from all expectation or claim; but she stopped me, saying, "You know what you now have from me:–the half of that I mean to continue."

Amazed and almost overpowered by a munificence I had so little expected or thought of, I poured forth the most earnest disclaimings of such a mark of her graciousness, declaring I knew too well her innumerable calls to be easy in receiving it and much more I uttered to this purpose, with the unaffected warmth that animated me at the moment. She heard me almost silently; but, in conclusion, Simply, yet strongly, said, "I shall certainly do that" with a stress on the that that seemed to kindly mean she would rather have done more.

The conference was in this stage when the Princess Elizabeth came into the room. The queen then retired to the antechamber. My eyes being full, and my heart not very empty, I could not then forbear saying to her royal highness how much the goodness of the queen had penetrated me. The sweet princess spoke feelings I could not expect, by the immediate glistening of her soft eyes. She condescended to express her concern At my retiring; but most kindly added, "However,

Miss Burney, go when you will, that you have this to comfort you, your behaviour has been most perfectly honourable."

LEAVE-TAKINGS.

This, my last day at Windsor, was filled with nothing but packing, leave-taking, bills-paying, and lessoning to Mlle. Jacobi, who adhered to my side through everything, and always with an interest that made its own way for her. All the people I had to Settle With poured forth for my better health good wishes without end; but amongst the most unwilling for my retreat stood poor Mrs. Astley.(344) Indeed she quite saddened me by her sadness, and by the recollections of that sweet and angelic being her mistress, who had so solaced my early days at that place.

Mr. Bryant, too, came this same morning; he had an audience of the queen: he knew nothing previously of my design. He seemed thunderstruck. "Bless me!" he cried, in his short and simple but expressive manner, "so I shall never see you again, never have the honour to dine in that apartment with you more!" etc. I would have kept him to dinner this last day, but he was not well, and would not be persuaded. He would not, however, bid me adieu, but promised to endeavour to see me some time at Chelsea.

I had then a little note from Miss Gomme, desiring to see me in the garden. She had just gathered the news. I do not believe any one Was more disposed to be sorry, if the Sight and sense of my illness had not checked her concern. She highly approved the step I was taking, and was most cordial and kind. Miss Planta came to tell me she must decline dining with me, as she felt she should cry all dinner-time, in reflecting upon its being our last meal together at Windsor, and this might affront Mlle. Jacobi.

The queen deigned to come once more to my apartment this afternoon. She brought me the debt. It was a most mixed feeling with which I now saw her.

In the evening came Madame de la Fite, I need not tell you, I imagine, that her expressions were of "la plus vife douleur,"; yet she owned she could not wonder my father should try what another life would do for me. My dear Mrs. de Luc came next; She, alone, knew of this while impending. She rejoiced the time of deliverance was arrived, for she had often feared I should outstay my strength, and sink while the matter was arranging. She rejoiced, however, with tears in her kind eyes; and, indeed, I took leave of her With true regret.

It was nine o'clock before I could manage to go down the garden to the lower Lodge, to pay my duty to the younger princesses, whom I Could not else see at all, as they never go to town for the Court-days. I went first up-stairs to Gomme, and had the mortification to learn that the sweet Princess Amelia was already gone to bed. This extremely grieved me. When or how I may see her lovely little highness more, Heaven only knows! Miss Gomme kindly accompanied me to Miss Goldsworthy's apartment, and promised me a few more words before I set out the next morning.

I found Mrs. Cheveley, at whose door, and at Miss Neven, her sister's, I had tapped and left my name, with Miss Goldsworthy and Dr. Fisher: that pleasing and worthy man has just taken a doctor's degree. I waited with Miss Goldsworthy till the princesses Mary and Sophia came from the upper Lodge, which is when the king and queen go to supper. Their royal highnesses, were gracious even to kindness; they shook my hand again and again, and wished me better health, and all happiness, with the sweetest earnestness. Princess Mary repeatedly desired to see me whenever I came to the Queen's house, and condescended to make me as repeatedly promise that I would not fail. I was deeply touched by their goodness, and by leaving them.

Wednesday.-In the morning Mrs. Evans, the housekeeper, came to take leave of me; and the housemaid of my apartment, who, poor girl, cried bitterly that I was going to give place to a foreigner, for Mrs. Schwellenberg's severity with servants has made all Germans feared in the house.

O, but let me first mention that, when I came from the lower Lodge, late as it was, I determined to see my old friends the equerries, and not quit the place without bidding them adieu. I had never seen them since I had dared mention my designed retreat. I told William, therefore, to watch their return from the castle, and to give my compliments to either Colonel Gwynn or Colonel Goldsworthy, and an invitation to my apartment.

Colonel Goldsworthy came instantly. I told him I could not think of leaving Windsor without offering first my good

wishes to all the household. He said that, when my intended departure had been published, he and all the gentlemen then with him had declared it ought to have taken place six months ago. He was extremely courteous, and I begged him to bring to me, the rest of his companions that were known to me.

He immediately fetched Colonel Gwynn, General Grenville, Colonel Ramsden, and Colonel Manners. This was the then party. I told him I sent to beg their blessing upon my departure. They were all much pleased, apparently, that I had not made my exit without seeing them: they all agreed on the Urgency of the measure, and we exchanged good wishes most cordially.

My Wednesday morning's attendance upon the queen was a melancholy office. Miss Goldsworthy as well as Miss Gomme came early to take another farewell. I had not time to make any visits in the town, but left commissions with Mrs. de Luc and Madame de la Fite. Even Lady Charlotte Finch I could not Call upon, though she had made me many kind visits since my illness. I wrote to her, however, by Miss Gomme, to thank her, and bid her adieu.

FAREWELL TO KEW.

Thursday, July 7.-This, my last day of office, was big and busy,- -joyful, yet affecting to me in a high degree.

In the morning, before I left Kew, I had my last interview with Mrs. Schwellenberg. She was very kind in it, desiring to see me whenever I could in town, during her residence at the Queen's house, and to hear from me by letter meanwhile. She then much Surprised me by an offer of succeeding to her own place,–when it was vacated either by her retiring or her death. This was, indeed, a mark of favour and confidence I had not expected. I declined, however, to enter upon the subject, as the manner in which she opened it made it very solemn, and, to her, very affecting. She would take no leave of me, but wished me better hastily, and saying we should soon meet, she hurried suddenly out of the room. Poor woman! If her temper were not so irascible, I really believe her heart would be by no means wanting in kindness.

I then took leave of Mrs. Sandys, giving her a token of remembrance in return for her constant good behaviour, and

Page 408 she showed marks of regard, and of even grief, I was sorry to receive, as I could so little return.

But the tragedy of tragedies was parting with Goter;(345) that poor girl did nothing but cry incessantly from the time she knew of our separation. I was very sorry to have no place to recommend her to, though I believe she may rather benefit by a vacation that carries her to her excellent father and Mother, who teach her nothing but good. I did what I could to soften the blow, by every exertion in my power in all ways; for it was impossible to be unmoved at her violence of sorrow.

I then took leave of Kew Palace–the same party again accompanying me, for the last time, in a royal vehicle going by the name of Miss Burney's coach.

THE FINAL PARTING.

I come now near the close of my Court career.

At St. James's all was graciousness; and my royal mistress gave me to understand she would have me stay to assist at her toilet after the Drawing-room; and much delighted me by desiring my attendance on the Thursday fortnight, when she came again to town. This lightened the parting in the pleasantest manner possible. When the queen commanded me to follow her to her closet I was, indeed, in much emotion; but I told her that, as what had passed from Mrs. Schwellenberg in the morning had given me to understand her majesty was fixed in her munificent intention, notwithstanding-what I had most unaffectedly urged against it–

"Certainly," she interrupted, "I shall certainly do it."

"Yet so little," I continued, "had I thought it right to dwell upon such an expectation, that, in the belief your majesty would yet take it into further consideration, I had not even written It to my father."

"Your father," she again interrupted me, "has nothing to do with it; it is solely from me to you."

"Let me then humbly entreat," I cried, "still in some measure to be considered as a servant of your majesty, either as reader, or to assist occasionally if Mlle. Jacobi should be ill."

She looked most graciously pleased, and Immediately closed in with the proposal, saying, "When your health is restored,– perhaps sometimes."

I then fervently poured forth my thanks for all her goodness, and my prayers for her felicity.

She had her handkerchief in her hand or at her eyes the whole time. I was so much moved by her condescending kindness, that as soon as I got out of the closet I nearly sobbed. I went to help Mlle. Jacobi to put up the jewels, that my emotion might the less be observed. The king then came into the room. He immediately advanced to the window, where I stood, to speak to me. I was not then able to comport myself steadily. I was forced to turn my head away from him. He stood still and silent for some minutes, waiting to see if I should turn about; but I could not recover myself sufficiently to face him, strange as it was to do otherwise; and Perceiving me quite overcome he walked away, and I saw him no more. His kindness, his goodness, his benignity, never shall I forget–never think of but with fresh gratitude and reverential affection.

They were now all going–I took, for the last time, the cloak of the queen, and, putting It over her shoulders, slightly ventured to press them, earnestly, though in a low voice, saying, "God Almighty bless your majesty!"

She turned round, and, putting her hand upon my ungloved arm, pressed it with the greatest kindness, and said, "May you be happy!"

She left me overwhelmed with tender gratitude.

The three eldest princesses were in the next room: they ran in to me the moment the queen went onward. Princess Augusta and Princess Elizabeth each took a hand, and the princess royal put hers over them. I could speak to none of them; but they repeated, "I wish you happy!–I wish you health!" again and again, with the Sweetest eagerness.

They then set off for Kew.

Here, therefore, end my Court annals; after having lived in the service of her majesty five years within ten days–from July 17, 1786, to July 7, 1791.

(333) By her "Visions" Fanny apparently means her desire of resigning her place at Court, and her hope of her father's concurrence.-ED.

(334) i.e., Attempts to induce him to procure for sundry strangers some acquaintance with his daughter.-ED.

(335) The Comtesse de Bouflers-Rouvrel and, probably, her daughter-in-law, the Comtesse Amélie de Bouflers. Madame de Bouflers-Rouvrel was distinguished in Parisian society as a bel-esbrit, and corresponded for many years with Rousseau. Left a widow in 1764, she became the mistress of the Prince de Conti. Her first visit to England was in 1763, when she was taken by Topham Beauclerk to see Dr. Johnson. She revisited this country at the time of the emigration, but returning to France, was imprisoned by the Revolutionists. The fall of Robespierre (July, 1794) restored her to liberty. Am6lie de Bouflers, less fortunate than her mother-in-law, perished by the guillotine, June 27, 1794.-ED.

(336) But is it possible, sir, that your daughter has no holidays?

(337) Burke's speech, delivered February 9, in a debate on the army estimates, in which he took occasion to denounce, with great vehemence, the principles and conduct of the French Revolution, which he contrasted, much to its disadvantage, with the English Revolution of 1688. "The French," he said, "had shown themselves the ablest architects of ruin that had hitherto appeared in the world." The sentiments uttered by Burke on this occasion delighted the ministerialists and friends of the Court as much as they dismayed his own party. As the debate proceeded he found himself in the strange position of a chief of opposition enduring the compliments of the prime minister and the attacks of Fox and Sheridan, who took a broader and juster view of the great events in France, though condemning equally with Burke the Excesses of the Revolutionists. Fox declared His grief at hearing, "from the lips of a man whom he loved and revered," Sentiments "so hostile to the general principles of liberty." This speech of Burke's may be said to mark the commencement of that disagreement between himself and Fox, which culminated in the total breach of their friendship.-ED.

(338) Dr. Burney was a member of this famous club, having been elected in 1784. Mr. Windham had been a member since 1778.-ED.

(339) "Reflections on the Revolution in France," published November 1, 1790. it was received by the public with avidity, and went through eleven editions within a year-ED.

(340) An allusion to the imperious interruption of the marriage of Cecilia, and young Delvile. See "Cecilia," book vii., ch. 7.-ED.

(341) Some weeks later Fanny has the following allusion to the ball: "The Princess Mary chatted with me over her own adventures on the queen's birthday, when she first appeared at Court. The history of her dancing at the ball, and the situation of her partner and brother, the Duke of Clarence, she spoke of with a sweet ingenuousness and artless openness which makes her very amiable character. And not a little did I divert her when I related the duke's visit to our party! 'O,' cried she, 'he told me of it himself the next morning, and said, "You may think how far I was gone, for I kissed the Schwellenberg's hand!"'"-ED.

(342) "On the evening of Saturday May 15 [1784], he [Dr. Johnson] was in fine spirits at our Essex Head Club. He told us, 'I dined yesterday at Patrick's with Mrs. Carter, Miss Hannah More, and Fanny Burney. Three such women are not to be found: I know not where I could find a fourth, except Mrs. Lennox, who is superior to them all.' " (Boswell.) This "occasional sally" cannot, of course, be taken as expressing Johnson's deliberate opinion of the relative merits of Fanny Burney and Mrs. Lenox. He was an old friend of Charlotte Lenox, and had written in 1752 the dedication for her "Female Quixote," a novel of singular charm and humour, though scarcely to be placed on a par with "Evelina" or "Cecilia."-ED.

(343) Fanny's successor in office.-ED.

344) The old servant of Mrs. Delany.-ED.

(345) Fanny's maid.-ED.

Page 410 '

SECTION 18. (1791-2.)
REGAINED LIBERTY.

Fanny's rambling journey to the west with Mrs. Ord was a pleasant restorative, to mind and body, and bore good fruit hereafter in the pages, of " The Wanderer." At Bath, in the course of this journey, she formed an acquaintance equally interesting and unlooked-for. It was certainly singular, to use her own words, "that the first visit I should make after leaving the queen should be to meet the head of the opposition public, the Duchess of Devonshire!" The famous Whig duchess was then in her thirty-fifth year. Fanny's description of her personal charms tallies exactly with the impression which we derive from her portraits by Reynolds and Gainsborough: that their celebrity was due rather to expressiveness and animation than to a countenance regularly beautiful. But the charming duchess, like most other people, had a skeleton in her closet. Notwithstanding her high spirits, and "native. cheerfulness," "she appeared to me not happy," writes our penetrating Diarist. What was the skeleton? Not gambling debts, although the duchess followed the fashion of the day, and Sheridan declared that he had handed her into her carriage when she was literally sobbing at her losses. Fanny gives us a hint, slight but unmistakeable. At their first meeting the duchess was accompanied by another lady–a beautiful, alluring woman, with keen dark eyes, who smiled, some one said, "like Circe." Lady Spencer introduced her daughter to Miss Burney with warm pleasure, and then, "slightly and as if unavoidably," named the beautiful enchantress–Lady Elizabeth Foster. It is only necessary to add that in 1809, some three years after the death of his first wife, the Duchess Georgiana, the Duke of Devonshire married again, and his second wife was Lady Elizabeth Foster.-ED.

RELEASED FROM DUTY.

Chelsea College, July.-My dear father was waiting for me in my apartment at St. James's when their majesties and their fair royal daughters were gone. He brought me home, and welcomed me most sweetly. My heart was a little sad, in spite of its contentment. My joy in quitting my place extended not to quitting the king and queen; and the final marks of their benign favour had deeply impressed me. My mother received me according to my wishes, and Sarah Most cordially.

My dear James and Charles speedily came to see me; and one precious half-day I was indulged with my kind Mr. Locke and his Fredy. If i had been stouter and stronger in health, I should then have been almost flightily happy; but the Weakness of the frame still kept the rest in order. My ever-kind Miss Cambridge was also amongst the foremost to hasten with congratulations on my return to my old ways and to make me promise to visit Twickenham after my projected tour with Mrs. Ord.

I could myself undertake no visiting at this time; rest and quiet being quite essential to my recovery. But my father did the honours for me amongst those who had been most interested in my resignation. He called instantly upon Sir Joshua Reynolds and Miss Palmer, and Mr. Burke; and he wrote to Mr. Walpole, Mr. Seward, Mrs. Crewe, Mr. Windham, and my Worcester uncle. Mr. Walpole wrote the most charming of answers, In the gallantry of the old Court, and with all its wit, concluding with a warm invitation to Strawberry Hill. Sir Joshua and Miss Palmer Sent me every species of kind exultation. Mr. Burke was not in town. Mr. Seward wrote very heartily and cordially, and came also when my Susanna was here. Mrs. Crewe immediately pressed me to come and recruit at Crewe Hall in Cheshire, where she promised me repose, and good air, and good society.

A WESTERN JOURNEY: FARNHAM CASTLE.

Sidmouth, Devonshire, Monday, Aug. 1.-I have now been a week out upon my travels, but have not had the means or the time, till this moment, to attempt their brief recital.

Mrs. Ord called for me about ten in the morning. I left my dearest father with the less regret, as his own journey to Mrs. crewe was very soon to take place. It was a terribly rainy morning, but I was eager not to postpone the excursion. As we travelled on towards Staines, I could scarcely divest myself of the idea that I was but making again my usual journey to Windsor; and I could with difficulty forbear calling Mrs. Ord Miss Planta during the whole of that well-known road. I did not, indeed, take her maid, who was our third in the coach, for Mr. de Luc, or Mr. Turbulent; but the place she occupied made me think much more of those I so long had had for my vis-'a-vis than of herself.

We went on no farther than to Bagshot: thirty miles was the extremity of our powers; but I bore them very tolerably, though variably. We put up at the best inn, very early, and then inquired what we could see In the town and neighbourhood. "Nothing!" was the concise answer of a staring maid. We determined, therefore, to prowl to the churchyard, and read the tombstone inscriptions: but when we asked the way, the same woman, staring still more wonderingly, exclaimed, "Church! There's no church nigh here!–There's the Prince Of Wales'S, just past the turning. You may go and see that, if you will."

So on we walked towards this hunting Villa: but after toiling up a long unweeded avenue, we had no sooner opened the gate to the parks than a few score of dogs, which were lying in ambush, Set Up so prodigious a variety of magnificent barkings, springing forward at the same time, that, content with having caught a brief view of the seat, we left them to lord it over the domain they regarded as their own, and, with all due Submission, pretty hastily shut the gate, without troubling them to give us another salute. We returned to the inn, and read B—'s "Lives of the Family of the Boyles."

Aug. 2.-We proceeded to Farnham to breakfast, and thence walked to the castle. The Bishop of Winchester, Mrs. North. and the whole family are gone abroad. The castle is a good old building, with as much of modern elegance and fashion intermixed in its alterations and fitting up as Mrs. North could possibly contrive to weave into its ancient grandeur. . . . I wished I could have climbed to the top of an old tower, much out of repair, but so high, that I fancied I could thence have espied the hills of Norrbury. However, I was ready to fall already, from only ascending the slope to reach the castle.

A PARTY OF FRENCH FUGITIVES.

We arrived early at Winchester; but the town was so full, as the judges were expected next morning, that we could only get one bed-chamber, in which Mrs. Ord, her maid, and myself reposed.

just after we had been obliged to content ourselves with this scanty accommodation, we saw a very handsome coach and four horses, followed by a chaise and outriders, stop at the gate, and heard the mistress of the house declare she- could not receive the company; and the postilions, at the same time, protested the horses could go no farther. They inquired for fresh horses; there were none to be had in the whole city; and the party were all forced to remain in their carriages, without horses, at the inn-gate, for the chance of what might pass on the road. We asked who they were, and our pity was doubled in finding them foreigners.

We strolled about the upper part of the city, leaving the cathedral for the next morning. We saw a large, uniform, handsome palace, which is called by the inhabitants "The king's house," and which was begun by Charles II. We did not, therefore, expect the elegant architecture of his father's days. One part, they particularly told us, was designed for Nell Gwynn. It was never finished, and neglect has taken place of time in rendering it a most ruined structure, though, as it bears no marks of antiquity, it has rather the appearance of owing its destruction to a fire than to the natural decay of age. It is so spacious, however, and stands so magnificently to overlook the city, that I wish it to be completed for an hospital or infirmary. I have written Mrs. Schwellenberg an account of its appearance and state, which I am sure will be read by her majesty.

When we returned to the Inn, still the poor travellers were in the same situation: they looked so desolate, and could so indifferently make themselves understood, that Mrs. Ord good- naturedly invited them to drink tea with us. They most thankfully accepted the offer, and two ladies and two gentlemen ascended the stairs with us to our dining-room. The chaise had the female servants.

The elder lady was so truly French—so vive and so triste in turn—that she seemed formed from the written character of a Frenchwoman, such, at least, as we English write them. She was very forlorn in her air, and very sorrowful in her counte-nance; yet all action and gesture, and of an animation when speaking nearly fiery in its vivacity: neither pretty nor young, but neither ugly nor old; and her smile, which was rare, had a finesse very engaging; while her whole demeanour announced a person Of consequence, and all her discourse told that she was well-informed, well-educated, and well-bred.

The other lady, whom they called mademoiselle, as the first madame, was young, dark but clear and bright in her eyes and complexion, though without good features, or a manner of equal interest with the lady she accompanied. She proved, however, sensible, and seemed happy in the general novelty around her. She spoke English pretty well, and was admired without mercy by the rest of the party, as a perfect mistress of the language. The madame spoke it very ill indeed, but pleasantly.

Of the two gentlemen, one they called only monsieur, and the other the madame addressed as her brother. The monsieur was handsome, rather tonnish, and of the high haughty ton, and seemed the devoted attendant or protector of the madame, who sometimes spoke to him almost with asperity, from eagerness, and a tinge of wretchedness and impatience, which coloured all she said; and, at other times, softened off her vehemence with a smile the most expressive, and which made its way to the mind immediately, by coming with sense and meaning, and not merely from good humour and good spirits as the more frequent smiles of happier persons. The brother seemed lively and obliging, and entirely at the devotion of his sister, who gave him her commands with an authority that would not have brooked dispute.

They told us they were just come from Southampton, which they had visited in their way from viewing the fleet at the Isle of Wight and Portsmouth, and they meant to go on now to Bath.

We soon found they were aristocrats, which did better for them with Mrs. Ord and me than it would have done with you republicans of Norbury and Mickleham; yet I wish you had all met the madame, and heard her Indignant unhappiness. They had been in England but two months. They all evidently belonged to madame, who appeared to me a fugitive just before the flight of the French king,(346) or in consequence of his having been taken.

She entered upon her wretched situation very soon, lamenting that he was, in fact, no king, and bewailing his want of courage for his trials. the queen she never mentioned. She spoke once or twice of son mari, but did not say who or what he was, nor where.

"They say," she cried, "In France they have now liberty! Who has liberty, le peuple, or the mob? Not les honn'etes gens; for those whose principles are known to be aristocratic must fly, or endure every danger and indignity. Ah! est-ce l'a la libert'e?"

The monsieur said he had always been the friend of liberty, such as it was in England; but in France it was general tyranny. "In England," he cried, "he was a true democrat, though bien aristocrate in France."

"At least," said the poor madame, "formerly, in all the sorrows of life, we had nos terres to which we could retire, and there forget them, and dance, and sing, and laugh, and fling them all aside, till forced back to Paris. But now our villas are no protection: we may be safe, but the first offence conceived by le peuple is certain destruction; and, without a moment's warning, we may be forced to fly our own roofs, and see them and all we are worth burnt before our eyes in horrible triumph."

This was all said in French. But the anguish of her Countenance filled me with compassion, though it was scarcely possible to restrain a smile when, the moment after, she" said she Might be very wrong, but she hoped I would forgive her if she owned she preferred Paris incomparably to London and pitied me very unreservedly for never having seen that first of cities.

Her sole hope, she said, for the overthrow of that anarchy in which the Unguarded laxity of the king had plunged the first Country in the world,—vous me pardonnec, Mademoiselle,—was now from the German princes, who, she flattered herself, Would rise In their own defence.

She told me, the next moment, of les spectacles I should find at Southampton, and asked me what she might expect at Bath of public amusement and buildings.

I was travelling I said, for my health, and Should visit no theatres, ball-rooms, etc., and could recommend none.

She did not seem to comprehend me; yet, in the midst of

naming these places, she sighed as deeply from the bottom of her heart as if she had been forswearing the world for ever in despair. But it was necessary, , she said, when unhappy, to go abroad the more, pour se distraire. In parting, they desired much to renew acquaintance with us when we returned to London. Mrs. Ord gave her direction to the monsieur, who in return, wrote theirs–"The French ladies, NO. 30, Gerrard-street, Soho."

They stayed till our early hour Of retiring made Mrs. Ord suffer them to go. I was uneasy to know what would become of them. I inquired of a waiter: he unfeelingly laughed, and said, "O! they do well enough; they've got a room." I asked if he could yet let them have beds to stay, or horses to proceed? "No," answered he, sneeringly: "but it don't matter for, now they've got a room, they are as merry and capering as if they were going to dance."

just after this, Mrs. Stephenson, Mrs. Ord's maid, came running in. "La! ma'am," she cried, "I've been so frightened, you can't think: the French folks sent for me on purpose, to ask t'other lady's name, they said, and they had asked William before, so they knew it; but they said I must write it down, and where she lived; so I was forced to write, 'Miss Burney, Chelsea,' and they fell a smiling so at one another."

'Twas impossible to help laughing; but we desired her, in return, to send for one of their maids and ask their names also. She came back, and said she could not understand the maids, and so they had called one of the gentlemen, and he had written down "Madame la Comtesse de Menage, et Mlle. de Beaufort."

We found, afterwards, they had sat up till two in the morning, and then procured horses and journeyed towards Oxford.

WINCHESTER CATHEDRAL.

Aug. 3.-We walked to the cathedral, and saw it completely. Part of it remains from the original Saxon building, though neglected, except by travellers, as the rest of the church is ample for all uses, and alone kept in repair. The bones of eleven Saxon kings are lodged in seven curious old chests, in which they were deposited after being dug up and disturbed in the civil wars and ensuing confusions. The small number of chests is owing to the small proportion remaining of some of the skeletons, which occasioned their being united with others.

Page 417 The Saxon characters are in many inscriptions preserved, though in none entire. They were washing a plaster from the walls, to discern some curious old painting, very miserable, but very entertaining, of old legends, which some antiquaries are now endeavouring to discover.

William of Wykham, by whom the cathedral was built in its present form, lies buried, with his effigy and whole monument in very fine alabaster, and probably very like, as it was done, they aver, before he died. Its companion, equally superb, is Cardinal Beaufort, uncle of Harry VI. William Rufus, slain in the neighbouring forest, is buried in the old choir: his monument is of plain stone, without any inscription or ornament, and only shaped like a coffin. Hardyknute had a much more splendid monument preserved for him; but Harry I. had other business to attend, I presume, than to decorate the tomb of one brother while despoiling of his kingdom another. An extremely curious old chapel and monument remain of Archbishop Langton, of valuable gothic workmanship. The altar, which is highly adorned with gold, was protected in Cromwell's time by the address and skill of the Winton inhabitants, who ran up a slight wall before it, and deceived the reformists, soi-disants. I could hardly quit this poor dear old building, so much I was interested with its Saxon chiefs, its little queer niches, quaint images, damp cells, mouldering walls, and mildewed pillars. One chest contains the bones entire of Egbert, our first king. Edred, also. I distinguished.

The screen was given to this church by King Charles, and is the work of Inigo Jones. It is very simple in point of ornament, very complete in taste and elegance; nevertheless, a screen of Grecian architecture in a cathedral of gothic workmanship was ill, I think, imagined.

STONEHENGE, WILTON, AND MILTON ABBEY.

Aug. 5.-We went to Stonehenge. Here I was prodigiously disappointed, at first, by the huge masses of stone so unaccountably piled at the summit of Salisbury Plain. However, we alighted, and the longer I surveyed and considered them, the more augmented my wonder and diminished my disappointment.

We then went on to Wilton, where I renewed my delight over the exquisite Vandykes, and with the statues, busts, and pictures, which again I sighingly quitted, with a longing wish

I might ever pass under that roof time enough to see them more deliberately. We stopped in the Hans Holbein Porch, and upon the Inigo Jones bridge, as long as we Could stand, after standing and staring and straining our eyes till our guide was quite fatigued. 'Tis a noble collection; and how might it be enjoyed if, as an arch rustic Old labouring man told u, fine folks lived as they ought to do!

Sunday, Aug. 7.-After an early dinner we set off for Milton Abbey, the seat of Lord Milton, partly constructed from the old abbey and partly new. There is a magnificent gothic hall in excellent preservation, of evident Saxon workmanship, and extremely handsome, though not of the airy beauty of the chapel. The situation of this abbey is truly delicious: it is in a vale of extreme fertility and richness, surrounded by hills of the most exquisite form, and mostly covered with hanging woods, but so varied in their growth and groups, that the eye is perpetually fresh caught with objects of admiration. 'Tis truly a lovely place.

LYME AND SIDMOUTH.

Aug. 8.-We proceeded to Bridport, a remarkably clean town, with the air so clear and pure, it seemed a new climate. Hence we set out, after dinner, for Lyme, and the road through which we travelled is the most beautiful to which my wandering destinies have yet sent me. It is diversified with all that can compose luxuriant scenery, and with just as much of the approach to sublime as is in the province of unterrific beauty. The hills are the highest, I fancy, in the south of this county–the boldest and noblest; the vales of the finest verdure, wooded and watered as if only to give ideas of finished landscapes; while the whole, from time to time, rises into still superior grandeur, by openings between the heights that terminate the View With the Splendour of the British channel.

There was no going on in the carriage through such enchanting scenes; we got out upon the hills, and walked till we could walk no longer. The descent down to Lyme is uncommonly steep; and indeed is very striking, from the magnificence of the ocean that washes its borders. Chidiock and Charmouth, two villages between Bridport and Lyme, are the very prettiest I have ever seen. During the whole of this post I was fairly taken away, not only from the world but from myself, and completely wrapped up and engrossed by the pleasures, wonders, and charms of animated nature, thus seen in fair perfection. Lyme. however, brought me to myself; for the part by the sea, where we fixed our abode, was so dirty and fishy that I rejoiced when we left it.

Aug. 9.- We travelled to Sidmouth. And here we have taken up our abode for a week. It was all devoted to rest and sea-air.

Sidmouth is built in a vale by the sea-coast, and the terrace for company is nearer to the ocean than any I have elsewhere seen, and therefore both more pleasant and more commodious. The little bay is of a most peaceful kind, and the sea was as calm and gentle as the Thames. I longed to bathe, but I am in no state now to take liberties with myself, and, having no advice at hand, I ran no risk.

SIDMOUTH LOYALTY.

Nothing has given me so much pleasure since I came to this place as our landlady's account of her own and her town's loyalty. She is a baker, a poor widow woman, she told us, who lost her husband by his fright in thinking he saw a ghost, just after her mother was drowned. She carries on the business, with the help of her daughter, a girl about fifteen.

I inquired of her if she had seen the royal family when they visited Devonshire? "Yes, sure, ma'am!" she cried; there was ne'er a soul left in all this place for going Out to See 'em. My daughter and I rode a double horse, and we went to Sir George Young's, and got into the park, for we knew the housekeeper, and she gave my daughter a bit to taste of the king's dinner when they had all done, and she said she might talk on it when she was a old woman."

I asked another good woman, who came in for some flour, if she had been of the party? "No," she said, "she was ill, but she had had holiday enough upon the king's recovery, for there was such a holiday then as the like was not in all England."

"Yes, sure, ma'am," cried the poor baker-woman, "we all did our best then for there was ne'er a town in all England like Sidmouth for rejoicing. Why, I baked a hundred and ten penny loaves for the poor, and so did every baker in town, and there's three, and the gentry subscribed for it. And the gentry roasted a bullock and cut it all up, and we all eat it, in the midst of the rejoicing. And then we had such a fine page 420 sermon, it made us all cry; there was a more tears shed than ever was known, all for over-joy. And they had the king drawed, and dressed up all in gold and laurels, and they put un in a coach and eight horses, and carried un about; and all the grand gentlemen in the town, and all abouts, come in their own carriages to join. And they had the finest band of music in all England singing 'God save the king,' and every Soul joined in the chorus, and all not so much because he was a king, but because they said a was such a worthy gentleman, and that the like of him was never known in this nation before: so we all subscribed for the illuminations for that reason, some a shilling, some a guinea, and some a penny,–for no one begrudged it, as a was such a worthy person."

This good Mrs. Dare has purchased images of all the royal family, in her great zeal, and I had them in my apartment–King, Queen, Prince of Wales, Dukes of York, Clarence, Kent, Sussex, Cumberland, and Cambridge; Princess Royal, and Princesses Augusta, Eliza, Mary, Sophia, and Amelia, God bless them all!

POWDERHAM CASTLE AND COLLUMPTON CHURCH.

Aug. 16.-We quitted Sidmouth, and proceeded through the finest country possible to Exmouth, to see that celebrated spot of beauty. The next morning we crossed the Ex and visited Powderham Castle. Its appearance, noble and antique without, loses all that character from French finery and minute elegance and gay trappings within. The present owner, Lord Courtney, has fitted it up in the true Gallic taste, and every room has the air of being ornamented for a gala. The housekeeper did not let us see half the castle; she only took us to those rooms which the present lord has modernized and fitted up in the sumptuous French taste ; the old part of the castle she doubtless thought would disgrace him; forgetting or rather never knowing–that the old part alone was worth a traveller's curiosity, since the rest might be anticipated by a visit to any celebrated cabinet-maker.

Thence we proceeded to Star Cross to dine; and saw on the opposite coast the house Of Sir Francis Drake, which was built by his famous ancestor. Here we saw a sight that reminded me of the drawings of Webber from the South Sea Isles; women scarce clothed at all, with feet and legs entirely naked, straw bonnets of uncouth Shapes tied on their heads, a

sort of man's jacket on their bodies, and their short coats pinned up in the form of concise trousers, very succinct! and a basket on each arm, strolling along with wide mannish strides to the borders of the river, gathering cockles. They looked, indeed, miserable and savage.

Hence we went, through very beautiful roads, to Exeter. That great old city is too narrow, too populous, too dirty, and too ill-paved, to meet with my applause. Next morning we breakfasted at Collumpton, and visited its church. Here we saw the remains of a once extremely rich gothic structure, though never large. There is all the appearance of its having been the church of an abbey before the Reformation. It is situated in a deep but most fertile vale; its ornaments still retain so much of gilding, painting, and antique splendour, as could never have belonged to a mere country church. The wood carving, too, though in ruins, is most laboriously well done; the roof worked in blue and gold, lighter, but in the style of the royal chapel at St. James's.We were quite surprised to find such a structure in a town so little known or named. One aisle was added by a clothier of the town in the reign of Edward VI.; probably upon its first being used as a protestant and public place of worship. This is still perfect, but very clumsy and inelegant compared with the ancient part. The man, to show he gloried in the honest profession whence he derived wealth for this good purpose, has his arms at one corner, with his name, J. Lane, in gothic characters, and on the opposite corner his image, terribly worked in the wall, with a pair of shears in one hand, so large as to cut across the figure downwards almost obscuring all but his feet. Till the cicerone explained this, I took the idea for a design of Death, placed where most conspicuously he might show himself, ready to cut in two the poor objects that entered the church.

GLASTONBURY ABBEY.

Aug. 19.-To vary the scenery we breakfasted at Bridgewater, in as much dirt and noise, from the judges filling the town, as at Taunton we had enjoyed neatness and quiet. We walked beside the river, which is navigable from the Bristol channel ; and a stream more muddy, and a quay more dirty and tarry and pitchy, I would not covet to visit again. It is here called the Perrot.

Thence, however, we proceeded to what made amends

all–the ruins of Glastonbury Abbey. These are the most elegant remains of monkish grandeur I have ever chanced to see,–the forms, designs, ornaments,—all that is left is in the highest perfection of gothic beauty. Five hundred souls, the people told us, were supported in this abbey and its cloisters.

A chapel of Joseph of Arimathea has the outworks nearly entire, and I was quite bewitched with their antique beauty. But the entrance into the main front of the abbey is stupendous; its height is such that the eye aches to look up at it, though it is now curtailed, by no part of its arch remaining except the first inclination towards that form, which shows it to have been the entrance. Not a bit of roof remains in any part. All the monuments that Were not utterly decayed or destroyed have been removed to Wells. Mere walls alone are left here, except the monks' kitchen. This is truly curious: it is a circular building, with a dome as high–higher I fancy–than the Pantheon's; four immense fireplaces divide it Into four parts at the bottom, and an oven still is visible. One statue is left in one niche, which the people about said was of the abbot's chief cook!

If this monastery was built by the famous old cruel hypocrite abbot, Dunstan, I shall grieve so much taste was bestowed on such a wretch.(347) We had only labourers for our informants. But one boy was worth hearing: he told me there was a well of prodigious depth, which he showed me, and this well had long been dried up, and so covered over as to be forgotten, till his grandfather dreamed a dream that the water of this well would restore him from a bad state of health to good; so he dug, and the well was found, and he drank the water and was cured! And since then the poor came from all parts who were afflicted with diseases, and drank the water and were cured. One woman was now at Glastonbury to try it, and already almost well! What strange inventions and superstitions even the ruins of what had belonged to St. Dunstan can yet engender! The Glastonbury thorn we forgot to ask for.

WELLS CATHEDRAL.

Hence we proceeded to Wells. Here we waited, as usual, upon the cathedral, which received our compliments with but

small return of civility. There was little to be seen without, except old monuments of old abbots removed from Glastonbury, so inferior in workmanship and design to the abbey once containing them, that I was rather displeased than gratified by the sight. They have also a famous clock, brought from the abbey at Its general demolition. This exhibits a set of horses with riders, who curvet a dance round a bell by the pulling a string, with an agility comic enough, and fitted to serve for a puppet-show; which, in all probability, was its design, in order to recreate the poor monks at their hours of play.

There is also a figure of St. Dunstan, who regularly strikes the quarters of every hour by clock-work, and who holds in his hand a pair of tongs–the same I suppose as those with which he was wont to pull the devil by the nose, in their nocturnal interviews.

The old castle of Wells is now the palace for the bishop. It is moated still, and looks dreary, Secluded, and in the bad old style.

At night, upon a deeply deliberate investigation in the medical way, it was suddenly resolved that we should proceed to Bath instead of Bristol, and that I should try there first the stream of King BladUd. So now, at this moment, here we are.

BATH REVISITED.

Queen Square, Bath, Aug. 20.–Bath is extremely altered since I last visited it. Its circumference is perhaps trebled but its buildings are so unfinished, so spread, so everywhere beginning and nowhere ending, that it looks rather like a space of ground lately fixed upon for erecting a town, than a town itself, of so many years' duration. It is beautiful and wonderful throughout. The hills are built up and down, and the vales so stocked with streets and houses, that, in some places, from the ground-floor on one side a street, you cross over to the attic of your opposite neighbour. The white stone, where clean, has a beautiful effect, and, even where worn, a grand one. But I must not write a literal Bath guide, and a figurative one Anstey (348) has all to himself. I will only tell you in brief, yet in truth, it looks a city of palaces, a town of hills, and a hill of towns.

O how have I thought, in patrolling it, Of my poor Mrs, Thrale! I went to look (and sigh at the sight) at the house on the North parade where we dwelt, and almost every Old place brings to my mind some scene in which we were engaged. Besides the constant sadness of all recollections that bring fresh to my thoughts a breach with a friend once so loved, how are most of the families altered and dispersed in these absent ten Years! From Mrs. Montagu's, Miss Gregory by a marriage disapproved, is removed for ever; from Mrs. Cholmley's, by the severer blow of death, Lady Mulgrave is separated; Mrs. Lambart, by the same blow, has lost the brother, Sir Philip Clerke, who brought us to her acquaintance; Mr. Bowdler and his excellent eldest daughter have yielded to the same stroke; Mrs. Byron has followed. Miss Leigh has been married and widowed; Lord Mulgrave has had the same hard lot; and, besides these, Mrs. Cotton, Mrs. Thrale's aunt, Lady Miller, and Mr. Thrale himself, are no more.

A VISIT FROM LADY SPENCER.

Aug. 31.-I found I had no acquaintance here, except Mr. Harrington, who is ill, Mrs. Hartley, who is too lame for visiting, and the Vanbrughs; and though Mrs. Ord, from her frequent residence here, knows many of the settled inhabitants, she has kindly complied with my request of being dispensed from making new visits.

Soon after we came, while I was finishing some letters, and quite alone, Mrs. Ord's servant brought me word Lady Spencer would ask me how I did, if I was well enough to receive her. Of course I begged she might come up-stairs. I have met her two or three times at my dearest Mrs. Delany's, where I met, also, with marked civilities from her. I knew she was here, with her unhappy daughter,–Lady Duncannon,(349) whom she assiduously nurses, aided by her more celebrated other daughter, the Duchess of Devonshire.

She made a very flattering apology for coming, and then began to converse upon my beloved Mrs. Delany, and thence to subjects more general. She is a sensible and sagacious character, intelligent, polite, and agreeable, and she spends her life in such exercises of active charity and zeal, that she would be one of the most exemplary women of rank of the age, had she less of show in her exertions, and more of forbearance in publishing them. My dear oracle, however, once said, vainglory must not be despised or discouraged, when it operated but as a human engine for great or good deeds.

She spoke of Lady Duncannon's situation with much sorrow, and expatiated upon her resignation to her fate, her prepared state for death, and the excellence of her principles, with an eagerness and feeling that quite overwhelmed me with surprise and embarrassment. Her other daughter she did not mention; but her grand-daughter, Lady Georgiana Cavendish, she spoke of with rapture. Miss Trimmer, also, the eldest daughter of the exceeding worthy Mrs. Trimmer, she named with a regard that seemed quite affectionate. She told me she had the care of the young Lady Cavendishes, but was in every respect treated as if one of themselves.

BATH SUNDAY SCHOOLS.

The name of Mrs. Trimmer led us to talk of the Sunday schools and Schools of Industry. They are both in a very flourishing state at Bath, and Lady Spencer has taken one school under her own immediate patronage. The next day, of course, I waited on her - she was out. But the following day, which was Sunday,, she sent me a message up-stairs to say she would take me to see the Sunday-school, if I felt well enough to desire it. She waited below for my answer, which, of course, I carried down in my proper person, ready hatted and cloaked.

It was a most interesting sight. Such a number of poor innocent children, all put into a way of right, most taken immediately from every way of wrong, lifting Up their little hands, and joining in those prayers and supplications for mercy and grace, which, even if they understand not, must at least impress them with a general idea of religion, a dread of evil, and a love of good ; it was, indeed, a sight to expand the best hopes of the heart.

I felt very much obliged to my noble conductress, with whom I had much talk upon the subject in our walk back. Her own little school, of course, engaged us the most. She told me that the next day six of her little girls were to be new clothed, by herself, in honour of the birthday of the Duke of Devonshire's second daughter, Lady Harriot Cavendish, who

was to come to her grandmamma's house to see the ceremony. To this sight she also Invited me, and I accepted her kindness with pleasure.

The following day, therefore, Monday, I obeyed Lady Spencer's time, and at six o'clock was at her house in Gay-street. Lady Spencer had Mrs. Mary Pointz and Miss Trimmer with her; and the six children, just prepared for Lady Harriot, in their new gowns, were dismissed from their examination, upon my arrival, and sent down-stairs to Wait the coming of her little ladyship, who, having dined with her mamma, was later than her appointment.

Lady Georgiana is just eight Years old. She has a fine, animated, sweet, and handsome countenance, and the form and figure of a girl of ten or twelve years of age. Lady Harriot, who this day was six Years old, is by no means so handsome, but has an open and pleasing countenance, and a look of the most happy disposition. Lady Spencer brought her to me immediately. I inquired after the young Marquis of Hartington. Lady Spencer told me they never trusted him from the Upper walks, near his house, in Marlborough-buildings. He has a house of his own near the duke's, and a carriage entirely to himself; but YOU will see the necessity of these appropriations, when I remind You he is now fourteen months old.

Lady Spencer had now a lottery--without blanks, you Will suppose- -of playthings and toys for the children. She distributed the prizes, and Lady Duncannon held the tickets. During this entered Lord Spencer, the son of Lady Spencer, who was here only for three days, to see his sister Duncannon. They had all dined with the little Lady Harriot. The duke is now at Chatsworth, in Derbyshire.

I thought of Lord Spencer's kindness to Charles, and I recollected he was a favourite of Mr. Windham. I saw him, therefore, with very different ideas to those raised by the sight of his poor sister Duncannon, to whom he made up with every mark of pitying affection; she, meanwhile, receiving him with the most expressive pleasure, though nearly silent. I could not help feeling touched, in defiance of all obstacles.

Presently followed two ladies. Lady Spencer, with a look and manner warmly announcing pleasure in what she was doing, then introduced me to the first of them, saying, "Duchess of Devonshire, Miss Burney."

She made me a very civil compliment upon hoping my
Page 427-
health was recovering, and Lady Spencer then, shortly, and as if unavoidably, said, "Lady Elizabeth Foster."

I have neglected to mention, in its place, that the six poor little girls had a repast in the garden, and Lady Georgiana earnestly begged leave to go down and see and speak with them. She applied to Lady Spencer. "O grandmamma," she cried, "pray let me go! Mamma says it all depends upon you." The duchess expressed some fear lest there might be any illness or disorder among the poor things: Lady Spencer answered for them; and Lady Georgiana, with a sweet delight, flew down into the garden, all the rest accompanying, and Lady Spencer and the duchess soon following. It was a beautiful sight, taken in all its dependencies, from the windows. Lord Spencer presently joined them,

GEORGIANA, DUCHESS OF DEVONSHIRE

To return to the duchess. I did not find so much beauty in her as I expected, notwith-standing the variations of accounts; but I found far more of manner, politeness, and gentle quiet. She seems by nature to possess the highest animal spirits, but she appeared to me not happy. I thought she looked oppressed within, though there is a native cheerfulness about her which I fancy scarce ever deserts her. There is in her face, especially when she speaks, a sweetness of good-humour and obligingness, that seem to be the natural and instinctive qualities of her disposition; joined to an openness of countenance that announces her endowed, by nature, with a character intended wholly for honesty, fairness, and good purposes.

She now conversed with me wholly, and in so soberly sensible and quiet a manner, as I had imagined incompatible with her powers. Too much and too little credit have variously been given her. About me and my health she was more civil than I can well tell you; not from prudery--I have none, in these records, methinks!- -but from its being mixed into all that passed. We talked over my late tour, Bath waters, and the king's illness. This, which was led to by accident, was here a tender Subject, considering her heading the Regency squadron; however, I have only one line to pursue, and from that I can never vary. I spoke of my own deep distress from his sufferings without reserve, and of the distress of the queen with the most avowed compassion and respect. She was extremely well-bred in all she said herself, and seemed willing

to keep up the subject. I fancy no one has just in the same way treated it with her grace before; however, she took all in good part, though to have found me retired in discontent had perhaps been more congenial to her. But I have been sedulous to make them all know the contrary. Nevertheless, as I am eager to be considered apart from all party, I was much pleased, after all this, to have her express herself very desirous to keep up Our acquaintance, ask many questions as to the chance of my remaining in Bath, most politely hope to profit from it, and, finally, inquire my direction.

Lady Elizabeth (Foster] has the character of being so alluring that Mrs. Holroyd told me it was the opinion Of Mr. Gibbon no man could withstand her, and that, if she chose to beckon the lord chancellor from his woolsack, in full sight of the world, he could not resist obedience!(350)

BISHOP PERCY.

Not long after our settling at Bath, I found, upon returning from the Pump-room, cards left for me of the Bishop of Dromore (Dr. Percy), Mrs. and the Miss Percys. I had met them formerly once at Miss Reynolds's, and once Visited them when Dr. Percy was Dean of Carlisle. The collector and editor of the beautiful reliques of ancient English poetry, I could not but be happy to again see. I returned the visit: they were out; but the bishop soon after came when I was at home. I had a pleasant little chat with him. The bishop is perfectly easy and unassuming, very communicative, and, though not very entertaining because too prolix, he is otherwise intelligent and of good commerce. Mrs. Percy is ill, and cannot make visits, though she sends her name and receives company at home. She is very uncultivated and ordinary in manners and conversation, but a good creature and much delighted to talk over the royal family, to one of whom she was formerly a nurse.

THE DUCHESS OF DEVONSHIRE AGAIN.

Three days before we left Bath, as I was coming with Mrs. Ord from the Pump-room, we encountered a chair from

which a lady repeatedly kissed her hand and bowed to me. I was too nearsighted to distinguish who she was, till, coming close, and a little stopped by more people, she put her face to the glass, and said "How d'ye do? How d'ye do?" and I recollected the Duchess of Devonshire.

About an hour after I had again the honour of a visit from her, and with Lady dowager Spencer. I was luckily at home alone, Mrs Ord having dedicated the rest of the morning to her own visits. I received them, therefore, with great pleasure. I now saw the duchess far more easy and lively in her spirits, and, consequently, far more lovely in her person. Vivacity is so much her characteristic, that her style of beauty requires it indispensably; the beauty, indeed, dies away without it. I now saw how her fame for personal charms had been obtained; the expression of her smiles is so very sweet, and has an ingenuousness and openness so singular, that, taken in those moments, not the most rigid critic could deny the justice of her personal celebrity. She was quite gay, easy, and charming: indeed, that last epithet might have been coined for her.

This has certainly been a singular acquaintance for me that the first visit I should make after leaving the queen should be to meet the head of the opposition public, the Duchess of Devonshire!

DR. BURNEY'S CONVERSATION WITH MR. BURKE: REMARKS BY Miss BURNEY.

"I [Dr. Burney] dined with Sir Joshua last week, and met Mr. Burke, his brother, Mr. Malone, the venerable Bishop of St. Pol de L'eonn, and a French abb'e or chevalier. I found Mr. Burke in the room on my arrival, and after the first very cordial civilities were over, he asked me, with great eagerness, whether I thought he might go in his present dress to pay his respects to Miss Burney, and was taking up his hat, till I told you were out of town. He imagined, I Suppose, you were in St. Martin's-street, where he used to call upon you. In talking over your health, the recovery of your liberty and of society, he said, if Johnson had been alive, your history would Page 430

have furnished him with an additional and interesting article to his 'Vanity of Human Wishes.' He said he had never been more mistaken in his life. He thought the queen had never behaved more amiably, or shown more good sense, than in appropriating you to her service; but what a service had it turned out!–a confinement to such a companion as Mrs. Schwellenberg!–Here exclamations of severity and kindness in turn lasted a considerable time."

If ever I see Mr. Burke where he speaks to me upon the subject, I will openly confide to him how impossible it was that the queen should conceive the subserviency expected, unjustly and unwarrantably, by Mrs. Schwellenberg: to whom I ought only to have belonged officially, and at official hours, unless the desire of further intercourse had been reciprocal. The queen had imagined that a younger and more lively colleague would have made her faithful old servant happier and that idea was merely amiable in her majesty, who could not Suspect the misery inflicted on that poor new colleague,

LITERARY RECREATION.

Chelsea College, October-.-I have never been so pleasantly situated at home since I lost the sister of my heart and my most affectionate Charlotte. My father is almost constantly Within. Indeed, I now live with him wholly ; he has himself appropriated me a place, a seat, a desk, a table, and every convenience and comfort, and he never seemed yet so earnest to keep me about him. We read together, write together,- chat, compare notes, communicate projects, and diversify each other's employments. He is all goodness, gaiety, and affection; and his society and kindness are more precious to Me than ever. Fortunately, in this season of leisure and comfort, the spirit of composition proves active. The day is never long enough, and I Could employ two pens almost incessantly, in my scribbling what will not be repressed. This is a delight to my dear father inexpressibly great and though I have gone no further than to let him know, from time to time, the species of matter that occupies me, he is perfectly contented, and patiently waits till something is quite finished, before he insists upon reading a word. This "suits my humour well," as my own industry is all gone when once its intent is produced.

For the rest I have been going on with my third tragedy.

I have two written, but never yet have had opportunity to read them; which, of course, prevents their being corrected to the best of my power, and fitted for the perusal of less indulgent eyes; or rather of eyes less prejudiced.

Believe me, my dear friends, in the present composed and happy state of my mind, I Could never have suggested these tales; but, having only to correct, combine, contract, and finish, I will not leave them undone. Not, however, to sadden myself to the same point in which I began them, I read more than I write, and call for happier themes from others, to enliven my mind from the dolorous sketches I now draw of my Own.

The library or study, in which we constantly sit, supplies such delightful variety of food, that I have nothing to wish. Thus, my beloved sisters and friends, you see me, at length, enjoying all that peace, ease, and chosen recreation and employment, for which so long I sighed in vain, and which, till very lately, I had reason to believe, even since attained, had been allowed me too late. I am more and more thankful every night, every morning, for the change in my destiny, and present blessings of my lot ; and you, my beloved Susan and Fredy, for whose prayers I have so often applied in my sadness, suffering, and despondence, afford me now the same community of thanks and acknowledgments.

SIR JOSHUA REYNOLDs's BLINDNESS.

November.-Another evening my father took me to Sir Joshua Reynolds. I had long languished to see that kindly zealous friend, but his ill health had intimidated me rom making the attempt; and now my dear father went up stairs alone, and inquired of Miss Palmer if her uncle was well enough to admit me. He returned for me immediately. I felt the utmost pleasure in again mounting his staircase.

Miss Palmer hastened forward and embraced me most cordially. I then shook hands with Sir Joshua. He had a bandage over one eye, and the other shaded with a green halfbonnet. He seemed serious even to sadness, though extremely kind. "I am very glad," he said, in a meek voice and dejected accent, "to see you again, and I wish I could see you better! but I have only one eye now,–and hardly that."

I was really quite touched. The expectation of total blind-

ness depresses him inexpressibly; not, however, inconceivably I hardly knew how to express either my concern for his altered situation since our meeting, or my joy in again being with him: but my difficulty was short; Miss Palmer eagerly drew me to herself, and recommended to Sir Joshua to go on with his cards. He had no spirit to oppose; probably, indeed, no inclination.

One other time we called again, in a morning. Sir Joshua and his niece were alone, and that invaluable man was even more dejected than before. How grievous to me It is to see him thus changed!(352)

AMONG OLD FRIENDS.

December.-I most gladly accepted an invitation to my good Mrs. Ord, to meet a circle of old friends. The day proved extremely pleasant. We went to dinner, my father and I, and met Mrs. Montagu, in good spirits, and very unaffectedly agreeable. No one was there to awaken ostentation, no new acquaintance to require any surprise from her powers; she was therefore natural and easy, as well as informing and entertaining.

Mrs. Garrick embraced me again and again, to express a satisfaction in meeting me once more in this social way, that she would have thought it indecorous to express by words. I thanked her exactly in the same language ; and, without a syllable being uttered, she said, "I rejoice you are no longer a courtier!" and I answered, "I love you dearly for preferring me in my old state!"

In the evening we were joined by Lady Rothes,(353) with whom I had my peace to make for a long-neglected letter upon my

"restoration to society," as she termed it, and who was very lively and pleasant. . .
.

Mr. Pepys, who came just at that instant from Twickenham, which he advanced eagerly to tell me, talked of Mr. Cambridge, and his admirable wit and spirits, and Miss Cambridge, and her fervent friendship for me, and the charm and agreeability of the whole house, with an ardour so rapid, there scarce needed any reply.

Mr. Batt gave me a most kindly congratulatory bow upon his entrance. I knew his opinion of my retreat, and understood it: but I was encircled till the concluding part of the evening by the Pepys and Lady Rothes, etc.; and then Mr. Batt seated himself by my elbow, and began. "How I rejoice," he cried, "to see you at length out of thraldom!"

"Thraldom?" quoth I, "that's rather a strong word! I assure you 'tis the first time I have heard it pronounced full and plumply."

"O, but," cried he, laughing, "I may be allowed to say so, because you know my principles. You know me to be loyal; you could not stand it from an opposition-man– but saints may do much!"

He is a professed personal friend of Mr. Pitt.

I then began some exculpation of my late fatigues, assuring him they were the effect of a situation not understood, and not of any hardness of heart.

"Very probably," cried he; "but I am glad you have ended them: I applaud–I honour the step you have taken. Those who suffer, yet still continue in fetters, I never pity;–there is a want of integrity, as well as spirit, in such submission."

"Those they serve," cried I, "are not the persons to blame; they are commonly uninformed there is anything to endure, and believe all is repaid by the smiles so universally solicited."

"I know it," cried he; "and it is that general base subservience that makes me struck with your opposite conduct."

"My conduct," quoth I, "was very simple; though I believe it did not the less surprise; but it all consisted in not pretending, when I found myself sinking, to be swimming."

He said many other equally good-natured things, and finished them with "But what a pleasure it is to me to see you here in this manner, dressed no more than other people! I have not seen you these five years past but looking dressed out for the Drawing-room, or something as bad!"

A SUMMONS FROM THE QUEEN.

January.-I had a very civil note from Mrs. Schwellenberg telling me that Miss Goldsworthy was ill, which made Miss Gomme necessary to the princesses, and therefore, as Mlle. Jacobi was still lame, her majesty wished for my attendance On Wednesday noon. I received this little summons with very sincere pleasure, and sent a warm acknowledgment for its honour. I was engaged for the evening to Mr. Walpole, now Lord Orford, by my father, who promised to call for me at the Queen's house.

At noon I went thither, and saw, by the carriages, their majesties were just arrived from Windsor. In my way upstairs I encountered the Princess Sophia. I really felt a pleasure at her sight, so great that I believe I saluted her ; I hardly know ; but she came forward, with her hands held out, so good humoured and so sweetly, I was not much on my guard. How do I wish I had gone that moment to my royal mistress, while my mind was fully and honestly occupied with the most warm satisfaction in being called again into her presence!

The Princess Sophia desired me to send her Miss Gomme, whom she said I should find in my own room. Thither I went, and we embraced very cordially; but she a little made me stare by saying, "Do you sleep in your old bed?" "No," I answered, "I go home after dinner," and she said no more, but told me she must have two hours conference alone with me, from the multiplicity of things she had to discuss with me.

We parted then, and I proceeded to Mrs. Schwellenberg. There I was most courteously received, and told I was to go at night to the play. I replied I was extremely sorry, but I was engaged. She looked deeply displeased, and I was forced to offer to send an excuse. Nothing, however, was settled; she went to the queen, whither I was most eager to follow, but I depended upon her arrangement, and could not go uncalled.

I returned to my own room, as they still call it, and Miss Gomme and Miss Planta both came to me. We had a long discourse upon matters and things. By and by Miss Gomme was called out to Princesses Mary and Amelia; she told them who was in the old apartment, and they instantly entered it. Princess Mary took my hand, and said repeatedly, "My dear Miss Burney, how glad I am to see you again!" and the lovely little Princess Amelia kissed me twice, with the sweetest air of affection. This was a very charming meeting to me, and I expressed my real delight in being thus allowed to come amongst them again, in the strongest and truest terms.

I had been but a short time alone, when Westerhaults came to ask me if I had ordered my father's carriage to bring me from the play. I told him I was engaged but would give up that engagement, and endeavour to secure being fetched home after the play.

Mrs. Schwellenberg then desired to see me. "What you mean by going home?" cried she, somewhat deridingly: "know you not you might sleep here?"

I was really thunderstruck; so weak still, and so unequal as I feel to undertake night and morning attendance, which I now saw expected. I was obliged, however, to comply; and I wrote a note to Sarah, and another note to be given to my father, when he called to take me to Lord Orford. But I desired we might go in chairs, and not trouble him for the carriage.

This arrangement, and my dread of an old attendance I was so little fitted for renewing, had so much disturbed me before I was summoned to the queen, that I appeared before her without any of the glee and spirits with which I had originally obeyed her commands. I am still grieved at this circumstance, as it must have made me seem cold and insensible to herself, when I was merely chagrined at the peremptory mismanagement of her agent. Mr. de Luc was with her. She was gracious, but by no means lively or cordial. She was offended, probably,–and there was no reason to wonder, and yet no means to clear away the cause. This gave me much vexation, and the more I felt it the less I must have appeared to merit her condescension.

Nevertheless, after she was dressed she honoured me with a summons to the White closet, where I presently felt as much at home as if I had never quitted the royal residence. She inquired into my proceedings, and I began a little history of my south-west tour,- which she listened to till word was brought the king was come from the levee: dinner was then ordered, and I was dismissed.

At our dinner, the party, in the old style, was -Mr. de Luc, Miss Planta, Mrs. Stainforth, and Miss Gomme; Mrs. Schwellenberg was not well enough to leave her own apartment, except to attend the queen. We were gay enough, I own my spirits were not very low in finding myself a guest at that table, where

I was so totally unfit to be at home, and whence, nevertheless,; I should have been very much and deeply concerned to have found myself excluded, since the displeasure of the queen could alone have procured such a banishment. Besides, to visit, I like the whole establishment, however inadequate I found them for supplying the place of all I quitted to live among them. O, who could succeed there?

During the dessert the Princess Elizabeth came into the T room. I was very glad, by this means, to see all this lovely female tribe. As soon as she was gone I made off to prepare for the play, with fan, cloak-, and gloves. At the door of my new old room who should I encounter but Mr. Stanhope? He was all rapture, in his old way, at the meeting, and concluded me, I believe, reinstated. I got off as fast as Possible, and had just shut myself in, and him out, when I heard the voice of the king, who passed my door to go to the dining-room.

I was quite chagrined to have left it so unseasonably, as my whole heart yearned to see him. He stayed but a minute, and I heard him stop close to my door, and speak with Mr. de Luc. The loudness of his voice assuring me he was saying nothing he meant to be unheard, I could not resist softly opening my door. I fancy he expected this, for he came up to me immediately, and with a look of goodness almost amounting to pleasure–I believe I may say quite–he inquired after my health, and its restoration, and said he was very glad to see me again. Then turning gaily to Mr. de Luc, "And you, Mr. de Luc," he cried, "are not you, too, very glad to see Miss Beurni again?"

I told him, very truly, the pleasure with which I had reentered his roof.–He made me stand near a lamp, to examine me, and pronounced upon my amended looks with great benevolence: and, when he was walking away, said aloud to Mr. de Luc, who attended him, "I dare say she was very willing to come!"

Our party in the box for the queen's attendants consisted of Lady Catherine Stanhope, Miss Planta, Major Price, Greville Upton, and Mr. Frank Upton. The king and queen and six princesses sat opposite. It was to me a lovely and most charming sight. The Prince of Wales, and the Duke of York and his bride, with the Duke of Clarence, sat immediately under us. I saw the duchess now and then, and saw that she has a very sensible and marked countenance, but no beauty.

Page 437 She was extremely well received by the people, and smiled at in the most pleasing manner by her opposite new relations.

At night I once more attended the queen, and it seemed as strange to me as if I had never done it before. The next day, Thursday, the queen gave up the Drawing-room, on account of a hurt on her foot. I had the honour of another very long conference in the White closet, in which I finished the account of my late travels, and during which, though she was very gracious, she was far less communicative than heretofore, saying little herself, and making me talk almost all. When I attended the queen again to-night, the strangeness was so entirely worn away, that it seemed to me as if I had never left my office! And so again on Friday morning

At noon the royal family set off for Windsor.

The queen graciously sent for me before she went, to bid me good- bye, and condescended to thank me for my little services. I would have offered repetition with all my heart, but I felt my frame unequal to such business. Indeed I was half dead with only two days' and nights' exertion. 'Tis amazing how I ever went through all that is passed.

MR. HASTINGS'S DEFENCE.

Feb. 13.-I found a note from Mrs. Schwellenberg, with an offer of a ticket for Mr. Hastings's trial, the next day, if I wished to go to it. I did wish it exceedingly, no public subject having ever so deeply interested me; but I could not recollect any party I could join, and therefore I proposed to Captain Phillips to call on his Court friend, and lay before her my difficulty. He readily declared he would do more, for he would frankly ask her for a ticket for himself, and stay another day, merely to accompany me. You know well the kind pleasure and zeal with which he is always ready to discover and propose expedients in distress. His visit prospered, and we went to Westminster Hall together.

All the managers attended at the opening, but the attendance of all others was cruelly slack. To hear the attack, the people came in crowds; to hear the defence, they scarcely came in t'ete- 'a-t'etes! 'Tis barbarous there should be so much more pleasure given by the recital of guilt than by the vindication of innocence!

Mr. Law(354) spoke the whole time; he made a general harangue

in answer to the opening general harangue of Mr. Burke, and he spoke many things that brought forward conviction in favour of Mr. Hastings; but he was terrified exceedingly, and this timidity Induced him to so frequently beg quarter from his antagonists, both for any blunders and any deficiencies, that I felt angry with even modest egotism, when I considered that it was rather his place to come forward with the shield and armour of truth, undaunted, and to have defied, rather than deprecated, the force of talents when without such support.

None of the managers quitted their box, and I am uncertain whether or not any of them saw me. Mr. Windham, in particular, I feel satisfied either saw me not, or was so circumstanced, as manager, that he could not come to speak with me; for else, this my first appearance from the parental roof under which he has so largely contributed to replace me would have been the last time for his dropping my acquaintance. Mr.

Sheridan I have no longer any ambition to be noticed by; and Mr. Burke, at this place, I am afraid I have already displeased, so unavoidably cold and frigid did I feel myself when he came here to me formerly. Anywhere else, I should bound forward to meet him, with respect, and affection, and gratitude.

In the evening I went to the queen's house. I found Mrs, Schwellenberg, who instantly admitted me, at cards with Mr. de Luc. Her reception was perfectly kind; and when I would have given up the tickets, she told me they were the queen's, who desired, if I wished it, I would keep them for the season. This was a pleasant hearing upon every account, and I came away in high satisfaction.

A few days after, I went again to the trial, and took another captain for my esquire— my good and ever-affectionate James. The Hall was still more empty, both of Lords and Commons, and of ladies too, than the first day of this session. I am quite shocked at the little desire there appears to hear Mr. Hastings's defence.

DIVERSE VIEWS.

When the managers entered, James presently said, "Here's Mr. Windham coming to speak to you." And he broke from the procession, as it was descending to its cell, to give me that pleasure.

His inquiries about my health were not, as he said, merely common inquiries, but, without any other answer to them than a bow, I interrupted their course by quickly saying, "You

have been excursioning and travelling all the world o'er since I saw you last."

He paid me in my own coin with only a bow, hastily going back to myself: "But your tour," he cried, "to the west, after all that-"

I saw what was following, and, again abruptly stopping him, "But here you are returned," I cried, "to all your old labours and toils again."

"No, no," cried he, half laughing, "not labours and toils always; they are growing into pleasures now."

"That's being very good, very liberal, indeed," quoth I, supposing him to mean hearing the defence made the pleasure but he stared at me with so little concurrence, that, soon understanding he only meant bringing their charges home to the confusion of the culprit, I stared again a little while, and then said, "You sometimes accuse me of being ambiguous; I think you seem so yourself, now!"

"To nobody but you," cried he, with a rather reproachful accent. "O, now," cried I, "you are not ambiguous, and I am all the less pleased."

"People," cried James, bonnement, "don't like to be convinced."

"Mr. Hastings," said Mr. Windham, "does not convince, he does not bring conviction home."

"Not to you," quoth I, returning his accent pretty fully,

"Why, true," answered he very candidly; "there may be something in that."

"How is it all to be?" cried James. "Is the defence to go on long, and are they to have any evidence; or how?"

"We don't know this part of the business," said Mr. Windham, smiling a little at such an upright downright question "it is Mr. Hastings's affair now to settle it: however, I understand he means to answer charge after charge as they were brought against him, first by speeches, then by evidence: however, this is all conjecture."

MR. LAW'S SPEECH DISCUSSED.

We then spoke of Mr. Law, Mr. Hastings's first counsel, and I expressed some dissatisfaction that such attackers should not have had abler and more equal opponents.

"But do you not think Mr. Law spoke well?" cried he, "clear, forcible? "

"Not forcible," cried I. I would not say not clear.

"He was frightened," said Mr. Windham, "he might not do himself justice. I have heard him elsewhere, and been very well satisfied with him; but he looked pale and alarmed, and his voice trembled."

"I was very well content with his materials," quoth I, "which I thought much better than the use he made of them; and once or twice, he made an opening that, with a very little skill, might most adroitly and admirably have raised a laugh against you all."

He looked a little askew, I must own, but he could not help smiling. . . I gave him an instance in point, which -was the reverse given by Mr. Law to the picture drawn by Mr. Burke of Tamerlane, in which he said those virtues and noble qualities bestowed upon him by the honourable manager were nowhere to be found but on the British stage.

Now this, seriously, with a very little ingenuity, might have placed Mr. Burke at the head of a company of comedians. This last notion I did not speak, however; but enough was understood, and Mr. Windham looked straight away from me, without answering; nevertheless, his profile, which he left me, showed much more disposition to laugh than to be incensed.

Therefore I proceeded ; pointing out another lost opportunity that, well saved, might have proved happily ridiculous against them; and this was Mr. Law's description of the real state of India, even from its first discovery by Alexander, opposed to Mr. Burke's flourishing representation, of its golden age, its lambs and tigers associating, etc.

Still he looked askew ; but I believe he is truth itself, for he offered no defence, though, of course, he would not enter into the attack. And surely at this critical period I must not spare pointing out all he will submit to hear, on the side of a man of whose innocence I am so fully persuaded.

"I must own, however," continued I, finding him still attentive, though silent, "Mr. Law provoked me in one point–his apologies for his own demerits. Why should he contribute his humble mite to your triumphs? and how little was it his place to extol your superior talents, as if you were not self-sufficient enough already, without his aid."

'Unless you had heard the speech of Mr. Law, you can hardly

imagine with what timid flattery he mixed every exertion he ventured to make in behalf of his client ; and I could not forbear this little observation, because I had taken notice with what haughty derision the managers had perceived the fears of their importance, which were felt even by the very counsel of their prisoner. Mr. Windham, too, who himself never looks either insolent or deriding, must be sure what I meant for his associates could not include himself. He did not, however, perfectly welcome the remark; he still only gave me his profile, and said not a word,-so I went on. Mr. Hastings little thinks what a pleader I am become in his cause, against one of his most powerful adversaries.

"There was still another thing," quoth I, "in which I felt vexed with Mr. Law: how could he be so weak as to beg quarter from you, and to humbly hope that, if any mistake, any blunder, any improvident word escaped him, you would have the indulgence to spare your ridicule? O yes, to be sure! when I took notice at the moment of his supplication, and before any error committed, that every muscle of every face, amongst you was at work from the bare suggestion."

He could not even pretend to look grave now, but, turning frankly towards me, said, "Why, Mr. Fox most justly observed upon that petition, that, if any man makes a blunder, a mistake, 'tis very well to apologize: but it was singular to hear a man gravely preparing for his blunders and mistakes, and wanting to make terms for them beforehand."

"I like him for this," cried James again bonnement, "that he seems so much interested for his client."

"Will you give me leave to inquire," quoth I, "one thing? You know my old knack of asking strange questions."

He only bowed–archly enough, I assure you. "

Did I fancy, or was it fact, that you were a flapper to Mr. Burke, when Mr. Law charged him with disingenuity, in not having recanted the accusation concerning Devy Sing? He appeared to me in much perturbation, and I thought by his see-saw he was going to interrupt the speech: did you prevent him?"

"No, no," he answered, "I did not: I did not think him in any danger."

He rubbed his cheek, though, as he spoke, as if he did not much like that circumstance. O that Mr. Burke–so great, so noble a creature–can in this point thus have been warped.

MR. WINDHAM ON THE FRENCH NATIONAL ASSEMBLY.

I ran off to another scene, and inquired how he had been amused abroad, and, in particular, at the National Assembly?

"Indeed," he answered, "it was extremely curious for a short time; but there is little variety in it, and therefore it will not do long."

I was in a humour to be just as sincere here, as about the trial; so you democrats must expect no better.

"I understand," quoth I, "there is a great dearth of abilities in this new Assembly; how then should there be any variety?"

"No, I cannot say that: they do not want abilities; but they have no opportunity to make their way."

"O!" quoth I, shaking my wise head, "abilities, real abilities, make their own way."

"Why, that's true; but, in that Assembly, the noise, the tumult– "

"Abilities," again quoth I, " "have power to quell noise and tumult."

"Certainly, in general; but not in France. These new legislative members are so solicitous to speak, so anxious to be heard, that they prefer uttering any tautology to listening to others; and when once they have begun, they go on with what speed they may, and without selection, rather than stop. They see so many ready to seize their first pause, they know they have so little chance of a second hearing, that I never entered the Assembly without being reminded of the famous old story of the man who patiently bore hearing a tedious harangue, by saying the whole time to himself, 'Well, well, 'tis his turn now; but let him beware how he sneezes."'

"A BARBAROUS BUSINESS!"

James now again asked some question of their intentions with regard to the progress of the trial. He answered, "We have nothing to do with its present state. We leave Mr. Hastings now to himself, and his own set. Let him keep to his cause, and he may say what he will. We do not mean to interfere, nor avail ourselves of our privileges."

Mr. Hastings was just entered; I looked down at him, and saw his half-motion to kneel; I could not bear it, and, turning suddenly to my neighbour, "O, Mr. Windham," I cried, "after

all, 'tis, indeed, a barbarous business!" This was rather further than I meant to go, for I said it with serious earnestness; but it was surprised from me by the emotion always excited at sight of that unmerited humiliation.

He looked full at me upon this solemn attack, and with a look of chagrin amounting to displeasure, saying, "It is a barbarous business we have had to go through."

I did not attempt to answer this, for, except through the medium of sport and raillery, I have certainly no claim upon his patience. But, in another moment, in a tone very flattering, he said, "I do not understand, nor can any way imagine, how you can have been thus perverted!"

"No, no!" quoth I, "it is you who are perverted!"

Here Mr. Law began his second oration, and Mr. Windham ran down to his cell. I fancy this was not exactly the conversation he expected upon my first enlargement. However, though it would very seriously grieve me to hurt or offend him, I cannot refuse my own veracity, nor Mr. Hastings's injuries, the utterance of what I think truth.

Mr. Law was far more animated and less frightened, and acquitted himself so as to merit almost as much 'eloge as, in my opinion, he had merited censure at the opening. It was all in answer to Mr. Burke's general exordium and attack.

DEATH OF SIR JOSHUA REYNOLDS.

Upon the day of Sir Joshua Reynolds's death(355) I was in my bed, with two blisters, and I did not hear of it till two days after. I shall enter nothing upon this Subject here; our current letters mentioned the particulars, and I am not desirous to retrace them. His loss is as universally felt as his merit is universally acknowledged, and, joined to all public motives, I had myself private ones of regret that cannot subside. He was always peculiarly kind to me, and he had worked at my deliverance from a life he conceived too laborious for me as if I had been his own daughter; yet, from the time of my coming forth, I only twice saw him. I had not recovered strength for visiting before he was past receiving me. I grieve inexpressibly never to have been able to make him the small tribute of thanks for his most kind exertions in my cause. I little thought the second time I saw him would be my last opportunity, and my intention was to wait some favourable opening.

Miss Palmer is left heiress,(356) and her unabating attendance upon her inestimable uncle in his sickroom makes everybody content with her great acquisition. I am sure she loved and admired him with all the warmth of her warm heart. I wrote her a few lines of condolence, and she has sent me a very kind answer. She went immediately to the Burkes, with whom she will chiefly, I fancy, associate.

March.-Sad for the loss of Sir Joshua, and all of us ill ourselves, we began this month. Upon its 3rd day was his funeral.(357) My dear father could not attend; but Charles was invited and went. All the Royal Academy, professors and students, and all the Literary club, attended as family, mourners. Mr. Burke, Mr. Malone, and Mr. Metcalf, are executors. Miss Palmer has spared nothing, either in thought or expense, that could render the last honours splendid and grateful. It was a very melancholy day to us; though it had the alleviation and softening of a letter from our dear Charlotte, promising to arrive the next day.

MR. WINDHAM TWITTED ON His LACK OF COMPASSION.

April 23.–I thought myself equal to again going to the trial, which recommenced, after six or seven weeks' cessation, on account of the judges going the circuit. Sarah went with me: I am now so known in the chamberlain's box that the door-keepers and attendants make way for me without looking at my ticket. And to be sure, the managers on one side, and Mr. Hastings's friends and counsel on the other, must pretty well have my face by heart. I have the faces of all them, most certainly, in full mental possession; and the figures of many whose names I know not are so familiar to my eyes, that should I chance hereafter to meet them, I shall be apt to take them for old acquaintances.

There was again a full appearance of managers to accompany

Mr. Burke in his entry; and again Mr. Windham quitted the procession, as it descended to the box, and filed off to speak with me.

He made the most earnest inquiries after the health of my dearest father, as well as after my own. He has all the semblance of real regard and friendship for us, and I am given to believe he wears no semblance that has not a real and sympathetic substance couched beneath. His manner instantly revived in my mind my intent not to risk, with him, the loss of making those poor acknowledgments for his kindness, that I so much regret omitting to Sir Joshua Reynolds. In return to his inquiries about my renovating health, I answered that I had again been very ill since I saw him last, and added, "Indeed, I believe I did not come away too soon."

" And now," cried I, "I cannot resist giving myself the pleasure of making my acknowledgments for what I owe to you upon this subject. I have been, indeed, very much obliged, by various things that have come round to me, both to you and Sir Joshua.–O what a loss is that!"

"What a wretched loss!" cried he: and we then united our warmest suffrages in his favour, with our deepest regret for our deprivation. Here I observed poor Mr. Hastings was brought in. I saw he was fixing him.

"And can you," I cried, fixing him, "can you have so much compassion for one captive, and still have none for another?"

"Have you, then, still," cried he, "the same sentiments?"

"Have you," cried I, "heard all thus far of the defence, and are you still unmoved?"

"Unmoved?" cried he, emphatically; "shall I be moved by a lion? You see him there in a cage, and pity him; look back to when you might have seen him with a lamb in his claws!"

I could only look dismayed for a moment. "But, at least," I said, "I hope what I hear is not true, though I now grow afraid to ask?"

"If it is anything about me," he answered, "it is certainly not true."

"I am extremely glad, indeed," cried I, "for it has been buzzed about in the world that you were to draw up the final charge. This I thought most cruel of all; You, who have held back all this time–"

"Yes! pretty completely," interrupted he, laughing.

"No, not completely," I continued; "but Yet YOU have made no direct formal speech, nor have come forward in any positive and formidable manner; therefore, as we have now heard all the others, and–almost enough–"

I was obliged to stop a moment, to see how this adventurous plainness was taken; and he really, though my manner showed me only rallying, looked I don't know how, at such unexampled disrespect towards his brother orators. But I soon went quietly on: "To come forth now, after all that has passed, with the eclat of novelty, and,-for the most cruel part of all,–that which cannot be answered."

"You think," cried he, "'tis bringing a fresh courser into the field of battle, just as every other is completely jaded?"

"I think," cried I, "that I am very generous to wish against what
I should so much wish for, but for other considerations."

"O, what a flattering way," cried he, "of stating it! however, I can bear to allow you a little waste of compliments, which you know so well how to make; but I cannot bear to have you waste your compassion."

A POINT OF CEREMONIAL.

May.-The 1st of this month I went again to Westminster Hall, with our cousin Elizabeth. Evidence was brought forward by the counsel for Mr. Hastings, and Lord Stormont was called upon as a witness. This produced some curious debating among the Lords, and with the chancellor. They spoke only for the ears of one another, as it was merely to settle some ceremonial, whether he was to be summoned to the common place where the witnesses stood, or had the claim of a peer to speak in his place, robed. This latter prevailed: and then we expected his speech; but no, a new debate ensued, which, as we gathered from the rumour about us, was that his lordship should have the prayer book, for his oath, belonging to the House of Peers. Here, also, his dignity was triumphant, though it cost the whole assembly a full quarter of an hour; while another prayer book was officially at hand, in the general post for plebeian witnesses.

Well! aristocrat as I am, compared with you, I laughed heartily at all this mummery, and yet it was possibly wise, at this period of pulling down all law and order, all privilege and subordination, however frivolous was its appearance.

Page 447 His testimony was highly favourable to Mr. Hastings, with regard to authenticating the intelligence he had received of an opening war with France, upon which hung much justification of the measures Mr. Hastings had pursued for raising supplies.

MRS. SCHWELLENBERG AND MLLE. JACOBI.

Thence I went to the Queen's house, where -I have a most cordial general invitation from Mrs. Schwellenberg to go by all opportunities; and there is none so good as after the trial, that late hour exactly according With her dinner-time.

She is just as she Was with respect to health; but in all other respects, how amended! all civility, all obligingness, all courtesy! and so desirous to have me visit her, that she presses me to come incessantly.

During coffee, the princess royal came into the room. She condescended to profess herself quite glad to see me; and she had not left the room five minutes before, again returning, she said, "Mrs. Schwellenberg, I am come to plague you, for I am come to take away Miss Burney." I give you leave to guess whether this plagued me.

May 2.-The following week I again went to Westminster Hall. Mlle. Jacobi had made a point of accompanying me, that she might see the show, as James called it to General Burgoyne, and I had great pleasure in taking her, for she is a most ingenuous and good creature, though–alas!–by no means the same undaunted, gay, open character as she appeared at first. Sickness, confinement, absence from her friends, submission to her coadjutrix, and laborious watching have much altered her.

The trial of this day was all written evidence in favour of Mr. Hastings, and violent quarrelling as to its admissibility on the part of Mr. Burke. Mr. Windham took his place, during some part of the controversy, and spoke ably and clearly as to the given point in dispute, but with the most palpable tremor and internal struggle.

A LONG TALK WITH THE KING AND QUEEN.

I attended Mlle. Jacobi to the Queen's house, where I dined ; and great indeed was my pleasure, during coffee, to see the Princess Elizabeth, who, In the most Pleasing manner

and the highest spirits, came to summon me to the queen. I found her majesty again with all her sweet daughters but the youngest. She was gracious and disposed to converse.

We had a great deal of talk upon public concerns, and she told me a friend Of mine had spoken very well the day before, and so had Mr. Burke. She meant Mr. Windham. It was against the new associates, and in favour of the proclamation.(358) Mr. Burke, of course, would here come forth in defence of his own predictions and opinions; but Mr. Windham, who had rather abided hitherto with Charles Fox, in thinking Mr. Burke too extreme, well as he loves him personally, was a new convert highly acceptable. He does not, however, go all lengths with Mr. Burke; he is only averse to an unconstitutional mode of reform, and to sanctioning club powers, so as to enable them, as in France, to overawe the state and senate.(359)

Soon after, to my infinite joy, the king entered. O, he spoke to me so kindly!–he congratulated me on the better looks which his own presence and goodness gave me, repeatedly declaring he had never seen me in such health. He asked me after my father, and listened with interest when I mentioned his depression, and told him that all he had done of late to soothe his retirement and pain had been making canons to solemn words, and with such difficulties of composition as, in better health and spirits, would have rather proved oppressive and perplexing than a relief to his feelings.

"I, too," said the king, after a very serious pause, "have myself sometimes found, when ill or disturbed, that some grave and even difficult employment for my thoughts has tended more to compose me than any of the supposed usual relaxations."

He also condescended to ask after little Norbury, taking off the eager little fellow while he spoke, and his earnest manner of delivery. He then Inquired about my friends Mr. and Mrs. Locke, and their expectations of the return of

Page 449 William. He inquired how I live, whom I saw, what sort of neighbours I had in the college, and many other particulars, that seemed to desire to know how I went on, and whether I was comfortable. His looks, I am sure, said so, and most sweetly and kindly.

They kept me till they went to the Japan room, where they meet the officers and ladies who attend them in public. They were going to the Ancient Music.

This dear king, nobly unsuspicious where left to himself, and where he has met no doubleness, spoke also very freely of some political matters before me–of the new association in particular. It gratified me highly.

MADAME DE GENLIS: A WOEFUL CHANGE.

I got home to dinner to meet Mrs. and Miss Mary Young,(360) who are in town for a few weeks. Miss Mary is sensible, and quick, and agreeable.

They give a very unpleasant account of Madame de Genlis, or de Sillery, or Brulard, as she is now called.(361) They say she has established herself at Bury, in their neighbourhood, with Mlle. la Princesse d'Orleans and Pamela, and a Circe, and another

young girl under her care. They have taken a house, the master of which always dines with them, though Mrs. Young says he is such a low man he should not dine with her daughter. They form twenty with themselves and household. They keep a botanist, a chemist, and a natural historian always with them. These are supposed to have been common servants of the Duke of Orleans in former days, as they always walk behind the ladies when abroad; but, to make amends in the new equalising style, they all dine together at home. They visit at no house but Sir Thomas Gage's, where they carry their harps, and frequently have music. They have been to Bury ball, and danced all night Mlle. d'Orl'eans with anybody, known or unknown to Madame Brulard.

What a woeful change from that elegant, amiable, high-bred Madame de Genlis I knew six years ago! the apparent pattern of female perfection in manners, conversation, and delicacy.

There are innumerable democrats assembled in Suffolk; among them the famous Tom Paine, who herds with all the farmers that will receive him, and there propagates his pernicious doctrines.

THE WEEPING BEAUTY AGAIN.

May 25.-This morning I went to a very fine public breakfast, given by Mrs. Montagu. . . . The crowd of company was such that we could only slowly make way, in any part. There could not be fewer than four or five hundred people. It was like a full Ranelagh by daylight.

We now met Mrs. Porteus, and who should be with her but the poor pretty S.S., whom so long I had not seen, and who has now lately been finally given up by her long-sought and very injurious lover, Dr. Vyse? She is sadly faded, and looked disturbed and unhappy; but still beautiful, though no longer blooming; and still affectionate, though absent and evidently absorbed. We had a little chat together about the Thrales. In mentioning our former intimacy with them, "Ah, those," she cried, "were happy times!" and her eyes glistened. poor thing! hers has been a lamentable story!—Imprudence and vanity have rarely been mixed with so much sweetness, and good-humour, and candour, and followed with more reproach and ill success. We agreed to renew acquaintance next winter; at present she will be little more in town.

MADAME DE LA FITE AND MRS. HASTINGS.

We went then round the rooms, which were well worth examination and admiration ; and we met friends and acquaintance every other step. . . . While we were examining the noble pillars in the new room, I heard an exclamation of "Est-ce possible? suis-je si heureuse?–Est-ce ma ch'ere Mlle. Beurni que je vois?"(362)

Need I say this was Madame de la, Fite ? or Mrs. Fitt, as, since the French Revolution, of which she is a favourer, she is called by some of the household to which I belonged.

I spoke so as to moderate this rapture into something less calling for attention, which her voice and manner were engaging, not unwillingly. I had not seen her since my retreat, and, if she had been less pompous, I should have been glad of the meeting. She kept my hand close grasped between both her own, (though her fan nipped one of my fingers till I was ready to make faces,) with a most resolute empressement, to the great inconvenience of those who wanted to pass, for we were at one of the entrances into the great new room; and how long she might have continued this fond detention I know not, if a lady, whose appearance vied for show and parade with Madame de la Fite's manner and words, had not called out aloud, "I am extremely happy indeed to see Miss Burney!"

This was Mrs. Hastings; and to answer her I was let loose.

I have always been very sorry that Mrs. Hastings, who is a pleasing, lively, and well-bred woman, with attractive manners and attentions to those she wishes to oblige, should have an indiscretion so peculiarly unsuited to her situation, as to aim always at being the most conspicuous figure wherever she appears. Her dress now was like that of an Indian princess, according to our ideas of such ladies, and so much the most splendid, from its ornaments, and style, and fashion, though chiefly of muslin, that everybody else looked under-dressed in her presence. It is for Mr. Hastings I am sorry when I see this inconsiderate vanity, in a woman who would so much better manifest her sensibility of his present hard disgrace, by a modest and quiet appearance and demeanour.

THE IMPETUOUS ORATOR.

Wednesday, May 30.-To-day I went to Westminster Hall again, to hear the evidence of Mr. Markham, which is so pleasantly in favour of Mr. Hastings, that all the friends of that persecuted man are gratified by all he deposes. Miss Ord accompanied me.

When the impetuous and ungovernable Mr. Burke was Interrupting the chancellor, in order to browbeat Mr. Hastings's evidence, Mr. Windham involuntarily exclaimed, "Hist!" just as if he had been at his elbow, and playing the kind part of a flapper. I could not help laughing, and half joining him: he echoed back my laugh, and with a good humour that took in all its meaning and acknowledged its sympathy with regard to Mr. Burke, nevertheless, he spoke not a word. Afterwards, however, he spoke when I had far rather he had been silent, for he went to the assistance of Mr. Burke.

Michael Angelo Taylor spoke also; but I observed with pleasure a distinction the chancellor made to Mr. Windham; for, when he answered their arguments, he singled him out as the person who had said what alone he meant upon that question to notice, by saying, "The honourable manager who spoke second."

But I am sure—I think so, at least—Mr. Windham as little approves the violence of Mr. Burke in this trial as I do myself. I see him evidently and frequently suffer great pain and mortification when he is so obstreperous.

BOSWELL'S MIMICRY OF DR. JOHNSON.

June 1.-This day had been long engaged for breakfasting with Mrs. Dickenson and dining with Mrs. Ord. The breakfast guests were Mr. Langton, Mr. Foote, Mr. Dickenson, jun., a cousin, and a very agreeable and pleasing man; Lady Herries, Miss Dickenson, another cousin, and Mr. Boswell.

This last was the object of the morning. I felt a strong sensation of that displeasure which his loquacious communications of every weakness and infirmity of the first and greatest good man of these times has awakened in me, at his first sight; and, though his address to me was courteous in the extreme, and he made a point of sitting next me, I felt an indignant disposition to a nearly forbidding reserve and silence. How many starts of passion and prejudice has he blackened into record, that else might have sunk, for ever forgotten, under the preponderance of weightier virtues and excellences!

Angry, however, as I have long been with him, he soon insensibly conquered, though he did not soften me: there is so little of ill-design or ill-nature in him, he is so open and forgiving for all that is said in return, that he soon forced me to consider him in a less serious light, and change my resentment against his treachery into something like commiseration of his levity ; and before we parted we became good friends. There is no resisting great good humour, be what will in the opposite scale.

He entertained us all as if hired for that purpose, telling stories of Dr. Johnson, and acting them with incessant buffoonery. I told him frankly that, if he turned him into ridicule by caricature, I should fly the premises: he assured me he would not, and indeed his imitations, though comic to excess, were so far from caricature that he omitted a thousand gesticulations which I distinctly remember.

Mr. Langton told some stories himself in imitation of Dr. johnson; but they became him less than Mr. Boswell, and only reminded me of what Dr. Johnson himself once said to me—"Every man has, some time in his life, an ambition to be a wag." If Mr. Langton had repeated anything from his truly great friend quietly, it would far better have accorded with his own serious and respectable character.

THE KING'S BIRTHDAY.

June 4.-The birthday of our truly good king.

As his majesty had himself given me, when I saw him after the queen's birthday, an implied reproach for not presenting myself at the palace that day, I determined not to incur a similar censure on this, especially as I hold my admission on such a national festival as a real happiness, as well as honour, when it is to see themselves.

How different was my attire from every other such occasion the five preceding years! It was a mere simple dressed undress, without feathers, flowers, hoop, or furbelows.

When I alighted at the porter's lodge I was stopped from crossing the court-yard by seeing the king with his three sons, the Prince of Wales, Duke of York, and Duke of Clarence, who were standing there after alighting from their horses, to

Page 454 gratify the people who encircled the iron rails. It was a pleasant and goodly sight, and I rejoiced in such a detention.

I had a terrible difficulty to find a friend who would make known to her majesty that I was come to pay my devoirs. At length, while watching in the passages to and fro, I heard a step upon the princesses' stairs, and, venturing forward, I encountered the Princess Elizabeth. I paid my respectful congratulations on the day, which she most pleasantly received, and I intimated my great desire to see her majesty. I am Sure the amiable princess communicated my petition, for Mr, de Luc came out in a few minutes and ushered me into the royal presence.

The queen was in her state dressing-room, her head attired for the Drawing-room superbly; but her Court-dress, as usual, remaining to be put on at St. James's. She had already received all her early complimenters, and was prepared to go to St. James's: the princess royal was seated by her side, and all the other princesses, except the Princess Amelia, were in the room, with the Duchess of York. Mr. de Luc, Mrs. Schwellenberg, Madame de la Fite, and Miss Goldsworthy were in the background.

The queen smiled upon me most graciously, and every princess came up separately to speak with me. I thanked her majesty warmly for admitting me upon such an occasion, "O!" cried she, "I resolved to see you the moment I knew you were here."

She then inquired when I went into Norfolk, and conversed upon my summer plans, etc., with more of her original sweetness of manner than I have seen since my resignation. What pleasure this gave me ! and what pleasure did I feel in being kept by her till the further door opened, and the king entered, accompanied by the Dukes of York and Clarence.

I motioned to retreat, but calling out, "What, Miss Burney," the king came up to me and inquired how I did,- and began talking to me so pleasantly, so gaily, so kindly even, that I had the satisfaction of remaining and of gathering courage to utter my good wishes and warm fervent prayers for this day. He deigned to hear me very benignly; or make believe he did, for I did not make my harangue very audibly; but he must be sure of its purport.

He said I was grown "quite fat" since he had seen me, and appealed to the Duke of York: he protested my arm was half as big again as heretofore, and then he measured it with his

Page 455 spread thumbs and forefingers; and the whole of his manner showed his perfect approbation of the step I had taken, of presenting myself in the royal presence on this auspicious day.

The queen soon after walked up to me, and asked if I should like to see the ball at night. I certainly should much like to have seen them "in all their glory," after seeing them thus in all their kindness, as well as to have been present at the first public appearance at Court of the Princess Sophia : but I had no means to get from and to

Chelsea so late at night, and was, therefore, forced to excuse myself, and decline her gracious proposition of giving me tickets.

MR. HASTINGS'S SPEECH.

Two days after, I went again to Westminster Hall with Miss Ord. Her good mother has a ticket for the Duke of Newcastle's box, in which she was seated. This -day's business consisted of examining witnesses: it was meant for the last meeting. during this session - but when it was over, Mr. Hastings arose and addressed the Lords in a most noble and pathetic speech, praying them to continue their attendance till his defence was heard throughout, or, at least, not to deny him the finishing his answer to the first charge.

He spoke, I believe, to the hearts of everybody, except his prosecutors : the whole assembly seemed evidently affected by what he urged, upon the unexampled delay of justice In his trial: silence was never more profound than that which his voice instantly commanded. Poor unhappy, injured gentleman! How, how can such men practise cruelty so glaring as is manifested in the whole conduct of this trial!

From hence, as usual, I went to dine at the Queen's house. Mrs. Schwellenberg took me to the queen after coffee.

She was writing to Lady Cremorne: she talked with me while she finished her letter, and then read it to me, exactly as in old times. She writes with admirable facility, and peculiar elegance of expression, as well as of handwriting.

She asked me, somewhat curiously, if I had seen any of my old friends? I found she meant oppositionists. I told her only at the trial. She kept me in converse till the dear king came into the room: he had a grandson of Lord Howe's with him, a little boy in petticoats, with whom he was playing, and whom he thought remembered me, I had seen him frequently

Page 456 at Weymouth, and the innocent little fellow insisted upon Making me his bows and reverences, when told to Make them to the queen.

The king asked me what had been doing at Westminster Hall? I repeated poor Mr. Hastings's remonstrance, particularly a part of it in which he had mentioned that he had already "appealed to his majesty, whose justice he could not doubt." The king looked a little queer, but I was glad of the opportunity of putting in a word for poor Mr. Hastings.

I went on regularly to the trial till it finished for this year.

Mr. Dallas closed his answer to the first charge, with great spirit and effect, and seemed to make numerous Proselytes for Mr. Hastings.

A WELL-PRESERVED BEAUTY.

Thursday, June 18.-After many invitations and regulations, it was settled I was to accompany my father on a visit of three days to Mrs. Crewe at Hampstead. The villa at Hampstead is small, but commodious. We were received by Mrs. Crewe with much kindness. The room was rather dark, and she had a veil to her bonnet, half down, and with this aid she looked still in a full blaze of beauty. I was wholly astonished. Her bloom, perfectly natural, is as high as that of Augusta Locke when in her best looks, and the form of her face is so exquisitely perfect that my eye never Met it without fresh admiration. She is certainly, in my eyes, the most completely a beauty of any woman I ever saw. I know not, even now, any female in her first youth who could bear the comparison. She uglifies everything near her.

Her son was with her. He is just of age, and looks like her elder brother! He is a heavy old-looking young Man. He is going to China with Lord Macartney.(363)

THE BURKES.

My former friend, young Burke, was also there. I was glad to renew acquaintance with him though I could see some little strangeness in him: this, however, completely wore off.

Page 457

before the day was over. Soon after entered Mrs. Burke, Miss F.,(364) a niece, and Mr. Richard Burke, the comic, humorous, bold, queer brother of the Mr. Burke, who, they said, was soon coming, with Mr. Elliot. The Burke family were invited by Mrs. Crewe to meet us.

Mrs. Burke was just what I have always seen her, soft, gentle, reasonable, and obliging; and we met, I think, upon as good terms as if so many years had not parted us.

At length Mr. Burke appeared, accompanied by Mr. Elliot. He shook hands with my father as soon as he had paid his devoirs to Mrs. Crewe, but he returned my curtsey with so distant a bow, that I Concluded myself quite lost with him, from my evident solicitude in poor Mr. Hastings's cause. I could not wish that less obvious, thinking as I think of it; but I felt infinitely grieved to lose the favour of a man whom in all other articles, I so much venerate, and whom, Indeed, I esteem and admire as the very first man of true genius now living in this Country.

Mrs. Crewe introduced me to Mr. Elliot: I am Sure we were already personally known to each other, for I have seen him perpetually in the managers' box, whence, as often, he must have seen me in the great chamberlain's. He is a tall, thin young man, plain in face, dress, and manner, but sensible, and possibly much besides; he was reserved, however, and little else appeared.

The moment I was named, to my great joy I found Mr. Burke had not recollected me. He is more near-sighted, considerably,- than myself. "Miss Burney!" he now exclaimed, coming forward, and quite kindly taking my hand, "I did not see you;" and then he spoke very sweet words of the meeting, and of my looking far better than "while I was a courtier," and of how he rejoiced to see that I so little suited that station. "You look," cried he, "quite renewed, revived, disengaged; you seemed, when I conversed with you last, at the trial, quite altered; I never saw such a change for the better as quitting a Court has brought about!"

Ah! thought I, this is simply a mistake, from reasoning according to your own feelings. I only seemed altered for the worse at the trial, because I there looked coldly and distantly, from distaste and disaffection to your proceedings; and I here

Page 458 .

look changed for the better, only because I here meet You without the chill of disapprobation, and with the glow of my first admiration of you and your talents!

BURKE'S CONVERSATIONAL POWERS.

Mrs. Crewe gave him her place, and he sat by me, and entered into a most animated conversation upon Lord Macartney and his Chinese expedition, and the two Chinese youths who were to accompany it. These last he described minutely and spoke of the extent of the undertaking in high, and perhaps fanciful, terms, but with allusions and anecdotes intermixed, so full of general information and brilliant ideas, that I soon felt the whole of my first enthusiasm return, and with it a sensation of pleasure that made the day delicious to me.

After this my father joined us, and politics took- the lead. He spoke then with an eagerness and a vehemence that instantly banished the graces, though it redoubled the energies, of his discourse. "The French Revolution," he said, "which began by authorising and legalising Injustice, and which by rapid steps had proceeded to every species of despotism except owning a despot, was now menacing all the universe and all mankind with the most violent concussion of principle and order." My father heartily joined, and I tacitly assented to his doctrines, though I feared not with his fears.

One Speech I Must repeat, for it is explanatory of his conduct, and nobly explanatory. When lie had expatiated upon the present dangers, even to English liberty and property, from the contagion of havoc and novelty, he earnestly exclaimed, "This it is that has made ME an abettor and supporter of kings! Kings are necessary, and if we would preserve peace and prosperity, we must preserve THEM we must all put our shoulders to the work! Ay, and stoutly, too!"

This subject lasted till dinner.

At dinner Mr. Burke sat next Mrs. Crewe, and I had the happiness to be seated next Mr. Burke, and my other neighbour was his amiable son.

The dinner, and the dessert when the servants were removed, were delightful. How I wish my dear Susanna and Fredy could meet this wonderful man when he is easy, happy, and with people he cordially likes! But politics, even on his own side, must always be excluded; his irritability Is so terrible on that theme that it gives immediately to his face the expression of a man who is going to defend himself from murderers. I can give you only a few little detached traits of what passed, as detail would be endless.

Charles Fox being mentioned, Mrs. Crewe told us that he had lately said, upon being shown some passage in Mr. Burke's book which he had warmly opposed, but which had, in the event, made its own justification, very candidly, "Well! Burke is right–but Burke is often right, only he is right too soon."

"Had Fox seen some things in that book," answered Mr. Burke, "as soon, he would at this moment, in all probability, be first minister of this country."

"What!" cried Mrs. Crewe, "with Pitt?–No!–no!–Pitt won't go out, and Charles Fox will never make a coalition with Pitt."

"And why not?" said Mr. Burke, dryly; "why not this coalition as well as other coalitions?"

Nobody tried to answer this.

"Charles Fox, however," said Mr. Burke afterwards, "can never internally like the French Revolution. He is entangled; but, in himself, if he should find no other objection to it, he has at least too much taste for such a revolution."

Mr. Elliot related that he had lately been in a company of some of the first and most distinguished men of the French nation, now fugitives here, and had asked them some questions about the new French ministry; they had answered that they knew them not even by name till now! "Think," cried he, "what a ministry that must be! Suppose a new administration formed here of Englishmen of whom we had never before heard the names! what statesmen they must be! how prepared and fitted for government! To begin by being at the helm!"

Mr. Richard Burke related, very comically, various censures cast upon his brother, accusing him of being the friend of despots, and the abettor of slavery, because he had been shocked at the imprisonment of the king of France, and was anxious to preserve our own limited monarchy in the same state in which it so long had flourished.

Mr. Burke looked half alarmed at his brother's opening, but,

when he had finished, he very good-humouredly poured out a glass of wine, and, turning to me, said, "Come then—here's slavery for ever!"

This was well understood, and echoed round the table with hearty laughter.

"This would do for you completely, Mr. Burke," said Mrs. Crewe, "if it could get into a newspaper! Mr. Burke, they would say, has now spoken out; the truth has come to light unguardedly, and his real defection from the cause Of true liberty is acknowledged. I should like to draw up the paragraph!"

"And add," said Mr. Burke, "the toast was addressed to Miss Burney, in order to pay court to the queen!"

This sport went on till, upon Mr. Elliot's again mentioning France and the rising jacobins, Mr. Richard Burke loudly gave a new toast—"Come!" cried he, "here's confusion to Confusion!"

Mr. Windham, who Was gone into Norfolk for the summer, was frequently mentioned, and always with praise. Mr. Burke, upon Mr. Elliot's saying something of his being very thin, warmly exclaimed, "He is just as he should be! If I were Windham this minute, I Should not wish to be thinner, nor fatter, nor taller, nor shorter, nor any way, nor in anything, altered."

Some time after, speaking of former days, you may believe I was struck enough to hear Mr. Burke say to Mrs. Crewe, "I wish you had known Mrs. Delany! She was a pattern of a perfect fine lady, a real fine lady, of other days! Her manners were faultless; her deportment was all elegance, her speech was all sweetness, and her air and address all dignity. I always looked up to her as the model of an accomplished woman of former times."

Do you think I heard such a testimony to my most revered and beloved departed friend unmoved?

Afterwards, still to Mrs. Crewe, he proceeded to say, she had been married to Mr. Wycherley, the author.(365) There I ventured to interrupt him, and tell him I fancied that must he some

Page 461

great mistake, as I had been well acquainted with her history from her own mouth. He seemed to have heard it from some good authority; but I could by no means accede my belief, as her real life and memoirs had been so long in my hands, written by herself to a certain period, and, for some way, continued by me. This, however, I did not mention.

A WILD IRISH GIRL.

When we left the dining-parlour to the gentlemen, Miss F- seized my arm, without the smallest previous speech, and, with a prodigious Irish brogue, said "Miss Burney, I am so glad you can't think to have this favourable opportunity of making an intimacy with you! I have longed to know you ever since I became rational!"

I was glad, too, that nobody heard her! She made me walk off with her in the garden, whither we had adjourned for a stroll, at a full gallop, leaning upon my arm, and putting her face close to mine, and sputtering at every word from excessive eagerness.

"I have the honour to know some of your relations in Ireland," she continued; "that is, if they an't yours, which they are very sorry for, they are your sister's, which is almost the same thing. Mr. Shirley first lent me 'Cecilia,' and he was so delighted to hear my remarks! Mrs. Shirley's a most beautiful creature; she's grown so large and so big! and all her daughters are beautiful; so is all the family. I never saw Captain Phillips, but I dare say he's beautiful."

She is quite a wild Irish girl. Presently she talked of Miss Palmer. "O, she loves you!" she cried; "she says she saw you last Sunday, and she never was so happy in her life. She said you looked sadly."

This Miss F- is a handsome girl, and seems very good humoured. I imagine her but just imported, and I doubt not but the soft-mannercd, and well-bred, and quiet Mrs. Burke will soon subdue this exuberance of loquacity.

I gathered afterwards from Mrs. Crewe, that my curious new acquaintance made innumerable inquiries concerning my employment and office under the queen. I find many people much disturbed to know whether I had the place of the Duchess of Ancastor, on one side, or of a chamber-maid, on the other. Truth is apt to lie between conjectures.

ERSKINE's EGOTISM.

The party returned with two very singular additions to its number–Lord Lough-borough,(366) and Mr. and Mrs. Erskine.(367) They have villas at Hampstead, and were met in the walk; Mr. Erskine else would not, probably, have desired to meet Mr. Burke, who openly in the House of Commons asked him if he knew what friendship meant, when he pretended to call him, Mr. Burke, his friend?

There was an evident disunion of the cordiality of the party from this time. My father, Mr. Richard Burke, his nephew, and Mr. Elliot entered into some general discourse; Mr.

Burke took up a volume Of Boileau, and read aloud, though to himself, and with a pleasure that soon made him seem to forget all intruders; Lord Loughborough joined Mrs. Burke and Mr. Erskine, seating himself next to Mrs. Crewe, engrossed her entirely, yet talked loud enough for all to hear who were not engaged themselves.

For me, I sat next Mrs. Erskine, who seems much a woman of the world, for she spoke with me just as freely, and readily, and easily as if we had been old friends.

Mr. Erskine enumerated all his avocations to Mrs. Crewe, and, amongst others, mentioned, very calmly, having to plead against Mr. Crewe upon a manor business in Cheshire. Mrs. Crewe hastily and alarmed interrupted him, to inquire what he meant, and what might ensue to Mr. Crewe? O, nothing but the loss of the lordship upon that spot," he coolly answered; "but I don't know that it will be given against him: I only know I shall have three hundred Pounds for it."

Mrs. Crewe looked thoughtful; and Mr. Erskine then began to speak of the new Association for Reform, by the friends of the people, headed by Messrs. Grey and Sheridan, and sustained by Mr. Fox, and openly opposed by Mr. Windham, as well as Mr. Burke. He said much of the use they had made of his name, though he had never yet been to the society; and I began to understand that he meant to disavow it; but presently he added, "I don't know whether I shall ever attend–I have so much to do–so little time: however, the people must be supported."(368)

"PRAY, will you tell me," said Mrs. Crewe, drily, "what you mean by the people? I never knew."

He looked surprised, but evaded any answer and soon after took his leave, with his wife, who seems by no means to admire him as much as he admires himself, if I may judge by short odd speeches which dropped from her. The eminence of Mr. Erskine seems all for public life; in private, his excessive egotisms undo him.

Lord Loughborough instantly took his seat next to Mrs. Crewe; and presently related a speech which Mr. Erskine has lately made at some public meeting, and which he opened to this effect:–"As to me, gentlemen, I have some title to give my opinions freely. Would you know what my title is derived from? I challenge any man to inquire! If he ask my

birth,–its genealogy may dispute with kings! If my wealth, it is all for which I have time to hold out my hand! If my talents,–No! of those, gentlemen, I leave you to judge for yourselves."(369)

CAEN-WOOD.

June 22.-Mrs. Crewe took my father and myself to see the Hampstead lions. We went to Caen-wood, to see the house and pictures. Poor Lord Mansfield(370) has not been downstairs, the housekeeper told us, for the last four years; yet she asserts he is by no means superannuated, and frequently sees his very intimate friends, and seldom refuses to be consulted by any lawyers. He was particularly connected with my revered Mrs. Delany, and I felt melancholy upon entering his house to recollect how often that beloved lady had planned carrying thither Miss Port and myself, and how often we had been invited by Miss Murrays, my lord's nieces. I asked after those ladies, and left them my respects. I heard they were up-stairs with Lord Mansfield, whom they never left.

Many things in this house were interesting, because historical but I fancy the pictures, at least, not to have much other recommendation. A portrait Of Pope, by himself, I thought extremely curious. It is very much in the style of most of jervas's own paintings. They told us that, after the burning of Lord Mansfield's house in town, at the time of Lord G. Gordon's riots, thousands came to inquire, if this original portrait was preserved. Luckily it was at Caen-wood.

We spent a good deal of time in the library,–and saw first editions of almost all Queen Anne's classics; and lists of subscribers to Pope's "Iliad," and many such matters, all enlivening to some corner or other of the memory.

AN ADVENTURE WITH MRS. CREWE.

We next proceeded to the Shakspeare gallery,(371) which I had never seen. And here we met with an adventure that finished our morning's excursions.

There was a lady in the first room, dressed rather singularly, quite alone, and extremely handsome, who was parading about with a nosegay in her hand, which she frequently held to her nose, in a manner that was evidently calculated to attract notice. We therefore passed on to the inner room, to avoid her. Here we had but just all taken our stand opposite different pictures, when she also entered, and, coming pretty close to my father, sniffed at her flowers with a sort of extatic eagerness, and then let them fall. My father picked them up, and gravely presented them to her. She curtsied to the ground in receiving them, and presently crossed over the room, and,, brushing past Mrs. Crewe, seated herself immediately by her elbow. Mrs. Crewe, not admiring this familiarity, moved away, giving her at the same time a look of dignified distance that was almost petrifying.

It did not prove so to this lady, who presently followed her to the next picture, and, sitting as close as she could to where Mrs. Crewe stood, began singing various quick passages, without words or connexion. I saw Mrs. Crewe much alarmed, and advanced to stand by her, meaning to whisper her that we had better leave the room; and this idea was not checked by seeing that the flowers were artificial. By the looks we interchanged we soon mutually said, "This is a mad woman." We feared irritating her by a sudden flight, but gently retreated, and soon got quietly into the large room when she bounced up with a great noise, and, throwing the veil of her bonnet violently back, as if fighting it, she looked after us, pointing at Mrs. Crewe.

Seriously frightened, Mrs. Crewe seized my father's arm, and hurried up two or three steps into a small apartment. Here Mrs. Crewe, addressing herself to an elderly gentleman, asked if he could inform the people below that a mad woman was terrifying the company ; and while he was receiving her commission with the most profound respect, and with an evident air of admiring astonishment at her beauty, we heard a rustling, and, looking round, saw the same figure hastily striding after us, and in an instant at our elbows.

Mrs. Crewe turned quite pale ; it was palpable she was the object pursued, and she most civilly and meekly articulated, "I beg your pardon, ma'am," as she hastily passed her, and hurried down the steps. We were going to run for our lives,

Page 466 when Miss Townshend whispered Mrs. Crewe it was Only Mrs. Wells the actress, and said she was certainly Only performing vagaries to try effect, which she was quite famous for doing.

It would have been food for a painter to have seen Mrs. Crewe during this explanation. All her terror instantly gave way to indignation; and scarcely any pencil could equal the high vivid glow of her cheeks. To find herself made the object of game to the burlesque humour of a bold player, was an indignity she could not brook, and her mind was immediately at work how to assist herself against such unprovoked and unauthorized effrontery.

The elderly gentleman who, with great eagerness, had followed Mrs. Crewe, accompanied by a young man who was of his party, requested more particularly her commands ; but before Mrs. Crewe's astonishment and resentment found words, Mrs. Wells, singing, and throwing herself into extravagant attitudes, again rushed down the steps, and fixed her eyes on Mrs. Crewe. This, however, no longer served her purpose. Mrs. Crewe fixed her in return, and with a firm, composed, commanding air and look that, though it did not make this strange creature retreat, somewhat disconcerted her for a few minutes. She then presently affected a violent coughing such a one as almost shook the room; though such a forced and unnatural noise as rather resembled howling than a cold.

This over, and perceiving Mrs, Crewe still steadily keeping her ground, she had the courage to come up to us, and, with a flippant air, said to the elderly gentleman, "Pray, sir, will you tell me what it is o'clock?"

He looked vexed to be called a moment from looking at Mrs. Crewe, and, with a forbidding gravity, answered her, "About two."

"No offence, I hope, sir?" cried she, seeing him turn eagerly from her. He bowed without looking at her, and she strutted away, still, however, keeping in sight, and playing various tricks, her eyes perpetually turned towards Mrs. Crewe, who as regularly, met them, with an expression such as might have turned a softer culprit to stone.

Our cabal was again renewed, and Mrs. Crewe again told this gentleman to make known to the proprietors of the gallery that this person was a nuisance to the company, when, suddenly re-approaching as, she called out, "Sir! sir!" to the younger of our new protectors.

He coloured, and looked much alarmed, but only bowed.

"Pray, sir," cried she, "what's o'clock?"

He looked at his watch, and answered.

"You don't take it ill, I hope, sir?" she cried.

He only bowed.

"I do no harm, sir," said she; "I never bite."

The poor young man looked aghast, and bowed lower; but Mrs. Crewe, addressing herself to the elder, said aloud, "I beg you, sir, to go to Mr. Boydell; you may name me to him—Mrs. Crewe."

Mrs. Wells at this walked away, yet still in sight. "You may tell him what has happened, sir, in all our names. You may tell him Miss Burney—"

"O no!" cried I, in a horrid fright, "I beseech I may not be named! And, indeed, ma'am, it may be better to let it all alone. It will do no good; and it may all get into the newspapers."

"And if it does," cried Mrs. Crewe, "what is it to us? We have done nothing; we have given no offence, and made no disturbance. This person has frightened us all wilfully, and Utterly without provocation; and now she can frighten us no longer, she would brave us. Let her tell her own story, and how will it harm us?"

"Still," cried I, "I must always fear being brought into any newspaper cabals. Let the fact be ever so much against her, she will think the circumstances all to her honour if a paragraph comes out beginning 'Mrs. Crewe and Mrs. Wells.'"

Mrs. Crewe liked this sound as little as I should have liked it in placing my own name where I put hers. She hesitated a little what to do, and we all walked down-stairs, where instantly this bold woman followed us, paraded Up and down the long shop with a dramatic air while our group was in conference, and then, sitting down at the clerk's desk, and calling in a footman, she desired him to wait while she wrote a note.

She scribbled a few lines, and read aloud her direction, "To Mr. Topham;" and giving the note to the man, said, "Tell your master that is something to make him laugh. Bid him not send to the press till I see him."

Now as Mr. Topham is the editor of "The World," and notoriously her protector, as her having his footman acknowledged, this looked rather serious, and Mrs. Crewe began to partake of my alarm. She therefore, to my infinite satisfaction, told her new friend that she desired he would name no names, but merely mention that some ladies had been frightened. . . .

We then got into Mrs. Crewe's carriage, and not till then would this facetious Mrs. Wells quit the shop. And she walked in sight, dodging us, and playing antics of a tragic sort of gesture, till we drove out of her power to keep up with us. What a strange creature!

AN INVITATION FROM ARTHUR YOUNG.

(Mr. Arthur Young to Fanny Burney.) Bradfield Farm, June 18, 1792. WHAT a plaguy business 'tis to take up one's pen to write to a person who is constantly moving in a vortex of pleasure, brilliancy, and wit,–whose movements and connections are, as it were, in another world! One knows not how to manage the matter with such folks, till you find by a little approximation and friction of tempers and things that they are mortal, and no more than good sort of people in the main, only garnished with something we do not possess ourselves. Now then, the consequence.

Only three pages to write, and one lost in introduction! To the matter at last.

It seemeth that you make a journey to Norfolk. Now do ye see, if you do not give a call on the farmer, and examine his ram (an old acquaintance), his bull, his lambs, calves, and crops, he will say but one thing of you–that you are fit for a court, but not for a farm; and there is more happiness to be found among my rooks than in the midst of all the princes and princesses of Golconda. I would give an hundred pound to see you married to a farmer that never saw London, with plenty of poultry ranging in a few green fields, and flowers and shrubs disposed where they should be, around a cottage, and not around a breakfast-room in Portman-square, fading in eyes that know not to admire them. In honest truth now, let me request your company here. It will give us all infinite pleasure. You are habituated to admiration, but you shall have here what is much better–the friendship of those who loved you long before the world admired you. Come, and make old friends happy!

(346) The flight of the king and his family from Paris, on the night of June 20-21. They reached Varennes in safety the following night, but were there recognised and stopped, and the next day escorted back to Paris.-ED.

(347) The reader will find in Green's "History of the English People," a widely different view of' the character of Dunstan. But Fanny knew only the old stories, and had, moreover, written a tragedy, "Edwy and Elgiva," in which Dunstan, in accordance with those old stories, appears as the villain.-ED.

(348) Author of the "New Bath Guide."-ED.

(349) Henrietta Frances, second daughter of John, first Earl Spencer, and younger sister of Georgiana, Duchess of Devonshire, married Viscount Duncannon in 1780. She died in 1821.-ED.

(350) Gibbon had good reason for his opinion of the power of Lady Elizabeth's charms. In 1787, he met her at Lausanne, a young widow of twenty-eight, and found her allurements so irresistible that he proposed marriage to her, and was rejected.-ED.

(351) Mrs. Ord was a yet more violent Tory than Fanny herself, and would believe no good of the Duchess of Devonshire, the queen of the Whigs.-ED.

(352) In the "Memoirs of Dr. Burney," Fanny writes in more detail of this her last visit to Sir Joshua. "He was still more deeply depressed; though Miss Palmer good-humouredly drew a smile from him, by gaily exclaiming, 'Do, pray, now, uncle, ask Miss Burney to write another book directly! for we have almost finished Cecilia again—and this is our sixth reading of it!'"

"The little occupation, Miss Palmer said, of which Sir joshua was then capable, was carefully dusting the paintings in his picture gallery, and placing them in different points of view.

"This passed at the conclusion Of 1791; on the February of the following year, this friend, equally amiable and eminent, was no more! (Memoirs, vol. iii. P. 144).-ED.

(353) The wife of Sir Lucas Pepys.-ED.

(354) Afterwards Lord Ellenborough: the leading counsel for Hastings.-ED.

(355) February 23, 1792.-ED.

(356) The greater part of Sir joshua's large fortune was left to his unmarried niece, Mary Palmer. Considerable legacies were left to his niece, Mrs. Gwatkin (Offy Palmer), and to his friend Edmund Burke. In addition to these legacies, his will provided for a number of small bequests, including one of a thousand pounds to his old servant, Ralph Kirkley. In the following summer Mary Palmer married the Earl of Inchiquin, afterwards Marquis of Thomond. "He is sixty-nine," Fanny writes about that time of Lord Inchiquin; "but they say he is remarkably pleasing in his manners, and soft and amiable in his disposition."-ED.

(357) He was buried in the crypt of St. Paul's Cathedral, near the tomb of Sir Christopher Wren.-ED.

(358) The recent proclamation by the Government against the publication and sale of seditious writings. The "new associates" were members of the societies of sympathisers with the principles of the French Revolution, which, under such titles as "Friends of the People." "Corresponding Society," etc., were now spreading all over England.-ED.

(359) The revolutionary clubs of Paris, the Jacobins' Club in particular, gradually acquired such power as enabled them to overawe the Legislative Assembly, and even, at a later date, the Convention itself. Their influence only ceased with the overthrow and death of their leader, Robespièrre, in 1794.-ED. (360) The wife and eldest daughter of Arthur Young, the well-known writer on agriculture. Mrs. Young was the sister of Dr. Burney's second Wife.-ED. (361) "Madame de Genlis's husband, the Count de Genlis, had become Marquis of Sillery by the death of his elder brother. He was a Revolutionist and member of the Girondin party: one of the twenty-two Girondins who perished by the guillotine, October 31, 1793. Madame de Genlis (or Brulard) had

come to England in October, 1791, with her young pupil, Mlle. d'Orléans (Egalité), the daughter of Philippe Egalité, Duke of Orleans, whose physicians had ordered her to take the waters at Bath. They remained in England until November, 1792, when they were recalled to Paris by Egalité. Arriving there, they found themselves proscribed as emigrants, and obliged to quit Paris within eight-and-forty hours. They then took refuge in Flanders, and settled at Tournay where Pamela was married to Lord Edward Fitzgerald, subsequently one of the leaders in the Irish Rebellion of 1798. In Flanders Madame de Genlis enjoyed the protection of General Dumontiez, but when he became suspected, with too good reason, by the Convention, she was obliged again to take flight, and found safety at last with Mlle. d'Orléans, in Switzerland.

Pamela was the adopted daughter of Madame de Genlis; some said her actual daughter by the Duke of Orleans; but this is at least doubtful. "Circe," or "Henrietta Circe," as Fanny afterwards calls her, was Madame de Genlis's niece, Henriette de Sercey (!), who subsequently married a rich merchant of Hamburg.-ED. VOL. 11.

(362) "Is it possible? Am I so happy? Do I see my dear Miss Burney?"

(363) Earl Macartney was sent as ambassador to China in 1793, for the purpose of concluding a commercial treaty with that power. He was unsuccessful, however, and, after spending some months in China, the embassy returned to England.-ED.

(364) "Miss French, a lively niece of Mr. Burke's." (.Memoirs of Dr. Burney, vol. iii, p. 157.)-ED.

(365) Burke was, of course, mistaken. When Wycherley died, at seventy-five (December, 1715), Mary Granville (afterwards Mrs. Delany) was in her sixteenth year. Wycherley, it is true, married a young wife on his deathbed, but it is certain that this was not Mary Granville; indeed, if Pope's account, given in Spence's "Anecdotes," may be trusted, it was a woman of very different character.-ED.

(366) Alexander Wedderburn, afterwards Lord Loughborough, was born in or near Edinburgh in 1733. He attained distinction at the bar, and entered Parliament early in the reign of George III. As a politician he was equally notorious for his skill in debate and his want of public principle. Previously a member of the opposition, he ratted to the Government in 1771, and was rewarded by Lord North with the Solicitor-Generalship. He defended Lord Clive in 1773. When Thurlow became Lord Chancellor (in 1778), Wedderburn succeeded him in the office of Attorney-General. In 1786 he was made Chief justice of the Court of Common Pleas, and called to the House of Peers by the title of Baron Loughborough. After this we find him acting as a follower of Charles Fox, and leader of the Whig party in the House of Lords. He supported Fox's views on the Regency question in 1788-9, but when the split in the Whig party on the subject of the French Revolution took place, Loughborough, like Burke, gave his support to the government. In January, 1793, he obtained the long coveted post of Lord Chancellor. He died January 1, 1805. A story goes that when the news of Loughborough's death was brought to George III., "his majesty was graciously pleased to exclaim, 'Then he has not left a greater knave behind him in my dominions.'" (Campbell's "Lives of the Chancellors," vol. vi., p. 334.)-ED.

(367) Thomas Erskine (born 1750, died 1823), "If less eminent in the law, was a far more respectable politician than Loughborough, although his parliamentary career was by no means so brilliant. He was a consistent Whig, with the courage of his convictions.

He lost his post of Attorney-General to the Prince of Wales through his defence of Thomas Paine, author of the famous "Rights of Man," in December, 1792. Fired by the example of the French Revolutionists, the friends of liberty in England were, about this time, everywhere forming themselves into political associations, for the purpose of promoting Parliamentary reform, and generally "spreading the principles of freedom." By the government these societies were regarded as seditious. Erskine was a member of one or more of these associations, and one of his most brilliant triumphs at the bar was connected with the prosecution by government (October, 1794), of Hardy Thelwall and Horne Tooke for high treason, as members of one of these supposed seditious societies. The prisoners were defended by Erskine and acquitted. Erskine became Lord Chancellor in 1806 after the death of Pitt.-ED.

(368) On his own admission Erskine was a member of the Society of Friends of the People about the end of 1792-ED.

(369) With all his talents Erskine was always noted for his inordinate vanity.-ED.

(370) The famous Lord Chief justice. He died in 1793, aged eighty-eight years.-ED.

(371) Alderman Boydell's celebrated "Shakspeare Gallery" in Pall Mall, contained paintings illustrative of Shakspeare by Reynolds, Romney, Fuseli, and many others of the most distinguished painters of the day. The entire collection, comprising one hundred and seventy works, was sold by auction by Christie, in May, 1805.-ED.

(372) For Arthur Young, see postea, vol. iii., p. 17. Bradfield Farm, his home was in Suffolk, in the neighbourhood of Bury St. Edmunds.-ED.

LaVergne, TN USA
17 May 2010
182924LV00003B/9/P